Life of Sir Henry Parkes, Australian Statesman

From Photo. by Falk, Sydney.]

LIFE

OF

SIR HENRY PARKES

G.C.M.G.

𝔄ustralian 𝔖tatesman

BY

CHARLES E. LYNE

(Formerly of the *Sydney Morning Herald*)

AUTHOR OF

"INDUSTRIES OF NEW SOUTH WALES," "NEW GUINEA," ETC., ETC.

WITH ILLUSTRATIONS

𝔏ondon

T. FISHER UNWIN

PATERNOSTER BUILDINGS

1897

[ENGLISH EDITION]

TO THE MEMORY OF

𝔐𝔶 𝔉𝔞𝔱𝔥𝔢𝔯

THIS BOOK IS AFFECTIONATELY

INSCRIBED.

PREFACE.

———◆———

THE following pages have been writt
the belief that a biography of Sir :
Parkes is called for, and that it will
interesting and instructive to all who app
important public services and admire great ca:

For nearly half a century Sir Henry :
was a conspicuous figure in Australian publ
and, for much of that period, by far the
prominent. By very many people he was re
as Australia's greatest statesman.

Primarily the labours of his long career
for the advancement of New South Wale
colony in which his lot was more directly
but many of his public acts have had a ber
influence upon the Australasian colonies as a
and, in benefiting Australasia, he assiste
progress of the British Empire. Throughc

life he was loyal to the mother land. While
faithful to the country of his adoption, he ever
remembered that "the crimson thread of kinship
runs through us all," and, foremost in the movement for Australian federation, the union he sought
was a "union under the Crown."

In many respects he was a remarkable man,
with an eventful history, full of incidents attractive to the ordinary reader, and of lessons useful
to the student.

C. E. L.

Sydney,
    11th November, 1896.

CONTENTS.

———— ◆ ————

LIST OF ILLUSTRATIONS.

CHAPTER I.

THE boyhood of Sir Henry Parkes was spent in the Parish of Stoneleigh, Warwickshire, England, where he was born in the year 1815. The son of an English farmer, the most dearly remembered pleasures of his childhood, he once told a country audience, were enjoyed in an old English farmhouse, situated "in the centre of England, only a few miles from the birthplace of Shakespeare, and within sight of the historical spires of Coventry."

From a boy he was a hard worker. Misfortune befalling his parents in his young life, at eight years of age he was compelled to earn his own living, and from that period to the end of his days, he was, either with his hands or his brains, one of the world's toilers.

This obligation to labour during his childhood and his early manhood, was an insuperable obstacle to his obtaining a suitable education; but he did what other remarkable men have done in their youth: he read every book within his reach, and reflected upon what he read, and he strove generally

B

to so inform himself that his mind should be familiar with everything going on around him. To the full extent of his power he cultivated habits of constant and careful reading and thinking, and with such success that though, at times, a want of educational polish was noticeable in his public utterances, they were remarkable for the wide range of information over which they extended, for their strong grasp of principles, and generally for the intelligent and convincing method employed in dealing with the subject under consideration. In respect of his being essentially a self-taught man, able to supply the deficiencies resulting from the want of proper educational training, so that he might with personal success and public advantage use his natural ability, he stood alone among the public men of New South Wales, and probably of Australia.

Men who were prominent in the early public life of New South Wales are, in comparison with those of the present day, sometimes regarded as giants. The comparison is extreme but not extravagant. Parkes, Wentworth, Lang, Cowper, Martin, Robertson and Dalley, are names which in the history of the colony will always stand high above those of their fellows. Others have been as much before the public, but none have planted themselves as firmly in the estimation of the community, or are so distinctly inscribed upon the roll of famous Australians. A nation had been born only a few years before these great colonists appeared in the country, and it fell largely to them to secure its welfare and progress both in its youth and in its maturity.

Sir Henry Parkes landed in Sydney in the capacity of an ordinary British workman, healthy and strong in mind and body, but poor in pocket. He sometimes told a public assembly of how useful to him was the finding of a sixpence in one of the streets of Sydney soon after he set foot for the first time on Australian soil. Previous to his coming to New South Wales he followed the occupation of a Birmingham mechanic,—a worker in ivory; and a glimpse of his life in the great English manufacturing town may be caught in the picture presented by some lines entitled, "Home of a Birmingham Artisan, twenty years ago," which appear in a small volume of poems he published in 1857 :—

> "One of a brick-built row in street retired,
> A lowly dwelling, so for comfort plann'd,
> No foot of room was lost; in nothing grand;
> Yet wanting nought which humble heart desired.
> Parlour,—with creeping plants the window wired,
> The furniture soilless kept by woman's hand,—
> In summer like some nook of fairyland,
> For winter nights, well hearth-rugg'd and coal-fired.
> Snug kitchen in the rear, with childhood's sports
> Gracing the threshold, and the home-cured flitch
> Within—fair picture 'gainst the poor man's wall !—
> Ope to a garden-plot, not crowded courts.
> Such our mechanic's home; nor wanted stitch
> His decent clothing; and content blessed all."

He arrived in the colony in 1839, an immigrant, with little to bind him to the land he had left but the ties of birthplace and kindred, and with nothing to temper the discouragements surrounding a stranger in a strange land but the hope of being able to find a more comfortable livelihood in a young and necessarily progressive community than seemed possible in England. He was what was called a "bounty immigrant." In those days two classes of immigrants came to New South Wales : Government immigrants and bounty immigrants. The former were brought to Sydney at the expense of the Government ; the latter came at the instance of the captains or agents of the ships which carried them, a bounty being paid the ships' representatives for each person whose qualifications were in accord with the Government regulations. The Government immigrants, on arrival, were provided with quarters in the Immigration Barracks, which were situated on the site of the present Government Printing Office, and there they were allowed to remain for a fortnight during which they were available for hire. The bounty immigrants were not so fortunate. No quarters were provided for them at the Immigration Barracks, and their only provision against discomfort, or, it might be, want, was the chance of immediate employment or the possession of a little money. Thus it was that on July 27th, 1839, the day after the barque Strath-fieldsaye entered Port Jackson with 203 immigrants on board, including Henry Parkes and his wife, and one child born off Cape Howe, this paragraph ap-peared in the *Sydney Herald* :—

" IMMIGRATION.—The following is an abstract of the immi-grants by the ship Strathfieldsaye, which arrived on Thursday, and is now lying off Walker's Wharf : 29 married and 54 single farm labourers and shepherds ; one married and 4 single carpenters ;

one single printer; 3 single gardeners; and one lawyer, one shoemaker, ONE TURNER, one painter, one whitesmith, one saddler, and one mason—all married; 21 dairymaids and female farm servants; 9 house servants and 2 needlewomen—singlewomen. These people having arrived by a bounty ship are not allowed by the Governor to enter the building erected for the use of immigrants, and therefore we earnestly recommend those persons who are in want of servants to engage them as early as possible in order to prevent them from falling into that distress which is inevitable if they remain long disengaged."

The young immigrant—he was but 24 years of age—suffered many hardships during the first few years after his arrival in Sydney. It was not easy for him to obtain permanent and suitable employment, and he followed two or three occupations before he was, in colonial parlance, able to settle down. After wandering about Sydney for several days he engaged himself as a labourer on the estate of the late Sir John Jamison, at Regentville, near Penrith, where he obtained the experience he was sometimes heard to say he possessed of washing sheep. Then he obtained employment in an ironmongery store, and afterwards in an iron foundry; and for a short period he was a tidewaiter in the Department of the Customs. The last-named position he relinquished in consequence of the results of his drawing prominent attention to what he regarded as malpractices or improprieties in some of the proceedings connected with the work of the Department.

Subsequently he betook himself to the trade he had acquired in England. Having apprenticed himself in Birmingham to an ivory and bone turner,

he had learned to use the lathe with skill and effectiveness; and now with a little money he had saved
during the time he had been in the colony he opened
a small turner's shop, first in Kent-street, and afterwards in Hunter-street, Sydney.

In an old Directory—the *City of Sydney Directory* for 1844-45—there is the name of " Henry
Parkes, Ivory and Bone Turner, Kent-street."   In
a second edition of the same publication, issued in
1847, but dealing with matters as they were in
the year previous, there is, among a list of fourteen
persons of similar occupation, the name of " Henry
Parkes, Ivory and Bone Turner, 25 Hunter-street,"
and in another part of the Directory an advertise-
ment of " Henry Parkes, Ivory and Toy Manufacturer, No. 25 Hunter-street," informing the public
that he always had on hand a long list of fancy and
useful little articles made from ivory or bone.

Few people now know where in Hunter-street
this little shop was situated, for not many are alive
who can remember the little shop-window showing
a lathe, and a tall, strongly built young man, with a
remarkable head and thoughtful countenance, hard
at work behind it, and a stall-board in front of him
containing the articles which were the products of
his labour.   It stood one door from Hamilton
Lane, close to Pitt-street, and until very recently
a building of the same kind, which adjoined it,
was still in existence, unaltered from what it was
fifty years ago.   Small in size, quaint in appearance, and encroaching upon the footpath, this relic
of the old days was very different from what is

usual in the modern style of business architecture ;
and with an assortment of goods in the window
somewhat varied from the curiosities it contained,
the shop of the turner of 1846 could easily have
been recognised.

From this place of business Henry Parkes
removed to a shop built for him, and still standing,
on the opposite side of Hunter-street, and near to
the George-street corner, where he continued the
manufacture and sale of fancy goods until journalism
bent his energies in another and more important
direction.

But while in the modest structure near Hamilton
Lane, and long before a journalistic career was
decided upon, it was a common thing to see the
young turner hard at work at his lathe, with, more
frequently than not, by his side or on the bench in
front of him, the newspaper, which as his work
would allow, he intently perused.   In those days
newspapers were neither so plentiful nor so easily
obtained as they are now, and the future statesman
was obliged to borrow the journal and read it as he
worked.   Even at the present time this habit of
reading in the opportunities afforded by his work is
spoken of in terms of admiration by some who
observed him at that struggling period.   Round
about him in his little establishment, displayed for
sale, was the collection of useful and fancy articles,
most of which his handiness at the lathe had
produced—billiard and bagatelle balls, chess and
backgammon men, card-counters and whist-markers,
ivory and bone whistles, paper knives, ladies' needle-

cases, egg-cups, knitting-pins, children's rattles, humming-tops, cups and balls, studs, buttons,—all kinds of little things which a turner in ivory and bone manufactures ; and in the production of such articles he was occupied day after day.

He was, however, no ordinary man, and those who were most intimate with him at that date, have asserted this most emphatically. One who knew him well, and can describe the interesting circumstances of the purchase by him of two whale's teeth, which he afterwards turned into bagatelle balls, declares that at all times he was in appearance and in manner superior to the usual type of men. His dress was better than that generally met with, and his bearing reserved and thoughtful. A story is told of him which is typical of his whole career. In the early lives of most distinguished men there have been incidents which have indicated their future prominence, and such are to be found in the early history of Sir Henry Parkes. Having assisted at the first election of Aldermen in the City Council, the part he had taken in the proceedings led a neighbouring tradesman to remark to him, in a conversation upon the result of the election— "Well, Mr. Parkes, we must put you up for Councillor."   " Mr. Smith," said the future Prime Minister, drawing himself erect, and speaking in a lofty and, as subsequent events proved, prophetic tone, "if ever I put up for anything it will be for something higher than Councillor;" and Mr. Smith's well meant intention came summarily to an end.

This apparent consciousness of future high position in the colony, which in various circumstances would assert itself, combined with a manner that stamped him as superior to most of his fellows, prevented him from being generally liked. He was respected,—he compelled respect, as he did throughout his life ; but for a time he did not make many friends.

When he left England that country was in the midst of the Chartist agitation, the English laboring classes clamouring for reform with a view to improve their means of existence, and threatening a revolution if they were not granted what they asked; and it was somewhat singular, and, as events proved, appropriate, that he should land in New South Wales amongst a people who not long afterwards were agitating vigorously for the redress of their grievances and not altogether averse to resorting to physical force if their demands were not satisfied.

No better opportunity for the employment of a strong mind of pronounced liberal tendency than that apparent at the period of Henry Parkes' arrival in the colony, could have presented itself to the young immigrant.

New South Wales was in its early youth, almost its infancy. It had passed through the worst of the experiences which attended the transportation system, and was commencing the struggle to free tself from any further taint of convictism. There was manifesting itself a deep desire for the purification of society, and for the introduction of free

institutions. It was beginning to be felt that the
time had arrived when the community should cast
off the fetters with which Imperial policy and
officialism had bound it, and assert its ability and
its right to go on in its own way regardless of all
but that which conduced to its prosperity. The
cry for self-government was heard. Years had yet
to pass before the darkness of the system which
then oppressed the colony was to give way to the
light of better things, but signs of the approaching
dawn were beginning to appear.

The general picture presented by the community
at this period was not pleasing. There was a
Legislative Council in existence, but the Governor
was paramount in it, and possessed powers that
made him virtually an autocrat. Transported felons
were to be seen at work in the streets, and at the
prison barracks, which the present generation of
colonists know as the Court of Bankruptcy and
formerly as the Immigration Barracks, the type
of convict depicted in the vivid pages of " His
Natural Life " might easily have been found. The
gaol fronted George-street, in the neighbourhood
of Essex-street, and the populace were in the habit
of congregating above Essex-street, on what was
called Gallows Hill, to witness the public execution
of condemned criminals.

Society was in a very unsatisfactory state. In
Sydney there was an unpleasant distinction of
classes, unavoidable perhaps in the circumstances of
the population being small and the convict element
extensive, but excessively irritating to the respect-

able immigrant unconnected with officialdom and untainted by the committal of any offence against the law.

Bushranging was very prevalent. "The arm of Justice has not been stayed," said the Governor, Sir George Gipps, at the meeting of the Legislative Council on June 11th, 1839, "for during the last Session the last sentence of the Law was passed upon eleven unfortunate beings, and acting under the advice of the Executive Council only two of these have been spared. Five have been executed, and four have been respited, because they asserted they could prove an alibi, but that having failed they are destined to meet the same fate as the others." The burden of the Governor's address on this occasion was crime and it punishment. "I believe," he declared, "it is too true that many deeds of rapine, blood, and villainy have lately been committed, and that there are now more armed depredators roaming about the colony than there have been for some months." Not very long before Dr. Wardell, a prominent colonist, was shot dead in an encounter with bushrangers on his private grounds in what is now the populous suburb of Petersham.

The City of Sydney and its environs were in a very primitive condition. There was no Circular Quay in existence. What is now a long line of well-appointed wharfs was, for most of its extent, a beach or muddy shore with the creek or water-course known as the Tank Stream flowing into it. Pinchgut (Fort Denison of to-day) was a rocky barren islet. Sydney

Cove, the site of the present Circular Quay, contained on the western side a wharf known as the Queen's Wharf, and another called Campbell's Wharf, and there were a few other wharfs scattered around Miller's Point and Darling Harbour. At the rear of Upper Fort-street was Walker's Wharf where Henry Parkes first landed on Australian soil.

The English and Foreign commerce of the Port for the most part was carried on in vessels so small that at the present day they would be considered as almost too insignificant for trading between the colonies.

Where the Town Hall and St. Andrew's Cathedral now raise their stately towers the old burial place of the colony stood, closed from further interments but intact, with quaint-looking weatherworn gravestones crowding the ground, and a brick wall which surrounded the cemetery projecting far into the street. This locality, in fact, so limited in extent was Sydney then, might be regarded as at that period quite out of town. St. Philip's Church crested the summit of Church Hill as it does now, and as the gaol and the principal military barracks were in close proximity, both prisoners and soldiers were in the habit of attending divine worship there. Charlotte Place was the chief official quarter of the town, and between Jamieson-street and Barrack-street, and facing George-street for almost the whole of that distance, the military barracks were situated.

The Church generally in the colony had begun to exert itself by the formation of religious organisations, but its efforts for the good of society were as yet very feeble. State aid to religion was in existence, and "Church and State, and may they never be separated," was a standard sentiment with Churchmen.

Newspapers were in their infancy, and though they displayed no small degree of ability, were outspoken, and exercised a certain influence, they had not at that period entered upon a career of continuous and solid advantage to the community.

Education had not been brought under a general and beneficial system, and schools were few, and for the most part inefficient. The Irish National System, which was subsequently introduced and retained until the present Public Schools came into existence, was being talked about, but some years had to pass before it was brought into operation. The future author of the Public Schools Act could see before him a clear field for the efforts which in 1866 were to lay for his name the foundation of an immortality.

The Drama, so far as it had been introduced into the colony, was in its earliest days. "The Theatre," said a newspaper notice of the period, "re-opens this evening, and if we may judge from the piece that is to be played the same description of trash that was brought out last season will be repeated." "If," it went on to say, "the 'Tempter,' and such pieces are kept up through the season it will have the effect of driving the few respectable people who still go to the theatre entirely away." And, proceeding to allude to the manner in which the performances were conducted, the notice remarked,—"Generally speaking the tragedy or comedy is presented to the

public without any care having been taken either as
to the dresses or scenery, and the whole of the
'business' is managed in the most slovenly manner."

The railway, the telegraph wire, rapid and safe
communication between one place and another, were
dreams of the future. The country was in a large
measure little better than a wilderness, but presenting opportunities of the highest kind for the
guiding hand of the future Member of the Legislature and Minister of the Crown.

CHAPTER II.

IN 1842 Sir Henry Parkes published his first volume of Poems under the title "Stolen Moments," with the quotation from Coleridge

> " Stolen
> From anxious Self, life's cruel taskmaster,"

and dedicated to Lieutenant-Colonel Gibbes "as a faint token of gratitude for services rendered." Colonel Gibbes was a friend of Henry Parkes. At the time of his employment in the Customs Department Colonel Gibbes was its head, and after the honest but perhaps indiscreet tidewaiter had left the service his chief, not forgetful of his merits, gave him high testimonials which he spoke of with satisfaction to his last day.

The book is interesting because it gives an insight into the writer's character, and some representation of his circumstances at the time when the poems appeared in this collected form. Most of them, the author tells us, in the preface to the little book, had seen the light previously in periodical publications in Australia or in England. Of those which had been published in New South Wales all but one had filled a place in the columns of the *Australasian Chronicle*, a newspaper at that time under the editorship of the late Mr. W. A. Duncan, and the one exception had appeared in the *Sydney* (now the *Sydney Morning Herald*). The expense of printing the little volume would seem to have been defrayed by subscription, for the book contains a long list of subscribers. As it appeared in 1842, the date of its publication was just three years after the author had arrived in the colony, and his ability to obtain the support of such a large number of persons as the list of subscribers represents, some of them men occupying positions among the highest in the land, indicates that in spite of adverse circumstances he had contrived to make himself both known and respected in the community.

In his preface he expressed the hope that his modest efforts to court the Muse might be of some little service to the cause of Australian Literature, by encouraging " some Australian bard to seize in earnest the unstrung lyre of his beautiful country," but though the desire to assist any legitimate literary enterprise may have been the incentive which elicited the support of some of the subscribers, most of them must have had a personal knowledge of, and some regard for, the writer. Evidently he had begun to make his way, and to prepare for the bolder movements and the higher flights in which his progressive mind and his strong will were to be engaged in the future. His subsequent success as a journalist with the *Empire* newspaper undoubtedly owed something to his efforts in writing verse, for these efforts, and the occasional production of prose articles, were perseveringly carried on for many years.

Some of the poems in "Stolen Moments" were written in Birmingham in 1834, when the age of the writer could not have been more than nineteen. Others were written in London in 1838. Nearly all, he said, were put together "in moments literally stolen from the time occupied by the ordinary duties of a not over-happy life," and a study of some of them will show how true this statement was.

In some "Retrospective Lines, written on the passage from England to Australia in the year 1839,"
we get a picture of an emigrant ship such as he journeyed in to Australia. "To complete the wretchedness of the crowded hole," he says, in a note, alluding to the 'tween deck experiences on board the vessel, "in which three or four hundred human beings are pent together for the space of four months, the ear is incessantly assailed by the coarse expressions and blasphemies of the profligate ; and the eye, let it turn where it will, is offended by some malignity or unnecessary unpleasantness in the conduct of those around."

We learn from the same "Lines" something of his habits in early manhood. As already mentioned, he was an ardent pursuer of knowledge. Whilst working hard for a livelihood as a mechanic :

"I mingled with the blessed few
Of Nature's children whom I ever knew,
Who strove with poverty, in bold pursuit
Of knowledge, and of freedom its best fruit.
*   *   *   *   *

c

I have watched the children of the poor,
Like Hunger's victims at the rich man's door,
Who turn not from denial, jeer, or threat,
But knock the louder till some bread they get,—
Yes! watched them oft to wisdom's waters come,
From toils ungenial, trials wearisome,
Press through all obstacles, to gain the brink,
Thirsting for knowledge, and resolved to drink.

          *   *   *   *   *

"Though 'gainst them their country's schools were barred,
Not all unblest were they with lot so hard,
They had—enough to make your boasters mute—
Their own self-reared Mechanics' Institute."

His verses breathe a deep love for England. He possessed to the full that veneration for the mother country as "home" which is characteristic of most emigrants from her shores, and some of his poems manifest an intense longing to return.

"It may come mine when future years are gone,
Yet in beloved England to possess
A home of peace, and think of all I've done,
Even with a keener tranquil happiness
Than if I could have passed through life with suffering less

And again :

"It may be here that Britons find
Scenes brighter than they leave behind ;
But, oh ! the counter-charm for home
Is found not yet, where'er I roam
O'er sea or land."

Equally strong with his love for England in these "Stolen Moments" was his loyalty to the Throne, and it is rather remarkable that an ode to the young Queen Victoria, published in this unpretending volume, should appear as a prominent

feature, used to considerable advantage, in an
eloquent speech delivered by the author of the poem
in the Legislative Assembly of New South Wales, on
the occasion of his moving an address of congratu-
lation to the Queen in the jubilee year of her reign,
nearly fifty years after the poem was written. The
lines are worth quoting for they are harmonious,
picturesque, and forcible.

> " High-destined daughter of our country, thou
> Who sitt'st on England's throne in beauty's morning !
> God pour His richest blessings round thee now ;
> And may the eyes that watch thy glory's dawning
> With hearts right glad and loyal, proudly scorning
> All that dare hostile to Victoria be,
> Daily behold new light thy name adorning !
> So may'st thou trust thy people's love for thee,
> Queen of this mighty land, Protectress of the Free ! "

" Stolen Moments " was published at five
shillings. In 1892 in Sydney, at auction, copies of
it were sold at from £5 to £7 each.

CHAPTER III.

SIR Henry Parkes was always a man of strong
political opinions, in close sympathy with the people,
and an earnest and active worker in all matters for
the progress and development of the country.

The hard lot of the working population of
England which, as a very young man, he had to share,
and the longing for that improvement which would
make the enjoyments of life less unequally distributed amongst the people, will be found depicted
in his earlier poems ; and coming to New South
Wales at a time when the social as well as the
political condition of the colony was in some
respects worse than anything of the kind in the
parent land, it was natural that his early impressions
should deepen, and that he should set himself to
reflect how things might be altered for the better.
With the wrongs in his native land, which the
Chartists were struggling against just before his
departure as a penniless emigrant, fresh in his
memory, a consciousness that the evils which he had
left need not under wise government be allowed to
exist in this newly peopled country, and the mental

and physical vigour requisite for the work of reform and progress, he wanted only the means through which he might do useful public service ; and almost from his arrival in Sydney he seems to have seen those means in a well conducted liberal newspaper press.

Arriving in New South Wales friendless and without money, it was not to be expected that he should be able to at once engage in this high occupation. It was necessary that he should first establish himself in the community and make himself generally known. This he very quickly did. The respect and confidence, which the list of subscribers to the book of poems published in 1842 shows he had won since his landing in Sydney, were not long in extending. Gradually these feelings towards him became more pronounced and wide-spread, and though at this early period of his life he was not without enemies, he made some warm friends. As opportunity offered he took part in public movements, and he wrote occasional articles for the press, his contributions appearing in the *Atlas*, or in the *People's Advocate*. All this attracted attention. He became known as a clever public speaker and a capable writer. Public meetings offered facilities for the exercise and display of his oratorical powers ; in journalism he saw the way to literary success. Friends with the means which were necessary to establish a newspaper did not hesitate to come to his assistance, and in December, 1849, in premises adjoining the shop in Hunter-street, on the south side of the street, the *Empire* was first published.

A year before this he was a prominent figure in the proceedings connected with an election of members to the Legislative Council. Mr. Robert Lowe, afterwards Lord Sherbrooke, was a candidate for the City of Sydney, and Henry Parkes, attaching himself to Mr. Lowe's committee, became one of the joint secretaries. Subsequently he interested himself in the agitations which were taking place for the discontinuance of transportation to the colony, and for the introduction of self-government.

At an open-air meeting, known afterwards as "The Great Protest Meeting," attended by 4000 persons, and held on vacant land near the Circular Quay, and in front of the old Colonial Secretary's Office, Henry Parkes was one of the principal speakers. Transportation, which for a time had ceased, had been resumed in a modified form, and the arrival of the first convict vessel under the new system was the cause of the meeting. This vessel — the *Hashemy* — entered the Heads on June 8th, 1849, and on the following day, in consequence of the arrival about the same date of several vessels with free immigrants on board, there was to be seen the singular and exasperating spectacle of a shipload of convicts in the midst of 1400 or 1500 newly-arrived free people. Popular feeling was deeply stirred, and a vigorously worded protest was adopted at the great public meeting. That protest, which, while expressing due loyalty to the British Crown, set forth in unmistakeably plain terms the grievance of the colonists, was written by Mr. Parkes.

He was very earnest in the part he took in this anti-transportation movement. Regarding the will of the majority of the colonists in the matter as entitled to the highest respect and consideration of the British Secretary of State, he denounced the indifference manifested by the resumption of transportation as a deep insult to the free community of New South Wales, and a serious obstacle to the progress of the country. "We wanted," he said in one of his speeches, in allusion to the qualifications necessary in a Government dealing with this colony, " men practically acquainted with every impulse, every transition and phase of our existence as a people," not those who were simply "raised to power or precipitated from office by the cumulative force of a series of accidents."

In the midst of this great movement for the total cessation of transportation to the colony, and for the right of the people to govern themselves through "Ministers chosen from and responsible to the colonists," this second demand springing naturally from the injustice which had prompted the other, the first number of the *Empire* appeared.

There were some who had not hesitated to charge Mr. Parkes and the others who were prominent in denouncing the indifference of the British Cabinet to the interests of the colony with disloyalty, and with endeavouring to bring about a " reign of terror." The same charge, for the circumstances were unaltered, might have been made in the early days of the *Empire*. But no foundation existed for it in either case. " I will yield to no man in feelings of

loyalty to the British Crown," Mr. Parkes declared
in a speech delivered at one of the anti-transportation
meetings in 1849; "but my loyalty does not teach
me to shut my eyes to the faults of Government.
It rather constrains me—and the stronger it grows
the more it constrains me—to seek a reform of
public abuses, that the Government may be established firmly and permanently in the affections of
a free people."

This declaration might have formed a statement
of the principles of the new journal, for it accurately
describes the paper's policy. It may even be regarded as a declaration of the policy of the speaker's
whole life, for loyalty to the Throne and an earnest
ever-present desire to benefit the people were the
chief characteristics of Sir Henry Parkes' career
throughout the long period of his public services.

At first the *Empire* was published as a broadsheet weekly. Very soon it began to appear as a
daily; not of large size, but containing a fair
quantity of news and with it a couple of vigorously-
written leading articles. The leading articles very
quickly became the great feature of the paper.
Regardless of whom it might offend, so long as the
complaint or censure were merited, abuse, wherever
it existed, or by whomsoever it might be committed,
was unsparingly exposed, and the perpetrator scari-
fied by an able and caustic pen. Independence,
honesty, and the public interest were the journal's
watchwords. "Clearly impressed with our duty,"
the editor announced, "we shall never allow our
minds to waver in its performance. It will be no

part of our business to study who may be gratified
or who displeased by our line of conduct. Persons
or parties may disown or assent to our opinions; we
shall maintain them with the same boldness and
singleness of purpose, so long as we believe them to
be correct." At once the paper attracted attention,
and won public favour.

The field for its operations was very wide.
Political affairs at the time were conducted in a
manner of little benefit to the colony; social matters
were in a condition far from satisfactory. The
Governor, Sir Charles Fitzroy, who, in those days,
virtually ruled the politics of the country, as well as
filled the position of leader of society, was, by a
large proportion of the colonists, neither liked nor
respected. Complaints, censure, ridicule, condemnation, even insult, directed at Government House,
were, in some of the public journals of the period,
almost as common as news. The *Empire* was an uncompromising opponent of Sir Charles Fitzroy, and
never lost an opportunity to criticise or condemn his
conduct or that of some of those by whom he was
surrounded in the administration of government.
Many of its contemporaries were prompt and warm
in its praise. "The *Empire* promises to become a
highly useful paper; in fact it appears to be just
the sort of paper which has long been required,"
said one. "We are glad to be able to admire the
tone and spirit of its arguments," said another. "Its
numerous leading articles are well and vigorously
written," was the opinion of a third; and others
were equally complimentary.

While the *Empire* was passing through the first few months of its career, gold was discovered in New South Wales, and the impetus which this immediately gave to business was not without its effect upon the fortunes of the new journal. Six months after its first issue it was enlarged to a double-demy broadsheet, the size of the *Sydney Morning Herald*, and its circulation and influence progressed rapidly.

Mr. Parkes became a man of considerable importance. The guiding spirit of a great newspaper necessarily occupies a high position in a British community, and Mr. Parkes as proprietor and editor of the *Empire* speedily became a prominent and well recognised figure. The journalistic instinct he possessed in a marked degree, and while he made his paper interesting he took care that its opinions should be felt. News, at that time, was not so available as it became some years later, but what there was to be had the *Empire* columns obtained ; and the strength and independence of the leading articles, combined with the fact that they were written in the public interest, caused the paper not only to be read but to be talked about.

Many stories are told of the editor's industry and smartness at this period of his life. At that time the greatest effort of the newspapers was to obtain at the earliest moment possible the latest news from England, which was brought by sailing vessel, the voyage occupying three or four months. The electric telegraph not being in existence it was necessary to meet the ship having the news on board, immediately she arrived within convenient distance of Sydney, and to do this the leading papers, the *Herald* and the *Empire*, were each obliged to have at hand a fast sea-going boat, like a whale-boat, with a competent crew. There was no working together, no mutual assistance, on the part of the two boats. Competition was the order of the day with them as it was with the papers, and every effort was made by each to be the first to secure the all important information. For miles outside Sydney Heads the boats would go at racing speed, each eager to be the first to reach the approaching vessel. Often the chief in the office of the *Empire*, determined to perform his share of the duty of giving the public the earliest intelligence, would remain at the office all night, awake and on the alert, for the "copy," which, if too late for the ordinary morning issue of the paper, would be most attractive matter for a second edition published towards the middle of the day. No labour was too arduous, no effort too great, so long as there was a prospect of the news columns being more than ordinarily interesting.

Naturally this close attention to his duties in the *Empire* office occupied the whole of his time, but his admirers believing him to be as well fitted for the Legislative Chamber as for the editor's chair, urged him to enter Parliament, to add the active life of the politician to the never-ceasing labours of the journalist, and ill-matched as the duties of the two positions seemed to be, eventually he consented.

CHAPTER IV.

The early portion of the parliamentary career of Sir Henry Parkes was passed in one of the most interesting and momentous periods of Australasian history, the period of the close of the struggle for the introduction of responsible government and its establishment.

Until 1843, when the Constitution Act which first introduced the representative principle in the Parliament of New South Wales came into force, the Legislature of the colony was a purely nominee body consisting of officials appointed to positions in the country by the Imperial Government, and nominated to the Legislature by the Governor for the time being. The Act of 1843 accorded the privilege of electing representatives to certain portions of the colony, and this was recognised as an important step towards full representation, but it was thirteen years from that time before representative government as it now exists in New South Wales became an established fact.

From 1843 to 1856 an incessant agitation for responsible government was carried on. Satisfactory as was in some respects the representation afforded the people by the Act of 1843, the nominee element in Parliament, whenever it cared to exercise its numerical strength, was successful in division, and this led the representative members and others of similar opinions outside the Legislature to do all in their power to bring about a change. In the Legislature there were William Charles Wentworth, Dr. Bland, George Robert Nichols, Charles Cowper, Terence Aubrey Murray, William Henry Suttor, and Edward Flood; and these formed the first advance guard of Liberalism. Later on Sir James Martin was elected to the Legislative Council, and he joined the party of Liberals, though with the liberal tendency of his opinions there was combined a conservative instinct which prevented him from going as far as the others in the advocacy of liberal measures.

Sir Henry Parkes entered Parliament for the first time in 1854, two years before the introduction of the system of government for which he, with the Liberal party in the colony, had been vigorously and persistently fighting. In later life he often alluded to the slow development of his parliamentary career towards the position of Minister of the Crown, as exemplifying the patience with which he performed the duties of a private member of Parliament before he thought of filling any office in the Government. He was similarly patient in awaiting the

time when he could fittingly enter Parliament.
Fifteen years had passed after his arrival in the
colony before he took a seat in the Legislature, and
for most of that period he had in one way or another,
largely as the conductor of the *Empire*, done useful
service in the public interest.   Unremittingly he
had worked, always for the good of the country,
with no definite intention of taking a special part in
politics, but at the same time, by the very nature of
his every-day duties, steadily qualifying himself for
the important part he was destined to perform in
Parliament.

Very quickly he attracted notice as a
public speaker.   The anti-transportation movement
was a suitable means for the encouragement and
growth of public oratory, and as a member of the
Anti-Transportation League he made some thoughtful and vigorous speeches, in which indications of
the eloquence for which in later years he became
remarkable are plainly to be seen.   Then came the
question of responsible government, and with that,
in due course, the subject of a new Constitution.

The latter question was brought prominently
before the public mind by what was known as
Wentworth's Constitution Bill.   This measure,
afterwards greatly altered and now with those
alterations the law under which New South Wales
enjoys self-government, contained in its original form
a number of very objectionable provisions which
aroused a feeling of indignation and protest from one
end of the country to the other.   The creation of a

colonial nobility with hereditary privileges, the
establishment of a nominee Upper House of Legislature, the giving of undue representation in the
Lower House to the country and squatting interests
at, it was considered, the expense of Sydney, and
the infliction upon the people of a heavy pension
list in the interests of those officers of the Government who on the introduction of a new Constitution
would be expected to retire from their offices,
were among its proposals. Mr. Wentworth, liberal-
minded as he was in most matters concerning the
colony and its progress, framed portions of his
great measure in a manner which met with almost
universal disapproval, and from being a very popular
man he became very unpopular. Eventually the
proposal for a colonial peerage was abandoned, but
the nominee Upper House exists now, and the
pension list also.

The bill was powerfully assailed by Mr. Parkes
on the public platform, and in the columns of the
Empire; and as vigorously did he denounce the proceedings of the Imperial Government of the day on
the transportation question. Inevitably he came to
be regarded as a prominent man in the community,—
an unflinching advocate of all that appeared for the
advantage of the people, an uncompromising opponent of everything detrimental to their interests, and
withal possessed of the power to express his opinions
effectively. While a capable journalist associated
with a well-conducted journal is a person of position
and influence in whatever part of the world his

work may be performed, when, in addition to his
public services by means of his journal, he exerts
himself unselfishly and in pure patriotism as a
speaker on the popular side, he becomes, particularly
in a young and progressive country like New South
Wales, a leader among his fellow-men, respected,
trusted, and honoured.

So it came to pass in the circumstances surrounding the position which Mr. Parkes had by this time
acquired in the community that he was urged to
allow himself to be nominated to a seat in the
Legislature vacated by Mr. W. C. Wentworth with
the intention of visiting England in support of the
Constitution Bill; and on the 2nd May, 1854, he
was triumphantly elected Member for the City of
Sydney.

The election was a more than ordinarily important one. Mr. Wentworth's Constitution Bill, and
the squatting system, by which appellation was
known a system in operation in the colony beneficial to the squatting class, and of little or no
advantage to anybody else, were the immediate
questions of the hour, and those upon which the
election was fought. "There never was an election
in this colony," said the *Empire* in its leading
article on the day the result of the polling was
published, " in which political principles were so
plainly the gauge of the contest as in that which
has just terminated. There never probably was an
election before, in which political principles so important to the future career of the colony were
brought to the issue of a contest."

There was some excuse for the tone of self-laudation in which the writer of the article had indulged. The contest had been severe ; the victory was unmistakable; the total number of votes polled by the successful candidate was larger by over a hundred than on any previous occasion in the colony had been recorded for a representative, and in every ward in the city Mr. Parkes had obtained a majority. He had been opposed in the election by Mr. Charles Kemp, a journalist like himself but not so clearly identified with the popular cause, and he defeated Mr. Kemp by 1427 votes as against 779.

Mr. Parkes' speech at the nomination of candidates is interesting, for it outlines the course of conduct which marked his political life from that time to the end.

" I am not one of those," he said, " who look out for persons of leisure to fill important public offices, for I believe that every one created in God's image must do what he conceives to be his duty, whether he have leisure or not; and whatever the sacrifices he may be called upon to make, a man must not shrink from discharging that duty."

He considered the power of the people should be paramount in a country such as New South Wales. " I believe that the danger here will be in limiting, not in extending, the power of the people. . . . . that the only danger which can accrue to the country will and must result from withholding that political power and those full privileges to which the people are entitled as free-born Britons."

D

On the question of education, he said,—" I have already declared myself, as systems at present stand, in favour of the National system. But so much importance do I attach to the work of mental training as the foundation of every social virtue, that I should be prepared to support any modification or alteration of that system which would more adapt it to the peculiar wants of the remote, thinly-populated, and scattered districts of the colony." Railways, he was of opinion, should, on a gigantic scale, be at once commenced, whatever the present cost, or whatever debt, within reasonable bounds, might result to posterity. "We must, however," he explained, "see first that the work is based upon sound principles, which, if carried out, will render the railways permanently useful." Of the vast importance to the country of public works of all descriptions he was very conscious.

He earnestly hoped he might prove "a valued member of the Legislature." "If it should be my fortune to be elected," he went on to say, "and I should find myself an uninfluential member of the House, my pride would not allow me to remain, whether you asked me to resign or not. That pride would compel me to retreat from a position for which I found myself unqualified, as much for my own sake as for the character of the constituency."

And with regard to his position in relation to the wealthy, as well as the poorer classes of the people, in the event of his election : " I would support the rights of the richest among you, but at the same time, with the same vigour, the same determination, the same energy, I would support the rights of the humblest and poorest. . . . I have ever set myself against class legislation of every kind. I would no more truckle to the working classes than to the highest; and at the same time I believe that among the lowest classes there is often to be found the largest share of those energies which are most valuable to a young country, and on which every institution of the country must depend."

There is much in these extracts from the nomination speech that marks the lines upon which the subsequent career of Sir Henry Parkes in Parliament was conducted, as there was much in the incidents of the election resembling the features of later contests when the triumph was equally pronounced. Shoulder high the future Premier was raised by his supporters at the close of the proceedings after the declaration of the poll; and, followed by an enthusiastic crowd, he was carried amidst vociferous cheering through the streets. It would almost seem from the manner of the crowd, the large support accorded in the voting, and the satisfaction expressed on all sides at the result of the contest, that there was abroad in the city a presentiment, if not a conviction, of the great public services which the successful candidate was destined to perform in Parliament, and of the high political position he was to attain. "This election," said the writer of the *Empire's* leading article in his concluding paragraph, "so full of strong and spontaneous support to the popular cause, so crushing to the faction of an old and corrupt misrule, we trust is the opening of a new era of progress for the country."

In his speech at the declaration of the poll, Mr. Parkes alluded to the circumstance of his having been elected the successor of Mr. Wentworth, whom he styled the greatest man who ever trod this country. "In assuming the position which he has vacated," he said, "I shall endeavour to copy all that was great in his political career, and avoid his errors." Great as Wentworth undoubtedly was in his services to the colony, not many years were to pass before the man who succeeded to his place in the Legislature would be acknowledged universally to be greater, and in important public services and statesmanship to have no superior in Australasia.

Mr. Parkes was sworn in a Member of the Legislative Council on 9th May, 1854, and for a few days he was silent.

The period was critical, for it was the eve of the Crimean War, and there was a feeling of alarm in Sydney at the unpreparedness of the city and of the port to resist attack. But Mr. Parkes, probably seeing that as a new member among a number of old and experienced legislators, his opinion expressed in the House might for the time have little or no effect, contented himself with saying what he had to say in the leading columns of his journal. So, for a time, though he was a regular attendant in the House, and took an active interest in everything, his voice was not often heard. He sat with the small band of elected members who were generally opposed to the official members or nominees, among them being

Charles Cowper, James Martin, Terence Aubrey Murray, J. B. Darvall, G. R. Nichols, Robert Campbell, W. Thurlow, Daniel Cooper, and Stuart Alexander Donaldson.

Cowper, active, adroit, and generally capable, aimed at securing the leadership of the Liberal Party; and, by the time the new Constitution of 1856 had been brought into existence, he had attained this position. Martin was a rising solicitor, young in years, slim in appearance, with considerable power of speech in which invective was frequently prominent, and generally recognised as a young man of very good ability. From his first election he had taken a very active part in the Council, and had shown indications of future prominence in legislative work. Murray (afterwards Sir Terence Aubrey Murray), though of pronounced liberal views, was aristocratic in appearance and in manner, and was not popular. The sharp lines by which society in the colony had been divided up to this time had thrown the gentlemen of the country together, and as a class they were very exclusive. G. R. Nichols, a solicitor, was a very able man and a very advanced radical; and Donaldson was a man of large financial knowledge combined with liberal views, the latter being tempered by a moderate conservatism.

John Robertson had not yet appeared as a public man, but he and Henry Parkes had met. One day a young man, with something of the rough appearance of the bush about him, entered the editor's room in the *Empire* office, and immediately set about

introducing himself. Extending his hand he grasped
that of the editor, and saying how glad he was to
see him and how he had long looked forward to the
meeting, announced himself as " John Robertson of
Yurundi." Not long afterwards young Robertson
was a witness before a select committee of Members
of the Legislative Council, of which Mr. Parkes
was chairman, on the state of agriculture in the
colony; and from that time until Sir John Robertson's death a more or less close acquaintance
existed between the two statesmen.

Henry Parkes' acquaintance with William Bede
Dalley commenced about the same time. Then a
very young man, Mr. Dalley was in the habit of
watching the proceedings in the Legislative Council
from the Strangers' Gallery, in the company of two
or three companions about the same age as himself,
and it was in the Strangers' Gallery that Mr.
Parkes first saw him. Introduced to each other, they
were at once intimate friends. Mr. Dalley became a
contributor to the *Empire*, writing frequently ; and
subsequently was appointed with Mr. Parkes to
visit England with a view to promote emigration to
New South Wales.

The first subject upon which Mr. Parkes
addressed the Legislative Council was the light-
house at Gabo Island ; not a very great matter
though undoubtedly important, for it had been
alleged that through a want of supplies the men on
the island had been reduced to a condition of
starvation, and there was danger of the light being
extinguished. It was not long before he took in

hand a much larger question. A little more than a month after he was sworn in, he gave notice of a series of resolutions for the establishment of a system of immigration from Great Britain and the countries of continental Europe, "based on sound economical principles, and having for its primary object a broad identity of interest between the individual immigrant and his adopted country;" and from that time, until the Legislative Council to which he had been elected was about to give way to the Parliament under the Constitution of 1856, he was among the most energetic of members.

CHAPTER V

THE year 1856 saw the fulfilment of the desires of the colonists in the direction of responsible government, and early in that year a general election took place under the new Constitution. Henry Parkes was elected one of four members for Sydney.

Previously to this he had made a determined effort to retire from political life, and devote himself, at least for a period, exclusively to the *Empire*. At the close of the session of the Legislative Council in 1855 he addressed to his constituents a letter, in which he informed them that as in the course of a week the Legislature to which he had been elected would virtually terminate its existence, the time had arrived when he ought to inform them of his intention not to present himself again as a candidate for their suffrages. The announcement took the citizens by surprise, and aroused widespread regret.

"During the two laborious sessions of my service as your representative," he wrote, "I have felt the

:onviction gaining strength, in despite, as I freely own, of some feeling of ambition, that neither my time nor whatever humble ability I might possess, would be sufficiently subjected to my will to enable me to discharge the high and responsible trust reposed in me, with that uniform devotion to the public interest which is implied in its acceptance. Though I have generally been in my place, I have attended the sitting by wrenching myself, as it were, away from other duties of an equally serious nature, which often left me wholly unprepared for the business of the Council; and in the part I have taken there, I have never felt conscious of my success to satisfy my sense of what is due from the representative to his constituents. . . . . .

"In making up my mind to stay outside I have had to conquer a strong feeling which my better judgment has told me ought not to be gratified; but the self-denial has been sweetened by the know-ledge that I have before me another field, fairly won by my own efforts, for future usefulness. I leave the Legislature, as I entered it, from a sense of duty alone. You opened the door for me against singular obstacles; I cheerfully close it with my own hand.

"If I am too poor to make the sacrifices incum-bent on a representative of the people, I am, at least, too proud to accept the honour and neglect the duties of that noble office."

This letter was written in December, 1855. A month later, at an important meeting of citizens, held in the Royal Victoria Theatre, he was chosen one of four candidates in the Liberal interest to represent the City of Sydney in the first Parliament under the new Constitution, by which action on the part of the people, he became committed to a Parliamentary career for life.

A weekly journal of the period, describing the proceedings at a public meeting which was held in the Royal Hotel a few days after the meeting in the Victoria Theatre, stated that there was nothing like general silence and attention until Mr. Parkes rose, that all the discordant elements of which the meeting, attended by the friends of various candidates, consisted, seemed to melt into harmony on his rising to speak ; and "he was not only well received, but welcomed with a perfect wildness of enthusiasm."

" His pale excited earnestness would probably have conquered the prejudices of any audience, and won a respectful attention. But his manifest conscientiousness and straightforward honesty were seconded in this case by a strong sympathy with his political principles, and the demonstration in his favour was genuine and emphatic."

Deeply moved by the earnest desire of the electors that he should go into the Legislative Assembly, he placed himself unreservedly in their hands. His own interests, he explained, and his wish to stand by for a season and " search his own heart and conscience to see how far he had been correct " in his public career, would have kept him aloof from this political conflict, but if the electors forbade him the interval of comparative seclusion

Thomas Parkes
my father
Henry Parkes

he would consult their wishes rather than his own views.

"He knew," he said, "that if he went into the next Legislature he should be for ever doomed to one tremendous struggle in behalf of this country. But if it were the wish of the city which had conferred upon him in former times distinctions, far above any merit he possessed, that he should go to the poll, he would do so, and if he were again elected as the representative of the city of Sydney, he would discharge the duties which would devolve upon him to the utmost extent of his power. One thing at all events he would promise—that he would never be absent when their liberties were at stake; he would never be absent when their money was to be voted away; he would never be absent when new laws might need his advocacy for the advancement of the welfare of their common country. He would promise more—he would never be absent at all so long as he had health to attend. He knew very well the sacrifice he should make—and he confessed that he desired to avoid that for a short time—the discharge of the public duties incumbent upon him would render him comparatively a stranger in his own family. That would be the extent of his sacrifice; but that sacrifice he was prepared to make rather than forfeit the good opinion of the citizens of Sydney, and shrink from a public duty if he was called upon to discharge it."

As was to be expected there were some who charged him with inconsistency, but his intention to retire from politics in the Legislature had been

earnest and genuine, and it was only in consequence
of repeated solicitations from influential sections of
the electors, and unequivocal expressions of approval
of his candidature from the citizens generally, that
he consented to be nominated for election to the
Legislative Assembly.   To use his own words, it
appeared to him that "he would be flying in the face
of the constituency if he were to refuse."   He was
confident of being elected, but he was equal to either
fortune.   If defeated he would feel at all events that
"the gates of Parliament were constitutionally
closed against him"; he could do as he pleased with
his time, and enjoy the pleasures of association with
his children.   But his position in the estimation of
the electors was too good for defeat to be possible.
At the close of his speech at the Royal Hotel he
called upon the meeting, if they really wished that
he should throw himself into the contest to tell him
so by a show of hands.   The appeal was instantly responded to, apparently by the whole meeting, amidst
general applause, and Mr. Parkes acknowledged the
demonstration by declaring he was at the service of
the city.

The contest, long and severe, ended triumphantly.
Six candidates entered the field, and Mr. Parkes, as
one of a "bunch" of four, the number to be
elected, was returned second on the poll, Mr. Charles
Cowper being first, 18 votes ahead, Mr. Robert
Campbell third, and Mr. J. R. Wilshire fourth.
Mr. J. H. Plunkett, who at the time was Attorney
General of the colony, and another candidate, were
defeated.   Mr. Plunkett was a strong man, and in

the election a dangerous opponent. His position in the community, and the fact that he stood alone in the contest as the representative of what had been the ruling class, were circumstances that indicated a great probability of his success, but he was defeated by over a hundred votes below the number recorded for the fourth candidate on the poll.

The nomination proceedings took place on the 12th, and the polling on the 13th March. On the night previous to the nomination a banquet was given to Mr. Charles Gavan Duffy (afterwards knighted, and now Sir Charles Gavan Duffy) in the Prince of Wales Theatre, and Mr. Parkes, a prominent figure on the occasion, delivered a speech in reply to the toast of " The land of our adoption," in which he declared that, under circumstances similar to those in which the Young Ireland party had acted, he would have been a rebel like Mr. Duffy. The declaration has often been quoted against him, and it is as well that his actual words should be given.

Mr. Duffy had recently arrived in Australia to make the country his home, and he had come here with the romantic patriotism of the Young Ireland party and the *Nation* newspaper surrounding him like a halo. Admirers flocked to him from all sides, and people of almost all shades of opinion sought to do him honour. In Sydney the feeling of the community led to the banquet in the Prince of Wales Theatre, the proceedings of which were marked with much enthusiasm. At such a time and in such company the wrongs of Ireland naturally became one of the topics of the speeches.

"Although, like our chairman," said Mr. Parkes, "I do not profess to enter into the spirit of Mr. Duffy's public life in his native country, I yet know this of Irish history and Irish wrongs, that had I been myself an Irishman, with Mr. Duffy's temperament and his principles, I believe I should have been a rebel like him. We all know," he continued, " that during Mr. Duffy's illustrious career one of the most terrible famines that ever passed over any fruitful country desolated Ireland, and that Mr. Duffy, with his fine imagination, his deep feeling of patriotism, must have seen in this famine terrible calls, terrible appeals to him to advocate the cause of his suffering country at every risk and every possible peril. And I only utter in public what I have often said in private, that if I had been born and reared as Mr. Duffy has been, and had been a witness of grinding want and poverty in a land which was intended by Providence to be one of plenty, I should have taken precisely the same course that he has taken."

These words are very plain and clear, but, to do the speaker justice in regard to them, they must be read with a recognition of the popular feeling concerning Mr. Duffy's arrival in the country, of the circumstance that Australia was not without experience of Imperial misgovernment and oppression, and in view of the undeniable loyalty that characterised the public life of Sir Henry Parkes throughout his long career.

The nomination and the polling for the City of Sydney were signal events in the history of the colony. Excitement was general ; the attendance at the hustings, which were in Hyde Park, then known as the Racecourse, was large ; and the proceedings were marked with much enthusiasm. Mr. Parkes' nomination speech contained some remarks of special interest, viewed in the light of events which have occurred since that time.

"I may say without affectation, without any parade of false feeling, that from the circumstances of my early life I have felt the want of education too painfully not to be well alive to its great importance, and I shall steadily labour, and use every energy, to promote education among the people upon a comprehensive and catholic basis." . . "I can assure you whether I am to-morrow night your representative or not, my great object throughout my life will be so to impress my name and my character and my influence on this country, that I may be remembered when I am dead and in my grave."

The chief interest in the election centred in the declaration of the poll. This was in favour of "the Bunch," but it was thought necessary, on the demand of Mr. Plunkett, to have a special examination of the votes, and the final declaration of the poll was not made till some days after the voting had taken place. The scene was very striking. For some reason, said to be the fear of a magistrate that the excitement of the populace would lead to the burning down of the structure, the hustings, which had been the centre of the triumphant proceedings of a few days previously, had been removed, and in its place a cart with an improvised handrail had been obtained. Offended by this, or professing so to be, the victorious " Bunch " refused to mount the cart either to hear the announcement by the Sheriff or to address the electors. They stood amongst the crowd, and the Sheriff, deeply mortified, was obliged to proceed with his duties, having only Mr. Plunkett, the defeated candidate, and one or two others to support him. The Sheriff was a courageous and zealous officer, with a keen sense of his dignity; but the position he was occupying at the time was new to him, and the occasion was marked by an importance such as he had never before experienced. The new-born power of the people ruffled the feathers of the officialism which had hitherto been the governing principle in the colony, and the old-time privileges of the ruling class were receiving some rude rebuffs. He did his best to induce the four elected candidates to ascend the nondescript hustings. He sought them in the crowd; requested, persuaded, entreated, apologised, almost implored them to come ; but they, strong in their success and their popularity, refused point blank, and were inexorable.

They stood together, a little group, not far from the cart, in the midst of a throng of their admirers. We can easily imagine them and their surroundings. Mr. Cowper, eminently respectable in appearance, dignified and condescending in manner ; Mr. Parkes, with the determination and general force of his

character expressed indelibly on his strangely powerful features; Mr. Robert Campbell, with the quiet
sternness of the successful man of business; Mr.
Wilshire, with a face in which satisfaction at the
result of the election was curiously blended with
indignation at certain charges which had been made
against him by opponents in the election;—four
striking figures, with a dense and excited crowd
around them stirred to the depths by the new
sensations of power and importance arising from the
exercise of the great privileges attending the choice
of their own representatives in Parliament. Hyde
Park has witnessed since that time many important elections, accompanied by great excitement
and much enthusiasm, but none more important or
more striking than this. Despairing at last of getting
the "Bunch" to do as he wished, the Sheriff
ascended the cart with Mr. Plunkett, and commenced to address the people. But the crowd
refusing to listen to any speech, wanted the result
of the election in a definite statement of the polling.
"Poll! Poll!" they shouted. "We want to know
the state of the poll!" And the Sheriff was obliged
to submit. The state of the poll, as it appeared
after the special examination which had been made
of the voting, was declared; the victorious "Bunch,"
were shown to be in a more triumphant position
than they were a week previously when the polling
took place; and the jubilation of the crowd was
unbounded.

Messrs. Cowper, Parkes, and Campbell, arm-in-
arm, and Mr. Wilshire, who was suffering from

E

lameness, in his gig, left the ground at the head of a large number of electors, and passing into Market-street, and thence down George-street, went to their committee rooms at the Exchange Hotel, from a window of which they addressed the electors.

"The main feature of the contest," said Mr. Parkes, "the primary and leading idea of it throughout has been Australian," and he expressed the hope that "all present, little boy and white-headed old man, would from that day forth be Australian in their feelings and their aims."

This satisfaction at Australians being the chief actors in all that is important to Australia was a prominent feature in Sir Henry Parkes' life. At the election of Sir J. P. Abbott to the office of Speaker of the Legislative Assembly of New South Wales, thirty-four years after the event of 1856, he gave expression to his satisfaction as an Englishman at the gratifying fact that Sir Joseph Abbot was a native-born Australian. "The time is coming," he said, "when we must all be Australians, and it is a gratifying circumstance to see the men born in the country aspiring to, and fitly qualified for, the highest offices in the State."

CHAPTER VI.

THE first Legislative Assembly in New South Wales was opened on 22nd May, 1856, and was dissolved on 19th December, 1857. Its life was short, for it was found difficult in the early days of the new order of politics, and in the desire to have the system of self-government proceed with the greatest public advantage, for Ministries to remain long in office. In the nineteen months during which the first Assembly was in existence four Ministries were in power, a dissolution of Parliament taking place three months after the fourth Ministry was appointed.

The instability of Governments at this period cannot be said to have been due to an unseemly scramble for office, though party feeling was very prominent. Discouraging as were many of the circumstances connected with the political life of the time, a high political morality pervaded the first Assembly. There were a sense of honour and an uprightness of conduct among most of the members which placed the public interest above personal advantage. The foundation of self-government

having been successfully laid, there was a very
general feeling that the edifice to be built upon it
should be symmetrical and lasting, and there was a
desire to make no false step, but to go forward in the
right direction from the outset.

Henry Parkes sat among a body of men many
of whom would have done honour to any political
assembly in the world. Cowper, Arnold, Darvall,
Donaldson, Forster, Hay, Jones, Macleay, Manning,
Martin, Murray, Nichols, Parker, Piddington,
Robertson, Dalley, Deniehy, and Plunkett, are
names that, in the history of New South Wales,
will ever be conspicuous among those of the men who
were the founders of the liberties which Australians
enjoy and of their wonderful advancement.

But the want of a stable ministry during the
period of the first Legislative Assembly made the
progress of the colony under responsible government, for the time, very slow. The rapid succession of Governments unsettled matters somewhat
seriously. The Donaldson Ministry, the head of
which was in all respects an English gentleman,
resigned after being in office only two months; "in
a fit of petulance" those annoyed at the resignation
described it, but largely because the highmindedness
of an honourable man declined to submit to attacks
prompted, he considered, in some quarters, by little
more than party spirit. He was succeeded by
Mr. Cowper, but no sooner had the Cowper
Government taken office than they were met by a
motion of want of confidence, and the motion was
carried. No time was allowed the hapless ministers

to either announce or initiate a public policy. The Parker Ministry who next came into power were almost equally unfortunate. Attempting land legislation and electoral reform, they failed in both ; and the rejection of their Electoral Bill brought their existence to a termination. Mr. Cowper, re-appearing as the head of an Administration, and having with him Mr. James Martin, Mr. Terence Aubrey Murray, and Mr. Richard Jones, again found it impossible to proceed effectively with public business, but he managed to remain in office until he could secure a dissolution. Introducing a Land Bill, the Government succeeded in passing its second reading by a majority of 36 in a House of 44 ; but so persistently was the measure attacked, both in and out of Parliament, that ultimately it had to be withdrawn. Then appeared a Judges Appointment Bill, which was rejected on the motion for leave to introduce it ; and, following this, a bill to provide for the assessment of stock on squatting runs, which, on the motion for the second reading, was defeated by a majority of one. This, and the difficulty on the land question, brought about a dissolution, and the Parliament went to the country in the hope that a general election would remove the obstacles to progress by sending back one party or the other with the majority necessary to enable them to rule.

Class jealousies and class interests were greatly at variance, the old squatting coterie being strongly opposed to the popular party which the new Constitution had sent into Parliament.

It was at this time that John Robertson was beginning to impress both the Legislature and the people with his scheme for dealing with the public lands of the colony on the principle of free selection before survey. Young and ardent, he lost no opportunity for putting forward his views upon this important question; and much of the difficulty experienced by the second Cowper Government, in their attempt at land legislation, was due to his persistent action. Sensible of the importance of such an opponent, Mr. Cowper considered how best he could be dealt with, and, before the meeting of the new Parliament, decided to accept his land scheme, and to offer him the position of Minister for Lands, which Mr. Robertson accepted. Land legislation on a popular basis became then the chief question of the hour, and the stability of the Cowper Government was assured.

Mr. Parkes sat in Parliament during the first few months of the session of 1856, an attentive observer of its proceedings. When he considered it necessary he was not backward in expressing his views upon the subject under discussion or on any matter claiming his attention, and he and his opinions were held in high respect; but he was not a frequent speaker.

He had been offered office in the Government, and had declined it. Mr. Donaldson, in the desire to secure a satisfactory position for his Administration, saw much to be gained by breaking up the party following Mr. Cowper, and this he thought could be done by including some of the best of them in his

Government. In pursuance of this idea, when forming his Ministry, he offered office to Mr. Cowper, and failing in that, he sought the assistance of Mr. Parkes, the medium of communication between the two being Sir Charles Nicholson. That gentleman seeing Mr. Parkes on the subject, submitted to him a list of names representing those it was desirable to have in the Government; and the list included the names of Mr. Parkes and Mr. Edward Flood. "A Government of that kind," Sir Charles Nicholson remarked, "will last twenty years." Mr. Parkes, however, explained that it was impossible for him to leave his friends, and that he did not approve of the coalition proposed; and Mr. Donaldson's Government existed for only a few weeks.

During this session Mr. Parkes was chairman of a select committee appointed to report upon the introduction of the electric telegraph into New South Wales. The colony of Victoria had done much in introducing and extending this means of communication through its own territory, and had proposed to run a line to connect Melbourne with Albury, on condition that New South Wales should connect Albury with Sydney. The committee regarded the matter as a question "of practical bearing and immediate necessity," calling for active measures to preserve the position of the colony in its various relations with the other Australian colonies, and recommended that the proposed connection between Sydney and Melbourne should be carried out, and also that Bathurst "as the industrial and commercial centre of an important rising district," should be connected by telegraph with Sydney.

Throughout this period of Sir Henry Parkes' life, earnest and zealous as he endeavoured to be in all he undertook, there could be seen very plainly the struggle between his ambition to excel as a politician and his desire to establish himself in a sound position in the community commercially. Between the demands upon his time and attention at the newspaper office, and those which made it indispensable that he should be regular in his attendance in the Assembly, and, if he desired to rise, take an active and intelligent part in the proceedings of Parliament, he was in a serious dilemma. Each being incompatible with the other, to satisfactorily perform the duties of both positions seemed impossible. The sacrifice of one or the other appeared inevitable, and yet to abandon either was as if to commit self-destruction. His position as a newspaper proprietor was essential to his means of livelihood ; his seat in Parliament was necessary to his success as a politician. Conscious of his capacity to excel in either, and yet impressed with the difficulties of adhering to both, he was tormented by the thought that one must be given up. Had he been possessed of a private income, or had the newspaper attained a position in which losses had given way to satisfactory profits, his mind would have been at ease. But it was still an uphill fight with the *Empire*, for though

eminently successful as a literary production it had
not yet succeeded financially, and close and un-
divided attention was the only means likely to
make it profitable.

Outside Parliament, among the people, his
worth as a public man and ultimate success as a
politician were settled convictions. To them he was
the champion from their own ranks specially fitted
to do great public service in protecting their interests
and extending their liberties. His courage and
capacity to attack abuses, and to advocate whatever
appeared for the public good, represented him as
just the kind of man wanted to drive the remnants
of the old official regime into permanent obscurity,
and to encourage the growth of the new order of
things which had brought constitutional government
and its attendant advantages into existence. He
himself was well aware of his abilities. He had not
up to this time done very much in Parliament, but
he had been a very useful member, and had given
much indication of what he might yet do. He knew
his strength, and was conscious of the services he
might perform in the future. He knew also that
when brought forward by the electors of East
Sydney, as one of their candidates for the Assembly,
he had declared that, if elected, he should consider
himself bound to a life-long service in Parliament.
But with all the desire to remain in the Legislature,
and the capacity to perform good work, the absolute
necessity to give something like proper attention
to his business affairs was so plain that an early

retirement from Parliament very quickly appeared impossible to avoid. It therefore came about that his seat in the first Assembly was not held for much more than a third of the period during which the Parliament existed.

CHAPTER VII.

BEFORE the first session of the Parliament of 1856 had closed, between six and seven months, in fact, after the session had opened, Mr. Parkes wrote a letter to the Speaker resigning his seat. The worry and anxiety attending his duties in the office of the *Empire* were now interfering greatly with his legislative duties, and, to his mind, an incomplete service in Parliament was inconsistent with a proper sense of public duty.

"A year ago," he wrote, to his constituents, "when the business of the late Legislative Council was about to close, I addressed a letter to you, informing you that it was not my intention to offer myself as a candidate for your representation in the new Parliament. In taking that step I was chiefly influenced by the conviction that my other engagements would not allow me to attend to the business of the Legislature so as to satisfy my sense of public duty, and that you had a right to expect from your representative a course of devoted service to the country unhampered by the pressure of his

personal affairs. The strong expressions of feeling
in my favour, and considerations urged upon me of
a purely political nature, induced me subsequently
to forego my purpose ; and on the day of election I
was returned to the Legislative Assembly as one of
your members. Highly as I deemed the distinction
thus conferred upon me, I could not even in the hour
of triumph conceal from myself the difficulties that
would surround a proper discharge of the duties I
had undertaken, though I hoped they would not be
greater than my power to overcome them. Since
then, however, the circumstances which presented
to my mind the desirability of my retirement have
grown of greater rather than of diminished force ;
and after the experience of another year, and an
anxious re-examination of the reasons for and
against the course I first proposed to pursue, I have
come to the conclusion it is clearly my duty to return into your hands the trust you have twice
confided to my keeping."

" Leaving the Legislature," the letter proceeded
"it may be well that I should say, to save my
conduct hereafter from misconstruction, that it is my
purpose also, for some years to come, to disconnect
myself entirely from public life. But while I live I
shall not forget that I have been honoured by
receiving your confidence ; and neither time nor
circumstance shall render the links that have united
us in higher relations, of less binding effect on my
ability to serve you as a private citizen. In return
for the first distinction I have enjoyed, I have
contributed little to the advancement of your interests ;

but at least I have not weakened the position of your representative by seeking to build up power to myself. Henceforth, I hope it will be my happiness to see others serve you who shall prove themselves worthy of the service."

The excellent tone of this letter at once attracted attention, and there was an almost unanimous expresssson of admiration and regret. People recognised in the man a sterling honesty,—a sense of duty of the highest kind; and this, coupled with the ability which he was known to possess, led them to regard his retirement from the Legislature as something like a public calamity.

Mr. J. H. Plunkett, a bitter opponent of Mr. Parkes during the election of 1856, and up to the time of the latter's retirement from the Assembly not on speaking terms with him, "was happy," he said in a public speech, "to bear testimony to the services Mr. Parkes had rendered. It would be difficult indeed for them to find a member so able, useful, and assiduous as he had been ; one who would throw, as Mr. Parkes had done, his whole heart and soul into the business of the country, or who would bring with him into the Legislature so much might and influence of character."

"I confess," wrote Sir Charles Cowper, in allusion to the resignation, and a letter he had received from Mr. Parkes on the subject at the time the letter announcing the resignation was written to the Speaker,—"I confess I read it with feelings of emotion, and I soon after went home with a heavy heart. The step which you have taken will deprive the Assembly of one of its most useful members, but I have hopes that good may come out of evil. I feel assured that many who have been the foremost in maligning you hitherto will deeply regret your absence from Parliament; they will now give you credit for motives, which, under feelings of party spirit, they have refused to acknowledge were guiding your actions."

"I trust your means of influencing the public mind," he also wrote, "will be increased rather than diminished, by your retirement. You wield (alluding to the *Empire*) a powerful engine, and by having more time to devote to this all but omnipotent instrument, I indulge the expectation that your usefulness will be felt, and acknowledged by the generous support of that public whom you have served so faithfully."

Dr. Lang regarded the resignation as a public calamity. "In common with all the right-minded portion of our community," he said, "I regret exceedingly your retirement from Parliament. We have so few men of the right stamp that to lose even one, and especially one of your weight and influence in the Legislature, is a public calamity. But I was not surprised at your procedure, from the overwhelming nature of your private avocations, as the head of so extensive an establishment."

Charles Gavan Duffy, at that time a member of the Victorian Parliament, told Mr. Parkes that the retirement could not and must not be more than temporary. "More than ever," he declared, with remarkable foresight, "I see no one else in New

South Wales to hope anything from for posterity."

In the Assembly there was a general feeling of regret, even among Mr. Parkes' political opponents ; and by the party with whom he had been associated the step was regarded with much concern. By some it was described as an "utter smashing of the Opposition ;" and Mr. Cowper and his followers waited with no little disquiet for further developments. "Much will depend upon your successor," he said, in his letter to Mr. Parkes, "and I wait with no little anxiety the announcement of his name. The malignity with which those are assailed who adhere faithfully to the cause of good government, is likely to deter many from venturing into public life. It often disheartens even me, and I doubt whether, if I were to begin a new career, I should face all the obloquy and calumny which I have been subjected to in acting up to my own sense of duty."

But the estimate in which Mr. Parkes had been held in Parliament was best expressed in a letter from the Speaker of the Assembly, Mr. (afterwards Sir) Daniel Cooper. "I cannot, he wrote "allow you to relinquish your seat in the Legislative Assembly, as one of the representatives of the City of Sydney, without briefly expressing to you the high opinion I entertain of your conduct as a member of the House, since I have had the honour to occupy the Speaker's Chair. Your industry, zeal for the public weal, manly independence, fairness, candour, and temper in debate, and unvarying respect for the Chair and forms of the

House, have been on all occasions most exemplary ;
and it affords me additional pleasure to be able to
add that I have frequently heard members of all
shades of political opinion give expression to a no
less flattering estimate of your Parliamentary
career."

Equally complimentary were the references to
the retirement in the press. " His untiring industry,
unceasing watchfulness, and manly independence as
a representative," said one journal, " will make his
loss deeply felt, and his like hard to be found. At
this stage of our affairs his retirement must be
deplored, but he may rest assured that the memory
of his past services will be cherished by the people
with reverence and gratitude." "Beyond all
doubt," said another, "he has been one of the most
valuable members in the House, and we believe
one of the most thoroughly honest and singlehearted.
Few men, indeed, in it give promise of higher
usefulness and greater eminence than he has done ;
for to our mind his is one of the improving spirits,
and he will be a better statesman five years hence
than he is now." In a lengthy notice of the subject,
a third journal declared that "the country owes
more to Mr. Parkes than many will be inclined to
acknowledge." "He has," it went on to say, "the
great merit of having been the first to organise here
a consistent political party. Before his entrance
into public life our politicians were remarkable for
anything but their consistency, voting merely as
their inclinations or interests led them, without any
regard to principles. . . . . We know of no

one in the House whose opinions on all subjects were delivered with greater earnestness or commanded more respect and attention from all parties. . . . . His industry and perseverance are above all praise. He is an example of what may be done by a man of talent and energy, relying solely upon his own exertions. Mr. Parkes has, perhaps, had less assistance from others in his career though life, than most men, yet he occupies a position in this rapidly advancing country second to none. It is to his honour that he has attained his position without sacrificing his independence or cringing to any class or person."

Another paper, similarly pronounced in its praise, said, that " short as had been Mr. Parkes' career in the Legislature it had stamped him as a consistent, honest, straightforward man, with a strict regard to political principle. But," the article continued, " Mr. Parkes is not merely an honest and consistent man—he is endowed by nature with a force of character and general ability which placed him among the foremost men in the House. There was a sincerity of purpose and earnestness of conviction, aided by intellectual power of no mean order, which would make themselves felt and respected in any deliberative assembly in the British Empire. Even his bitterest political opponents have faith in his integrity, and the attention with which he was invariably listened to, both in the Legislature and out of it, affords the strongest proof of the estimation in which his parts and character are held by all classes. . . . . . .

G

Men of Mr. Parkes' stamp can be ill spared by the country, and whatever the circumstances which have rendered his withdrawal from public life inevitable, we hope that the day is not far distant when he will again be enabled to take his place among the legislators of his adopted country."

Many other such notices of the retirement appeared, all breathing a feeling of deep regret at the step which Mr. Parkes had found it necessary to take, and of high appreciation of the public services he had performed. But the actual words of only one other need be quoted. The paper was the *Freeman's Journal*, and it said, " Much as we are opposed to, and hard as we have often hit, Mr. Parkes, we regret his resignation extremely. He was the 'noblest Roman of them all' on the Opposition benches."

One outcome of this almost universal expression of regret and goodwill was a strongly supported proposal to raise and present to Mr. Parkes a great public testimonial. On all sides it was admitted that, if ever circumstances justified such a proceeding, they did in his case, and the desire was to so arrange that the testimonial, whatever might be its form, should come from the people of the colony generally, —" some form of testimonial," it was remarked at the time, " in which the people can all take part, in which thousands can have a share, and which Mr. Parkes' children can one day point to with honourable pride."

A preliminary meeting was held at the Royal Hotel, George-street, for the purpose of forming a committee, and making other arrangements preparatory to the calling of a public meeting. Complimentary speeches were made, and resolutions in accordance with the object of the meeting were passed. Very quickly matters were so complete that ultimate success was certain. But before the public meeting could be held, a letter was received by the committee from Mr. Parkes declining the testimonial, and therefore putting an end to the movement. The letter was addressed to the hon. secretary of the committee, and was as follows :

"SYDNEY, *January 21st, 1857.*

" MY DEAR SIR,

" Until I saw the report of the meeting held yesterday, at the Royal Hotel, I did not know who were interesting themselves on my behalf in getting up this proposed testimonial, and I did not see my way to interfere in the business. I think it is right, however, that I should now communicate to you, in order that you may explain to the committee that has been appointed, my feelings on the subject.

In the first place, I think the public should be slow to stamp the services of any man with a special mark of their approval, for honours of this kind can only retain their value by reason of the just claims of the persons on whom they are bestowed. Entertaining this opinion, I cannot persuade myself that I have any merits to entitle me to a distinction so altogether personal. If I have been fortunate enough to effect any amount of good in the share I have taken in public life, I would rather have it entirely lost sight of than over-estimated by my fellow-citizens. In either case the good could not in reality be made greater or less ; but it would be more grateful to one's self-respect to rest upon something that remained for ever unacknowledged than to feel conscious of having accepted a distinction undeserved. On the broadest ground that can be assumed, I think my friends would best consult the public interest and my individual reputation by abandoning their intention in regard to me.

In the second place, even if I could believe that my claims to public consideration were greater than my warmest friends can possibly make them out to be, I have a kind of horror of testimonials. My sense of justice, I am bound to say, is against them. Merit, wherever it exists, will work out its own most fitting reward. If men cannot achieve something to stand as a memorial of their own lives, it is best that they should pass away without any attempt of friendly hands to magnify their littleness. I am quite content to submit myself to that inexorable trier of men's actions, Time ; and to take my chance of being swept away.

Moreover, I desire above all things, just now, to be allowed to work in quiet. The duties that lie nearest to me require this for their performance. I am gratefully sensible of the kindness of my friends, which I shall ever remember ; but that kindness will manifest itself in the form most desired by yielding to the wishes expressed in this letter.

I am, my dear Sir,

" Yours very truly,

" HENRY PARKES."

" Mr. C. G. Reid, Secretary to Committee
appointed at the Royal Hotel."

This letter stopped the testimonial, but it raised the writer higher than ever in public esteem. Such a true sense of duty, such an unselfish estimate of the value of important services, was new in a community where personal advantage had, in most instances, been the principal object in public life. The letter was read with admiration, and though no one denied the justness of the sentiments it expressed, it seemed to many to be of that character which should assist in pushing forward the movement that had been commenced rather than in bringing it to a termination.

Dr. Woolley, Principal of the University of Sydney, writing to Mr. Parkes at the time, said it was only natural there should be a wish on the part of the people to express their sense of his past public services, and their earnest and cordial anticipations of a long future, which should secure him in the hearts of all generations of Australians "*monumentum œre perennius.*" "I cannot help adding," Dr. Woolley wrote, "that I am delighted, and not surprised, at the manly and generous sentiments contained in your letter to Mr. Reid : they come like the fresh breeze from a free mountain side. It does one good to think that we have some *real men* amongst us. God grant, my dear sir, that you may be spared to take that part in the development of the moral and material interests of this country, which I know you desire, and which, I am confident, will make your name as familiar to our children as that of Hampden and Cromwell."

It is not one of the least remarkable features in Sir Henry Parkes' career that, at this early period, when he had done comparatively little in the public interest, the promise of future great services was universally recognised.

In a spirit similar to that in which Dr. Woolley penned his letter, a large number of prominent men attended another meeting at the Royal Hotel to determine whether, in deference to the wish of Mr. Parkes, the proposed testimonial should be abandoned, or whether, notwithstanding that wish, the movement should be allowed to proceed. Eventually it was abandoned, but not at this meeting, nor until a determined effort had been made to push it forward regardless of Mr. Parkes' objections.

At the instance of Mr. John Robertson the meeting resolved,—

"That while this meeting desires to express its unfeigned sense of admiration of the noble and patriotic motives by which Mr. Parkes has been actuated in writing the letter just read, and in sensitively shrinking from any acknowledgment of his public services, it is of opinion that those services have been such as to demand the public recognition which it was determined at the preliminary meeting of Mr. Parkes' friends should be given to them"

The speeches on the occasion could not have been more eulogistic. In fact, read to-day in the light of a comparison of what the subject of the eulogy had up to that time done, with the public services he afterwards rendered, they seem little short of extravagant. But they were evidently the honest sentiments of the speakers. Mr. Richard Jones, Mr. Charles Cowper, Mr. John Robertson, and Mr. William Forster, joined in these complimentary utterances. The peculiarities of public life brought about, in after years, a change in the relations between at least two of these well-known men and Mr. Parkes, but at this time there was scarcely any limit to their admiration. In common with the people generally, there seemed to be no compliment too great to pay the man whom everybody was disposed to honour.

His services in the Legislature had been of a kind in which all his efforts had been directed towards the public good, and no vestige of self-interest appeared. He had been regular in attendance, fairly active in debate, watchful in voting, and industrious in instituting inquiries into several subjects important to the public welfare. He had not accomplished much, if what he had done were judged by actual record, but he had been conscientious, painstaking, and self-sacrificing, and these were qualities which met with public approval, for they were wanted in a Legislature where the principles of self-government had just come into operation.

On the Press his services had been longer than his services in Parliament, and undoubtedly they had been important. His work on the *Empire* had given a prominence to public questions which, before, was not imparted to them ; and by a system of independent and able criticism, he had never lost an opportunity of safeguarding and promoting the public interest. Added to this was the fact that he had improved the tone and stimulated the enterprise of the Press of the colony generally. In this way he had done great public good, and the people were grateful.

The result of the resolution to proceed with the movement for raising the testimonial was a public meeting in the Lyceum Theatre, York-street. Mr. Charles Cowper presided, and the principal speakers were Mr. W. B. Dalley, Mr. Richard Jones, Dr. Woolley, Mr. John Robertson, Mr. John Campbell, and Mr. W. C. Windeyer (now His Honor, Sir William Windeyer). The same feeling was apparent as at the previous meetings. Everyone was eager to praise the proposed recipient of the testimonial, and determined to make the testimonial one worthy of acceptance. It had been arranged that the following resolutions should be submitted to the meeting :—

1. That this meeting is unanimously of opinion that the public services of Henry Parkes, Esq., in the patriotic efforts which he has made for many years past to advance civil liberty, social progress, and good government, demand the sincere and grateful acknowledgment of every Australian colonist.

2. That upon Mr. Parkes' retirement, probably for a long period, from public life, this meeting desires that a suitable and permanent memorial should be established of the high estimation of his public virtues by his fellow-colonists, and that a subscription be opened for the purpose of raising funds for the purchase of an estate, to be vested in trustees for the benefit of Mr. Parkes' family.

3. That the earnest co-operation of the Australian colonists, in promoting the objects of this meeting, be solicited, and that gentlemen favourable thereto be invited to aid in forming local committees, and in soliciting subscriptions in aid of the proposed testimonial."

These resolutions would have been carried, and the movement pressed on with every prospect of success; but the proceedings were again checked by a protest from Mr. Parkes. The chairman of the meeting, Mr. Cowper, was obliged to announce, on taking the chair, that though it had been hoped after what had taken place at the meetings at the Royal Hotel, that Mr. Parkes would have consented to waive his objections to what was being done, it was found not only that he had not done so, but that he had stated to most of his friends his objections with greater force than before, and in a manner that almost compelled them to defer to his wishes.

The proceedings, therefore, came to an end. Mr. Dalley expressed his deep regret that the intended "great public distinction" had been declined, but consoled himself with the reflection that " at all events when the curtain fell between him (Mr. Parkes) and the public—that curtain which for a time concealed him from them as a public man—it was rung down with the universal applause of the country." Mr. Richard Jones, while agreeing with the course taken by Mr. Parkes in declining the testimonial, said " it would be difficult indeed for them to make an adequate return for the many and important services which he had rendered to the community." Dr. Woolley spoke of the glorious career which would one day unite Mr. Parkes' name " with those of the guardians of liberty in America and elsewhere." Mr. Robertson declared that in " every hamlet, village, and town " in the country the most popular man was Mr.

Parkes ; and Mr. W. C. Windeyer, this occasion
being his first appearance in public, urged that, as
the proposal for a testimonial was to be abandoned,
they should at least present an address, signed by
all, " to bear testimony to the love, admiration, and
respect which they felt towards Henry Parkes."
A resolution was adopted,

> " That an address be presented to Henry Parkes, Esq., late
> representative of the city, on his retirement from Parlia-
> ment, expressing the feelings of the citizens of Sydney
> and the colonists at large in reference to his eminent
> public services ; "

and the meeting terminated.

CHAPTER VIII.

Not long after his retirement from the Legislative Assembly in 1856, Mr. Parkes published a second volume of poems, entitled, "Murmurs of the Stream," with the following dedication :—

THE VERSES UNDER THIS HEAD,

CONTAINING

RECORDS OF FEELING

SCATTERED OVER FIFTEEN YEARS,

ARE DEDICATED

TO THE

3057

ELECTORS OF SYDNEY,

WHO RETURNED THE AUTHOR

TO THE

LEGISLATIVE ASSEMBLY,

MARCH 13th, 1856.

The little book—it contained 107 pages—showed no particular advance upon the previous volume in poetic conception or skilfulness of versification, but it revealed the yearnings of a soul impelled to utterance by the same deep love and reverence for England, and passionate desire for the well-being of Australia. It opened with a poem on "Fatherland :"

"The brave old land of deed and song,
  Of gentle hearts and spirits strong,
  Of queenly maids and heroes grand,
  Of equal laws,—our Fatherland!"

And, after recounting some of the splendid characteristics of England, it proceeds :

"Shall Cromwell's memory, Milton's lyre,
  Not kindle 'mong us souls of fire,
  Not raise in us a spirit strong—
  High scorn of shams—quick hate of wrong?

"Shall we not learn, Australians born!
  To smile on tinselled power our scorn,—
  At least, a freeman's pride to try,
  When tinselled power would bend or buy?

"The brave old land of deed and song,
  We ne'er will do her memories wrong!
  For freedom here we'll firmly stand,
  As stood our sires for Fatherland!"

Politics in the days when some of these poems were written did not, in all respects, commend itself to the writer, and the Donaldson Cabinet, the first Administration under the new Constitution Act of 1856, did not please him. Especially did he view with disfavour the appointment of the late Mr. Thomas Holt to the position of Colonial Treasurer. And he wrote :—

"Here men leap forth, the statesmen of an hour,
  With one untutored bound to highest place,
  Who yesterday had never dreamt of power,
  Whom none had named for mad ambition's race.

"Here men are called to rule,—ah, self-deceived!
  Because, if for a cause the thing can be—
  They have neglected most and least achieved,
  To found a State or set a people free."

Not inapplicable are these verses to what has been the case in some Ministries since 1856, and must continue to be so until sufficient time shall have passed for a race of politicians to exist in the colony, natives of the soil, and trained in politics and parliamentary procedure from their youth upwards.

"Poor land!" he exclaimed in some lines "suggested by political changes in men and power and men out of power in 1856,"—

> "Poor land! of what avail for thee
> Thy summer wilds and skies resplendent,
> If all this light still lifeless be,
> And man grow here a thing dependent."

And in a poem entitled "The Australian Maiden to her Brother," in which he deplores the debasing effect of much that, at this period, marked the institutions connected with the government of the country, he says, alluding to the condition of lands possessed of the blessings of freedom, and urging that every effort be made to raise Australia to the same level,—

> "Hast thou forgot our evening, morning,
> And midday dreams, of isles less fair,
> Where Freedom dwelt, the world adorning,
> And Truth made man her gifted heir!

> "And how our loved Australia yet
> Might rise among those names of light,
> Brighter than star e'er rose, which set
> Within the old world's troubled night?

"Did we not dream how thou should'st stand,
　　Though even alone, a patriot true,
　And late and early, for our land
　　Toil on as patriots only do ?

" And art thou worn with nights of thought,
　　For her so steeped in crime and fear ?
Hast thou all means of justice sought
　　To raise her up—our country dear ?

" In manhood's dawn—in sport of fame,
　　Thou, with the poet's skill, did'st twine
A garland round her sullied name,
　　As proud to call such country thine.

" But is this all ?—and can'st thou brother
　　Australia's abject suffering see ?
And live one hour for any other
　　Than the great purpose—her to free ?

" Go—through her sun-bright forests gaze—
　　Go, and determine which shall share—
A people free for better days,
　　Or lord or serf—God's bounty, there.

" Ask not what sorrow wears my breast,
　　Seek not again to comfort me,
While still our country sinks oppressed,
　　Without a helping hand from thee."

There are other verses in the book expressing similar sentiments to these, but at the same time full of hope of the glorious future which the author saw clearly from the first awaited this land.

" We live in hope—we have no past—
　　Our glory's to be won !
And come it will, in spite of ill,
　　Sure as to-morrow's sun."

In some lines called " The Strength of Life " we
have a picture of the poet himself, drawn with such
clearness that the portrait cannot be mistaken.

" The dreams of boyhood all were passed,
　　The gorgeous light that shone through all
Had faded from life's track at last,
　　Like sunshine from a prison wall :
He stood alone, and faced the world—
　　The wide, bleak world without a star ;
And every scorner's lip was curled ;
　　And heart was faint ; and hope was far.

" But—faint with disappointment's pang,
　　And trust deceived, and efforts foiled,—
And bleeding now from misery's fang,—
　　That heart yet firmly beat and toiled.
He gazed upon the desert way,
　　And drew fresh life from resolute will ;
For hope still smiled, though pale her ray,
　　And Heaven was bending o'er him still.

" And never failed that trustful heart,
　　In conflict dark and suffering long,—
Still striving for the higher part,—
　　By every struggle waxing strong.
The grim realities of life
　　He met, with front as fixed and grim ;
But well he cherished, through the strife,
　　All gentle thoughts that came to him.

" And when, far up the sunny mount,
　　He rested like a traveller tired,
His dearest joy was to recount
　　The dreams that first his spirit fired.
The glory of those dreams returned,
　　All pure and tranquil, bright and free,—
Not one rich hue that early burned
　　Tinged by the trail of misery."

No truer or better description of Mr. Parkes'
life, up to the time when these verses were written,
could be given than is set forth in these lines.   His
friendlessness when he came here, his struggles to
improve his position, the sneers of the envious
or the unfriendly, the pangs of disappointment
or of failure, the pleasures of hope, the faith in the
future, the determination to go on : all are depicted
with strength and vividness.

The book contains also a rather lengthy poem
addressed " To an Australian Child," and the verses
have a deeply pathetic tone.   The child who had
inspired the poet to pen the lines, was his first born
son ; they were written in the warmth of a father's
affection, and the brightness of his anticipation of the
boy's future ; and, alas ! the boy's life was a
disappointment.   He lived a commonplace existence;
he died in early manhood ; and the father's cherished
hopes were unfulfilled.   The poem is too long to
quote *in extenso*, but a few verses are sufficient to
show with what fond expectation the future of " my
own blue-eyed boy " was regarded.

" How bright is the morning, young creature of mirth,
    As 'twere the fresh dawn on a paradise wild,
  Out-bursting in smiles o'er the land of thy birth !
    But the beauty of Eden had ne'er reconciled
  Thy sire to his exile, if never those eyes
    Had pleaded in innocent love for its claim !
  For, oh ! these are not the green woods and blue skies
    Which my childhood rejoiced. nor these wild flow'rs the same.

*   *   *   *   *   *   *

" But the sun in his rising, benignly resplendent,
    Thy land, little Southerner ! flooding with smiles,
Ever wakes fresher feelings—pure, proud, independent,
    That link us anew to this fairest of isles !
And right regally She, in the morning's rich light—
    My boy's native city—now looketh the Queen,
With the sea at her feet lying tranquil and bright,
    Skirted still by her forests of dark evergreen !

" And grandly her future, my fair-fortuned boy !
    Shall unfold o'er Australia's wild mountains and glens,
With effulgence of mind, and pervasion of joy !
    That shall startle the world from its pomp of old sins.
Yes ! Freedom her prime more august shall renew,
    With the spirit of Sparta, the sway of first Rome,
Where now the green desert lies shut from man's view ;
    Or the desert's dark tribes, in sole mastery, roam.

" And high is thy birthright, entitling to share
    In her patriot's labours—the work yet unplanned
Of some Hampden, perchance, now by mother's fond care
    Cradled safe 'mong the mountains afar in the land ;—
To claim when thy country shall rank with the nations,
    An honour-marked place by the side of her chiefs,
With a soul that has fed on her proud aspirations,
    And pined 'neath the weight of her national griefs ! "

  The boy might have risen to manhood's estate
high in the Government service, had his father so
chosen, but it was one of the principles of Sir Henry
Parkes' life not to appoint his relatives to positions
under the Government, and his sons had to make
their way in the world independently of this aid, and
by their own efforts. The eldest, following in the
footsteps of his father when he was conducting the

Empire, became a printer. He died at the age of 37, and was buried at Faulconbridge, Sir Henry Parkes' mountain home, his grave being the first that was made there.

On the day before the funeral the present writer received the following letter, dated from Faulconbridge, which contains some interesting references to the verses just quoted, and some touching observations regarding him to whom the lines had been addressed.

" Faulconbridge,

" January 4, 1880.

" My dear Mr. Lyne,

" At page 75 of the accompanying little volume you will find some verses which more than 34 years ago I addressed to my poor dead son, then a child 2½ years old. At that time I was myself an unknown young man with no thought of entering upon a public career. The verses were written in 1846. I took part in public proceedings for the first time in 1848, at the election of Mr. Robert Lowe for Sydney.

" Looked at from the present day, through the changes of the intervening years, the political character of the verses has a curious interest for myself, and in this sense and in connection with my loss they might be of interest to the public. I am too much absorbed in my own little world to be a judge of this.

" Throughout my poor boy's boyhood I had great hopes of his future. All this ended in sad disappointment, but he was one of the kindest and gentlest creatures that ever lived.

" Faithfully yours,

" HENRY PARKES."

There was a touching simplicity, and yet a picturesqueness, about the funeral.   The remains of the deceased were conveyed to Faulconbridge by train, and on arriving at the railway platform there the coffin was taken from the train, and carried to the grave by six of the workpeople employed by Sir Henry Parkes and the late Sir James Martin, then Chief Justice, on their mountain estates, the men being dressed in spotlessly white attire, and wearing a band of crape around the left arm and another around the hat.   Preceding the coffin was the clergyman, an old friend of the family, and following it were Sir Henry Parkes, his son Mr. Varney Parkes, Mr. James Watson, then Colonial Treasurer, Mr. G. A. Lloyd, Mr. W. Neill, and a few others.   On reaching the grave, which had been dug in a spot shaded by a wild nutmeg tree, about a quarter of a mile from the Faulconbridge railway platform, though but a very short distance from the railway line, a beautiful cross of flowers composed of rare white roses and maiden hair fern, some equally beautiful floral wreaths, and some wild flowers were laid upon the coffin ; and bearing these tributes of regard and affection, the body was lowered into its last resting place.   The floral cross and wreaths were sent by the Governor, Lord Augustus Loftus; the wild flowers were gathered by hands prompted by loving hearts, about the rocks and dells of Faulconbridge.

"Murmurs of the Stream," closes with some

ATTEMPTS
IN
SONNET WRITING,
DEDICATED
TO
SIR CHARLES NICHOLSON, K.B.,
AS
A LINK
OF
A VALUED FRIENDSHIP.

They are not unsuccessful, and the little book generally, though it exhibits some crudities of expression and rhyme, is musical, thought-inspiring, and pleasing. Writing in 1878 with reference to some books he was sending me, one of them being this volume of poems, Sir Henry Parkes said :—

"I shall feel gratified if you will accept the accompanying volumes in remembrance of a very pleasant journey we performed together last month.

"The speeches were published chiefly as a record of opinion extending over some 25 years. The book has had a value attached to it by others, both here and in England, which I can say most sincerely I do not attach to it myself.

"The smaller volume ("Murmurs of the Stream") has been severely condemned by the critics, but that too has had a good word said of it by a great poet, the late W. C. Bryant.

"I offer the books to you, good or bad, as part of myself."

But the book, and more recent volumes of poems, have had a " good word" said for them by a greater poet than W. C. Bryant. Lord Tennyson spoke well of them, and another authority, famous for his genius with the sculptor's chisel rather than the poet's pen, but recognised as a poet of consider- . able talent, Mr. Thomas Woolner, R.A., also alluded to some of them in terms of praise. Not very long before Mr. Woolner's decease Sir Henry Parkes received from him, in acknowledgment of a copy of " Fragmentary Thoughts," a letter in which he said—" The poems give a most interesting glimpse of your inner aspirations, and, above all, the warm and passionate desire you have always felt to improve the hard fate of the poor, and bestow upon them your sympathy, which, in some respects, is by them even more highly valued."

CHAPTER IX.

A few months after the events which followed
Mr. Parkes' resignation from the Legislative
Assembly in 1856, the *Empire* was in difficulties.
The commercial department of the paper had not
been successful. Its literary character had been
excellent throughout, and it had exercised an important and beneficial influence upon the community;
but from one cause and another the journal, from a
pecuniary point of view, had not been carried on
profitably.

Probably Mr. Parkes' election to the Legislature
had so drawn him away from his duties at the
Empire office that he was prevented from giving to
the office that supervision which, in any such case,
to be of use must be unremitting. His work on
the *Empire* was that not only of an editor but also
of a proprietor, and it needed constant attention.
Not being a practical printer he was open to the
many evils, attended by loss of money or business,
which a man trained to the printing trade can, in
most instances, with little difficulty avoid. His
only chance of escaping them was by regular atten

dance in his office, and active personal acquaintance with everything going on there. Even then he must have been to a large extent at the mercy of others directly charged with departments of work which he could not well understand.

He had received some assistance in money from friends when the paper was started, and almost from the first the business columns of the journal obtained a fair share of advertisements. The paper steadily advanced in circulation, and the price of it was fourpence. But through most of its career the cost of production was very great—for a considerable period as much as £100 a day—and there was a constantly increasing amount of book debts. Money owing to the office did not come in as it ought to have done. The general public regarded the paper with high approval, but, as is frequently the case, many of those with whom it had business relations showed little concern as to its means of existence. Consequently, instead of progressing satisfactorily in this most material part of a great newspaper enterprise, it went backward. At different times it was found indispensable to seek pecuniary assistance from persons willing to lend money to enable the paper to overcome its difficulties, and these appeals had met with a prompt response. The great good the paper was doing was recognised, and there was seen no reason why, when it had surmounted the obstacles never absent from the first years of a large newspaper business, it should not return a satisfactory profit.

But as time went on it was found from certain
circumstances, unforeseen, that the hope of the
ultimate pecuniary success of the journal was
delusive.   Where there are a number of creditors
in an estate it is not always that they act in unison.
It is not unusual to find one or two whose opinions
as to a proposed course regarding the property
concerned are opposed to the opinions of the rest ;
that, while a large majority are disposed to assist
to the fullest extent of their power, the small
minority are doggedly determined to do the very
opposite.   So it turned out to be in this case.

At the time when Mr, Parkes retired from the
Legislative Assembly in 1856 the liabilities of the
paper amounted to fully £50,000, a very large sum
to ordinary eyes, but not so to the eyes of those
who know what the liabilities of great newspapers
sometimes are.   This £50,000 included a mortgage
for £11,000, and the mortgagee pressing for payment, the matter went into the Supreme Court.
Very soon possession was taken of the property
for the mortgagee, and the paper was advertised
for sale.

In this condition of affairs Mr. Parkes called a
meeting of his creditors, and explained the situation
to them.   To a certain extent the result was
satisfactory.   It showed that most of the creditors
were satisfied of the integrity and the ability of the
proprietor of the paper, and of the ultimate success
of the journal.   They were willing to agree to Mr.
Parkes' proposals, and to wait.   But this general
decision on the part of most of those to whom the

paper was indebted was made abortive by the one or
two creditors who had taken up an antagonistic
position, and who had declined to give away.

At this point the whole staff of the paper
abandoned their work ; and for a few days the very
appearance of the paper was jeopardised. A new
staff could not be obtained, and for a time the
situation seemed a hopeless one. But in his extremity there were a few persons who came to the aid of
the editor, and with th ⋅ ⋅ assistance the paper
appeared day by day,—not, certainly, in its usual
complete form, but sufficiently complete to pass
current ; and in that way this new difficulty was
surmounted. The staff did not leave from hostility
to Mr. Parkes. They were careful to explain that
their relations with him, up to the period of the
present embarrassments, had always been cordial and
satisfactory ; but as at this time some arrears of wages
were due to them, and as it had been explained to
them that inasmuch as the mortgagee had taken
possession of the property they must look to him for
payment of what was due to them, and he had
declined to pay them, they left the office.

The condition of affairs now became very
critical. The prospect of being able to go on under
such a load of difficulties as had accumulated was
very slight ; yet every consideration urged that a
strong effort should be made to prevent complete
disaster. The six years of incessant labour in the
establishment and the conduct of the paper had
been too great, and in their effect upon the community too beneficial, to be lightly set aside. The

paper had done signal service under the old order of
government ; it was doing equally good service
under the new. Meetings were held by persons
interested, chiefly from patriotic motives, in the
well-being of the journal, to consider what was best
to be done ; and it was determined to take steps to
to pay off the mortgage. The money was raised by
subscription ; the mortgage was redeemed ; and the
pressing trouble which had threatened the existence of the paper under Mr. Parkes' management
was removed.

So far this was satisfactory, especially to the
paper's many friends ; but the relief of the journal
from the mortgage debt does not appear to have
been brought about with Mr. Parkes' consent. In
1868 he alluded to the matter in a speech in the
Legislative Assembly. " There was a mortgage on
the paper," he explained, " of some £11,000, to Sir
Daniel Cooper, and a number of persons proposed to
take it up from that gentleman, but in a manner to
which I objected. I stated my objections in writing,
and was never a consenting party to the transaction,
except in endeavouring to work it out after it was
done. I wished to be left alone to deal with my estate
as other people do with theirs." Though requested to
name persons who might assist in the movement he
had declined to name anyone, not believing that any
good could result from the course that was being
taken. He did not approve of what was being
done, and declined to be a party to it. An explanation, similar to this, he also made when, as far as
Pai decis concerned, the publication of the paper came
nd in 1858.

A letter written at the time by Mr. Parkes to one of the most earnest and active of the friends who brought assistance to the embarrassed journal, indicates very forcibly his feelings on the subject. The letter bore date " Saturday afternoon, March 21, 1857," and was as follows :

My dear Mr. Montefiore,

After I saw you yesterday I again had much trouble with parties connected with the office, which occupied my attention nearly the whole afternoon. In the evening I saw Mr. Jones, and had a long conversation with him on the subject of my unfortunate affairs. Thus, much of my time was consumed, and I was left in a frame of mind little fitted to think of what you desired me to think of. I cannot but feel that the *Empire* has few friends who would render the extraordinary assistance required, and I cannot think of any I should be justified in naming.

Since Mr. Jones left me I have spent some anxious hours endeavouring to realise the future, in case your arrangements with Mr. Cooper were to be completed. It is clear I should live in a new world of thought and feeling—my relations with men entirely changed—the public men of the country all standing in an altered light, some whom I have hitherto regarded as opponents or with indifference now assuming the character of benevolent protectors—my very existence depending on the wealth of a gentleman who a few weeks ago told me to my face that he would rather 'crush' the *Empire* than suffer personal annoyance from his connection with it.

It were unwise not to ask myself calmly and searchingly am I strong enough to bear all this—to outlive the moral imprisonment to which I should be consigned—my judgment and my integrity alike distrusted and myself suspecting everyone.

In ordinary cases this might be borne,—if the ends in view were only the accumulation of money. But I should be expected to maintain a high ground of independence, to infuse fire and vigour into the political life of the country, to appear at the door of my own dungeon every morning as a spirited defender of freedom.

I am not seeking to conjure up gloom and difficulty, but to ascertain by the severe light of reason what would in reality be my future position, and what would be my prospect of surmounting my difficulties with a new burden of so irksome a nature placed upon my back, and with only one motive to action—the hope of paying my debts—in the place of all those warm and stirring ones which animated me in my past struggles.

The obstacles that stood before me on the first of January appear to me now of tenfold greater magnitude; the spirit that sustained me then I feel is now half extinguished. The public canvass of my affairs which has taken place will sit upon my energies like a hideous nightmare; and I know too well the natural action of the public mind not to foresee that the idle sympathy which has been created will be transient and will dissipate itself in a chilling mist of pity and suspicion.

This kind of public support of a public journal, believe me, will prove as perilous as the clasp of those shrubs which in most cases destroy the tree to which they cling. The public—that monster of a thousand conflicting passions—ought to be compelled to respect a public journal, not asked to look upon it with commiseration.

Looking at the frightful extent to which my difficulties have been aggravated and complicated by recent occurrences, and the deadly blow which has been struck at the prestige of the *Empire* throughout the world, my confidence for the first time forsakes me, and I feel· I ought to let you know the state of almost despair in which I find myself.

I have sent for Mr. Wilshire with the view of making a last appeal to him to take the thing into his own hands. That is the only way which I can see to carry the paper through its troubles. The help which you and other friends, by your great kindness and the great waste of your time which it has caused, have succeeded in raising, would be just sufficient to drag me to the dust—to affix to the *Empire* the stigma of dependence on eleemosynary aid, but, I seriously apprehend, as it would be rendered on conditions subversive of my self-respect, it would be utterly insufficient to save me from destruction.

I reveal to you these apprehensions because it is right that you should know them. I do not wish them to be interpreted as my final decision in a matter of such high moral concern to me, and in which I feel myself in such a fearful state of doubt and difficulty. But I beg that you will do nothing without letting me know the distinct conditions to which I am to be subject, as I am most anxious not to deceive you by undertaking what would be too much for my strength hereafter.

With a thousand thanks for the trouble you and all have taken,

Believe me,

Yours truly,

H. PARKES.

The haunting fear so well expressed in this letter, that in the new circumstances of its existence the paper could never again be what it had been, was far from being groundless. The *Empire* did not long survive the period of its fallen fortunes. The

mortgage being paid off, the man in possession
departed, and for a time the paper went on in most
respects as formerly.   Expenses were curtailed
where it was practicable to do so, and the business
arrangements generally were improved, largely with
the object of obtaining money, the total amount of
which was very considerable, from persons indebted
to the office as subscribers or advertisers.   But
these efforts did not meet with success. The money
did not come in as it ought to have done ; the
expenses of the paper were beyond its income ;
liabilities pressing upon it could not be materially
reduced.   The publication of the journal was
henceforth, until it ended, a continuous struggle ;
the great burden of the paper's difficulties causing it
to rapidly lose, with no prospect of ever regaining it,
its old familiar garb of high literary ability, far-
reaching criticism, comprehensive information, and
public usefulness.

CHAPTER X.

EARLY in 1858 Mr. Parkes re-entered Parliament,
being returned at the general election in this
year for a constituency known as the North
Riding of Cumberland.

His retirement from Parliamentary life at the
close of 1856 had not been as prolonged as he had
anticipated. He had made a determined effort to
free himself, for at least some years, from the
obligations attending the possession of a seat
in the Legislature. Twice he had voluntarily
returned the trust confided to his care by the
electors of the City of Sydney, and each resignation
had been followed by a closer attention to his duties
in the office of the *Empire*. With his great newspaper established on firm foundations, and enjoying a
prosperous career, Parliamentary labour would
have been a delight; with the journal struggling to
free itself from its load of indebtedness it was
unsatisfactory and burdensome. But his efforts to
keep out of the Legislature until he should be able
to command more leisure proved futile. Important
as unremitting attention to the interests of the

Empire was acknowledged to be, there were those among his friends, who, recognising his peculiar fitness for political life were always urging him to seize the earliest occasion for re-entering the Legislative Assembly. These importunities naturally had some effect, though of themselves they were not sufficient to draw him from the course he had resolved to take. But when his efforts to reorganise the *Empire* office, and make some satisfactory arrangement with the creditors of the paper, had failed, and permanent success in his newspaper enterprise was seen to be, under the circumstances, very doubtful, if not impossible, there seemed to be no reason why he should remain away from Parliament a moment after the opportunity for his return presented itself. So it came about that he re-entered the Legislative Assembly as one of two members for the North Riding of Cumberland.

He might have stood for Sydney, the electorate which had previously returned him, or for two or three other constituencies, but there were weighty reasons why he should present himself for election in the North Riding. At this time he was living at Ryde, an important part of this constituency, and he had many friends there. Some of these friends, without making proper preparations to ensure success, injudiciously nominated him as a candidate for the electorate at a bye-election which took place a few months before the general election at which he was afterwards returned. The result was that he was defeated. This was unpleasant, but as the causes of the defeat were not such as to show that the constituency as a whole was adverse to his representing it, he determined to submit himself to the electors of the North Riding a second time rather than become a candidate for any other electorate.

His determination was supported by a requisition from the electors, numerously and influentially signed. "I may fairly claim," he said in his reply to this requisition, "a place among our oldest public men who are still before the country, and therefore my character, to some extent, may be tried by the test of time. My votes recorded in nearly every division of two Legislatures, and my expressed sentiments on nearly every subject that could be submitted for debate, are open to the severest review, and I am content to stand or fall by such examination."

At this period he had been actively engaged in public life for ten years, and the nature of the political situation at this general election was such as to justify a claim on the electors based upon long and valuable service in the public interest. Responsible government, so far as it had been tried, had not produced the good results which at its introduction had been anticipated. It had been in operation for twenty months ; and during that time four Ministries had been in office, parties in Parliament had become disorganized, and legislation was at a standstill. The first popular Parliament in the country had ended in "nothing effectual, nothing real, nothing tangible," and there was a general feeling of disappointment. In the appeal to the constituencies which followed, this feeling was apparent

by a disinclination on the part of prominent
colonists for public life. It was a time when
men who, like Mr. Parkes, could point to several
years of labour in behalf of the people, were wanted.

Parliament had been dissolved at the instance of
Mr. Cowper, on the land question, though the
matter on which the Government had sustained
actual defeat was the Assessment Bill, a measure
which sought to continue a charge upon the
squatters of the country by an assessment upon the
stock depasturing on the runs. The principal
feature in the programme for the new Parliament
was electoral reform, by which there would be a
larger number of members in the Assembly, an
equalization of the electoral districts,—representation being based upon population,—and an
extension of the franchise. With an amended
electoral system, it was believed there would be
much better means available for dealing successfully
not only with the land question, but with such
questions as the abolition of State aid to religion,
the improvement of the means of education, prison
reform, the better management of asylums for
lunatics, and of Government charitable institutions,
railway and road construction, and an equitable
system of finance.

Mr. Cowper and his colleagues were not in high
favour, and there was some danger of their meeting
with disaster in the elections. They strengthened
their position by admitting Mr. Robertson to the
Cabinet as Secretary for Lands and Public Works,
but they had more difficulties to meet than those

connected with the land question.   So insecure did
the position of the Government appear that Mr.
Dalley, then young and ardent, implored the electors
of Sydney, where he with the Premier and two
others formed the Government bunch of candidates,
to return Mr. Cowper whatever else they might do.
Mr. Cowper was elected, but he was fourth on the
poll; and Mr. Dalley and another of the Government
bunch, and Mr. J. K. Wilshire, were rejected.

Mr. Parkes, not being one of those who professed to approve of everything the Government
had done, or one who had been accustomed in his
public career to refrain from expressing his disapproval of that which merited condemnation, was
charged by some with being an advocate of violent
measures, a Radical of the extremest type.   But he
appealed to the facts of his public life in repudiation
of the charge.

"I have ever been opposed," he said, in his
address to the electors of the North Riding, "to
experimental legislation, and believe that the Parliament of a new country has no graver duty to
perform than guarding against the accumulation of
special enactments which, introduced upon paltry
grounds to meet particular cases, are often at variance with the maxims of common law; and, while
they encumber the statute book with unintelligible
complications, are calculated to impede the healthful
working of the great natural laws so clearly laid
down for the moral government of society.   Acting
upon this conviction, if elected by you, I shall subject all measures, from whatever quarter they may

proceed, to those indisputable principles established
by a long course of political reasoning, and those
great practical truths deduced from legislative experience, which the statesmen of England and
America accept as their common landmarks.   The
liberalism I have ever professed, and ever acted upon,
is in reality the true conservatism of mind and intelligence in our institutions—of justice and equity
in our laws."

 Sir Charles Gavan Duffy, not then knighted,
writing from Melbourne at this time to Mr. Edward
Butler, the well-known barrister of a few years ago,
referred to Mr. Parkes as a man who had won
general confidence by public services performed in the
interests of the entire people.   The letter is remarkable for its recognition of the important position
in politics which, at this period, Mr. Parkes had
attained, and for its expressed belief in his future
eminence.

"I wish I knew how, without impropriety," Sir
Charles wrote, "I could aid you in securing the
election of Mr. Parkes for North Cumberland.   I
would gladly go to Sydney with that object, if my
interference was not liable to be considered un-
warrantable.   And I am the more anxious because
some of our countrymen, you tell me, hesitate to
support him.   I should be sorry to see the Irish
citizens of these colonies separate themselves in any
respect from the general muster of Australians;
but such a separation would be painful and humili-
ating, if it were directed against a man who has won
general confidence, by public services performed in

the interest of the entire people. Mr. Parkes is pre-eminently such a man, and his labours obliterate from all generous minds the recollection of such casual mistakes or misunderstandings as cloud the life of every public man.

" Our friends were angry with him for resisting the election of Mr. Plunkett, for Sydney, in March, 1856. So was I. But the day after that event, or any day since, if I were living in Sydney, I would have felt it my duty to aid, abet, and co-ope-rate with him in politics, as one of the wisest and most disinterested public men that Australia can boast. I am not much in the habit of accepting opinions ready-made from any man; but if I were to select the man on your side of the border, with whom I hold most principles in common, I would name him. And to the right opinions he adds that subtile moral force (combined of genius and integrity) which turns opinions into facts. I am confident that ten years hence, and I do not doubt that ten generations hence, the name which will best per-sonify the national spirit of New South Wales in this era will be the name of Henry Parkes.

" At this distance your contemporary annals fall into the perspective of history to us, as those of England do to you; and the shame and regret which the exclusion of Bright and Cobden from the English Parliament must have created in Sydney, would be felt by some of the best men here at the exclusion of Henry Parkes from your Legislature. I cannot doubt that there are many constituencies which would be rejoiced to

have him ; but the difficulty of the contest which he
has undertaken is a touching evidence to me of a
generous and lofty character.   He is conscious of
public integrity, and he scorns to select a friendly
jury to pronounce on his career."

And the letter concluded :

"If there be among the constituency any
political or personal friends of mine, entreat them to
range themselves on the side of Parkes.   In all the
elections throughout these colonies, there is not one
contest in which I would have less difficulty in taking
_my side, whoever stood on the other, for there is no
man entitled to exclude him. , And I would hear
with the intensest pain and humiliation, that those
in whom I have the interest of a common origin,
ranked themselves against a man for whom I have
not only the highest esteem as a personal friend,
but the completest confidence as a legislator and a
statesman."

Mr. Parkes was elected for the North Riding
of Cumberland, with Mr. Thomas Whistler Smith.
He was returned second on the poll, by a small
majority ; but the contest was severe, and he had
many difficulties to contend against. The features of
his success lay in the facts that the election cost him
nothing, he was not required to make any pledges,
and he proved to the community generally that his
previous defeat in the constituency was not a correct
representation of the feelings of the majority of the
electors.

" If Mr. Smith," said Mr, Parkes at the official
declaration of the poll, " can feel a sentiment of just

pride in being returned for the North Riding of Cumberland, how much more may I, who have been before the country some ten years, who, by the course I have taken, have created large numbers of hostile opponents,—who having taken a most active course in public life, cannot have failed, by the very fact of my having taken so decided a course, to have raised up a large and powerful opposition against me—how much more, under such circumstances, may I feel justly proud of being returned by the constituency which may be considered least favorable to my election."

"The principles on which I have acted," he also said, "are the principles which some of the most enlightened and best men are seeking to carry out in the Government of our fatherland. Those principles I shall not swerve from. I shall to the best of my ability, with whatever energies I possess, seek to carry them out. Though I do not profess to be altogether indifferent to party, believing as I do that responsible government must be carried on by something like constitutional parties, still I will not do violence to my judgment— violence to what I conscientiously believe to be right —for the sake of any party whatever."

In this spirit was he determined to pursue his parliamentary career.

CHAPTER XI.

THE second Parliament under responsible government sat for little more than twelve months, its
principal work being the passing of a new electoral
law.

Not more than half of this short period had gone
by when Mr. Parkes again resigned his seat in the
Assembly, this time in consequence of the difficulties
of the *Empire* having reached a point which forced
the property into the Insolvency Court.

For the short period during which he sat in this
second Assembly he took a prominent part in its
work, and in various ways showed his ability and
usefulness as a legislator.

Early in the session he was instrumental in
saving the Cowper Government from a necessity to
resign on a motion which was virtually one of
censure. By an indiscretion on the part of the
Governor, Sir William Denison, the House had
been offended in its dignity, and Mr. Cowper,
accepting responsibility in the matter, ran great
risk of being sent out of office.

The incident is interesting as it is the first instance, under responsible government in New South Wales, of a Governor coming into conflict with Parliament.

The Indian Mutiny had just broken out, and the Governor-General of India was looking in all directions for troops. A regiment of infantry and a company of artillery were, at the time, stationed in Sydney, and Lord Canning thought the colony might easily spare them for the. urgent service of assisting to quell the rebellion in India. Sir William Denison thought so too, and sending a message to the Assembly, covering a despatch from Lord Canning, he asked the Assembly to consent to the immediate despatch of the troops to Calcutta, and at the same time to make provision for the purchase of the horses necessary to enable the artillery upon landing to take the field. The colony was paying for the services of these Imperial troops, for it was then considered essential that a properly trained and disciplined force should be maintained in Sydney for the purpose of its defence. The infantry consisted of the 77th Regiment, and the Assembly was willing that it should go to India; but objection was raised to the artillery leaving the colony, and the proposed expenditure in the purchase of horses, £3,640, was refused the moment it came before the House in definite form. Regarding the proposal as one to assist the East India Company, a wealthy corporation, well able to bear the cost of these horses, the majority of members declined to sanction the expenditure, and the Government were

of course bound to acquiesce. The decision of the
House was annoying. It was a rebuff to the
Government for bringing forward the proposal, and
it was not complimentary to the Governor. But
there was no intention to show disloyalty to the
Crown. At the very time the Assembly refused
the money for the purchase of the artillery horses, a
movement was in progress in Sydney for relieving
the distress of sufferers in India from the effects of
the Mutiny, and there was every reason to believe
that, in the aggregate, the contributions would be
very large, and, when forwarded to India, very
beneficial.

Mr. Parkes, on this occasion, was with the
opponents of the proposal, and it was withdrawn.

Sir William Denison, angry at what had taken
place, for he had committed himself in the matter
so far as to have informed Lord Canning that the
troops would be despatched with the horses required
for the artillery, sent to the House a message of
remonstrance in terms which were considered to be
unjustifiable and insulting ; and the House, resenting
the Governor's conduct, referred the message to a
select committee, and then adopted a report from
the committee in which the message was strongly
condemned. Very properly, the Government
assumed all responsibility in the matter as between
the Assembly and the Governor, and, regarding the
course taken by the House as a vote of censure,
were obliged to consider their position, and would
have resigned if Mr. Parkes had not come to
their assistance with a motion of confidence. This

was passed by a majority of nearly two to one, for, though the Government were not in great favour, there was no general desire for a change, and the position of Mr. Cowper and his colleagues was, for the time, materially strengthened.

One important result of these proceedings was that they served to establish definitely in the eyes of Parliament and the public, the responsibility of Ministers in all proceedings between the Governor and the Assembly. For all time it was placed beyond question that, in all his acts in his relations with Parliament, the Governor should proceed with the advice of his Ministers, and that for the consequences of those acts Ministers are fully responsible. The incident was also an important assertion of the independence of Parliament. The old order of politics and the domination of Government House, it was shown had passed away, and the rule of the Governor had given place to the will of the people expressed through their representatives in the Legislature.

Mr. Cowper rose in public estimation by his announcement of ministerial responsibility, though many persons regarded the admission as unnecessarily exposing the Government to the risk of disaster; and, on the whole, it resulted to him in considerable advantage. To Sir William Denison the proceedings were a cause of much discomfort, for the course taken by the Assembly had the appearance of a rude rebuke. Unfortunately for him, he had not become properly conscious of the

great change which the Constitution of 1856, and
the election of the first popular Assembly, had
brought about; and, although on the whole he endeavoured to conform to the new order of things,
his actions at times indicated something of the old
system of arbitrariness and almost absolute power.

One of the measures introduced by Mr. Cowper
at this period, was a bill to restrict Chinese immigration, and in the debate on the motion for the
second reading Mr. Parkes expressed, for the first
time, his views on the subject. They were very
similar to what they were thirty years later, when
he carried through Parliament the Act which
virtually prohibits Chinese immigration into New
South Wales. Very few in number as the Chinese
in the colony in those days were, compared with the
number here now, they had begun to make themselves obnoxious, and an impression was abroad
that unless their influx were in some way checked
they might very soon over-run the country.
Mr. Cowper proposed a poll tax of £3 on each
Chinese arriving in the colony, and the proposal
received the sanction of the Assembly, but the bill
was defeated in the Council. Mr. Parkes was of
opinion that the measure should be prohibitory,
and consistently with that opinion he managed to
pass such a measure thirty years afterwards.

Throughout the period during which he sat in
the second Parliament, Mr. Parkes was constant
in his attendance in the House, and very active in
the performance of the duties of his position. The
difficulty of the "unemployed" made its appearance

in Sydney; and while the *Empire* advocated sending as many persons as possible into the country, in order that they might be judiciously distributed through the districts where employment was probably to be found, its conductor endeavoured as far as he was able to bring about in the Assembly a reduction in the general public expenditure. He thought retrenchment possible, and, in view of the condition of the country at the time, desirable. He did not contend that the officers employed in the public service were too numerous, or the salaries paid them too high, but he considered that a very desirable saving might be effected by a reorganization of the departments. There were, for instance, at the time, two ministers attached to the Crown Law Offices, and yet not at the head of a department. Another minister had the management of the public lands and the public works of the country.

In moving resolutions on the subject, Mr. Parkes argued that, since the time when the salaries then paid were fixed, rents had fallen 50 per cent., the prices of provisions and clothing, which had risen very largely during the excitement attending the discovery of gold, had decreased so much that the market was glutted and sales were being effected at a positive loss; and, in view of the general depression, as much economy in the Government expenditure as was possible should be exercised. Ministers of the Crown, as well as officers of the Civil Service, he proposed, should come under the general revision. He did not think any salary the country could pay could be sufficient remuneration to a minister who properly discharged his duty. Ministerial salaries, he contended, could only be considered as "some kind of nominal recognition of the minister's services." But he was alive to the danger of a growing extravagance in the public expenditure, and he thought that ministers should be paid an equal salary, and that the salary should not amount to more than £1200 a year. His resolutions were :—

"(1.) That a reorganization of the departments, which shall place the duties of public employment more equally under the control of ministers, and secure their more economical performance, is urgently required and ought not to be delayed.'

"(2.) That the estimates of expenditure for the ensuing year ought to be framed upon the basis of reduction, according to amount in each case, considered in reference to the nature of the service proposed."

"(3.) That the salaries paid to the responsible Ministers of the Crown ought to be equal in amount, and not higher than £1200 per annum."

The resolutions were not passed by the House. They were opposed by the Government, who suggested that the matter might be referred to a select committee; and this course was adopted. Mr. Parkes was careful to explain that, while he believed the expenditure had unnecessarily increased, he regarded it as impolitic that public service should be underpaid. What he desired was to restrict the Government to the expenditure which was absolutely necessary for the public service ; and he followed

up his resolutions by moving for a return of the
annual expenditure of the Civil Service of the
colony for the seven years 1850—1858, showing the
separate cost of each department, and the proportion
of the total to each head of the population, with an
accompanying explanation of the cause of increase
or decrease in any department.

About this time the country became interested
in a dispute between the Government and Mr. J. H.
Plunkett, which led to his dismissal from the office
of Chairman of the Board of National Education,
and his resignation from the position of President of
the Legislative Council. Originating in a difference
of opinion as to the powers of the Board of Education in relation to the issue by the Board of certain
rules and regulations in connection with non-vested
schools, the dispute led to a sharp correspondence
between the President of the Board and the
Colonial Secretary, Mr. Cowper, in which Mr.
Plunkett used expressions such as the Government
considered it impossible to overlook , and steps were
taken to bring about his removal.

In common with other prominent public men
Mr. Parkes endeavoured to effect a reconciliation.

Mr. Plunkett was an old colonist who had
done good public service, and was very generally
esteemed. Coming to New South Wales in 1832
as Solicitor-General, and afterwards filling the office
of Attorney-General for nearly twenty years, he
had become conspicuous in the public life of the
country; and his appointment to the position of
President of the Board of National Education had

given general satisfaction. He was a Roman
Catholic, but he was a man of liberal mind, and he
enjoyed the respect and confidence of a large proportion of the Protestant community. For ten
years he had sat at the head of the Board of
Education, and in that office his labours had undoubtedly been beneficial. It was therefore with
something like universal regret that it was learned
that he had left the post where he had been so
useful.

The matter came before the Assembly in a
series of resolutions moved by Mr. James
Macarthur, and after a debate extending over
several days, during which excitement in and out of
the House ran high, the difficulty was brought to
an end by a compromise. Sympathy was expressed
with Mr. Plunkett, and the Government was not
directly censured; but, in an amendment moved by
Mr. Parkes, and adopted, it was hoped that such
steps would be taken as would enable the Government to restore Mr. Plunkett to the position from
which he had been removed.

In putting forward this amendment, its author
was actuated by the double motive of acting fairly
with Mr. Plunkett and defending the Government
in a case the merits of which he considered were in
their favour. He could not close his eyes to the
circumstance that some of those who were loud in
the support of Mr. Plunkett, were moved less by a
wish to befriend him than by a desire to injure
Mr. Cowper and his Government; and, while he
recognised Mr. Plunkett's distinguished services, and

the desirableness of bringing him and the Govern
ment together again on friendly terms, he declined
to admit that the Government had done wrong. A
reconciliation, however, would be in the interest of
society, and for the benefit of the cause of education;
and this he was able to bring about. The country
could not afford, he said, to deal carelessly or
lightly with its public men, who were one of the
greatest elements of its moral worth; and it was
equally undesirable to censure a Government that
had taken in this matter the only course a proper
sense of its dignity would allow.

Mr. Plunkett did not return to the Board of
National Education, but he publicly expressed his
regret for that portion of his correspondence with
the Government which had led to his dismissal.

A few months previous to this George Robert
Nichols had passed away. For something like a
quarter of a century he had been a prominent
figure in politics. In various ways he had rendered
important public service, and had exercised considerable influence. He had been a Minister of the
Crown. Several of the most prominent lawyers in
the community owed to him much of their advancement. One who was well able to speak of him
said "Scarcely any member of the Legislature had
laboured so zealously, so devotedly, and so contin-
uously as he." Especially useful were his services
in committee, his great legal knowledge and acumen
being employed to much advantage in the criticism
and amendment of bills. He had some of the
virtues and some of the failings of Goldsmith. A
K

story is told of how a distressed friend called upon
him on one occasion for relief, a bailiff having been
put in the friend's house in consequence of a debt
of £60. Curiously enough there were bailiffs in
Nichols' house at the time, consequent upon a debt
which Nichols had not been able to pay of £120,
but he had been able to get together a sum of £60
towards meeting the liability. With the appearance
of the friend, however, his intentions with regard
to the £60 changed ; and, handing the money to his
fellow sufferer, he said : "Take it! it is of no use
to me in the circumstances, and it is just the sum
you want." He died almost in poverty, leaving a
little property, but with heavy mortgages hamper-
ing it; and a public meeting was held to collect
subscriptions for his widow and younger children.

Many years afterwards, at the instance of
Mr. Parkes, the name of George Robert Nichols was
inscribed with those of other prominent politicians of
the early days, in the vestibule of the Legislative
Assembly, where it is to be seen at this day.

CHAPTER XII.

ON the 6th May, 1858, Mr. Cowper introduced in the Legislative Assembly his Electoral Law Amendment Bill, which contained among its chief provisions the principles of representation on the basis of population, manhood suffrage, and vote by ballot.

The bill was strongly opposed by the old conservative party, in whose eyes it threatened to bring about something like anarchy and ruin; and the fact that this settlement of the land question, on the basis of the principles advocated by Mr. Robertson, was to be the chief measure to come before the reformed Parliament increased the bitterness felt by the squatters. Mr. Donaldson opposed the Electoral Bill as a revolution and not a reform, a measure utterly ruinous to property. So offensive did it appear to him that he declared, if it passed, he would immediately pack up his things and leave the country. To Mr. (afterwards Sir John) Hay it was a bill likely to lead to great mischief. It left the good old English path, he said, and was an indication that the government of the country was on a downward course towards democracy and the tyranny of an unthinking majority. Yet in reality the colony was simply passing from a system of restriction and stagnation to a condition of freedom and progress.

Mr. Parkes regarded the measure as in spirit a thoroughly English one. The democratic power proposed to be given by the bill was not, he argued, so great as that which at the time existed in the House of Commons, and if the inclination towards popular rule was so great in England, how much greater ought it to be in New South Wales, where the very nature of society and the genius of our institutions were essentially democratic. In his opinion danger could only arise from placing too great a restraint upon the democratic tendencies of the country.

The second reading of the measure was carried by 36 votes to 14, and not long afterwards the great principles of the bill were brought into operation.

Looking back over the period that has since passed, it is interesting to note that the increased power given to the people has, on the whole, been accompanied by the progress of the country. The fears respecting manhood suffrage still exist. There are many persons in the colony who regard this privilege with disapproval. But in a country where class distinctions now exist more in name than in reality, where men are more equal than in any other part of the globe, it would not be possible to have any other voting qualification. From the time of the introduction of self-government under the Constitution of 1856 the colony has been marching towards an absolute democracy, and, with the rule of the people, the inseparable evils of the popular system of government have had to be, and must still be, borne. The wonder is that in such a free and vigorous community these evils have not been much greater than they are. Undesirable persons appear as candidates at elections for Parliament, and sometimes are elected; the educated and wealthy men of the country, as a rule, hold themselves aloof from politics; and the waste of time in the performance of Parliamentary work is sometimes lamentable. But in spite of this the country has been constantly moving ahead. Population has greatly increased; trade has largely extended; industries have grown; wealth has accumulated enormously. Mr Donaldson's alarm has not been realised; and the "good old English path," so admirable in the eyes of Mr. Hay, instead of being widely divergent from the broader Australian road, has itself gradually changed in accordance with the Australian example until it has become virtually identical.

While Mr. Cowper, as head of the Government, was pushing forward the work of reforming the Legislative Assembly, Mr. Parkes did something towards altering the nature of the Legislative Council from that of a nominee, to that of an elective, chamber. Mr. Robertson had already moved in this direction, and at his instance the Assembly, in 1857, had passed a resolution affirming "that all deliberative bodies entrusted with legislative functions ought to be elected by the people in their primary assemblies." Furthermore, the

resolution had been recognised by two Governments
as referring to the Legislative Council, and had been
twice alluded to in vice-regal speeches as a matter
to which the attention of the Government would be
directed, with a view to the principle which it advocated being carried into effect.   But as no further
action was taken, though Mr. Robertson had become
a member of the Government, Mr. Parkes brought
the subject forward in the first session of 1858, in
order that Mr. Robertson's resolution might be
re-affirmed.

Doubts had existed in the mind of Mr. Parkes
as to the desirableness of having a Legislature composed of two Houses, but this feeling had arisen
more from the operation of the Constitution up to that
time than from any positive dislike of the dual system of legislation.   Reflection showed him that what
was regarded as unsatisfactory in the working of
the Legislative Council might be traced to a specific
cause, and that cause removed.   That which, in
his opinion, was most desirable, was to bring the
second chamber into closer association with the
people ; not to make it a mere reflex of the
Assembly, or, in its alteration, to introduce in any
extreme degree the principles of democracy, but to
place it on such an elective basis as would bring
into the House " that class of persons whose length
of service, great ability, and private virtue, consti-
tute them the moral aristocracy of the country."

On many occasions since he expressed the
same idea.   At various times in his later career he
had occasion to complain of the Council taking, with

regard to measures sent there by the Assembly, a course which probably would not have been followed if the House had been directly responsible to the people; and twice he brought forward a bill to make the Council elective. Yet it cannot be denied that notwithstanding the obstacles which, by the action of the Upper Chamber, have been placed in the way of some proposals having the support of a majority in the Assembly, the Legislative Council has done good service to the country. Frequently it has checked or improved legislation hurriedly passed by the Lower House; it has originated valuable measures; and in all its proceedings it has displayed an extensive knowledge of political questions, and a clear view of the necessities of the case in the matter under discussion, with, on most occasions, a patriotic desire to do the best thing possible under the circumstances.

The course taken by Mr. Parkes in 1858, in seeking to have Mr. Robertson's resolution reaffirmed, was approved by the Assembly; and it was decided that, in the opinion of the House, "the Legislature of the colony ought to be composed of two Houses, both elected by the people."

In some quarters at the time an impression existed that this decision of the Assembly was intended as a hint to the Council of the course that might be taken if that House should prove hostile to the new Electoral Bill,—that it was in reality a threat intended to coerce the Upper Chamber in the consideration and passing of the measure. But, as far as Mr. Parkes was concerned, there is nothing to show that it was anything more than consistent action on a subject with reference to which he had been of one opinion all his life.

Railway construction in the colony was attracting attention at this period, and the Government were casting about for the best method of having the work carried out with stability and economy. Ten years previously there was not a mile of railway in New South Wales. Now Campbelltown had been reached on the Great Southern line, Parramatta on the Western, and West Maitland on the Northern. Crossing the mountain ranges, and penetrating far into the distant interior, were dreams of the future. The mail coach, built for strength rather than comfort, lumbered along the rough bush roads of the colony, spending many nights and days on journeys which now occupy less than twenty-four hours, and not infrequently having the monotony of its movements rudely interrupted by the appearance of a gang of bushrangers who rifled the mailbags and robbed the passengers. Everyone favoured the pushing on of the railways. Mr. Cowper, desirous of doing as much as possible in the matter, sought the authority of Parliament to carry on their construction under special agreement, instead of by contracts entered into after public competition for the work. Railway contractors were not then as numerous or as capable of carrying out their contracts as they are now, and Mr. Cowper's desire was to have the railways constructed by men like Sir Morton Peto, who was willing, if sufficient inducement offered, to send out the necessary plant and skill from England. Parliament gave Mr. Cowper the authority he asked for, but, at the instance of Mr. Parkes, with the understanding that any special agreement entered into should be laid before both Houses, if in session, fourteen days before the agreement was ratified.

While the Government were giving their attention to opening up the interior of the country by means of railways, Mr. Parkes took in hand the question of adequate communication with Europe and America by the establishment of a satisfactory mail and passenger service *via* Panama. A service by way of India was in existence, but in several respects it had not been satisfactory, and, by the adoption of the Panama route, Mr. Parkes saw prospects of regular and rapid communication with England and Europe, a considerable extension of trade, particularly with America, and probably the introduction of large numbers of desirable immigrants. In relation to the last subject he was one of those who thought that immigration to the country would be what it ought to be "just in proportion as it embodied in its volume a due proportion of capital and labour to carry on the operations of a civilized country." For that reason, believing at the same time it was only by means of a large population the colony could be benefitted, and its people enjoy permanent prosperity, he thought immigration should be entirely voluntary and spontaneous. Some years afterwards it was found wise to adopt a system of assisted immigration, but the "voluntary and spontaneous" method, so far as

it has operated, has undoubtedly been the more
beneficial.

It was argued by Mr. Parkes that the Panama
service would bring to the colony a large population of the best class; and that it would infuse
a new spirit into the commerce of the country,
by which its resources would be developed, its
reputation increased, and a position gained for it
that would be the first in this part of the world.
The Cowper Government agreed with the proposal, and the resolutions were passed by a large
majority; but it was seven years later before what
they recommended was carried into effect.   Then the
Pacific Ocean was " bridged " by a fleet of steamers
equal to any at the time afloat, under a joint subsidy
from the Governments of New South Wales and New
Zealand ; and, though the service was not successful
to the extent anticipated, it placed Australia and
New Zealand in close and regular communication
with America, and has been followed by many good
results.

The Parliament of 1858 had the further privilege
of moving in the direction of the establishment of a
naval station at Sydney.   The question had been
raised as long before as 1851, when Mr. James
Martin advocated the maintenance of a force of two
frigates.   It was now brought forward by Mr.
Donaldson, who proposed that there should be a
naval squadron stationed in New South Wales
waters, consisting of one fifty-gun frigate and three
corvettes.   But the proposal did not meet with
general favour.   It was thought that, if the

Imperial Government could be induced to send the vessels, the colony would have to pay for their maintenance ; and this it was believed would amount to perhaps £50,000 a year, an expense which New South Wales was not then prepared to incur. The Legislative Assembly, therefore, when the matter was under consideration, disposed of the subject by carrying the previous question.

The Electoral Bill was still before Parliament, and Mr. Parkes was assisting to the best of his ability in the debates upon its important provisions, when there appeared in the *Empire* an announcement forcibly indicating the embarrassments which, in connection with that journal, were troubling him at this period.

"The state of suspense," the notice stated, "in which this journal has for the last three weeks been issued, will be brought to a termination in the course of a few days, either by the restoration of the *Empire* to its former size and style of publication, or by its being permanently reduced ; in which latter case a corresponding reduction will be made in the price, and the typographical arrangement and character of the paper will be materially altered." Then giving a statement of how the wages of printers had increased, causing the receipts of the establishment, amounting to more than £26,000 for the year, to be swallowed up in wages and other expenses of publication, it was explained how Mr. Parkes had proposed to the printers to reduce the rate he had been paying them, convinced after long experience that either this reduction must be submitted to or the publication itself reduced. The printers refused to agree to the reduction, and," said the notice, "it could not reasonably be expected that the proprietor should go on year after year, contending with complicated and undiminished difficulties, with all the anxiety and burden of collecting £26,000 or £27,000 a year from the four quarters of the globe, simply to pay it away for paper, ink, rent, and labour."

"It may be," the notice went on to say, "after all, that the colony cannot afford to support two daily papers on the scale of the morning journals hitherto published in Sydney. In that case the proprietor of the *Empire* is at last willing to give up the field to the older journal, and to reduce its publication to a secondary character. He certainly is not quite prepared for this final step, though more than weary of a struggle which has been disastrous to himself and those most closely connected with him, whatever may have been its other results ; but a few days may determine its adoption."

The few days passed, and there seemed some hope that the increased difficulties might be surmounted, for another announcement appeared stating that the necessary mechanical arrangements would be completed not later than the following week, to enable the paper to be brought out permanently in its former size. It was not, however, so to be. Instead of the difficulties being removed, they became greater than ever ; and he who had done so much by his journal for the good of the colony was forced into the Insolvency Court, and his career as a journalist came to an end. The last issue of the *Empire* was on 28th August, 1858, and three days afterwards there appeared, in the *Herald's* record of the business of the Insolvency Court, the information that Henry Parkes, of Ryde, newspaper proprietor, had surrendered his estate " on petition and affidavit," the liabilities being estimated at £50,000, and the assets at £48,500.

The same day were published as advertisements two communications from Mr. Parkes, one to the readers of the *Empire*, and the other to his constituents of the North Riding of Cumberland. The former was a plain but dignified statement of the reasons why the *Empire* had ceased to appear.

" The public journal established by me in November, 1850, and conducted by me up to last Saturday, has ceased to exist. I wish to say a few words which the public have a right to expect in explanation of its sudden stoppage. I still hold to the opinion I formerly expressed on different occasions, that the *Empire* during the first six years of its existence was eminently successful as a young journal. I know of no instance where a daily paper of equal magnitude, in so short a time, has risen to a higher position of circulation and influence, and received more frequent acknowledgments of ability and character. Its early embarrassments arose from inadequacy of means, and not from any natural condition of failure in the undertaking itself. But I firmly believe it would have surmounted all difficulties if the state of its affairs had not been brought before the public eighteen months ago.

"Of all things in the world a public journal is the very last to bear an exposure of this kind. It must command public respect, not depend upon public sympathy. I felt all this at the time of the first crisis in the *Empire's* affairs, and so expressed myself to the gentlemen who at so much personal inconvenience interested themselves publicly on my behalf. When matters were arranged for the continuance of the publication from April 1st, 1857, I accepted the obligation to go on and do the best I could for the property, though I was fully convinced that things were changed greatly to my disadvantage in the business.

"Since that period I feel conscious that I have done all that man could do, by continuous labour and systematic economy, to preserve the *Empire* in existence; and, though at last overborne in my efforts, I have succeeded in keeping its liabilities where they were at the commencement of this last struggle—showing how near it had risen to a position of safety when the first public shock came upon it.

"Independent of the injury sustained by the occurrence to which I have alluded, and from which the paper never appeared to recover, a variety of other circumstances arising out of that crisis in its existence, together with the general stagnation of business, have been unfavourable to success. Still, however, as the expenditure was very considerably reduced, I think the *Empire* would have floated through the bad times and its smaller difficulties, if it had not been for the apparent indifference of a large number of

its readers in neglecting to pay their accounts.
For example, I received by the post this morning
several letters containing each the sum of £1 due
on the 30th June for a quarter's subscription.
In each of these cases while that debt of 20s. was
accumulating the publication cost me upwards of
£6000. Since I have been waiting for the payment
of that debt of 20s. it has cost me £4000 more.
Indeed, up to the present moment, we have not
received 2s. 6d. in the pound on the total amount
of the accounts demandable, beyond the limits of
Sydney, on the 30th June. In these unpleasant
facts may be discovered the immediate cause of the
stoppage of the *Empire*." And the announcement
closed with an appeal to those indebted to the paper
to remit the amount of their accounts to the trustees
"for the benefit of those whose pecuniary interests
are involved in my misfortunes."

In these circumstances Mr. Parkes' career as a
journalist closed, for, though at various times, in the
subsequent years of his life, he contributed to the
Press, he did not again take part in the conduct
of a newspaper.

Henceforth his abilities were to be devoted
to politics. So far as he had proceeded he had
won for the *Empire* a very prominent position, and by its aid had in many ways done good
service to the country. Well conducted it was from
the issue of the first number, but its best days from
journalistic and literary points of view may be said
to have been during the years 1854-1856. By that
time it had become in every sense a great newspaper,
and had attracted to its service many of the ablest

writers in the colony.   Sir James Martin, Mr.
William Forster, and Mr. Edward Butler were
among the contributors to its pages.   Men skilful
with the pen, and earnest in the desire to use it to
the advantage of the colony, admired the outspoken
tone of the paper, and coveted the privilege of
writing for its columns.   And so it flourished, and
its importance in the community grew.   If it had
continued, and its conductor had never entered on a
Parliamentary career, he would, as a great journalist,
have always been a conspicuous figure among the
prominent men of his time, and held in general
esteem as a public benefactor.

Mr. Parkes' insolvency made it necesary for him
to resign his seat in the Assembly for the North
Riding of Cumberland, and in taking leave of his
constituents he explained to them his position.   He
had worked hard in the House during the few months
he had been their representative, assisting to the
utmost of his ability to make the Electoral Bill a
fair and useful measure.   He had voted in every
division on its clauses, always on the side of practical
reform, and had taken part in all important
discussions.   On other questions also he had in all
instances endeavoured to act in the public interest.
Now, for a time at least, retirement into private life
was inevitable.   "Circumstances of private difficulty," he wrote, "known to you at the time of my
election, which it was thought would terminate more
fortunately, have, contrary to my hopes, assumed a
weight beyond my strength to support, and involved
me in absolute and irretrievable ruin."

CHAPTER XIII.

IN THE PARLIAMENT OF 1859—FIRST ELECTION FOR
EAST SYDNEY.

THE first election under the Electoral Act of 1858
took place in June, 1859, and for the first time
East and West Sydney appeared as electoral districts, each entitled to return four members. Under
the new Act the city of Sydney, forming previously
one constituency returning four members, was
divided into two constituencies returning eight
members.

Mr. Parkes came forward as a candidate for
East Sydney. Between the time of his resignation
from the Legislative Assembly in 1858, in consequence of the misfortunes of the *Empire*, and the
general election of 1859, he did not take any
prominent part in politics. For almost the whole
of that period his affairs were before the Court of
Insolvency, and it was only a few days previous to
the general election that he obtained his certificate
of discharge. Much of his time had been occupied
by the proceedings in relation to his insolvency, and
the remainder had been spent chiefly in the establishment of a business of a kind somewhat similar to
that which he had relinquished for the profession of

L

a journalist. He had been offered, in relation to the
proposed mail service *viâ* Panama, a lucrative
position which would have placed . him above
necessitous circumstances, but it would have obliged
him to leave the colony, and this obligation led him
to refuse it. Upon mature consideration he determined, notwithstanding his reverses of fortune, to
remain in the country which, as he said in alluding
to the circumstance, had upon the whole treated
him well and showered distinctions upon him.

The proceedings in connection with his insolvency
were of a very trying nature. Immediately the
Empire terminated its career the enemies of Mr.
Parkes increased, and he was bitterly assailed. It
is safe to kick a dead lion, and in various ways those
unfriendly to him harassed him. In the endeavour
to continue the publication of the *Empire*, in spite
of the difficulties which in the later period of his
proprietorship had accumulated around it, he had,
under responsible advice, adopted, in association with
the monetary arrangements of the paper, a method
which, when the publication of the paper had ceased,
formed, in the hands of his opponents, the groundwork
for virulent attack. Though completely exonerated
by the judge—Chief Commissioner Purefoy—who
presided in the Insolvency Court, from even the
suspicion of any act of impropriety in his business
operations, he was then, and afterwards, when
political ends were to be gained by it, subjected to
bitter abuse and innuendo.

It was objected in the court, by those who
opposed the issue to him of a certificate of discharge,

that he had obtained goods and credit by means of cheques, well knowing that there were no funds to meet them, and that they could not be paid. But it was pointed out by the judge that there was no evidence to sustain this charge. No witness was called to whom a cheque of this description had been given, or to whom any pretence of the kind indicated had been made.

Then it was said that he had been in the habit of drawing two kinds of cheques, one to be paid on presentation at the bank, and the other not. This, however, it was shown by the judge, had been done in pressing circumstances, under advice from the bank, and without any fraudulent intent.

In April, 1857, Mr. Parkes' creditors, the evidence proved, consented to give him five years to pay off his then existing debts, and at that time several cheques were outstanding and unpaid. The current expenses of the *Empire* made it necessary that cheques should be drawn every week, or oftener, for wages, paper, and other purposes; and the fund from which those cheques had to be honoured consisted of money paid into the bank, as it was received at the *Empire* office, in the course of business day by day. This money, so paid into the bank, was found insufficient to meet all the expenses of the establishment; and, at the suggestion of the bank, it was arranged that cheques, the payment of which, as the judge explained it, " was urgent, and which, so to speak, had a moral or necessary claim to preference over others," should be initialled by Mr. Parkes, so that they might be distinguished from other cheques, " the payment of which was temporarily postponed."

Mr. Parkes declared on oath, that he fully intended to pay every cheque as funds were placed in the bank from time to time, but the sudden and unexpected stoppage of the paper, by the mortgagee taking possession, frustrated his hopes and expectations; and the judge believed him.

In His Honor's opinion there was no fraudulent intent in what had been done; the course adopted had been rather "for the purpose of keeping the paper in circulation, and endeavouring to meet and possibly overcoming the difficulties" which, at the time, were pressing heavily on Mr. Parkes. To the judge it appeared clear that Mr. Parkes had entertained a reasonable and *bona fide* hope of being able, within the time allowed him by his creditors in 1857, to pay everybody in full; and that this hope was not unreasonable could be seen in the circumstance that, for the last four quarters previous to the stoppage of the paper, it had cleared, over all expenses, above £3000. The good debts, at the time the publication of the paper ceased, were sworn by the accountant to be worth £9000, and Mr. Edward Butler, considered by the judge to be fully competent to form an opinion on the matter, estimated the commercial value of the paper, at the time the mortgagee took possession, at £50,000, supposing its debts were paid. "Could it be said, then," asked the judge, "that, under such circumstances, Mr. Parkes was not justified in using every possible exertion to keep the *Empire* in circulation, and that, in adopting the mode referred to of paying some cheques in preference to others, he was not anxious only to attain that end and not to defraud his creditors in any way ? " Such a practice as that followed with regard to the cheques might have been irregular, but there was no fraudulent intent apparent in it.

A third objection to the issue of the certificate was that the insolvent " had appropriated trust funds or other property of which he was only the agent or trustee." This was based on the circumstances that Mr. Parkes had obtained, from different persons, renewal promissory notes, for the purpose of retiring other notes which had been given him for the business requirements of the *Empire*, but, instead of using the renewal notes for this object, he had, through extreme pressure of the demands upon him at the time, applied the proceeds of the renewals to meeting some of these demands, "leaving the original bills or notes unpaid, and, in some few instances, the makers of these notes had to take up both."

But, here again, it was pointed out by the judge, that though, according to the evidence, it was understood between the parties giving these notes and Mr. Parkes, that the first notes were to be paid or retired with the proceeds of the second, and that Mr. Parkes, in some instances, promised to do so, the notes had been given merely for the convenience and benefit of Mr. Parkes; the proceeds of the second bills were applied strictly to the business purposes of the *Empire*; and, "when Mr. Parkes explained the circumstances under which he had been compelled to deviate from his promise as to the appropriation of the money, the makers of the notes admitted the exigency, and approved of the payments made." No complaint was made by them as to any misappropriation of the money.

A fourth objection was that Mr. Parkes had contracted debts without intending to pay, or having at the time any reasonable or probable expectation of paying them,—in fact, well knowing that he could not pay them ; and there were several others. All, however, were overruled, His Honor giving it as his opinion that the rapid growth of the *Empire*, and the aid and encouragement, pecuniary and otherwise, which Mr. Parkes had received from numerous and influential friends, had been sufficient to create the most sanguine hopes of ultimate success, and ability to discharge all his monetary obligations.

In this position Mr. Parkes appeared before the electors of East Sydney at the general election in 1859. Overwhelmed with business embarrassments a few months previously, he had, though with the loss of the *Empire* and his prestige as the proprietor and editor of a great newspaper, passed through them unscathed, and now was prepared to re-enter the political arena, comparatively free from the difficulties by which he had been hampered in his early Parliamentary career.

He came forward as a candidate at the solicitation of friends. Vilified, oppressed, penniless it may be said, there was no one to deny his political ability and the consistency of his character. Depressed, as he had been by his business complications, compelled, under peculiar circumstances, to retire from active political life, he was yet in the community a conspicuous figure in whom the public recognised an abiding power to act in the interests and for the benefit of the country. Even his enemies felt this. The *Herald*, bitter in those days in its cleverly written and merciless leading articles, referring to his insolvency and the result of the proceedings in the Insolvency Court, said that, while in England bankrupts were whitewashed, in New South Wales they were "Purefoyed;" but it admitted he was a man of power and influence in the country, and the leader of the democracy. "Who has the right to say," it asked, " he is not qualified to be a representative of the people ? . . . Unquestionably there is no man before the electors who would represent a larger amount of popular aspirations or who would represent them with greater intelligence and discretion."

Though for some weeks previous to the election he was urged to permit himself to be brought forward as a candidate for East Sydney, it was not until the nomination proceedings were very near that he consented. His reluctance was not due to fear of failure. It was rather owing to a disregard of the whole matter, born of the weariness and worry which had been associated with his previous career in the Legislature. Conscious of his ability to serve the colony, and willing—even ambitious—to be in its service, he yet could not be forgetful of the unsatisfactory nature of the conditions that had attended his past political life. He had done much,

but it had fallen far short of what he had set himself
to do.   Now, when he was free from the business
career which had harassed him, when he was more
master of his time, as he himself explained it, than
ever he had been before, when "if he went into the
Legislature again he should have a ten-fold strength,
as it were, to serve the country," he saw no reason
why he should not consent to the solicitations of
his friends, and appear as a candidate for East
Sydney, part of the important constituency which
had elected him twice before.

He announced, that if elected, he would go into
Parliament thoroughly independent,— "a follower
of no man, a flatterer of no man, but an independent
democrat, determined to support that Administration which shall be true to the principles of progress
and to the democratic genius of the age,—to support that Administration and none that falls short
of that."   Not long ago, in the glamour of
the appearance in the political world of the new
Labor Party, it suited some of his opponents to
close their eyes to the democratic professions of his
earlier political career, and to his strict adherence to
democratic principles throughout his life.   Yet he
never swerved from the line of duty marked out
by himself from the first.

In the Parliament of 1858 he had been friendly
to Mr. Cowper and of considerable assistance to his
Government.   But the support had never been
given in any subservient manner, or on mere party
grounds ; and, towards the end of the period during
which he occupied a seat as a member of that

Parliament, he saw reason to modify his support, and to act more as an independent critic than had before appeared necessary. Mr. Cowper, though undoubtedly one who, in all he did as the head of the Government, had the interest of the country at heart, sometimes acted in a manner which had the effect of weakening the confidence of his friends and alienating their support. They doubted his sincerity. He was a singular mixture of various qualities. That he was a highly honourable christian gentleman no one would be disposed to deny, and yet it would be equally difficult to say that he was not as capable, as any one in his position might be, of resorting to all the tricks and devices necessary to retain a hold of office and power. In many of his acts and purposes which professed to aim at the progress and the welfare of the colony he was undoubtedly sincere, and yet he was so insincere that he came to be known by the sobriquet of "Slippery Charley." Such a portrait as this might be taken to represent politicians since the time of Mr. Cowper, but the inexperience of the colony, at this period of its existence, in the ways of government under a popular Constitution, would probably make the defects in the character of a prominent public man much more conspicuous than they may appear in such a person now.

Mr. Cowper appeared before the electors at the general election of 1859 as the head of a Government which had passed the new Electoral Act, but the Government were not received with any display of enthusiasm. Their land policy—that which a few

years later was passed by the persistent efforts of
John Robertson—was the principal measure in their
programme for the future, and some of its main
provisions were not generally approved, perhaps,
not rightly understood.   Even friends of the
Government refrained, for the time, from expressing
their concurrence in the proposed new system.
Robertson, convinced himself on the subject, and
enthusiastic in its advocacy, put the matter before
the country in a manifesto, and, with his colleagues,
carried it to the hustings, where it was destined for
some time to remain.   Its chief principle was free
selection before survey, or, as Mr. Cowper described
it, "provision to enable a person of small means
to obtain his farm and settle himself without the
delays of office."

Next to the land question was the subject
of education.   Though the towns of the colony
were well supplied with schools under the
National system, the country districts, especially
those in which the population was small and
scattered, were greatly deficient in the means for
the teaching of children; and the extension of the
means of education throughout the country was
one of the leading questions in the election.

The reconstruction of the Legislative Council was
also a measure which the Government contemplated
having to deal with in the new Parliament.   Attempts
to bring about this reconstruction had already been
made, but they had not been successful, and the
Government favouring the plan of placing the
Upper Chamber upon an elective basis, were inclined to try again.

Another matter of importance, though not of such moment as to demand immediate attention, was the question of State aid to religion, and the advisableness of reducing all religious bodies in the colony to the voluntary or self-supporting principle.

Mr. Parkes was liberal in his views on each of these questions, but he did not blindly follow what the Government put forward. He did not see his way clear to assent altogether to Mr. Robertson's land scheme, nor to the whole of the principles put forth at the time by a Land League which had been formed in Sydney. He expressed himself generally in favour of the American land system, which was similar to Mr. Robertson's in regard to permitting people to settle on the land where and when they chose, irrespective of survey or anything else, but not the same in what was afterwards required to be done. There was more definiteness and safety in the American system as to residence, improvement, and subsequent ownership by the settler, than there was in the scheme advocated by Mr. Robertson. By the American system the settler was duly protected and the country benefitted; by Mr. Robertson's plan it was not certain that either of these results would be attained.

In common with all who sought the real progress of the colony in regard to its lands, Mr. Parkes favoured agricultural settlement, and all measures that would assist such an object; but, at the same time, he did not desire to act unjustly towards the squatters. He recognised the fact that, though they were a powerful class in the community, influenced frequently by self-interest, they were undoubtedly one of the mainstays of the country, and he was willing that full justice should be accorded them. But he wanted such a revision of the system under which they had the use of the public lands, as would make it impossible for them to hold the lands against the advance of population.

The question of education he regarded as intimately connected with the subject of the public lands; and having always been a staunch supporter of the National school system, he intimated that, in any revision of the system of public instruction in the colony, he should adhere to the maintenance " of those broad principles of the National system which had already been shown to possess so much usefulness."

At the same time it seemed to him that greater facilities "should be given to ministers of religion to impart religious instruction to the children attending the schools, and to satisfy the consciences of those who complained of the system in this particular." If such facilities could be given, he said to the electors of East Sydney, without impairing the usefulness of the schools, the plan should have his cordial support. Since that time the tendency has been to make education in the State schools of the colony almost wholly secular, and Sir Henry Parkes conformed to the general feeling in this direction; but, in 1859, he was more in favour of a system on the basis of the National school system, (which was not much dissimilar from our present public school system), with ample provision for religious instruction in the schools.

With respect to the Legislative Council, he was favourable to seeing a system of election applied to it, with a suffrage similar to that required for the Legislative Assembly; but though ready to make the basis of the two Houses common so far as the suffrage was concerned, so that the Council should be free from the objections that would be urged against it if the suffrage were of a more restrictive character, he was in favour of some restriction as to the age of a candidate for the Upper House; and he thought it a question worthy of consideration, whether some period of service in the Lower House should not be required as a qualification for the higher Chamber. While strongly in favour of a second House, he thought the two Houses should be composed of similar elements, with the exception "that the Council ought to gather up the ripened intellect, the valuable experience, of the country."

A firm believer in the democratic institutions of the colony, it was impossible, he was of opinion, for us to progress with any other system of government; but, at the same time, it ought to be our endeavour to infuse into our institutions a high spirit, and a nice discriminating sense of honour. For these reasons, he pointed out to the East Sydney electors, every effort should be made to put honest, faithful, and able men into the new Parliament, and to educate the children of the country so that when they should come to man's estate they should be able to perform the duty of free citizens, with a full consciousness of the importance of that duty, and a deep sense of the necessity for preserving the liberties of the country and building up a great and honourable national character. This sound advice he was never tired of instilling into the minds of the people at any period of his life, whenever and wherever he may have been addressing them.

His faith in the importance of the democratic spirit of the country was equalled only by his belief in the value of its natural resources. In his eyes New South Wales was far richer than any of the other colonies, and he saw an important future before it, not only as a country of great production, but as one of manufactures. " I will never rest," he said, " until I see that we have not only a great producing interest, that we are not only developing the raw material for manufacturing, but that we have a sound, enlightened, and extensive commerce, and, in addition, that great basis of national prosperity, a great manufacturing interest. For the country to be safe it ought to have as its three bases, a great producing interest, a great manufacturing interest, and a great commerce, and I would not attempt to serve the interests of the one at the expense of the other, but to foster the three alike so that there shall be many outlets for the energies of our children."

These words are not exactly those which might be expected from a freetrader, and yet they are not antagonistic to freetrade. Mr. Parkes' views on the question of freetrade and protection were not, at this period of his life, as distinct as they became later on.

At this time he was not so much a freetrader as he was what has since been called a fair trader. But, as he himself has explained, his views on the subject were then immature. Longer experience and deeper reflection taught him that progress and prosperity are best found under a policy in which commerce is entirely free, and manufactures are not fostered artificially. At the same time he was never averse to assisting the manufacturing interest when it could be done consistently with the principles of commercial freedom.

To the electors of East Sydney he described his opinions on these points in words which were sufficiently plain for them to understand his position. "I have for twenty years," he said, "been a freetrader; but I am not one of those who ridicule the efforts or the opinions of those who are called protectionists. I am a practical freetrader as against theoretical freetraders, and I would maintain the principles of freetrade to this extent: that I would resist all legislation that would seek to restrict the supply of the main commodities of human existence or in any way limit the well-being of the community."

Dr. Woolley, who was present at the meeting, and took some part in it, regarded Mr. Parkes "as a freetrader with a good deal of protection in him," and this was the generally accepted view of the matter.

As it proceeded the election created much interest. There were eight candidates: Mr. Cowper, Mr. Parkes, Mr. James Martin, Mr. John

Black, Mr. Richard Driver, Mr. W. B. Allen, Mr. W. Benbow, and Mr. Charles Kemp. Mr. Parkes was, in some respects, regarded as the rival of Mr. Cowper. Each desired to top the poll, and it was thought that Mr. Parkes aimed at the leadership of the Liberal Party in Parliament. For this important position he was not regarded as unfitted. Some of the opinions of the leading journal on his fitness have already been quoted. As the day of nomination drew nigh the paper appeared to be more than ever impressed by the prospect of his future eminence. That he was destined to be a great popular leader and the head of a Government appeared to the *Herald* more than probable.

"Looking about us," it wrote, "at the indications of feebleness and uncertainty which mark the movements of public life—the disposition of men to pick up the articles of their political creed out of any current of popular feeling which sweeps by them, we are not sure that a man of strong will and considerable popular influence may not make his way upwards to the highest position. All we hope is that if Mr. Parkes should be so fortunate as to gain that position, to which he undoubtedly aspires, he may have power to infuse into the policy of the future some of those moderating principles which he has so freely recognised."

"No man among us," the *Herald* said on the same occasion, "knows better where to find the heart of the dark-browed and the rough-handed. The solemnity of his manner, the very tone of his voice, and the expression of his countenance, all

combine to corroborate his influence over them, and
if we are not greatly mistaken, he is marked out by
the hearty vows of many—and they the most
active and persevering—to be the future chief of the
democracy and its legislators."

The speeches delivered by Mr. Parkes at this
time were much above the average of those of other
candidates in the election. They were marked by
great breadth of view and much evidence of
thoughtfulness, and, in their delivery, there was an
earnestness of manner which showed that in what
was said expression was given to strong convictions,
and that what was advocated was conscientiously
believed to be for the public good.

A prominent feature in them was the
aphoristic style of language adopted. This
kind of phrase was used with frequency, and
doubtless with effect. So nicely were the sentences arranged, so well did they convey the ideas
embodied in them, that to-day, reading from
a musty volume of newspapers over thirty years
old, they appeal to the understanding as eloquently,
and as forcibly, as they must have done when they
leaped with the freshness and strength of new life
from the lips of the orator. " My motto has always
been," he said, speaking on the subject of education,
" fewer gaols and fewer policemen, more schools and
more schoolmasters." "It is much better to educate
your children into intelligent, enlightened, obedient,
and industrious citizens than to attempt to coerce
them into the observance of, and servile obedience
to, crude and impolitic laws." " My motto is few

M

laws, and those laws embodying sound principles
and of universal application." That these are words
of wisdom, admirably expressed, and such as appeal
with forcibleness to those who listen or those who
read, who will deny ?

The declaration of the polling showed Mr.
Cowper to be at the head of the list with 2,064
votes, Mr. Black, who had been running with Mr.
Cowper, second with 1,682 votes, and Mr. Parkes,
with 1,654 votes, third. The fourth candidate
elected was Mr. Martin, whose votes numbered
1,349. At the nomination proceedings, Mr. Parkes
was by far the most popular of all the candidates,
and obtained the largest show of hands ; but in the
voting the Government party proved the strongest,
and secured the first two places. Mr. Parkes took
a philosophic view of the situation. Though
third in the order of those elected, he did not
regard himself as the representative of any particular class, or even as specially representing
Sydney, but accepted his election as placing him in
the position of a representative of the whole body
of the people and of the interests of the whole
country.

Parliament opened on the 30th August, and
the Government, doubtful of their chances of remaining long in office, endeavoured to secure
support by putting forward an attractive programme.

Mr. Parkes gave notice of a motion for the
immediate repeal of the duties on tea and sugar.
These duties, first imposed in 1851, and four years

afterwards doubled, the increase being made for revenue purposes, were the work of an irresponsible Legislature, and they had never been popular with the constituencies. Mr. Cowper had been one who had opposed their increase, and now that there was a Government in power, under a popular system, at the head of which was one who had denounced the duties in their present shape, Mr. Parkes expected to see some step taken towards their repeal. He advocated their repeal because they were opposed to established principles of political economy ; they had been imposed by a Government irresponsible to the people; the Government now in power had been sufficiently long in office to be in a position to deal with the question ; and as the Governor's speech at the opening of Parliament had stated that the revenue was in a prosperous condition, there could not be a more favourable opportunity for taking the course proposed.

Mainly through indecision in the matter the Government caused the motion to be carried, though only by a majority of one; and their resignation was announced, their hope lying in the belief that their opponents would be unable to form a new Administration. In this view they were correct. Mr. T. A. Murray was sent for by the Governor, and he was unsuccessful; the efforts to form a new Government failing through a want of cohesion among the members of the Opposition.

In later days Mr. Parkes would have been entrusted with the task of forming a new Administration, but at this time his democratic tendencies were regarded by many as somewhat dangerous. Consistent in principle and in conduct he had always been, and was admitted to be; but, in influential quarters, there was a feeling of aversion to seeing "the greatest democrat of the colony," as Mr. Robertson styled him in the debate on the tea and sugar duties, in power. "As public men," the *Herald* observed in reference to this point, "we may prefer, for instance, Mr. Parkes to Mr. Cowper, and this, because as a legislator, Mr. Parkes has always been steady to his principles and true to the political programme he announced. He has been the same man as a journalist, as a candidate, and as a member of the Assembly; but if the question be whether the principles espoused by the more intimate supporters of the Ministry, or those advocated by Mr. Parkes, should become the ruling policy of the country, we should certainly have no hesitation in voting with Mr. Cowper. We must have a Government, and if we cannot have that which we prefer, it is mere folly to go with the extreme section of the Opposition."

The impossibility of forming a Government from the Opposition having been proved, Mr. Cowper induced the House to rescind the resolution passed for the repeal of the tea and sugar duties, and remained in office; but in less than two months his Government was again in difficulties.

CHAPTER XIV.

THE Cowper Government met their fate in a defeat on a bill introduced by them to deal with the subject of education ; and a Ministry under Mr. William Forster conducted the affairs of the country, until, at the end of four months, they were succeeded by the Robertson-Cowper Administration, famous in the political history of the colony for its land legislation on the principle of free selection before survey.

About this time Mr. Parkes began to turn his attention to the subject of immigration, and the best means for bringing a desirable class of immigrants from the mother country to New South Wales. Until very recent years there was a great dearth in the colony, and, in fact, in Australia generally, of that class of population who are possessed, not only of the energy to do what can be done in developing the resources of the country, but of the capital to enable them to do it. There was also a scarcity of mechanics and labourers, and of domestic servants. Until as late as 1860 this was very marked. Among the labouring classes

there were some, who, notwithstanding the scarcity
of population, thought, or professed to think, that
no more people were wanted; but there had not been
shown by the working classes generally the spirit,
which has since been exhibited, in the efforts made
by labour organizations to discourage all immigration
to the country.   Generally, people recognised that
they were few in number and limited in means; and,
though surrounded by almost boundless natural
resources, were unable to properly take advantage of
them.   As a consequence they were not averse to
giving their attention to the desirableness of
adopting, in addition to the means then existing,
some plan by which the population and the capital
of the country might be judiciously increased.

Mr. Parkes had long been impressed with the
necessity for more people and more money, and was
convinced that without them the country must be
materially hindered in its progress.   As far back as
1854 he had sat as a member of a select committee
which had expressed itself strongly in favour of
immigration ; and now, with the construction of
railways, the introduction of the electric telegraph,
and the establishment of ocean mail services, an
increased population was wanted, if only to prevent
the burden of meeting the public necessities from
pressing too heavily upon the comparatively few
people in New South Wales.

Much, he thought, might be done by spreading
a knowledge of the colony in England.   The
ignorance of the English people respecting Australia
was very marked.   Very few were aware of any

difference between the country of this period and the Botany Bay of the convict days, while the vast majority were entirely oblivious of its existence. If persons in the position of public lecturers could be sent to England, and there make known to the British people the great advantages offering to those who emigrated to the colony, probably, Mr. Parkes thought, there would be a considerable influx of population. The climate was all that could be desired ; the facilities for obtaining land under the new land law, it was believed, would prove very satisfactory ; the colony was particularly suited for various important industries ; and English institutions and habits existed throughout the land. There was, therefore, much to attract the emigrant ; and it seemed very reasonable to think that amongst the large population of the mother country there were a considerable number of persons, with the means of emigrating, who, when convinced that they might improve their condition in life by removing to New South Wales, would not hesitate to leave their native land and come out to Australia.

Impressed with these ideas, and following a provision contained in an Act relating to Immigration, then recently passed by Parliament, Mr. Parkes, on May 1st, 1861, proposed in the Assembly that £5000 should be expended on the establishment "of immigration agencies and lectureships in Great Britain and Ireland," the money to be distributed as follows : £2000 in salaries for twelve months for two lecturers and general agents, £1000 to meet the travelling expenses of the lecturers, £500 in

payment to shipping agents in the principal British
ports for collecting and imparting to intending
emigrants information as to vessels sailing for
Australia, and £1500 to cover the expense of printing,
in a cheap and popular form, copies of the Land Acts
and other trustworthy information relating to the
colony.   A scheme of this kind, in his opinion,
would induce a spontaneous emigration to New
Sonth Wales, which would be large and satisfactory;
and, in this opinion, he was supported by the
Government and by the Legislative Assembly.
With an amendment, which left to the Government
the details as to the distribution of the £5,000, the
motion was passed without division.

The following morning the *Sydney Morning
Herald*, writing upon the subject, remarked that no
one would be so suitable as Mr. Parkes to address
the working classes of England; and, very shortly
afterwards, it was announced that the Governor,
with the advice of the Executive Council, had
appointed Mr. Parkes and Mr. W. B. Dalley to
proceed to England in accordance with the terms of
the Assembly's resolution.

Comment and criticism now began to appear.
Mr. Parkes having been a strong opponent of the
Government, their ever watchful foe and keenest
critic, and Mr. Dalley a colleague and staunch
supporter, an idea prevailed, in some quarters, that
instead of being prompted by a desire to benefit the
country through additional immigration, the Government had been influenced in making the appointments by the unworthy object of getting rid of an

enemy and serving a friend. The *Herald* making further reference to the matter, though again complimentary to Mr. Parkes, plainly indicated its opinion that an able opponent of the Government had been adroitly disposed of.

The appointment of Mr. Parkes, the article remarked, was expected the moment his resolution received the support of the Government; and, it added, "no one could be so suitable to carry out the plan which he had submitted." But, in alluding to the position which he had filled in relation to the Government, it said: "That he proposed the plan of sending lecturers to England, was a suggestion to the Ministry both to accept the relief which it promised them, and to grant the compensation by which that relief is repaid. Mr. Parkes, lately a determined opponent of the Government—a few weeks ago armed with a resolution which would have demolished one member of the Ministry at least, if not the Cabinet of which he is a member—more lately silent upon political subjects, is now in the service of the Crown, under the auspices of Mr. Cowper."

The paper, however, still refrained from condemning the appointment. "We do not condemn the appointment of Mr. Parkes in itself," it said. "He is qualified for the task if anyone could fulfil it." And further: "Mr. Parkes will be better fitted to serve the country on his return than on his departure. . . . Mr. Parkes has many valuable qualities—great industry and indomitable perseverance, and an oratory which,

though not adapted to the schools, tells with great
effect upon the masses.   His work, if it prove
successful, will entitle him to the public thanks, and
doubtless interest in his future career many who
may be induced by his persuasion to seek this
country as their future home.   Had we much
greater reason to complain of his career than we
have hitherto admitted, we should at the present
moment withdraw them, and only express our desire
that, having rendered on the whole considerable
service to the country, he may be successful in the
mission he has undertaken, and return hereafter to
complete the circle of public labour which his
ambition has doubtless contemplated, and to which,
comparing him with his competitors, it is not unreasonable he should aspire."

He and his colleague Mr. Dalley were not long in
setting forth upon their mission.   The appointment
rendered necessary the resignation of Mr. Parkes' seat
in Parliament, and this step having been taken,
preparations were made for departure.

The day upon which the two commissioners
left Sydney, an address from his friends and
admirers, headed by Dr. Woolley, was presented
to Mr. Parkes.   It was the outcome of a meeting
of citizens held a few days previously, and it
was read and presented to the recipient on
the deck of the steamer *Wonga Wonga*, just
before her departure for Melbourne, where the
commissioners were to catch the mail steamer for
England.   Time had not permitted of anything
more elaborate or demonstrative.

" We cannot allow you," the address was worded,
" to leave the colony without expressing the confidence which we feel in your ability to carry out
the object of your important mission to the mother
country."

This, in itself, was a great compliment. Not
very many years previously Mr. Parkes had stood
on the deck of another vessel, in the same
harbour, among a crowd of others, a friendless,
almost penniless, immigrant, with all the years of
toil and hard experience to bring him to his present
position before him.

" Your public life," the address proceeded,
" consistent throughout in adherence to fixed
principles, your untiring energy and perseverance,
the warm interest which you have ever taken in
social questions, and your expressed attachment to
the country, are a sufficient guarantee that the
advocacy of the colony will be safe in your hands.

" We earnestly hope that as an accredited
representative of the country, your efforts will be
successful, not only in dispelling much ignorance
with regard to New South Wales as a field for
industry, enterprise, and capital, but in exposing
the misrepresentations of any who depreciate our
institutions and cast a doubt upon the future
development and progress of the colony."

And the address concluded by wishing him a
safe return to the country, for which he had
" laboured so long and so earnestly."

In his reply, Mr. Parkes explained his position.
He believed, he said, that he had done right in

proceeding to Europe. He had toiled hard for eight or ten years. His health, though in its foundation strong, was somewhat impaired by over-anxiety and prolonged labour ; and the change he was about to enjoy would probably establish his health, and confer on him a great physical benefit.

But independently of all personal considerations, he went on to explain, the object which he was about to assist in carrying out, he had ever regarded as one of great importance and interest. The records of the Legislature would show that it had been his settled belief that what was wanted to keep this colony, if not actually in advance, at least abreast of the other colonies, was giving sufficient publicity in Great Britain to its natural resources and attractions.

He was convinced that there was nothing that would remove the embarrassment from which the country was suffering, but an increase of the classes engaged in the various avocations of production ; and the only way, in his opinion, to extend the great producing interests of the country was to diffuse labour throughout them.

In going to England, his intention was not simply to introduce into the colony wage-earning labourers. His object would be to represent to the British public of all classes, rich and poor, high and low, settled and unsettled, men with capital, and men without capital, the real character of the country as a field for general immigration. " My object," he said, " is to attract rich men here as well as poor men, so that a spontaneous volume of immigration may visit us, bringing with it, as a great element of prosperity, labour and capital combined, so that we shall have as it were a slice of old England in this country."

Of his past career he said but two or three words, but they were words of weight. " I have learned to value above all things the test of time as applied to a public man, and if any little services that I have rendered to the country will not stand the test of time I say—let them perish."

This interesting little ceremony, which most persons would think should have elicited the approval of everybody, excited displeasure in some quarters, and was followed by unfavourable comments in the press. The leading journal appeared to have arrived at the conclusion that, at last, it was clear the appointment was not pure and in the public interest.

The morning after the presentation on the steamer it appeared with an article in which it said :—" The appointment itself and all the circumstances under which it was made points out its true character. Mr. Parkes has been the most formidable opponent of Mr. Cowper, but he has been compelled to surrender, like many a strong fortress, under the pressure of starvation. Mr. Cowper, being in better quarters and having the revenues of the country at his back, could have carried on this war for some months longer. Mr. Parkes was fairly exhausted. There was, however, in his public character a latent strength which might under any accident display itself and command

the wavering majority of the Assembly.   The coast
was clear.   He moved for a grant of £5000 for the
appointment of lecturers, £1000 as salary, £500 as
travelling expenses, and the remainder to enable
them to distribute tracts or whatever might be
otherwise convenient and desirable.   Mr. Cowper
accepted the terms, and the appointment was made,
Thus, in the course of a few days, one of the most
prominent and consistent of the radical party, a
man, who, whatever may be his faults, did more to
secure its organization and consolidation and early
triumphs than all the rest put together, was
removed from the arena.   It is in vain to look to
immigration as the object of this compact — no
light will come from that quarter.   The whole
thing combines in itself all the characteristics of a
job, *and it is a job.*"

These strictures only provoke a smile now.   The
editor of the *Herald*, and undoubtedly many other
persons, found it difficult to reconcile the appointment with Mr. Parkes' vigorous and sustained
criticism of the Government and their actions, unless
on the hypothesis that the one had been made to
put an end to the other.

Of Mr. Dalley, as the colleague of Mr. Parkes
in the mission to England, very little was said.   He
had not then risen to prominence.   He was known
and recognised as a clever speaker, as a man of
considerable natural ability and eloquence, but he
had not impressed himself upon the proceedings of
the colony at this time in anything like the manner
that elicited the approbation and aroused the

popularity which surrounded his career in later years. He had been a staunch supporter and friend of Mr. Cowper, and a member of one of Mr. Cowper's Governments; and he had done much to save Mr. Cowper from rejection at the hands of the electors at a critical time. His appointment as joint commissioner with Mr. Parkes was regarded as a reward for useful services, and beyond that little was thought of it.

He was, however, a more conspicuous figure in the matter than was generally thought, for it was at his instance, and in response to his persuasion, that Mr. Parkes accepted the position when it was offered to him. Mr. Dalley was on terms of friendship with Mr. Parkes. From the time of their being introduced to each other they had been very close friends, partly through contributions which Mr. Dalley made to the columns of the *Empire*, and partly for other reasons. The visit to England attracted the attention of Mr. Dalley very soon after the proposal of Mr. Parkes, as expressed in his resolution, was made public, and he was desirous of securing one of the appointments for himself. The other he thought could not be given to a more suitable person than Mr. Parkes. Especially suitable would the two appointments be to Mr. Dalley, as Mr. Parkes was his friend, and travelling to England on a lecturing tour with a friend was in prospect much more pleasant than travelling with a stranger. So Mr. Dalley came to Mr. Parkes, and urged him to go.

"I can safely say," said Mr. Parkes, on one occasion when talking of this incident in his life, "that when I moved that resolution the thought of going myself never entered my head." Mr. Dalley was not in Parliament at the time. He had lost his seat in the general election, when, as a candidate for East Sydney, he had sacrificed himself to secure the return of Mr. Cowper. Being free from Parliamentary requirements, there was nothing of any importance to call upon him to remain in the colony, and he had but to mention his desire to go to England to induce Mr. Cowper and his colleagues in the Government to consent. His friendship with Mr. Parkes, his power of persuasion, and a circumstance in relation to Mr. Parkes himself at this time, prevailed, and Mr. Parkes consented to go.

This other circumstance, which, apart from Mr. Dalley, induced Mr. Parkes to consent to accept the appointment, was pecuniary embarrassment. "I was in needy circumstances," Mr. Parkes has since frankly said, "and I thought it would be a fine thing if I could do some good, and I yielded; but I never should have gone if it had not been for Dalley." So desirous was Mr. Dalley that Mr. Parkes should go, that he declared if anyone but Mr. Parkes should be appointed he would not go. His acceptance of the position depended entirely upon that of Mr. Parkes, although he very much wanted the appointment.

As the published correspondence shows, Mr. Parkes did not approach the Government on the subject.   The first intimation of the appointment being within his acceptance came from them, in a confidential letter from the Secretary for Lands, Mr. John Robertson.   This letter, and Mr. Parkes' reply, with two letters which followed on the question of precedence in relation to Mr. Parkes and Mr. Dalley, and the minute of the Executive Council, confirming the appointments, have a historic interest.

Mr. Robertson's letter, dated 11th May, 1861, from the Department of Lands, and marked "confidential," was as follows :—

Department of Lands,
11th May, 1861.

My dear Mr. Parkes,

It is the intention of the Government to appoint forthwith, at a salary of £1,000 a year and allowances, two gentlemen, to proceed to the Mother Country as Commissioners of Emigration ; and my colleagues and myself are desirous of placing one of those appointments at your disposal.   Will you, therefore, say whether or not you are willing to comply with our wishes ?   It is unnecessary for me to describe for you the nature of the duties of the office, as the proposal, sanctioned by Parliament, originated upon your own motion.

It may, however, be proper to mention that a similar communication to this has been made to Mr. W. B. Dalley.

I am, &c.,
JOHN ROBERTSON.

To this, Mr. Parkes wrote in reply :—

Sydney, 13th May, 1861.

My dear Mr. Robertson,

I beg to acknowledge the receipt of your letter of the 11th instant, offering me, on behalf of yourself and col-

N

leagues, the appointment of Commissioner of Emigration in England.

After mature consideration, I have determined to accept the appointment, principally with the hope that I may be of material use in successfully carrying out the important undertaking sanctioned by Parliament. I beg the Government to accept my assurance that I shall enter upon the duties of my office with an earnest and anxious purpose to disseminate a correct knowledge of this colony, to exhibit its real advantages as a field for the better class of emigrants, and to raise its reputation in the estimation of the British people.

I have this morning resigned my seat in the Legislative Assembly, and shall be prepared at once to receive the instructions of the Government, and to proceed to England by the first opportunity.

I have, &c.,

HENRY PARKES.

The appointments were notified to the public, in a Supplement to the *Government Gazette,* on the day after the receipt by the Secretary for Lands of Mr. Parkes' letter; and, so far, everything appeared to be satisfactory. But, inasmuch as Mr. Dalley's name appeared in the *Gazette* notice before that of Mr. Parkes, and the circumstance seemed to indicate that Mr. Dalley was regarded by the Government as occupying the superior position of the two Commissioners, the question of precedence arose, and for a time threatened some difficulty.

Five days afterwards, Mr. Parkes wrote to Mr. Robertson on the subject. His letter was dated from " Werrington," his place of residence near Ryde, on Sunday, 19th May, and, after dealing with some matters of business necessary to be attended to with promptness to enable the Commissioners to start on their mission, went on to say :—

> "I notice in the *Gazette* of our appointments, that precedence has been given to the name of Mr. Dalley; and I infer from this, that in any communications addressed to us jointly by the Government, the same deference will be shown to that gentleman. I presume this distinction must have been intended, as it could hardly have arisen from seniority in years, greater prominence in public life, or more intimate connection with the subject of our mission. Though this consideration, if it had been hinted at previous to my acceptance of the appointment, would have determined me in declining it, I should not now allude to the matter were it not that it may lead to some embarrassment hereafter ;—for instance, if we are to make joint reports to the Government, I shall decline to sign my name after Mr. Dalley, unless I am instructed to do so."

At the same time he was not disposed to raise such a difficulty as would affect the chances of the mission being a success. What he wanted was an authoritative statement from the Government as to whether one Commissioner was to be regarded as the superior of the other, or whether they were equal.

> "If the Government, however," the letter continued, "consider Mr. Dalley has superior qualifications for the direction of our movements in England, I shall raise no objection whatever to such an arrangement, but shall implicitly obey your instructions in acting under the advice of that gentleman as my duly appointed superior. All I desire to know before leaving the colony is, our precise positions in matters of courtesy as well as action, and our relative responsibilities."

To this, Mr. Robertson sent a very cleverly-worded reply. With each of the Commissioners he was on terms of friendship, and though Mr. Dalley had been more closely in association with him as a friend and supporter of the Government, and on that ground merited special regard, yet he was not disposed to overlook the claim to consideration on the side of Mr. Parkes. He desired to be just to each, to offend neither, and to maintain the position he occupied in the matter as the Minister charged with the arrangements for the carrying out of the mission. He wrote to Mr. Parkes as follows :—

Lands, 20th May, 1861.

My dear Mr. Parkes,

I have your note of yesterday, and will have all the arrangements relative to money matters and the commissions ready for you, at the time you mention.

I regret very much to find the view you take of the relative positions of yourself and Mr. Dalley; and especially I regret the tone and temper of your observations thereupon.

You assume that one of the Emigration agents will have functions superior to those entrusted to the other; an idea which I confess appears to me not only new, but unnecessary.

You also say that if it (this supposed preference of Mr. Dalley) had been hinted previously to your acceptance of the appointment, you would have declined it.

To me the necessity for these statements is quite unintelligible. I look in vain for anything that has been done, warranting the supposition that Mr. Dalley is placed in a position of superiority to yourself.

As to your reference to the absence of any hint on the subject, previous to your taking office, of course there

could have been none, it never having been intended
that any superiority should exist.   It seems, however,
evident, that had your name appeared first in the *Gazette*,
you would have claimed something of the kind ; why so,
I do not understand, as I am sure no hint of mine ever
justified it.

One of two names necessarily appeared first, and the
usual custom, in cases where it is intended that gentlemen
shall hold equal positions, is to give alphabetical precedence ; and as D stands before P, Mr. Dalley's name
would appear before yours.   But there is another ground
for his nominal precedence, and one that I am not
disposed to overlook ;—it is that he has held high office
in the colony, having been Solicitor-General, and a
Member of the Cabinet, with several Members of the
present Government.

You speak of your determination not to sign joint
reports after Mr. Dalley, unless specially instructed on
that behalf.   I have too much confidence in your good
sense to suppose that you will not speedily see that a statement of that kind is unworthy of you.   At any rate I feel
quite sure that no difficulty will arise—that Mr. Dalley
will have too much regard for the important interests
intrusted to him, to allow them to be impeded by refusing to you any comfort that you may desire from
signing first, on such occasions ; I shall therefore give no
order in the matter.   In great haste—

I am, &c.,

JOHN ROBERTSON.

This smartly written letter effectually disposed
of the question of precedence, for nothing more
concerning it appeared in correspondence ; and the
completion of the arrangements for the despatch of
the Commissioners was pushed on rapidly.

On the 28th May, the appointments were confirmed
by the Executive Council. According to the Council's
minute, each of the Commissioners was to be paid a
salary of £1,000 a year, and an allowance of £500
a year to cover travelling and all other personal
expenses, including the cost of passage to and from
England; and they were to receive an advance of
three months' salary and allowance prior to leaving
Sydney. At the same time, provision was made
against continuing payment to them after it
should be considered by the Government necessary that they should be recalled; and they were
informed that the salary and allowance would be
continued for a period of three months, and no
longer, after the delivery at their official address in
London, of a notice from the Government that their
mission was at an end.

Under these arrangements the Commissioners
left Sydney. In a letter of instructions the Minister
for Lands stated generally the wishes of the Government in regard to the manner in which the work of
the Commissioners should be performed, but, necessarily, the method of carrying out the duties
attached to their mission was largely left to themselves.

While, however, practically leaving to their
own discretion the precise manner in which they
should endeavour to secure the results aimed at by
the Government and the Legislature, Mr. Robertson
suggested that it was of the first consequence
to the success of the undertaking, that they should,
as early as possible after arriving in England,

associate themselves with, and seek the co-operation of, gentlemen having local influence among
those portions of the community it was especially
desirable to attract to the colony.   These were,
he explained, small capitalists, and such of the
labouring classes as had the means of defraying the
cost of their passage to New South Wales.

"To place before such persons the advantages
which it is conceived this colony possesses as a
field, as well for the man with small means as for
the industrious mechanic and labourer, is, of course,"
he wrote, "the very essence of your mission.
Whether you effect this by means of lectures, or
pamphlets, or by means of the public press, or by
viva voce addresses, is a matter which must be left,
and which is confidently left, to your own discretion.
Whatever meed of success may attend this experi-
ment, the Government are fully assured it will not
fail from the want of able and zealous advocacy."

The two Commissioners landed in Liverpool on
Sunday, August 4th, and immediately set about
their work; Mr. Parkes going to Birmingham, and
Mr. Dalley to London.

But though from that time they were very
closely occupied, Mr. Parkes visiting several parts
of England and Scotland, and the principal centres
in Ireland, they had not been long engaged at their
work before they became aware of a disposition
among the propertied classes of England to discourage emigration.

In the humbler walks of life they found generally
a desire for information respecting the colonies, and

in many cases a strong inclination to remove to
Australia ; but they were handicapped by the peculiar nature of the plan under which it was hoped
people would be induced to emigrate to New South
Wales. Each emigrant, unless able to pay the whole
of his or her passage money, was obliged to lodge
the portion necessary under the assisted immigation
regulations, in the Colonial Treasury at Sydney ;
and this it was not easy to do. It was difficult also
to arrange for suitable accommodation on ships
sailing for the colony, unless a certain number of
passengers were guaranteed, and another obstacle
was the fact that some of the other colonies were
offering to emigrants greater inducements in the
way of concessions than New South Wales was
prepared to offer.

The Commissioners did not, however, despair.
They opened offices in London, and styled them-
selves "New South Wales Government Emigration
Agents."

Sir John Young, who, at this time, was Governor
of New South Wales, had given them letters of
introduction to Mr. Gladstone, Lord Brougham,
and the Duke of Newcastle ; describing Mr. Parkes
as a gentleman who "had occupied a seat in the
Legislative Assembly for several years, and acquired
much distinction by his ability and various exertions,
especially by those he has made for the moral and
social improvement of his fellow citizens," and
Mr. Dalley as a highly talented gentleman, a native
of New South Wales, and a barrister-at-law who
had held, for a considerable time, a seat in the

Legislative Assembly, and was, in the year 1859, Solicitor-General and a member of the Cabinet. These eminent persons, and others, they waited upon, and as far as could be done were assisted in their mission. They addressed a large number of public meetings; had personal interviews with individuals and families; answered much correspondence; distributed thousands of circulars and pamphlets; and published information in the press.

From time to time they forwarded to the Secretary for Lands, in Sydney, reports of their proceedings, and these, though somewhat hopeful in tone, were generally very plainly expressive of the difficulties they found in their way. The more they extended their operations, the clearer did they see the indisposition of the wealthy classes to emigration of any kind but that, perhaps, of the criminal portion of the population. The sympathies of landed proprietors and of large employers of labour were not with them.

In one of his reports, Mr. Parkes described a conversation he had with a wealthy manufacturer and influential politician on the subject of New South Wales. "It is a fine country," this gentleman said, "it sends us amazing quantities of wool and gold, and is a splendid customer for our manufactures. I do a good trade with Sydney myself. Don't you think the colonists could be persuaded to take our convicts again?"

At this period, it was not at all uncommon for persons of influence in the political arena of Great Britain to manifest an adverse feeling towards the

Australian colonies; and Mr. Parkes found that they were afraid of "stimulating" emigration, because it was the best class of people who emigrated.

The chances of the success of his mission appeared to be greatest in personal communication with the emigrating class ; · " frankly explaining to them the condition of the colony, and their own prospects of success as colonists, and advising them according to the different circumstances of their cases."

Frequently, he had interviews with families of this class. "Men come to me," he wrote, "with their wives, and a son or daughter, or perhaps a friend, lay their case before me, apparently with the utmost confidence, and explain their views in wishing to emigrate, which sometimes discover a long course of thought and inquiry on the subject. I am at present in communication with several families, who reckon that, after removing themselves to Australia, they would have little capitals, ranging from £100 to £600 ; and I have reason to believe that their lot will be cast among the inhabitants of New South Wales next year. In this way—travelling, corresponding, and giving personal interviews, I have been much occupied of late, and shall be for some time to come, in the Midland and Northern Counties."

CHAPTER XV.

In the earlier period of his Parliamentary career, Sir Henry Parkes did much good work in connection with select committees, which he was instrumental in having appointed, and of which he was, in most instances, Chairman.

Several of the ˙principal of these committees sat in 1859-1861. One of them was that the report of which formed the foundation of the charge made against Sir Henry Parkes˙ of being favourable to a protective fiscal policy. This committee was appointed to inquire into the condition of the working classes of Sydney—the want of employment among them, the subject of wages, the class of house accomodation available, and the existence and extent of juvenile vagrancy. It was appointed on 30th September, 1859, and it sat from the 7th October of that year, until 18th April, 1860.

. The condition of affairs it disclosed was a very sad one. It is interesting at this time as a picture of degraded life which, existing at the period of this inquiry, has, to a large extent, since then disappeared. Destitution and immorality are still amongst us, but the homes of the masses are much better, and their lives purer and brighter than was the case thirty-five years ago.

Sir Henry Parkes, when he moved his motion for the appointment of the committee, could not have been fully aware of the state of things his inquiry disclosed, and yet his speech on the occasion showed that he possessed a considerable grasp of the subject. The object he had in view— " giving a more healthy character to society and a better direction to the industrial energies of the population "—had led him to acquaint himself with very much of what was going on around him.

Several years before, he had done what he could towards reforming the juvenile vagrants of the metropolis, by having a select committee appointed to consider the propriety of establishing a nautical school, in which many of the male portion of these waifs and strays ought to be placed and trained into useful citizens. Now, his efforts were directed to the improvement of life among the parents as well as the children. He desired to see the children taken from the slums and by-ways, where dirt and vice were ever present; and this he knew could only be effected by improved house accommodation, better moral training, the spread of education, and increased means of livelihood so that the adult portion of the male population might be more constantly in employment and earning higher wages.

And what was the state of affairs disclosed by the select committee's inquiry ? It was so shocking that it cannot be read without a feeling of horror.

Want of employment existed amongst the working classes to a large extent, and no doubt contributed much to degrade the life which a great proportion of these classes were living. Decent houses are not obtained from landlords without the payment of adequate rent; wholesome food and good clothes are not bought for less than their value; and, in the absence of decent houses, and good food and clothes, family life must go backward, and pass from bad to worse.

The gold-fields of the colony, at this period extensively worked, had unsettled the lives of numbers of men, and withdrawn them from their families in Sydney, the wives and children being in many cases left without protection, or any means of subsistence; and this had produced a large amount of destitution and misery. The impossibility of finding employment, experienced by a large proportion of the men not attracted from Sydney by the glitter of the gold-fields, produced more.

The house accommodation of the working classes was deplorably bad. Drainage and ventilation were scarcely thought of. Sanitary precautions were almost entirely neglected. It was not uncommon at this time to find large families, with sometimes a lodger or two, in small weatherboard structures, containing two rooms of not more than 10 feet by 11 feet each, their ceilings not more than six or seven feet high, and possessing little or no means of ventilation, except the door or window. "Hundreds of houses in Sydney," the Master of the Benevolent Asylum stated to the committee, " are totally unfit for human habitation."

The suburbs in this respect were, to a great extent, in the same condition as the city. In a block of twenty or twenty-five wretched hovels, accommodation, such as it was, was obtained for, perhaps, a hundred people, old, middle-aged, and young; married and single. Not only were the houses for occupation by the working classes constructed without regard to the requirements of comfort or health, but they were grossly overcrowded in consequence of high rents. A tenement, deserving of no better name than a den, of two rooms, might be occupied by as many as fourteen persons—seven men and seven women. Seventy persons had been found herded together in a common lodging-house of six rooms; and, in one of the Chinese quarters, one building proved a lodging house for no fewer than 315 celestials.

With these conditions of life existing, it is not surprising that intemperance, destitution, and vice among old and young abounded, or that the committee should consider that, in this disordered state of things, the social happiness of the community was fast becoming undermined.

The committee made certain recommendations, and among them, the famous protectionist proposal which ever afterwards attached itself to Sir Henry Parkes.

"Your committee," the report stated, "are also of opinion that the connection of cause and effect is in some measure to be traced between the fiscal laws of the colony and the existing social evils, and they consider a revision of our entire taxation

a matter of necessity.   We have the authority of
eminent economists in support of raising revenue
in a new country by the imposition of duties that
would tend to foster manufacturing enterprise, and
such encouragement to our own people within
well-considered limits would not be inconsistent
with practical freedom in our commercial intercourse with the world, while no nation affords us
an example of the establishment of manufactures
without encouragement."

From this recommendation, which was not only
an expression of opinion from the committee as a
body, but may be regarded as peculiarly Sir Henry
Parkes' own, inasmuch as the report was signed by
him as chairman, it is plain that, at this period of
his life, Sir Henry Parkes entertained protectionist
ideas.   But the circumstance is not unnatural,
and can be easily explained.   Indeed, he himself
explained it, on more than one occasion, when it
was used as a weapon against him by his opponents.

At this time he had been but six years in Parliament.   His political knowledge had been chiefly
acquired in the intervals of a busy life, which did
not afford him too many opportunities for reading
and reflection.   In his youth and early manhood, he
had experienced all the hardships attendant upon
want of employment or low wages.   Moreover, he
had imbibed to a certain extent the fiscal doctrine
apparent in a well-known passage in the writings of
John Stuart Mill.   Was it at all strange that he
should, under such circumstances, have thought that
unrestricted freedom of commerce was not, in all

conditions of a country's existence, the best for its welfare?   Further observation and study of the subject, and an interview with Richard Cobden during a visit to England in 1861-2, disclosed to him the fallacies of protection ; and with the clear view of the whole matter, which this more matured examination of the question put before his mind, he became what since that time he always was—a staunch supporter and advocate of free trade.

During his later life, in the struggle which certain industries have had in this country to firmly establish themselves, and, in response to earnest solicitations for some assistance on their behalf, there were occasions when, as head of the Government, he indicated his willingness to assist those industries to the extent of a certain preference over manufacturers outside the country in the tendering for work required by the Government to be done ; and this has been characterised by some persons as protection.   But it would be difficult to prove that the concessions offered in this manner went, in any instance, beyond what was justifiable in the interests of either free trade or the general welfare.

If the excess in price of a New South Wales tender, as compared with the tender of an English firm, be no more than would be represented by freight, insurance, and other charges incidental to obtaining the required articles from England, and the quality of the articles made in the colony be equal to that of the articles manufactured in England, there can be no valid objection to accepting the colonial tender in preference to the English one; and this Sir Henry Parkes was always willing to do.

Strongly free trade in its fiscal opinions, the Legislative Assembly refused to adopt the Committee's report.

Mr. Parkes moved its adoption in an able and distinctly protectionist speech. "He held that the country, to be prosperous, must rest upon something more than their industry employed in the production of raw products. There was only one base for a prosperous community, and that was the three-fold base of producing raw material, of manufacturing it, and of trading in it; or, in other words, agriculture (taking that term in its wider sense as including all the products of the soil), and manufactures and commerce. . . . . And, in passing, he might say that the whole doctrine of free trade (and perhaps he was as thorough a free trader as most members of the House) was at least a theory. It rested upon assumptions. Its reasoning was all of a deductive nature. There was, however, this in favour of the out-and-out protectionists : that their doctrine to a great extent depended upon the actual rise of nations. . . . . It was absolutely necessary for the employment of the human mind, and all the faculties belonging to our nature, that the modes of employment should be as varied within the country as possible."

Quoting largely from authorities in support of the contention that it is desirable to produce within our own towns as much as possible of the commodities we consume, and as to the justification of

o

imposing duties for the establishment of manufactures, he went on to say :—"The mere traders
of a community, though highly honourable and
useful in their proper relations, it must be borne in
mind were non-producers, and, as far as they were
concerned, the world would die out in all the
elegancies and refinements of life. So that, necessarily, a large proportion of the population would
be unproductively employed. Thus it would be
impossible for us to keep abreast of the age. . .
. . . Our only chance if we wished to bring out
the talents of the rising generation, and to run a
fair race with other parts of the world in all the
attainments which dignify human life, was by introducing other modes by which the inventive faculties
of the country would be brought into full play."

The motion for the adoption of the report was
negatived by so large a majority as 27 votes to 6 ;
but the matter did not end there. By the unemployed portion of the citizens of Sydney, the decision
of the Assembly was viewed with much dissatisfaction ; and for several nights hostile demonstrations
were made by a mob outside the Assembly Chamber.

On the third night following that during which
the report was rejected, the gathering was so large
and threatening, that something like a riot—certainly a serious disturbance—occurred. Torches
were burned; members favourable to the report
were cheered, and those unfavourable to it groaned
at and hooted. Inflammatory speeches were delivered, and attempts were made to penetrate into
the enclosure in front of the Parliamentary

buildings, and effect an entrance where the House was sitting.

In the Assembly Chamber, Members were fearful that the Chamber was about to be rushed; and the attention of the Speaker was called to the circumstance, a debate upon the subject taking place. Meanwhile, the efforts of the crowd to pass the entrance gates becoming more persistent and determined, a conflict arose between the crowd and the police. The guardians of the law drew their batons; blows were struck freely; and several persons were severely injured. Still the mob endeavoured to reach the gates; and it was only when police reinforcements—including a detachment of mounted police—arrived on the scene, that the people could be beaten and driven back, and the street cleared.

These demonstrations by a portion of the populace made Mr. Parkes throughout this agitation a prominent figure; but he gave no encouragement to what was done, and was not slow to describe it as ill-advised, and not justifiable.

He made another attempt to carry the report of the committee through the Assembly, but again failed. On the 22nd May, 1860, he endeavoured to have the provisions of the report adopted, by moving a series of resolutions embodying the proposals made in it; but after some discussion the resolutions were shelved by the House adopting the previous question.

The report did not again see the light. Not long afterwards, Mr. Parkes went to England, and there his protectionist ideas disappeared under the benign free trade influence of Richard Cobden. Very recently he referred to the circumstance, and entered into a detailed explanation of his old protectionist error. Speaking chiefly of his protectionist views in 1860, he said not without pathos: " My case is this ;—I was not educated at a University. Unhappily for me, I was not educated at all. I never was at school more than three months in my life, and whatever I have attained, I have attained in circumstances of bitter poverty. Some allowance might be made for me who have had to educate myself every day of my life from my cradle until now. . . . . I started in life as a free trader. I dare say that much of my opinions was caught up from those around me. I dare say that I imbibed my free trade opinions very much as many persons imbibe their religion. I admit that in the year 1859 or 1860, I was misled by that fatal, that mischievous, passage in John Stuart Mill's book, in which he lays down the doctrine that protectionist duties are pardonable to support new industries in a new country. And, about the same time, I read one or two American economists who confirmed that view. Mine was a case of pure backsliding. . . . . I went to England, and the person who converted me finally, and put me into the groove where I have remained ever since, was that illustrious Englishman, Richard Cobden. I spent a few days at Mr. Cobden's house. On a cold winter's night, which I remember well, and shall ever remember,

Mr. Cobden invited me into his room. We sat down by the fire, and had a conversation of two hours on the question of protection in Australia; and he satisfied me that the view I was then taking was in error. If I admit that he was my converter, I shall only admit that I was converted by the man who converted Sir Robert Peel. But now," he went on to say with some triumph, "comes my vindi cation. From that day until the present time, I have been a steady consistent free trader; and surely thirty years ought to protect me from any reference to that early period. When, as I tell you, with a confession that costs me a good deal to make, I have had to educate myself every day of my life from my very childhood, I might be pardoned for straying into the paths of error; because when I got true knowledge, I retraced my steps."

Another important select committee appointed at the instance of Mr. Parkes, and of which he was chairman, was one to inquire into and report upon the state and management of the public prisons in the city of Sydney and the county of Cumberland.

The arrangements for the confinement and treatment of prisoners at this period were very incomplete and unsatisfactory. Though an improvement upon what existed in the very early days of the colony, they were far short of what was necessary. Overcrowding, want of cleanliness, and the absence of any inducement to reform, had such a brutalising effect upon the prisoners that they became terrible in their depravity, resorting to

unspeakable practices and indulging without hesitation in the committal of serious crimes.

At this period Cockatoo Island was the largest
prison in the colony, though the new gaol at
Darlinghurst was in use ; but Darlinghurst, though
containing many prisoners was only partially built,
and Cockatoo Island was full to overflowing. At
times there were as many as 500 prisoners on the
island, and a large proportion were always of the
very worst class.

The passenger in the Parramatta River
steamboats, which call nowadays at Cockatoo as
regularly as at other places on the river, can still see
sufficient to send his thoughts back to the period
when hundreds of hardened criminals were there.
Only some remnants of the old·prison buildings are
now standing, but these and two or three stone sentry
boxes close to the water's edge, deserted and
weather worn, suggest with much force the grim
nature of the place thirty-five years ago.

The Committee made a number of recommendations with a view to improvement in the condition
of the gaols and the management and treatment of the
prisoners.   Among these recommendations was the
appointment of an inspector of prisons, who should
be a man of ability and high character, entrusted
with the entire supervision and direction of the
prison system of the colony.   This officer was
ultimately appointed, and the prison system greatly
improved.   Now there is a Comptroller-General of
Prisons ; and, at the present time, the prisons of the
colony are equal in every respect to the prisons of
any other country.

A copy of the Committee's report, with the evidence upon which it was based attached, was forwarded by Mr. Parkes to Charles Dickens, who wrote the following letter in reply :—

> Gad's Hill Place,
>
> Higham by Rochester, Kent,
>
> Tuesday, twenty-sixth August, 1862.
>
> Sir,—
>
> I beg to acknowledge the safe receipt of your very obliging letter, and its accompanying report and evidence. I have perused that public document with great interest and not a little horror, and with a sincere admiration of the spirit in which the whole inquiry was conducted. It is very honourable to the gentlemen concerned and to the great country they represent.
>
> Faithfully yours,
>
> CHARLES DICKENS.
>
> Henry Parkes, Esq.

Various other matters important to the good government of the colony were inquired into and reported upon by select committees appointed on the motion of Mr. Parkes, and assisted by him in their labours. From his first entry into Parliament he saw in the select committee a means of great usefulness ; and, up to the period of his official life as a Minister of the Crown, he used this means whenever he thought it was required, to the great advantage of the country.

CHAPTER XVI.

RETURNING to Sydney from England in January, 1863, in response to a resolution of the Legislative Assembly in June, 1862, recalling him and his colleague, Mr. Dalley, from their positions as emigration agents and lecturers, Mr. Parkes resumed business in Sydney, and awaited an opportunity for re-entering Parliament.

He had lost none of his popularity; public opinion of his great capacity and his political integrity was as strong as ever; and a seat for him in the Legislature was assured. He had only to await the occurrence of one of the political crises so numerous in those days, and then to choose his constituency.

The opportunity came in April, 1864, when Mr. Parkes was returned as Member for Kiama in the place of the late Mr. Samuel W. Gray.

Previous to this he made an effort to obtain the seat for East Maitland, rendered vacant by reason of Mr. J. B. Darvall accepting the office of Attorney-General in the Cowper Government, and going before his constituents for re-election.

The step was not a wise one, for not only was it unsuccessful, but the contest proved one of the bitterest in political annals. The amount of vituperation introduced into the speeches of the candidates was unequalled. Both able men and powerful speakers, they were recklessly unmerciful in their denunciation of each other.

, Mr. Darvall, usually polished and refined in his oratory—for he claimed to be and was an educated gentleman—allowed himself for once to adopt a style which, while unsurpassed in skilfulness and effect, was coarse and even revolting. Tucking up his sleeves on the hustings, in the manner of a callous surgeon, he proceeded to describe the previous career of Mr. Parkes, as the surgeon would dissect an unsavoury body.

Mr. Parkes was equally severe, though in a different manner; and both writhed under the torture. So intense, indeed, was the feeling engendered, that at the close of the election when in addition to the unmeasured abuse heaped upon him, he had to endure the disappointment of defeat, Mr. Parkes called upon the electors if they believed him to be the guilty character his opponent had described, to hound him and stone him to death immediately he left the hustings.

Doubtless Mr. Darvall was excessively annoyed at being opposed at all. Unless there be very special reasons for a contrary course, the re-election of a Minister is generally allowed to go without opposition. The practice is universal, and not without its advantages. Mr. Parkes owed some consideration to Mr. Cowper, and having returned only a few months before from his visit to England as an Emigration Commissioner, he might well, it was thought, have refrained from embarrassing the Government. Mr. Robertson went to him, and sought to induce him not to come forward as an opponent of the Attorney-General. " There will be other opportunities before long," Mr. Robertson urged ; "several seats will be available shortly." But Mr. Parkes declined to withdraw. He disapproved of the proceedings of the Government as a whole, and therefore considered himself justified in opposing the re-election of their Attorney-General.

Probably he was also annoyed at a rumour which had been spread that he had applied unsuccessfully to the Cowper Government for an appointment, at this time about to be made, of Inspector of Prisons. This appointment had been recommended by Mr. Parkes. Commissioned by Mr. Cowper to make inquiry while in England respecting the English prisons, Mr. Parkes had done so ; and one result of his inquiry was a recommendation that a high inspecting officer should be appointed in Sydney.

People naturally thought Mr. Parkes suitable for the position, and with equal readiness considered that he would get it. Mr. Cowper was ready to give it him; but having already been charged with buying him off, by means of the emigration commissionership, he was reluctant to offer any second appointment. Mr. Parkes did not ask for it. That he desired it is not at all likely, for great as were the possibilities of his political success before he went to England, the information and experience gained during his sojourn there, made those possibilities very much greater; but it is not improbable that he would have been glad to have had the refusal of it. This was not absent from Mr. Cowper's mind, and was an additional reason why he did not make the offer. So the two came together several times, and talked of prisons and prison inspectorship; but though each was anxious that the other should make some move in the direction of an offer or a request, no offer or request was made; and the inspectorship eventually went to somebody else.

The Kiama election, in 1864, which sent Mr. Parkes back to the Legislative Assembly, was not very exciting; but his speeches during the contest indicated that his visit to England had not been without an effect upon his mind, which, while being beneficial to it, was certain to be of advantage to the political life of the colony.

He was still the same uncompromising liberal, the same keen critic and denouncer of political incapacity and wrong, the same able and persistent advocate of social reform; but the association which, during his stay in England, he had enjoyed with prominent men in politics, literature, and society, had enlarged his views, increased his stock of information, and improved his style.

He has told us since that one of the great Englishmen with whom he was intimate at this time in England was Richard Cobden; and that conversations with him dissipated from his mind for

ever the protectionist fallacies which had made an
entry there in the early years of his political career.

To one destined to be the leader of Governments
in New South Wales, over a period longer than that
of any other Prime Minister in the political history
of the colony, association with such men as Cobden,
even for the transitory period covered by a short
visit to England, must have been invaluable.   And
it is not unlikely that Cobden learned something
from Mr. Parkes.   His arrival in England, fresh
from the self-governing young Australian community, his mission to promote emigration to New
South Wales, his strong democratic opinions, the
important part he had taken in Australian public life
—all this would be of deep interest to Mr. Cobden,
and make Mr. Parkes' company as agreeable as
Cobden's company was to Mr. Parkes.

It did not need an eye of much discernment to
see in Mr. Parkes the probabilities of future
eminence.   His detractors professed to observe
nothing but vanity and superficialness.   Impartial
observers saw with clearer vision, and were sometimes not slow to say what they saw.

At the Kiama election he read a letter he had
received from Charles Gavan Duffy, who, in those
days, was ever ready to bear testimony to the probable greatness of Mr. Parkes' future.   The letter
was written at a time when Mr. Parkes was defeated
in an election at Braidwood, and it was produced at
Kiama in reply to a charge made during the election
there that he was an enemy to the Irish Roman
Catholics.

" I read in the Sydney telegram to-day," wrote Mr. Duffy, "that you have lost your election by a few votes ; and be sure that though sometimes a silent, I am never an indifferent, spectator of your affairs. Ah, my dear friend—if you will permit me to moralise the occasion—you might have been anything in this new world, if you had only made up your mind once for all what it was to be. You may do anything still on the same conditions."

Re-entering Parliament as Member for Kiama, Mr. Parkes did not take his seat as a supporter of the Government, which was then under the premiership of the late Sir James Martin. His political sympathies, he had told his constituents, were not in that direction. He could not see, in the course which had marked the political conduct of the Government in power, any avowed and distinct principles. There was a want of agreement among them on the main questions of the day. They were at variance on the subject of the land laws ; some were protectionists and others freetraders; and they were divided on the subjects of State-aid to religion and education. To such an incongruous body Mr. Parkes could not give his assistance, and he became what he described as an " independent neutral member."

Yet, in less than two years afterwards, he found it in the public interest for him to join some of these ministers, in a Government which proved to be one of the most useful in passing measures to promote the welfare of the country.

In November, 1864, Parliament was dissolved ;
and it re-assembled on 24th January, 1865, Mr.
Parkes again taking his seat as Member for Kiama.

To him the new Parliament was destined to be
one of great importance. It was to mark his entry
into official life, in which he did not, as is usual with
those taking ministerial office for the first time,
accept a subordinate position, but at one bound rose
to the highest and most influential, for he became
Colonial Secretary.

Parliament opened with the Martin Ministry in
office, though not in power, for they had been badly
beaten in the elections, and their retirement was
only a question of a day or two. They were
succeeded by a Ministry under Mr. Cowper, and the
proceedings of this Ministry provided the means by
which, after a long and exceedingly useful career as
a private member, Mr. Parkes was enabled to apply
his great abilities to the actual government of the
country.

The Cowper Ministry, though indicating when
it entered office a very capable administration,
fell in the course of a few months into serious
difficulties through the necessity for reconstruction.
Mr. Robertson, in consequence of difficulties connected with his private affairs, was obliged to
relinquish his position of Minister for Lands ; and
Mr. W. M. Arnold, who was holding the office of
Minister for Works, succeeded him. Mr. Thomas
Ware Smart, who was Colonial Treasurer, was
removed to the Works Department, a new Treasurer
being found in Mr. (afterwards Sir) Saul Samuel.

A few days subsequently Mr. Arnold was elected Speaker of the Legislative Assembly, and Mr. Robertson returned to the Lands Office.

These changes greatly embarrassed Mr. Cowper, and seriously interfered with the well-being of the Government; but it was left for a further change to bring matters to the point of a crisis.

Mr. Samuel, in his capacity of Treasurer, made his Financial Statement on 29th November, 1865, and proposed a taxation scheme which the House virtually rejected. He at once resigned. Mr. Cowper, sensible enough of the gravity of the situation, was anxious to make another effort to place the finances of the country in a satisfactory condition before relinquishing office; and looked around for a new Treasurer. The field of choice open to him was small. The Government were not popular either in the House or outside. Additional taxation appeared to be absolutely necessary, and a Government upon whom the duty of taxing the community falls is not likely to be popular. Furthermore, there was a general impression that the Ministry could not last long, and that it would speedily give way to another.

Mr. Cowper was one of those men not easily cast down by difficulties; and he had at his back, in the person of Mr. Robertson, a man still more resourceful. It did not seem easy to find a new Finance Minister, but it was not impossible. On a previous occasion it had been quite as difficult for Mr. Cowper to find an Attorney General; and yet he was at last discovered in a gentleman just landed from a vessel which had arrived from England.

Curiosity was aroused now as to whence Mr. Samuel's successor would come.   Name after name was mentioned, and the chances of the persons considered eligible for the office discussed.   But none of those in Parliament regarded as suitable were willing to undertake the duties of Treasurer at this particular time, and under the circumstances surrounding the ministerial position.

Mr. Cowper was compelled to fall back upon an outsider, a Treasurer who would be a Treasurer in name only.   He announced that the office had been accepted by Mr. Marshall Burdekin. This gentleman was not known either to have had the experience or to possess the ability to enable him to fill the position of Finance Minister satisfactorily, and his appointment was regarded with much disfavour.   Mr. J. H. Plunkett, Attorney-General in the Government, absent from Sydney when the appointment was made, resigned his office immediately the name of the new Treasurer reached him.

In the Assembly, with the approval of Mr. Martin, the matter was taken in hand by Mr. Parkes.

On the 9th January, 1866, Mr. Cowper moved that the seat of Mr. Marshall Burdekin be declared vacant by reason of his acceptance of office, and thereupon Mr. Parkes moved—" That, in declaring such vacancy, the House feels it to be its duty at once to express its entire disapproval of Mr. Burdekin's appointment."

A short but sharp debate ensued; and the amendment was carried by 25 votes to 10, the original motion, as amended, being passed by 21 to 11.

This expression of opinion was a direct vote of censure; and though Mr. Cowper was inclined to evade it, he very quickly found himself compelled to act in accordance with its real nature. The Assembly adjourned, and, at its next meeting, was informed that the Government had advised a dissolution, but that the Governor had not accepted this advice, and consequently Mr. Cowper and his colleagues had resigned.

Mr. Parkes' opportunity had now arrived. The prospect of his becoming a member of the Government in a high and influential position was at once greater than ever before. The fear of the effects of his ardent radical opinions, and of his tendency to encounter and overthrow established forms and institutions wherever they interfered with what he considered to be the welfare of the country, was disappearing before the sense of his great ability and of his patriotism.

Almost from his entry into the Legislature he was well fitted for office; but, for the powerful Conservatives of those days, he had always gone too fast in the direction of reform, and fear that ministerial power might induce him to run riot in the endeavour to improve, where improvement might be needed, had made Cabinet-makers very chary of admitting him to their ranks.

At last, however, it was recognised that he ought

P

to be in the Government; that he was entitled to it on
every ground of fitness except the pace at which he
Had travelled in his efforts for social and political
advancement, and that even this characteristic might,
after all, not be so bad as to some persons it had
seemed.

It was not, therefore, with alarm that the resignation of the Cowper Government was seen to indicate the probable inclusion of Mr. Parkes among
their successors. To a large proportion of the
community it gave great satisfaction, and those who
were not quite satisfied were not without hope
that his appointment would prove beneficial.

The Governor, Sir John Young, was not, appar
ently, as confident of the success of Mr. Parkes in
high office as many of Mr. Parkes' friends were. In
the ordinary course of things, Mr. Parkes should have
been commissioned to form the new Government.
Instead of that, Mr. Martin was sent for. But Mr.
Martin and Mr. Parkes were in consultation and
agreement as to the new Ministry, and though
Mr. Martin was to be Premier, he gave Mr. Parkes
a choice of the other offices, including that of Colonial
Secretary.

The new Ministry proved a very strong one, and
it remained in office for nearly two years, passing
during that time some of the most beneficial of the
measures under which the country for the last thirty
years has been advancing. Mr. Martin was Attorney-
General and Premier ; Mr. Parkes, Colonial Secretary ; and Mr. Geoffrey Eagar, Colonial Treasurer.
The other offices were filled by Mr. John Bowie

Wilson, Minister for Lands; Mr. James Byrnes, Secretary for Public Works; Mr. Robert Macintosh Isaacs, Solicitor-General; and Mr. Joseph Docker, Postmaster-General.

All have since passed away, and the names of several may be said to be forgotten; but the legislation they, as a Ministry, were able to bring into operation will ever live conspicuous in the political history of the colony.

There was, of course, criticism of the new Government, favourable and unfavourable. Some people professed not to understand how Mr. Parkes could enter the same Cabinet as Mr. Martin, especially with Mr. Martin as Premier. The two had not been very friendly in the Assembly, and in 1864 a quarrel occurred between them, which lasted twelve months. "With respect to several of the more important questions that had engaged the attention of Parliament and the public," it was said, " the new Ministers have occupied the most opposite positions, whilst they have denounced each other's conduct in the strongest language." And the combination was regarded as having been brought about with a view to securing the support of different sections in the Assembly, rather than as the result of agreement on any distinct line of policy.

But the one led to the other. Once certain of the necessary support in Parliament, it was easy to formulate a policy upon which there should be general agreement.

Mr. Parkes, in his address to his constituents, made some allusion to the causes of the

the coalition. "One result," he said, "of the perverse and tortuous courses pursued in political life of late years is the obliteration of nearly all party distinctions, so that it is now quite impossible for any six public men to associate together without making mutual concessions and sinking differences of opinion which, under circumstances more favourable to a healthy state of party action, would present a broad ground of disagreement. In the present juncture it is felt to be obligatory on persons who regard the public interest as superior to personal consideration to make such concessions."

The financial circumstances under which the new Government entered office were somewhat auspicious, notwithstanding a gloomy outlook when the Cowper Government went from power. The Treasurer was able to put before the House a statement so satisfactory, that it showed, instead of a deficiency on the year's transactions and a necessity for increased taxation, as indicated by his predecessor, a considerable surplus. This, however, was largely due to the receipts from *ad valorem* duties brought into operation by the Cowper Government, and the advantages from which the Martin-Parkes Government were reaping.

From a state of something like alarm into which the community had drifted through the periods of successive Governments, the public were beginning to realise a feeling of hopefulness and confidence.

At that date the finances of the colony were, of course, of as much importance to the general public as the finances of the present period are to the people of to-day ; but, compared with what they are now the public accounts of 1865 were little short of insignificant. The charges for the year, inclusive of a sum of £20,000 for a postal service, a large expenditure for such a purpose at that period, amounted to £1,932,745, and those to be provided for by loan £820,500. The estimated revenue for the year was £2,084,511. Nowadays the figures for estimated expenditure and estimated revenue reach £9,000,000. Another remarkable difference between the circumstances of the two periods is to be seen in relation to the public debentures. At the present time they can be sold readily at a high price. In 1865, they were not only exceedingly difficult of sale, but were disposed of for what they would bring. In that year, by an agreement between the Cowper Government and the Oriental Bank, the bank had absolute power to sell the debentures which it held as security at any price to cover its cash advances; and though the sum due by the Government to the bank was only £940,000, against which it held debentures of the nominal value of £1,716,300, it refused to make the advance necessary to pay the interest on the public debt due in London in July, 1866.

The Ministry proposed to do nothing in their first session but pass the estimates. The great measures of their programme were to stand over until the session following. Though of much importance, these were not so urgent as to make it necessary to interfere with the desire to get the financial matters of the country into thorough order.

By having a short session to deal solely with the estimates, the necessary monetary arrangements for the year could be made, and, after a brief recess, Parliament, unembarrassed by financial matters, could proceed calmly and deliberately with the principal parts of the ministerial policy. This was done. The session commencing on 20th February, 1866, lasted about six weeks, and Parliament went into recess until July.

Mr. Parkes spent a portion of his time in visiting some of the country districts. Bushranging was very troublesome at this period, and, as the minister at the head of the Police Department, he was instrumental in administering to it a very salutary check. He possessed, in a marked degree, the faculty of discernment of character. More appointments to high and responsible positions in the colony were, through his life, made by him than by any other person who has held the office of Minister, and his appointments, it may be said, were invariably satisfactory. During one of his tours through the country at this period of his career, he exercised his power of judging the capabilities of men by suddenly picking out, from his police guard, an ordinary policeman, and commissioning him to search for and capture the two most bloodthirsty and notorious of the scoundrels then infesting the interior. The man, who was naturally fitted for such work, but had never before had the opportunity to show what he could do, accepted with alacrity the duty so unexpectedly placed upon

him, and in a very short time captured the bushrangers and earned a sub-inspectorship.

Another instance of excellent judgment of character and capacity, which occurred about the same
period, with very beneficial results to the colony,
was in relation to the asylums for lunatics. Mr.
Parkes had not been long in office as Colonial
Secretary, before he ascertained that these asylums
were in a very imperfect and unsatisfactory state.
They were, in fact, little better than prisons. He
saw the necessity for improvement ; and one thing
the Government did, on his recommendation, was
to lay out the grounds at Gladesville, so that the
patients might enjoy to a proper extent fresh air
and exercise among beautiful surroundings.

More, however, required to be done. Accident threw Mr. Parkes into acquaintance with
a gentleman who was a surgeon on one of the ships
of war on the Australian station, and this gentleman, he discovered, was very conversant with the
treatment of lunatics. Frequent conversations with
him, led to the conclusion that he was the man
wanted in connection with the New South Wales
asylums ; and, overtures being made to him, he left
the Navy to enter the public service of the colony.
Then, with the approval of his colleagues in the
Ministry, Mr. Parkes commissioned him to go through
Europe and America, and examine the construction,
and methods of management, of the principal
asylums for lunatics in those countries, and to report
the results to the Government. This he did, at
considerable expense, but very effectively, and his

report is regarded as one of the most valuable contributions to the literature relating to the treatment
of lunacy.

This gentleman is Dr. Manning, the present
Inspector-General of the Insane in New South
Wales; and the state of perfection to which
the asylums for lunatics in the colony have been
brought by him is well-known to everybody. Referring to this subject in a speech made in 1883, Mr.
Parkes remarked that he took the important step
of sending Dr. Manning on his tour of observation
and inquiry, without waiting for Parliamentary
authority. " I risked the censure of Parliament,"
he said. " If I had waited for Parliamentary
authority, Dr. Manning would have sailed away in
the ship of war, and his services would never have
been obtained."

CHAPTER XVII.

THE great fact in the career of the Martin-Parkes Ministry was the passing of the Public Schools Act.

Education in the colony had not been neglected, and had produced fairly good results. But the system in operation, beneficial in some respects, was not by any means as satisfactory as was desirable. The plan adopted for its administration was cumbrous and expensive, and, being based on a wish to meet the religious prejudices of some classes of the people, rather than upon a determination to afford the fullest educational advantages to the people as a whole, the standard of instruction was necessarily inferior. The schools were similar to the Irish national schools, that system having been introduced into the colony in 1844, and they were divided into two classes—the national schools and the denominational schools. Each class of schools was controlled by a Board, and maintained at the expense of the State; but beyond this, and the necessity that a certain average educational standard should be observed, they were practically distinct.

One class consisted of secular schools, the other of church schools. As far as possible, each went its own way, doing the best for itself, and caring nothing for the welfare of the other. The rivalry between the supporters of the one and the adherents of the other was virtually a struggle between popular rights and sectarian suspicion and jealousy. While one party wanted the education of the young directed for the good of the State, the other saw little advantage to be gained unless it were associated with a strengthening of the power of the church.

It is easy to see that with such conflicting interests at work the results to the community as a whole were certain to be the reverse of satisfactory.

Another serious defect in the educational system of the period was that its operations were not as far-reaching as it was necessary they should be. The schools were confined to the large towns and principal centres of population. The children of the inland districts, where the people were few and scattered, were, in many instances, wholly without the means of education.

Men taking up blocks of land under the new Land Law, and, with their families, establishing permanent homes, saw their children growing up ignorant even of the common rudiments of systematic knowledge, and exposed to all the evils which want of education induces.

It was estimated in 1866 that fully 100,000 children under the age of fourteen years were in the colony receiving no instruction whatever. The population at the time stood at about 400,000, and the number of uninstructed children represented, therefore, one-fourth of the population. Government after Government had tried to remedy this, and had not succeeded. Political exigencies, arising from party struggling, had proved a serious obstacle, and, so far, all attempts to improve the State school system had failed.

Mr. Parkes and his colleagues in the Ministry considered, as other Governments had, that the time had arrived when a limit should be put to the assistance given by the State to denominational schools. Mr. Parkes himself had long given close attention to the subject. From the circumstances of his own career, he could not but be deeply conscious of the importance of an adequate system of popular instruction. As a journalist he had seen the evils arising from the inefficiency of the system in the colony, in those districts where schools and schoolmasters were most needed. As a member of the Legislature he was familiar with all that had been done to exchange the existing system for a better.

He knew of no higher duty before him or before Parliament than to devise improved means of education, and extend them to every corner of the land. Want of education led to crime. "If parents are not alive to their own responsibility, and will allow their children to grow up without any education," he argued, "we cannot be surprised if the fire in their young blood finds a vent, or if, removed from the better influences of society, they turn out offenders against law and swell the roll of bushrangers." To prevent crime, the people must be enlightened. Better have schoolmasters, he was fond of saying, than gaolers; better schools than gaols.

Sentiments such as these were not likely to pass lightly across the minds of a population scattered far and wide over many hundreds of miles of wild bush. The evils of ignorance and crime were too apparent around the infant settlements of the interior for men to shut their eyes or close their ears to the advantages derivable from educational improvement. Where the schoolmaster ought to have been, the highwayman roamed; and the boy, whom education would have made a good and useful citizen, was, in too many instances, instructed in little more than the gain to be obtained by a career of robbery and murder.

It could not be for a moment doubted by anyone who knew the country, said Mr. Parkes when moving the second reading of his great measure, if education had been extended to the unfortunate young men who had during the preceding few years suffered the extreme penalty of the law for bushranging, they might have been still alive, enjoying liberty and using that liberty well.

At the same time, no one than Mr. Parkes was more fully aware of the difficulties in the way of improving the existing condition of things. He fully recognised the important fact that the two great religious bodies in the colony—the Anglican and the Roman Catholic Churches—were leagued in a determination to resist to the uttermost all proposed change. Yet, while conscious of the strength of these opposing parties, he saw a way through their opposition, by which it appeared to him he might, to a large extent, meet their prejudices. and, at the same time, secure most of the advantages obtainable from a greatly-improved and well-arranged. secular system.

As the time did not appear ripe, or the possibilities of success sufficiently assured, for suddenly depriving the denominational schools of all State support, the wisest course to take seemed to be the adoption of a system which should be a fair compromise. The denominational schools might still be maintained at the public expense, but conditions. must be introduced by which all aid from the State should cease, if the standard of instruction fell below that in the purely State schools, or the attendance of scholars became smaller than a fixed number. Every encouragement that was justifiable should be given to the denominational schools, and the conditions imposed upon them should be no more than consistent with what was believed to be the desire of a majority of the people,—that there should be one educational system of a uniform standard maintained from the public funds. Schools showing that standard should be assisted ; schools below that standard should be closed, or remain in operation at their own expense.

In this spirit the Public Schools Act was framed. Instead of having two controlling boards it was proposed that there should be one, to be called the Council of Education, no two members of which should be of the same religious persuasion. Denominational schools might operate wherever they were strong enough to do so; but to entitle them to the public money they must show a certain attendance of children, a certain efficiency of instruction, and be a certain distance from a public school. Where the public school was sufficient to meet the educational requirements of a locality, no assistance would be given to a denominational school establishing itself in the vicinity. Religious instruction in denominational schools would, in the main, not be interfered with; but in all such schools receiving State aid the full benefit of the secular education imparted in them must be afforded all children applying for it without any compulsion upon them to receive instruction in religious matters.

While, however, there was this apparent restriction upon religious instruction in the denominational schools, there was a provision that one hour a day might be set apart in the public schools for instruction in religion. This also was not to be compulsory. The hour for religious instruction would be occupied in that manner at the discretion of clergymen voluntarily attending; and it was to be optional with the children in the school whether they should attend the classes in religion or remain at their secular studies.

In regard to the question of religious instruction the bill was very cleverly drafted. It kept in view the desirableness of having as far as possible only one kind of State-supported schools throughout the colony, and aimed at bringing this about;

but its provisions were framed so that the desired change should be effected gradually and without harshness. Denominational schools were doomed; but there was no wish to close them arbitrarily, or in a manner to unduly irritate and create excitement. Reasonable compromise was likely to be a much more effective weapon than blunt force; and this was the prime feature of the measure. The bill sought to improve the quality of the education imparted in the colony, to extend it in all directions, and to have, as far as was justifiable, only one class of schools ; and in endeavouring to secure these great advantages, the author of the measure, while not backward in paying due respect to the feelings of denominationalists, did not lose sight of the best interests of the whole community.

Mr. Parkes moved the second reading of the bill on the 12th September, 1866, in a speech which was a masterpiece of well chosen details, telling argument, and eloquent language. The actual state of the country, the necessities of the rising generation, and the duty upon the Government to do something to extend, to those who did not now possess them, the advantages of education, were the strong points of his case ; but he had carefully ascertained the condition of affairs with regard to education in other countries, particularly those of Europe, and this information greatly strengthened his position.

He was, he said, exceedingly anxious in addressing himself to the question to temper his own opinion with the results of experience, and to consider the opinions of others with every possible respect. The disadvantages of the system in operation in the colony were that education was unnecessarily expensive, inferior in quality, calculated to engender jealousies and uncharitable feelings among the different sections of society, and, in an alarming manner, limited in its supply. These defects he earnestly desired to remove.

To him it was clear that the schools established to educate the children of the colony should not be engaged in an unnatural competition. If the Government undertook the great duty and responsibility of educating the children, they should do it in a manner to be effectual, both in teaching as many children as possible, and in providing a quality of education as high as it could possibly be raised. At the same time, the money available for the purpose should be so economised, that a single shilling more than necessary should not be spent in the work.

"It must be wrong," he contended, "nay, positively sinful, to spend a single shilling unnecessarily upon educating 50,000 children so long as other 50,000 children are destitute of education. It must be wrong to administer the Parliamentary grants in a way that shall, in any respect, interfere with the quality of education; and it must be wrong to administer them in a way that shall in any degree interfere with the extension of this education."

He did not seek to hide his opinion of the baneful effects upon education, which sectarian interference produces. The reason for the multiplicity of small inefficient schools was, he explained, the contention amongst religious bodies to have schools of their own. " The clergy of the various churches, in this as well as in the mother country, are the most inveterate and the most powerful enemies that popular education ever had."

How differently they might act, and with what good results, he was equally plain in stating. " If, in a locality," he said, "where there is only a sufficient number of children to form one good school, they would exercise in a proper spirit that christian charity which ought to be the chief feature of their religion, and consent to their children being educated side by side, extravagance would be avoided, and the means of education would be extended to a number of other children who, whilst ministers of religion are cavilling over a division of the spoils, are left to moral destitution—to the gaols, and, unfortunately, sometimes to the gallows."

He was inclined to consult the interests of the great denominations, even, to some extent, to consult their predjudices ; but he was determined to put an end to all that stood in the way of the desired reform. With this resolve, the Government had framed the bill so that the difficulty should be met in the most practical manner they could desire.

The soul of the bill, as Mr. Parkes described it, was in the clauses which made provision for the establishment of a public school in any locality where, after due inquiry, the Council of Education was satisfied there were at least twenty-five children who would regularly attend such school, and for the
Q

establishment of denominational schools in all cases
where children enough could be found to fill them ;
the Government giving full permission for the
teaching of religion in the denominational schools,
and only insisting on the number of children and
that the standard of secular education taught should
be as high as in the other schools.

A new proposal in the bill was a provision for
the appointment of itinerant teachers in districts
where, from the scattered condition of the population,
or from other causes, it was not practicable to establish a public school ; and the great benefit this has
been to many families in the far interior is well
known to all who have had any acquaintance with
provisional or half-time schools.

" To save the children and make them useful
members of society " was the grand feature of the
speech from the beginning to the close ; and the
close was an unusually fine burst of eloquence.

" This cause," said Mr. Parkes, "cannot suffer
from the feebleness of my appeal.   The voices of a
hundred thousand children appeal to you, and im-
plore you not to allow any secondary consideration
to impair your generous exercise of power in saving
them from neglect and ignorance.   By what you
do now you may render a service that will be felt
hereafter in the aspirations of a hundred thousand
human lives—of that unknown multitude arising in
our midst who have yet to employ their faculties in
moving the machinery of society, and who, for good
or evil, must connect the present with the future.
They will come after us, in the field and in the

workshop, in the school and in the church, on the judgment seat and within these walls—a mighty wave of intelligence that must receive its temper from you, but whose force you will not be here to control. I leave with you this question, so pregnant with social consequences, relying on your enlightened patriotism to approach it in a temperate spirit, to consider it dispassionately, and to arrive at a decision upon it which shall inspire the people with renewed confidence in the wisdom and integrity of Parliament."

The debate extended over five nights ; and the division list showed the House to be in favour of the bill by nearly three to one.

It was generally understood, after Mr. Parkes' speech, that the measure was safe, and certain to be passed by a substantial majority. Its chief opponents were men of extreme denominational tendencies, and some of them were not slow to bitterly denounce the measure and its author.

Mr. Macpherson, who followed Mr. Parkes in the debate, had struggled desperately, only a short time before, by a resolution, and by a judicious canvas and banquetting of members, to re-establish the system, previously in force, of State aid to religion. In that attempt he had failed completely ; but, conceiving that the rejection of this bill would at least be beneficial to the State-aid principle, by keeping within the grasp of the churches the power they exercised over a large proportion of the schools, he opposed the measure vehemently. In the bill as introduced, it was proposed that the Council of Education should consist of five persons, with the Colonial Secretary, for the time being, as ex-officio President.   To Mr. Macpherson, this proposal to place the Colonial Secretary at the head of the Council was to make him "the Pope of education, with five Cardinals under him."   Another member, equally rabid in his opposition, characterised the bill as a monstrous measure, one that sought "to remove the Deity out of his place."

But while the bill had some bitter opponents, it had also some powerful friends.   Dr. Lang came to its support with the strength of an intellectual giant.   To his mind, it was a great and important step in the advancement of the colony, likely to introduce a new era in colonial history, and to promote in a much higher degree the intellectual, moral, and religious welfare of the community.

Outside Parliament, the struggle between the supporters and the opponents of the bill was marked with much vigour, and not a little unscrupulousness.

The two leading religious organizations in the colony joined in a common onslaught upon the measure.   Each denounced it from the pulpit, and pulpit denunciations were followed, or accompanied, by pastorals or addresses which were published far and wide.

The Bishop of Sydney (Dr. Barker) described the bill as "one to extinguish the denominational system," except in a few of the largest towns, and as destructive of religious instruction.

The Roman Catholic Archbishop and his clergy regarded it as something that would "destroy the principles of religion and morality in the public schools of the colony," and merited the severest condemnation. A pastoral on the subject, issued by the Archbishop, was printed and circulated for "the guidance and encouragement" of Roman Catholics "in the present emergency, when the Public Schools' Bill, now before the Legislative Assembly, again threatens to deprive us of one of the dearest portions of our liberty."

Not content with attacking the bill on religious grounds, the extreme denominationalists declared that it would largely and unduly increase the power of the Colonial Secretary, and greatly swell the public expenditure without adequate cause. These charges, joined with that which declared the bill to be, in some of its provisions, destructive of religion in the community, formed a serious indictment.

But the very nature of this indictment was sufficient to prevent it from having any important effect in the direction intended by those who made it. Reduced to the necessity of seizing upon any pretext likely to support their position, the opponents of the bill went too far.

Those of the public, who thought for themselves, could see there was very little in the charges when they came to be examined. Religious instruction in the schools was not abolished ; the arrangements connected with it were merely altered. The power of the Colonial Secretary, instead of being improperly extended, was simply enlarged, so that he

might sit as the official head of the body who were
to administer the Act; and that this was not
regarded as an essential feature of the bill, was
afterwards seen in the fact that it was omitted. As
to the increase in the public expenditure, the great
majority of the people were of Mr. Parkes' opinion,—
that it was better to spend money in providing
schools than in building gaols, and upon schoolmasters than upon gaolers. Public money spent in
educating the children of the colony under one well-
arranged system was public money well spent,
whatever the sum might be. So most people
thought.

But the denominationalists laboured on; continuing the fight during the whole time the bill was
before Parliament.

Among their proceedings was the presentation
to Parliament of a large number of petitions.
Many names were attached to these documents; but neither these nor the documents
attracted much attention. What was generally
regarded as the most significant thing about them
was the manner in which the names had been
obtained. Numbers of them were said to have been
collected at church doors, and under inflammatory
harangues from the pulpits. It was scarcely probable
they would influence in the direction desired, to any
appreciable extent, the minds of those who were bent
upon dealing with the bill in the public interest.

The numbers in the division upon the motion for
the second reading were 36 to 14; and, among
those who voted with the ayes, were Dr. Lang,

William Forster, John Robertson, Saul Samuel, and John Stewart. In committee the bill was subjected to close examination and criticism ; but it stood the ordeal well, and emerged slightly amended though in no respect with its principal features altered. One of the amendments, and perhaps a desirable one, was the omission of the proviso that no two of the five members of the Council of Education should be of the same religious persuasion.

A final effort against the measure was made by denominationalists in the Legislative Council. On the motion for the second reading, Mr. Plunkett moved that the bill be referred to a select committee, who should inquire into and report on the state of education in the colony, on the alleged defects in the system in operation, and on the causes and remedies thereof ; and a week was spent before the House came to a decision in the matter.

The amendment was rejected by 22 votes to 3, and the bill was then read the second time. Some rather important amendments were introduced in committee ; and these, when the bill was returned to the Assembly, threatened for a time something like a deadlock between the two Houses. Eventually an amicable arrangement was arrived at ; and the bill was assented to by the Governor, and became law on 21st December, a little more than three months after the date of its introduction.

Very soon afterwards Mr. Parkes commenced, and continued at intervals, through several years, what may be said to have been a unique proceeding in relation to an Act of Parliament. He began educating the people respecting the principles and provisions of the great measure which had been passed.

The course observed in the introduction and passing of a bill through Parliament is rendered so tortuous by conflicting opinions, mystifying speeches, and party scheming, and the newspaper reports of the debates are often so abridged, that, in many cases, it is not easy for the ordinary citizen to properly comprehend what is adopted and what rejected.

Mr. Parkes set himself to the task of explaining to the people what the provisions and the advantages of the new law really were. He took to travelling in the country; and, wherever he travelled, some opportunity presented itself, of which he could take advantage, for speaking on the new educational system. Sometimes the opportunity was offered by a public dinner given to him. At other times it was presented through an invitation to open a new public school. Occasionally he was in the position of being obliged to deliver a political speech on matters generally. But wherever he was, or whatever might be the circumstances under which he was called upon to speak, he never failed to do his utmost to instruct the general public respecting the provisions and the operation of the new law.

The consequence was that the Public Schools Act which, under ordinary conditions, might, like most measures passed by Parliament, have been placed among the statutes of the colony and speedily

forgotten, became the best known of the laws of the
country, and the most popular. An appeal to the
people by its author, based upon the great privileges
it conferred, never failed since then to excite their
minds and arouse their enthusiasm. Frequently it
influenced, at critical times, debates and divisions
in Parliament. It won many elections. It
gave Mr. Parkes an impregnable position in public
esteem.

The enemies of the Act did not, with its passing,
cease their hostility to it. Efforts of various kinds
were made to render it unpopular, or to hamper its
operation. In many instances, pressure was brought
to bear on parents to prevent them from sending
their children to the public schools.

But, in spite of all opposition, the schools
rapidly increased in number ; the attendance of
children grew with the growth of the schools ;
and the quality of the instruction imparted showed
great improvement.

The Council of Education, well chosen in its
personnel, worked with energy and wisdom. Mr.
Parkes was its President. No man, it was considered, could understand the Act better than he ;
no one was more capable of administering it. On
those grounds, and as a compliment in respect of
the valuable services he had rendered the cause of
education, he was offered, and he accepted, the most
influential position on this important Board. His
colleagues were Mr. George Allen, a Member of
the Legislative Council ; Mr. William Munnings
Arnold, the Speaker of the Legislative Assembly ;

Mr. James Martin, the Attorney-General and Premier; and Professor John Smith, of Sydney University. They were well fitted for the important work of bringing the Act into operation, and conducting it through its initial difficulties. Well known men, in whom the public had confidence, they were firm without being violent; not likely to be set aside from their duty by any consideration whatever, they were at the same time anxious to administer the Act with as little harshness to its opponents as possible.

The Council of Education had very large powers. It was the sole authority in the expenditure of all sums of money appropriated by Parliament for elementary instruction. It established and maintained all public schools, and granted aid to the denominational schools. It appointed all teachers and school inspectors. It had the power to frame regulations, which had the force of law unless disallowed by express resolution of both Houses of the Legislature. In this way it was able to make good any omission, to repair any defect in the Act, as between what the Legislature actually passed and what it desired to pass but unintentionally overlooked. In other words, without altering the provisions of the Act as passed by Parliament, the Council was able, by framing regulations, to make the Act fully effective.

Perhaps its most important duty was the choice, training, and classification of teachers; and of this Mr. Parkes entertained a very strong and very proper opinion. Having the requisite number of

children in the locality to justify the establishment
of a school, the first necessity was a competent
teacher.

In Mr. Parkes' view, no person should be
appointed to the position of teacher simply because
he or she was a protégé of a minister of religion,
or was unable to earn a living in any other walk
of life.   Furthermore, he was well aware that men
might be accomplished scholars, and yet quite unfit
to teach little children.   They might be highly
educated, he once pointed out, and yet have none
of "that aptitude, that patient power of control,
that peculiar sense of responsibility to parents
and to society, which are necessary in the management of children.   They may know nothing of the
varying forms of development of the human mind :
and, without some knowledge of the capacity of the
mind to receive instruction, no man or woman can
teach little children."

It was the duty of the Council of Education
to teach the accepted candidates for the
position of teacher the art of teaching ; and,
having gone through the prescribed training,
course they were classified not merely upon their
ordinary educational attainments but upon their
skill in teaching.   This has been of enormous benefit to the educational system of the colony from
the time of the passing of the Public Schools
Act until now.   It has brought into existence in
the community an army of teachers, who in natural
fitness for their duties, in educational accomplish-
ments, and in technical skill, compare favourably with

In some of the proceedings of this remarkable period of New South Wales history are to be found circumstances which at intervals, for many years afterwards, were made the gound work, inside and outside Parliament, for virulently attacking and denouncing Mr. Parkes. Not, in fact, until those who sat as members in the Parliament of 1868 had disappeared from the arena of politics by death or retirement, and a new generation had made its appearance, did these attacks materially weaken or the denunciation cease.

As Colonial Secretary Mr. Parkes was at the head of the police; and it consequently fell to his lot to be acquainted with everything relating to the attempted assasination of the Duke of Edinburgh. No other minister of the Crown, nor any public official, was in so good a position for knowing the whole of the circumstances connected with the crime.

About the middle of 1868, after the Prince had recovered and left the colony, and O'Farrell had been executed, Mr. Parkes visited his constituents at Kiama; and, in the course of a speech he delivered there, he said " that he held in his possession, and could produce at any moment, evidence attested by affidavits, which left on his mind the conviction that, not only was the assassination of the Duke of Edinburgh planned, but that someone who had a guilty knowledge of the secret, and whose fidelity was suspected, had been foully murdered." And this evidence, he declared, would carry the same conviction to the mind of any impartial person.

These statements created a sensation. Some persons professed to doubt their truth ; most people believed them. Later on, they were nicknamed by some of Mr. Parkes' political opponents, " The Kiama Mystery," and, by others, " The Kiama Ghost."

In the beginning of 1869, the statements at Kiama formed the subject of an inquiry by a select committee of the Legislative Assembly. A short time previously, Mr. Parkes had retired from the Government, in consequence of a disagreement with his colleagues respecting the censure and dismissal of a high public officer ; and the Martin Government had given place to one under Mr. Robertson. Mr. Parkes was chosen by the Opposition to move a motion of want of confidence in the new Government, and, immediately this became apparent, the statements at Kiama were seized upon and used against him with great bitterness. Parliament met on 8th December, 1868, and on the same day, Mr. Parkes gave notice of his want of confidence motion. On the following day the motion was proposed, and the debate, which was protracted over twelve days, did not end until 22nd December.

During one of the intervals in the proceedings, and in the course of a series of tactics by the party supporting the Government, resorted to with the object of discrediting the Member for Kiama, and so bringing about the defeat of his motion, the select committee was appointed. It was appointed at the instance of Mr. Macleay, and it was " to

R

inquire into, and report upon, the existence of a conspiracy for purposes of treason and assassination, alleged by a former Colonial Secretary to have existed in this country, and to receive all evidence that may be tendered or obtained concerning a murder alleged by the same person to have been perpetrated by one or more of such conspirators, the victim of which murder is stated to be unknown to the police."

The select committee was a somewhat remarkable one, and has a curious history in the legislative annals of the colony. It reported dead against Mr. Parkes, declaring that there was no evidence to support the statements he had made before his constituents at Kiama; and requested that its conclusions might be forwarded to the Secretary of State for the Colonies. The report was adopted by the committee, on the vote of Mr. Macleay as Chairman, the numbers in the division being equal, and three of those voting for the adoption of the report being Ministers. Mr. Parkes, when the report came before the Assembly, secured its rejection, and had it expunged from the records.

The conclusions of the committee, as stated in their report were as follows :—

" (1.) That there is no evidence to warrant the belief that the Government was aware of any plot or intention to assassinate His Royal Highness, the Duke of Edinburgh, before his arrival in this country, or at any time previous to the attempt upon his life.

(2.) That it does not appear that any extra-ordinary precautions were taken for the preservation of the life of His Royal Highness, either on the occasion of his landing, or at any period during his stay in this country, up to the moment of his attempted assassination.

(3.) That there is no evidence to warrant the belief that the crime of O'Farrell, who attempted to murder the Duke of Edinburgh, was the result of any conspiracy or organization existing in this country, or, as far as the Government had or have any knowledge, the result of a conspiracy or organization existing elsewhere.

(4.) That there is no evidence whatever of the murder of any supposed confederate in the alleged plot.

(5.) That the foregoing resolutions be embodied in an Address to the Governor, with a request that His Excellency will forward the same to Her Majesty's Secretary of State for the Colonies."

Mr. Parkes induced the House by a substantial majority to set the resolutions of the committee aside, and to adopt the following :—

"(1.) That the report of the select committee, appointed on the 15th December, 1868, to inquire into the existence of a conspiracy for purposes of treason and assassination, presented by the chairman on the 3rd inst., contains numerous statements and inferences not warranted by the evidence, and is made an instrument of personal hostility against a member of this House, in disregard of the authorised objects of the inquiry, and manifestly for party purposes.

(2.) That the evidence shows that several principal officers of the Government,—who from their official position and experience, were best qualified to form a correct judgment of the occurrences, and the state of public feeling during the time of excitement, previous and subsequent to the attempt to assassinate the Duke of Edinburgh,—were and are still of opinion, that meetings of seditious persons were held in the colony; that the criminal O'Farrell was not alone and unaided in his attack upon the life of His Royal Highness; and that persons openly sympathised with the attempted assassination.

(3) That the evidence shows that rumours of intended violence towards His Royal Highness, more or less definite, were in circulation before the 12th March, 1868; and that some such rumours have proceeded from sources unknown to the Government at the time, and that, therefore, they supply independent evidence in support of the statements of the official witnesses.

(4) That the important results of the inquiry set forth in the preceding second and third resolutions, and also other matters of serious

moment, which ought to have been faithfully
represented to this House, have been either
set aside altogether, or improperly and
prejudicially dealt with in the report.

(5.) That this House expresses its disapprobation
of the said report, and directs that it be
expunged from the proceedings of the select
committee."

The opinion of the majority of the members of
the Legislative Assembly, at the time Mr. Parkes
secured this signal triumph over his political foes,
may be said to be the general opinion now. A
quarter of a century has passed since the attempt
upon the life of the Prince, and it is not now difficult
to so calmly and carefully consider the evidence
relating to O'Farrell's crime and its surroundings,
as to arrive at a just conclusion. Few persons, now
living, who remember the incidents of the attempted
assassination, the magisterial inquiry, and the trial
of the prisoner, are disposed to deny that there was
much more evidence to support Mr. Parkes' statements, than there was to justify the conclusions of
the select committee.

The statements of O'Farrell were themselves
sufficient to show this. He was not insane, and he
repeatedly declared that the crime he had committed
was the outcome of action on the part of a
disloyal organization who had allotted the duty
to him. The first shot from his revolver took
effect in the Prince's back; and his intention
was to fire a second shot at the Prince as he
lay on the ground, and then kill himself. This

he stated at the magisterial inquiry held soon after his arrest. On the same occasion, in answer to a question from the magistrate he said :—" I have nothing to say but that the task of executing the Duke was sent out and allotted to me."   Asked by the Crown Solicitor to repeat this, he answered again,—" the task of executing the Prince was sent out to me ; but I failed, and I am not very sorry that I did fail."   " Everybody," it was remarked at one of the public meetings held at the time, " in-stinctively guessed the source of the treason."   " I am sorry I missed my aim," O'Farrell remarked to a police-sergeant on the way to Darlinghurst Gaol. "I don't care for death. I am a Fenian. God save Ireland."

The *Herald* argued that there could be little doubt that Dublin being the headquarters of the Fenian conspiracy, it must have been from Dublin that "the task," as O'Farrell termed it, was sent out, if it were sent out at all. That was where the plot was originally hatched, and the head central organization there was responsible for the crime. But it was exceedingly improbable that O'Farrell himself was nominated in Dublin. He could not be sufficiently well-known to be trusted by the rebel authorities there. The story of his life showed that he had spent only a small portion of his existence in Ireland, and that he had for a long period been a resident of Victoria. If, therefore, "the task" were sent out from Ireland it must have been sent to some branch Fenian organization in Australia—probably in Victoria.

This inference may have been correct. At least it appears, from the evidence, certain that, for some time, the possible assassination of the Prince was a matter of rumour in New South Wales, and was made known to the police in Sydney. The period was one in which Fenianism in Ireland and America was active, and in its far-reaching operations there was nothing very surprising in the sending of a mandate to one or more of its emissaries in Australia.

Undoubtedly Fenian sentiments were entertained by people in New South Wales. A witness before the select committee described a number of Fenian meetings at which he had been present. In the year 1867, while living at Shoalhaven, he began to attend meetings of the Irish settlers in the neighbourhood. These meetings were partly social and partly political. "The young people indulged in dancing whilst the old people talked politics and treason." The arrival of the mail with the latest Irish newspapers was always the signal for one of these gatherings. On one occasion, after some derogatory remarks concerning the Royal family, this witness was asked by one of those present what he should think if he should hear of His Royal Highness the Duke of Edinburgh being shot. Laughing at the idea, he inquired if it were thought anybody would be so foolish or so madbrained as to do it. "Oh," was the reply, "some one will be found that will do it." That it was "no sin to put anyone to death who stood in the way of the purposes of Fenianism" was an observation often made. "It had been frequently said," this witness stated in his evidence, "that they did not consider it any sin to exterminate any person whatever that stood in the way of those who were standing up for the rights of old Ireland. They said the Royal family were in the way, and would soon be exterminated."

A landholder at Penrith heard a neighbour, on the occasion of a visit to that town by the Duke of Edinburgh, say, in allusion to the Prince, " It's all very well now ; he is joyous enough now with the red flag waving over him, but the black flag will wave over his corpse before he leaves the country."

Irish disaffection has never been fortunate ; and one of the misfortunes invariably attending it, has been that disclosures from some one not loyal to the cause have enabled the authorities to put in force effective precautionary measures.   It was so in the course of the Fenian movement in Ireland.   It was equally so in these ebullitions of disloyalty in New South Wales.   The Government were fairly well informed of what was going on. Their information was not as minute as was desirable, but it was more than sufficient to put them on the alert.   Mr. Martin, when moving the suspension of the standing orders to allow of the rapid passing of the Treason Felony Act, told the Legislative Assembly, that a great quantity of information had been placed before the Government tending to show that there were persons in the colony engaged in a conspiracy against the British Crown.   "There are persons here," he said, "agents of persons in other parts of the world, and in correspondence with societies who have entered into a conspiracy against the British Crown. We have been informed that these persons have their places of meeting where there are, no doubt, papers connected with the conspiracy or where such papers are supposed to exist."

No arrests were made as a result of this information, nor were any important documents discovered and secured ; but that does not prove the information supplied to the Government to have been unreliable. The passing of the Treason Felony Act in a country like New South Wales was similar to the suspension of the *Habeas Corpus* Act in a country like Ireland. Under it, the liberty of no man could be said to be absolutely safe. Arrest and imprisonment might take place upon the mere surmise of a justifiable reason. One important effect from the passing of such a law would therefore be that disloyal meetings would cease. Compromising documents would be destroyed. Bands of conspirators would disperse. The speed at which the Treason Felony Act was passed through the New South Wales Parliament and made law, was within a few hours that at which the House of Commons, in 1866, two years before, suspended the *Habeas Corpus* Act in Ireland. The object of the two Parliaments was the same ; the results were similar.

It was said that the attempted assassination of the Duke of Edinburgh was an act of revenge for the execution of the Manchester Fenians. We know that the hanging of those men gave an additional impulse to Fenianism. The execution took place on November 23rd, 1867. The shooting of the Prince occurred on March 12th, 1868. The despatch of instructions from the Fenian head quarters in Ireland immediately after the execution at Manchester, would be a very natural proceeding. It was known that the Duke of Edinburgh intended to visit Australia, and a more effective reply to what, not only the Fenian brotherhood, but many loyal Englishmen regarded as excessive punishment, than the taking of the life of a son of the Queen, could not have appeared to the minds of the Fenian leaders.

Two days after the attempted murder of the Prince, the warder of Darlinghurst gaol specially charged with the care of the prisoner O'Farrell, reported that, in the course of conversation, the prisoner had remarked that, the Queen had very little feeling or compassion for the Manchester Fenians, who had been wrongfully executed. But the day before this, and the day following the shooting of the Prince, O'Farrell stated to the Chief Warder of the Gaol, that immediately after the news arrived in Australia of the Manchester executions, " a Fenian body was organized in Melbourne, composed of some Ballarat men, under the leadership of a person who came out from England for that purpose, when it was agreed upon that Prince Alfred was to be shot. They came over here (Sydney), and recruited their ranks some two dozen, but losing confidence in some of their members, the band was reduced to ten, who drew lots to whose part it should fall to assassinate the Prince and the Earl of Belmore."

Lord Belmore appears to have escaped by becoming patron of St. Patrick's Regatta, at that time an annual celebration in Sydney Harbour. Immediately after the determination to murder the Prince and the Earl, Lord Belmore became, O'Farrell explained, "the patron of some society that was favourable to them, or they were favourable to it. Lots were again drawn, to know who was to shoot the Prince, only, and the lot fell to O'Farrell.

Some days after these statements by the prisoner he was seen by Mr. Parkes, in his capacity of Colonial Secretary. O'Farrell conversed freely, and the details of the conversation were recorded by a shorthand writer. Much that the prisoner said confirmed the view which had been taken of his crime and its cause; but, ultimately, he sought to withdraw his statements concerning the existence of an organized conspiracy which had directed him to the committal of the crime, and to take the blame for what he had done solely upon himself.

The strongest evidence in support of the statement that the Government had been warned, and believed that an attack might be made upon the Prince, is to be seen in the precautions taken to protect him. Special constables were sworn in before his arrival. Two troopers were specially directed to ride abreast of him. The officer at the head of the police, when giving these men the order as to their duty, remarked to them, that if the Prince was fired at, they would receive the shot.

How necessary some such protection was came to light after O'Farrell's arrest. It then became known that his first intention had been to shoot the Prince on the occasion of his official landing. Hiring a room from which he could view, within easy distance, the procession from the landing place, he managed to convey a loaded gun there. This gun he actually levelled at the Prince, but did not fire because he found it impossible not to risk shooting one or other of the two protecting troopers.

In defending himself from the aspersions contained in the select committee's report, Mr. Parkes closed a carefully considered and effective speech with some impressive sentences.

" I shall content myself," he said, " with nothing less than is set forth in my resolutions. I will not submit to having a report, so dishonest and so scandalous as I have shown this to be, still remaining among the records, to be unfairly quoted at any moment by persons whose capabilities of unfairness we have so often witnessed—to be made a handle of in a nefarious way at the general election, when it is desirable that the verdict of the constituencies should be honestly taken. I take my stand upon this ground,—that I am above reproach in this matter ; that the committee, with all its malignity and ingenuity, have failed to substantiate a charge against me ; and that the charges recoil upon themselves by the unanswerable testimony I have adduced before the House. The laws of honourable feeling are against the authors of this report. The law of God declares " Thou shalt not bear false witness against thy neighbour "; and I will not submit to that which will stamp our proceedings with disgrace, and which, if I submit to it, may at some future time fall upon the head of a worthier man."

The conclusion of the speech was followed by a burst of cheering from most of the members of the House; and, on the passing of Mr. Parkes' resolutions, three cheers were given with enthusiasm for Her Majesty the Queen. The occupants of the Strangers' Gallery, which was crowded, joined with members in this extraordinary demonstration by waving hats and handkerchiefs; and, outside the House, received Mr. Parkes with many demonstrations of approval. The honourable member for Kiama, in this matter, undoubtedly had the support of the general public.

CHAPER XIX.

LESS than a month after he had made to his constituents his famous "Kiama Mystery" speech, Mr. Parkes resigned his office of Colonial Secretary. This he did in consequence of the Cabinet, at the instance of the Colonial Treasurer (Mr. Eagar), dismissing Mr. W. A. Duncan from his position of Collector of Customs, and making such arrangements to fill his place as did not meet with Mr. Parkes' approval.

Parliament, at the time, was in recess. A quantity of goods imported by a Sydney tradesman had been seized, by the order of the Collector of Customs, on the ground that the nature of the packages having been improperly described the goods were undervalued, and an attempt was made to defraud the Customs revenue.

Regarding the case as one requiring severe treatment the Collector, having seized the goods, recommended their confiscation and the imposition of a heavy fine on the importer. To this the approval of the Colonial Treasurer was not given. Mr. Eagar, after representations had been made to him by the importer, was of opinion that, as far as the importer was concerned, there had been no attempt at fraud ; and he directed that the seizure be cancelled and the goods restored. Payment of the amount of duty, calculated on the proper value of the goods, he considered sufficient to meet the ends of justice. The Collector refused to deliver up the goods. He considered the course he had taken to be that not only authorised but directed under the law, and deemed it his duty to abide by the law rather than obey the order of the Colonial Treasurer.

A repetition of the order from Mr. Eagar had no more effect than the first. Firm in the belief that the law directed the seizure, and that this was superior to any mandate of a Minister, the Collector was obdurate. Angry correspondence took place; and Mr. Duncan wrote a minute which Mr. Eagar viewed as a gross act of insubordination and disrespect to him as the Minister having the control of the Customs Department. He directed the suspension of Mr. Duncan; and took steps to bring the matter before the Cabinet. Mr. Duncan refused to be suspended. He declared that it was not in the power of the Colonial Treasurer to suspend him ; that such a suspension could only be ordered by the Governor and the Executive Council. Mr. Eagar, knowing more than Mr. Duncan appeared to know of the power of a Minister of the Crown over the Department of which he is the official head, insisted on the suspension, and threatened to resort to police assistance to eject Mr. Duncan from his office. This proved effectual.

The threatened forcible ejection induced Mr.
Duncan to leave the Custom House; and he immediately forwarded a statement of his case to Mr.
Parkes. With Mr. Parkes he had been on terms of
close friendship for many years. The intimacy had
commenced in Mr. Parkes' struggling days, when
occasional poems, afterwards published in the volume "Stolen Moments," were admitted by Mr.
Duncan into the columns of the *Australian
Chronicle*; and it had grown to firmly rooted
feelings of esteem. Mr. Duncan thought he could
count upon Mr. Parkes' friendship as a weapon
against Mr. Eagar. He asked Mr. Parkes, as
Colonial Secretary, to interfere with what he considered the inconsiderate conduct of the Treasurer.

Mr. Parkes sympathised with Mr. Duncan, but
disapproved of what he had done. Refusing to
interfere, he pointed out that it was not possible for
him to do so. He wrote to Mr. Duncan two letters,
of interest to everybody who may care to clearly
understand the position and power of a Minister of
the Crown under Responsible Government.

"As I explained to you on Saturday (the letter
stated) it is quite impossible for me to interfere in
the case represented by the papers which you sent
to my office. I and Mr. Eagar stand upon an equal
footing as members of the Government, and I should
simply put myself in a false position by presuming
to interfere in the Department of the Public Service
under his Ministerial control. A Minister is responsible to Parliament alone for his management;
and *his* judgment must guide, and his decision be

final, so far as those who serve the Government are concerned."

A few days afterwards he wrote again, regretting that it was not in his power to serve Mr. Duncan in his difficulty, and saying, that he did not see Mr. Duncan's way out of it.

" I wrote to you last Monday " (the letter went on) " from a sincere desire to point out to you, so far as I might presume to remind you of what you should know quite as well as myself, that *Government must govern*, and that it is not for the *servants of the Government*, whatever their rank, to dictate the course of action which should be pursued by those, who for the time being, represent and hold the powers of the Constitution.   It has often appeared to me that the public servants in this colony have failed to comprehend the full force of the change that has taken place in the management of our affairs—that all power of local government has been transferred to the responsible Ministers of our own Legislature.   As one of those Ministers responsible to Parliament alone, the Colonial Treasurer, in dealing with the Department placed under his control, acts with the whole weight and authority of Government.   It is this Minister, thus constitutionally clothed with authority, whom you have disobeyed, treated with contempt, accused of illegal conduct, and threatened with correction from his colleagues in power. . . . I repeat all I said to you, when I last saw you, of my sincere respect for your personal character and attainments; but if I had received the minute which you sent to

8

the Colonial Treasurer, I should have suspended
you instantly, and I am quite sure Mr. Martin would
have done the same. Under any circumstances, in
such a case as the present, I should consider it my
duty to support my colleagues in the Government,
or retire from office. In these particular proceedings
I am convinced that you are entirely in the wrong,
and that the Treasurer had no other course open to
him, consistent with the respect which is due to his
office, than the one he has taken."

Up to this time, the relations between
Mr. Parkes and Mr. Eagar were most cordial.
Mr. Eagar had informed Mr. Parkes of the circumstances of the Duncan case, and consulted him in
the matter. The two Ministers were thoroughly in
accord as to the insubordination of the Collector,
and the necessity for adequate punishment.

But, after his suspension, Mr. Duncan retracted
and apologised ; and this, in Mr. Parkes' opinion,
gave to the matter a new and important aspect.
He thought the Treasurer might, without loss of
dignity, accept the apology, and restore Mr. Duncan
to his position. Mr. Martin thought so too. Other
members of the Cabinet, and also the Governor,
were of a similar opinion. Mr. Parkes, in the desire
to lay this view before the Treasurer, wrote to Mr.
Eagar the following private note :—

" My dear Mr. Eagar,

I called to see you yesterday morning, but you were not at the
moment at the Treasury. Mr. Duncan has sent in an uncon-
ditional apology, and Lord Belmore has written a long private
note to me on this matter, in which he refers to a similar case at

home. I think you would probably like to see what is said on this point.

My object, however, in writing this note is to offer you *my opinion* simply as *mine*. You have gained everything in compelling Duncan to acknowledge that you have been right and he wrong. You are in the highest position that any man in power can occupy, when you can afford to be magnanimous, and refrain from punishing where you have the power to punish and where punishment has been deserved. Your position is even still better—you can save a man from ruin, where no consideration at your hands has been merited. It is not often that men have an opportunity of acting with this sweet and abiding sense of satisfaction. If I were in your place, I should do what I have ventured to suggest. Having thus hastily unburdened my mind, I shall not go behind your back to express my opinion to your colleagues, and I am quite sure you will appreciate my speaking plainly to yourself."

Most people would see little or nothing in a letter of this kind at which to be angry. They would recognise in it, the friendly counsel of a colleague, as well as a desire to serve an erring friend. Few persons would say that the good counsel of the colleague was used merely as a means for serving the friend.

Mr. Eagar, however, took offence at the letter. Though up to this point, there had been no interruption of the good relationship between the two Ministers, Mr. Eagar appeared to view this private note of friendly advice as something grossly offensive. Communication between him and Mr. Parkes, personally, or by letter, at once ceased; and Mr. Eagar began to treat Mr. Parkes with what the latter regarded as contempt. Cabinet meetings,

which hitherto had been held in the office of the
Colonial Secretary, were now held elsewhere; and, in
many other ways, the ill-will of Mr. Eagar and his
influence in the Cabinet were shown.

Mr. Martin was of the same opinion as Mr.
Parkes, respecting Mr. Duncan's apology, but he
allowed himself to be swayed by Mr. Eagar.

The Premier was anxious to avoid taking the
extreme course of removing Mr. Duncan from his
office; and, in the endeavour to accommodate
matters, and prevent the Collector from being
dismissed, several meetings of the Cabinet were
held, and the ultimate decision of the case put off
from time to time, in the hope that the Treasurer
would be induced to accept Mr. Duncan's apology.
But this, Mr. Eagar firmly declined to do; and Mr.
Martin, rather than lose the services of a colleague
with whom he had been politically associated for
some years, and who, next to Mr. Martin, was, of
the Premier's party, the most prominent Minister
in the Government, sided with Mr. Eagar, and Mr.
Duncan was dismissed.

Mr. Parkes viewed this dismissal as an act of
great harshness, but he did not immediately resign.
Probably, he contemplated resignation; but it was
not until other proceedings in relation to the office
of Collector of Customs took place in the Cabinet,
that he determined to forward his resignation to
the Governor.

Mr. Eagar considered that the position of
Collector of Customs had been one of too much
independence of action. In his opinion, it was

desirable to make it more amenable to the
Treasurer's control. He therefore urged the
Cabinet to reduce the salary of the Collector,
and to make the office more subordinate than it
was in the time of Mr. Duncan ; and the Cabinet
agreed.

To Mr. Parkes, this seemed a degradation of
the office of Collector, harsh and unwise in itself,
and not at all necessary in the public interest.
Moreover, he did not regard the decision as one
arrived at after unbiassed deliberation of the
Cabinet. He would not agree to it, and as a
consequence, determined to relinquish his office of
Colonial Secretary.

Mr. Martin tried to dissuade him from taking
this step, and then to reconsider his decision. But
he was immovable. He allowed a day or two to
pass, and then wrote that he had taken time to
weigh the various considerations pointed out to him,
with the result that he believed he was right in the
course he was pursuing.

" I believe," he said, " I am right in my view
of the special case and of the public interests
affected by it, and that entertaining those views,
and having been made the object of Mr. Eagar's
marked contempt, I am not simply justified in the
course I propose to pursue, but I could scarcely
take any other, and preserve my self-respect."
Mr. Duncan, the letter went on to say, " has not
only acknowledged himself in the wrong, and
unreservedly apologised, but has thrown himself on
the mercy of the Government in consideration of

his long service, his advanced years, and his helpless family. I know Mr. Duncan to be a man of integrity and unblemished life, and I cannot view his humbled position as it has been viewed by you and your colleagues. Then, again, if Mr. Duncan were removed, I could not assent to the arrangements that are to follow."

He severed his connection with Mr. Martin very regretfully.

" Believe me, my dear Martin," he wrote, " that I separate from you at this moment with feelings of deep regret, so far as I am concerned myself, and of warm esteem towards you, which has been strengthened by every day's experience since we have been associated together."

Mr. Martin sacrificed the Collector of Customs simply because he thought it to be his duty rather to be loyal to his colleague, the Treasurer, than generous to a public officer.

"As you are aware," he wrote to Mr. Parkes, "it would have been most gratifying to me if Eagar could have been prevailed .upon to accept the retractation and apology of Mr. Duncan, and no pains were spared by me to bring about such a result. The determination of Mr. Eagar, however, to insist on the removal of Mr. Duncan, and to withdraw from office unless that removal took place, presented to me the alternative of either standing by an officer whose conduct justified his removal, or supporting a colleague of more than four years' standing in a course which, in my opinion, he was perfectly warranted in pursuing."

And the letter concluded : " I need not tell you how much it would have gratified me if you had consented to remain with us during our term of office. Notwithstanding occasional differences of opinion, which in any combination must be expected to arise, I have been enabled cordially to co-operate with you, for nearly three years, under circumstances of no common difficulty, and in spite of efforts perseveringly made to induce us to distrust one another. Those efforts have in every instance proved unavailing, and, while I regret the loss of a colleague whose energy and ability have conferred so much benefit upon the public, and have been of such great advantage to the Government, I am glad to be enabled to say that that loss has not been occasioned by any difference, personal or political, with myself."

Public opinion was with Mr. Parkes in the matter. The course he had taken was almost universally approved. The leading journal, alluding to it, said that throughout the incident he had acted with prudence and humanity.

" His interference was limited to that kind of persuasion which men who meet each other and are not on terms of enmity are accustomed to use to prevent an evil or to accomplish a good. The letter of Mr. Parkes setting forth his views before Mr. Eagar is couched in terms which do him infinite credit. Every man not embittered by public life, and conscious of human infirmities, will approve of his recommendation to Mr. Eagar, both as to its form and substance."

Not long did the Government survive the resignation of Mr. Parkes. Probably it would not have
lasted much longer if he had remained. It had
been in office two years and nine months, a period
greater than in the case of any Administration but
one—the Robertson-Cowper Ministry of 1860-1863
—since the introduction of responsible government,
and beyond what is regarded as the average life of
Ministries in the colony. It had done good work;
but a certain proportion of the Assembly had
begun to tire of it, and others were hostile because
of the passing of the Public Schools Act. Twice it
had met with a serious reverse. It had been defeated on its railway policy, and upon a bill to
amend the Land Laws. So pronounced was the
opposition to the Land Bill that Mr. Martin
obtained the adjournment of the House to enable
the Government to consider its position. It did not
resign, and the rejection by the House of a direct
motion of want of confidence enabled it to go on,
but it had been greatly shaken. The worrying
tactics of some of the Opposition made matters
worse.

The Government was undoubtedly tottering to
its fall, but the withdrawal of Mr. Parkes materially hastened the end. Mr. Parkes resigned on
17th September; Parliament reassembled on 13th
October; and on 20th October the Government
went out of office. Defeated on an amendment moved by Mr. Robertson on the Address-in-
Reply to the Governor's Speech at the opening of
Parliament, Mr. Martin endeavoured to secure a

dissolution, but this the Earl of Belmore refused to grant, and the Ministry resigned.

To Mr. Parkes the defeat of the Government in a vital division was, in one sense, highly complimentary, for Mr. Robertson's amendment was based on the dissatisfaction of the House with the Ministry after Mr. Parkes' retirement. Mr. Robertson moved the following addition to the Address-in-Reply.

"But we feel that we should be wanting in our duty if we did not, on the earliest opportunity of which we can avail ourselves, respectfully express to your Excellency our regret that, on the retirement of the late Colonial Secretary, your Excellency did not secure an Administration having the confidence of this House."

The debate, preceded by an explanation of the Duncan incident by Mr. Martin, and a statement from Mr. Parkes, was brought to an end the same evening. Three points of importance appeared in the speeches of the Opposition. They disapproved of the dismissal of Mr. Duncan ; they regarded the Government as irretrievably weakened by the resignation of Mr. Parkes; and they refused to consent to the position of Colonial Secretary being given to a member of the Legislative Council, where Mr. Martin had found, in the person of Mr. Joseph Docker, Mr. Parkes' successor. The division was equal, and the Speaker gave his casting-vote with the Government; but it was impossible for the Ministry to continue. It had been undoubtedly condemned, chiefly because without Mr. Parkes it

was not considered deserving of support; and Mr.
Robertson, who had skilfully used the retirement of the Colonial Secretary for his own purpose,
took Mr. Martin's place at the head of a new
Administration.

CHAPTER XX.

For the greater part of three and a half years following the defeat of the Ministry in which he had held the office of Colonial Secretary, Mr. Parkes occupied, in the Legislative Assembly, the position of a private member. As had always been his habit, he was very regular in his attendance, very watchful of the proceedings, and ever on the alert to keep Ministers from overstepping the bounds of constitutional practice.

The Robertson Government of 1868 he tried to displace immediately it appeared in the Assembly; and, for a few days, there was a prospect of his being successful and becoming the head of an Administration formed by himself. Extraordinary efforts on the part of the Government alone saved it.

Though the Martin Ministry had outlived its support in the popular branch of the Parliament, its successor, on its entrance to office, was not received with general approval. The new Government had been formed somewhat incongruously; it had made but a weak announcement of policy; and, for some time its chief objects seemed to be the raking up of every charge possible against the Martin Government, and the publication of these with unlimited abuse. The Opposition, with the members of the late Martin Government at their head, determined to see, in a definite manner, to what extent Mr. Robertson and his colleagues had the support of the House. It was believed that they and their friends were in a minority.

The principal members of the Ministry were Mr. Robertson, Mr. Forster, and Mr. Samuel. Mr. Robertson and Mr. Samuel had been together in a previous Government, as had Mr. Forster and Mr. Samuel; but Mr. Robertson had never before been associated in a Ministry with Mr. Forster. They had been regarded as relentless opponents rather than bosom friends.

Mr. Forster, once described as " disagreeable in Opposition, insufferable as a supporter, and fatal as a colleague," had a very bitter tongue. Though an educated and cultured man of considerable ability, it seemed to be his nature to be disagreeable and to say unpleasant things. It was at least exceedingly difficult, and certainly most unusual, for him to say anything pleasant or agreeable. He revelled in cynicism, which he brought into use in every debate and applied to every subject. He had said many unpleasant things of Mr. Robertson, and Mr. Robertson had flung back unpleasant things at him. Mr. Forster had likened Mr. Robertson to a certain insect " so offensive that it could only be touched by a pair of tongs," and which, " if pinched according to its deserts, emitted a very unpleasant odour."

"Unless, therefore," he proceeded with his unsavoury illustration, "I can figuratively lay hold of the honourable member with a pair of tongs. and carry him outside without the risk of contact with what is extremely offensive, I shall not, if I consult my own feelings, have anything to say to him."

Mr. Robertson had said of Mr. Forster that he was always holding with the hare and running with the hounds, that he could not take a straightforward and consistent course. " No one," Mr. Robertson declared on one occasion, " enunciated more liberal opinions, and no one more frequently recorded his vote with those who were opposed to all progress."

Before the reassembling of Parliament after the Ministerial re-elections the Opposition held a meeting, and decided that a test want-of-confidence motion should be moved. It was also determined that Mr. Parkes should move it. He urged that the duty could be more fittingly performed by others. Mr. Martin, for instance, as the head of the previous Government and the leader of the present Opposition, was, in Mr. Parkes' view, the person in whose hands the motion should be placed. But the choice of the party fell on Mr. Parkes, all his colleagues in the Martin Ministry approving; and he consented.

On 9th December, 1868, he moved, " That the present Administration does not possess the confidence of this House; " and, in a speech of ability and force, scathingly attacked the Government on their want of agreement amongst themselves, their incapacity for governing, and their failure in possessing or putting forward a definite policy.

The debate and its attendant proceedings were unique. Neither before nor since has anything similar taken place. A challenge, by direct motion, of the right of Ministers to occupy their positions on the Treasury benches, coming from a prominent and influential member of the House, is generally regarded as a signal to stop business until the hostile motion has been disposed of. When, in the matter, the member moving the motion is the chosen mouthpiece and leader of the Opposition, the cessation of all business, to permit of the debate upon the motion proceeding without interruption, is imperative. Unless upon some subject which, in the public interest, it would be unwise to delay, not even a question is answered. Everything awaits the decision of the House upon the movement of the Opposition. Consequently a Government, when challenged in this manner, immediately adjourns the House until the day appointed for making the motion, and then proceeds day by day with the debate upon it, until it is brought to a vote.

In this case, the Government and its supporters took a very different course. Everything that could be thought of by Ministers and their friends was brought forward to block the progress of the debate, delay the decision of the House, and weaken the effect of Mr. Parkes' indictment.

There was a general impression, based on a careful counting of members, that in the division the Opposition would have a majority of five or six; and, in the interests of the Government, it was necessary to do all that was possible to effect an alteration. If the debate could be prolonged, some members inclined to vote against the Government might be induced to waver and vote the other way. Time to deal with these flexible gentlemen was essential.

The question was how to gain the necessary time. If, in addition to gaining time, the position of the mover of the hostile motion could be materially shaken, so much the better. Mr. Parkes' attitude in the O'Farrell incident had raised, in some quarters, a bitter feeling against him. Some persons honestly believed he had been guilty of gross exaggeration, if not deliberate misstatement, in his public utterances respecting O'Farrell and his crime. Others, more directly inimical to him, if they did not actually believe this, professed to do so, and joined with those who did. Besides this combination of unfriendly persons, there was a party of influence and activity, who had never forgiven him for what he had done in establishing the Public Schools Act, and undermining the existence of Denominational Schools.

Here were the directions in which, with advantage, he might be attacked, and the decision of the Assembly upon his want-of-confidence motion delayed. The Government resolved to take this course.

The debate upon Mr. Parkes' motion had not proceeded beyond the first night, when it was interrupted by a motion moved by Mr. William Macleay, and a long discussion upon it, for the production of all papers having reference to the attempted assassination of the Duke of Edinburgh. Appeals to have this postponed, in order that the debate on the want-of-confidence motion might be continued without interruption, were altogether vain. The Government and their supporters pressed Mr. Macleay's motion forward, and attacked Mr. Parkes upon some of his proceedings as Colonial Secretary, during the time of the O'Farrell incident, with a virulence unknown before.

One of a number of charges brought against him, was the removal and retention from the Colonial Secretary's Office, of certain papers relating to matters connected with O'Farrell's crime. Mr. Thomas Garrett, then, and all his life, a firm supporter of Mr. Robertson, declared that the proper way of getting these papers, was to issue a search warrant, and have it executed by a common constable ; and Mr. Robertson went so far as to say that, if the papers were not returned to the Colonial Secretary's Office by the following day, he would put the criminal law in motion. " I will have them to-morrow, if the criminal law will give them to me," he said. " If the law will enable me, I will put him in custody."

These words indicate the nature of the debate. The removal of the papers was easily explained, and was justifiable ; but the anger and resentment, which actuated the Government party at the time, made them deaf to explanation, and drove them at the mover of the hostile motion with the savagery of a pack of wolves.

The larger portion of Mr. Robertson's speech, in answer to Mr. Parkes, consisted of a series of charges against him which he had sought to hide, Mr. Robertson averred, by bringing forward his motion; and most of the speakers on the Ministerial side adopted a similar course. The main idea of almost everyone appeared to be to pile up the charges, and so crush the delinquent effectually. The sins of the whole of the Government of which he had been a member, as well as his own shortcomings, were heaped upon him; and, as he afterwards said, in his speech in reply at the close of the debate, it almost seemed as if the motion the House was considering was one condemnatory of the honourable member for Kiama, rather than one inviting the House to censure the Government.

During the debate there was a curious disclosure with regard to some expenditure by the Martin Government for political purposes of their own. It was said that they spent £20 in cab hire, to bring up their supporters from their homes at night, when they were wanted in the House for a division.

Mr. Eagar, the Treasurer in the Government, admitted the truth of the charge, and candidly defended it. He had authorised the expenditure, and saw no harm in doing so. "Honourable members of the Opposition," he explained, "were forming little conspiracies and endeavouring to surprise the Government by an adverse vote; and he considered it necessary to send round messages to collect the Government supporters together." For this purpose he had employed certain cabs, and had ordered

T

the payment of the cab hire from the Treasury. He had gone further. On some nights of important debate, he had caused a number of cabs to be retained in the vicinity of the House, and had used them in sending for members as they were wanted. This he considered to be necessary in order to keep business in a proper state. " It was no personal interest of his," he told the House ; " but, in order to bring members to the House, it was necessary to send messages to their private residences. It was, in fact, part of the system of the Government."

The unjustifiable character of this expenditure it is needless to point out, and Mr. Parkes did not defend it. In his opinion it could not be justified.

But he himself was charged with having been paid from the Treasury a large amount, for expenses in travelling, while Colonial Secretary ; and it was said that his Government had given a lunch at a cost of £98 which had been defrayed from the same source. This charge even went on to assert that a quantity of wine, left over from the lunch, was sent to the private residence of one of the Ministers, and that the money for it was not paid in to the Treasury until after the new Government had come into office.

The charge against Mr. Parkes was trivial, and easily answered. He had travelled about the country, principally to make himself acquainted with the state of education in the colony, so that the knowledge thus acquired might be used to advantage in the preparation, and in the conduct through Parliament, of the Public Schools Bill. He had done so with the approval of his colleagues, and with their expressed sanction to the payment of his expenses.

Mr. Robertson entertained great respect for Mr. Parkes' ability, but professed that he was not to be trusted. He was a man of remarkable power, Mr. Robertson said during this debate, but one whose support was dangerous to any Government. When taking office, after the fall of the Martin Ministry, Mr. Robertson was advised to endeavour to get the support of Mr. Parkes to the new Administration; but the advice Mr. Robertson asserted, was not taken. There is no doubt the new Premier recognised the fact that any such attempt would result in failure. But, in stating the circumstance to the House, he made the most of the situation. " I have been incautious sometimes," he declared, " but I have not been so incautious as to let the enemy within the walls."

The debate extended over twelve days, and resulted in a majority for the Government, the division being twenty-five for the motion, and twenty-nine against it. Virtually, the Government were defeated, as several members who voted with them expressed a want of confidence in them, and six out of nine members who did not vote in the division, were understood to approve of the motion.

Eleven months afterwards, Parliament was dissolved; and Mr. Parkes came back from the elections triumphant—at the head of the poll, in the most important of the constituencies, and undoubtedly the most popular man in the country.

Very little business was done in the Legislative
Assembly by the Robertson Government, and the
Parliamentary record, generally, for the period
between the want-of-confidence motion in 1868, and
the dissolution of Parliament in 1869, was not satis-
factory.   But some notable events occurred during
the year.   Mr. Duncan was reinstated as Collector
of Customs.   Mr. Michael Fitzpatrick, who years
afterwards occupied the position of Colonial
Secretary in a Ministry formed by Mr. J. S.
Farnell, retired from the office of Under Secretary
for. Lands.   Mr. James Martin and Mr. T. A.
Murray were knighted ; Mr. Charles Cowper and
Mr. J. B. Darvall were made Companions of the
Order of St. Michael and St. George ; and Mr.
Geoffrey Eagar and Mr. J. Bowie Wilson received
permission to assume the title of " Honourable "
within the colony.   The Duke of Edinburgh visited
Sydney for the second time in H.M.S. *Galatea*,
and laid the foundation stone of the pedestal in
Hyde Park, upon which now stands Woolner's fine
statue of Captain Cook.   The Australian Library
at the corner of Bent and Macquarie Streets was
purchased by the Government, and opened as a
Free Public Library ; this last mentioned event
being preceded by the opening at Newtown of the
first public library established in New South Wales,
at which the ceremony was performed by Mr.
Parkes.

The member for Kiama had been in evidence
throughout the year.   In the Assembly, on some
important occasions, he had been by far the most
conspicuous figure there.

He had especially thrust himself into notice by
the outspoken attitude he assumed on the question
of Irish immigration. The Roman Catholics of the
community became bitterly hostile to him. The
dislike of him aroused by the passing of the Public
Schools Act and his uncompromising defence of
that Act, and increased by his proceedings as
Colonial Secretary during the O'Farrell incident,
grew to positive hatred. Nothing was too bad to
say of him ; scarcely any course too extreme to take
in the desire to check his progress or destroy his
position in public life. But, while one section of
the community detested him, another adored him.
The Protestants flocked to his support, and hailed
him as their champion. The evil of the whole thing
was that the population of the colony became
transformed into two hostile religious camps, the
effects of which are apparent even now.

Yet it would not be right to say that Mr. Parkes'
course on the question of Irish immigration was not
justified by circumstances. For many years, from
one cause or another, Irish immigrants had arrived
in the colony, at the public expense, in undue proportion to those from England, Scotland, or Wales.
As far back as 1858, the question had been prominently before the public. In that year, it had
formed the subject of a petition to the Legislative
Assembly, and of an inquiry by a select committee.

Much of the complaint at that time respecting
the Irish immigrants was directed against the Irish
girls brought to the colony for domestic service.
For this position in life, it was held they were quite

unfitted. The Immigration Agent reported that "they were unsuited to the requirements of the community, and distasteful to the majority of the people;" and it was not an uncommon thing to see in advertisements for domestic servants, "No Irish need apply." The subordinate positions in the public service, such as those of messenger, cleaner, or caretaker, were, in the large majority of cases, filled by immigrant Irishmen; and, in the police force, they were numerous. Very few entered into the productive industries of the colony.

So noticeable did this become, that strong feelings were aroused among other sections of the community; and a bill, introduced by the Robertson Government, but afterwards withdrawn, to extend the existing system of assisted immigration, was denounced as a measure offering a premium to the Roman Catholic hierarchy to Romanise the territory.

Mr. Parkes was not opposed to Irishmen or Irishwomen forming part of the general community, nor to their introduction as assisted immigrants; all he wanted was that they should not be brought to the colony at the public expense in undue proportion to immigrants from England, Scotland, and Wales.

"I am as anxious," he told the electors of East Sydney, in December, 1869, "that the people of Ireland should come here as any other class of persons; I am as anxious that Roman Catholics should come as any other persons; but I am opposed to their coming here in excessive numbers,—I am

opposed altogether to their coming in such undue
streams as to lead to change in the social character
of the country." "Let them come," he said again,
"to this free land, from England, from Scotland,
from Ireland, from any other country under the
sun; but let them come on equal terms, to be
Australian colonists."

It was easy to join to this immigration outcry
the question of religion; but Mr. Parkes was
equally emphatic in denying a want of due consideration on his part for the religious belief and
practices of any portion of the community.

"I am attached to our common Protestant
religion," he explained in the speech just quoted
from, "broadly on these great social grounds; that
I believe it is identified with the freedom of men
and the progress of the world. . . . I believe
that Protestantism is identified with universal
liberty. But this in no way puts me in the position
of denying to any man the right to worship his God
in his own way. I would be the last—I would
rather lose my life than I would be a party to
imposing disabilities on any man on account of his
faith. Let every man enjoy his own opinion, and
worship God in his own way; but do not let any
section of persons attempt to ride rough-shod over
the rest of the community."

These sentiments won Mr. Parkes wide support;
and, as Protestantism and the Public Schools Act
seemed to very many people inseparably connected,
it was little wonder that East Sydney, at this time
elected him their senior member with acclamation.

He was returned at the head of the poll with 3397
votes ; Sir James Martin being second with 3158,
Mr. David Buchanan third with 2765, and Mr.
George King fourth.   Mr. Cowper was fifth on
the poll, and, of course, defeated.

The leading article of the *Herald* the next
morning, on the result of the election, is worth
attention.

" Mr. Parkes heads the poll," it said. " There
is no possiblity of mistaking the significance of this
fact.   Mr. Parkes, on the present occasion, has
been a representative man.   His name is indentified
with the Public Schools Act ; he introduced and
carried it ; and, as President of the Council of
Education, he has continued to watch over its
operation.   His warmest admirers do not pretend
that that Act was a purely original conception, or
that the merit of framing and passing it belongs
exclusively to himself.   Nor has he, though not
deficient in self-appreciation, ever claimed any such
monopoly of merit.   But this is certain,—that
however much he may have done for the Act, he
has certainly suffered for it.   In certain quarters he
has been unsparingly abused for his connection with
it.   His public and his private character have both
been attacked ; and, from some things that have
been said and written, it might almost have been
inferred that he was little better than the author of
all evil for having been the author of the Act. For
some time past no uncertain intimation had been
given that, at the general election, a determined effort
would be made to reverse the public educational

policy, and repeal or modify the obnoxious law. This intimation has provoked a counter-movement. Organization has been met by organization. The rival parties have tried their strength against each other, and now we have the first result. The Public Schools Act is at the head of the poll."

The change of tone in the leading journal towards Mr. Parkes, indicating, as it did, from a source not previously given to paying him compliments, a fairer and fuller recognition of his services and his merits, was, equally with the firm hold his great system of public education had secured in the hearts of the people, a sign of the strong position he had attained in the political world and of his future progress and success.

CHAPTER XXI.

THE year 1870 was one of very chequered experiences to Mr. Parkes.

Before two months of it had gone he had resigned his seat in the Legislative Assembly for East Sydney, choosing to sit there for another constituency which, like East Sydney, had, at the general election, returned him to Parliament as its representative. A few days afterwards, he was the unsuccessful defendant in a slander action. Later on, he severed his connection with the Council of Education, where he had worked earnestly and well in the interests of the Public Schools Act for four years. About the same time, through financial difficulties in the commercial business in which he was then engaged, he was obliged to retire completely from the Assembly. A fortnight subsequently, he was re-elected to Parliament, the election taking place on November 3rd. On December 9th, for the third time during the twelve months, he relinquished his position as a member of the House; and the year closed with him out of Parliament, and out of public life. The ups and

downs in this short period of his career were frequent and vexatious.

His resignation early in the year, as one of the
members in the Legislative Assembly for East
Sydney, was due to his having been returned at the
General Election by both East Sydney and Kiama.

At the time of the election at East Sydney, he
was a candidate for Kiama, and had expressed his
determination to go to the poll there, in order that
the electors of Kiama, who were his constituents in
the previous Parliament, might deliver their verdict
upon his character and proceedings in Parliament in
relation to the select committee obtained by Mr.
Macleay respecting the crime of O'Farrell. Their
verdict was an emphatic approval; and, notwithstanding the flattering manner in which the premier
constituency of the colony had dealt with him, he
determined to remain among the electors with whom
he had been in association, through the period which
had been marked by some of the most harassing
of his troubles and some of the greatest of his
triumphs.

One thing only dimmed the lustre of his public
position at this time, and that, but temporarily. In
his speech in the Assembly upon the report of Mr.
Macleay's select committee, he had alluded to one
of the witnesses examined by the committee, in
terms which could not afterwards be justified. Supplied with information which, on what he considered
to be satisfactory assurances, he believed to be correct, he used it; and the speech being afterwards
published and circulated by him in pamphlet form,

an action was brought against him for slander, with the result that a verdict was obtained against him, with damages, to the extent of £100.

The case excited much interest, and the verdict was a subject of comment far and near. It gave much satisfaction to the enemies of Mr. Parkes, but it did not lessen the number of his friends. To them, the voluntary stepping forth from the shelter of the privilege that protected him, so long as the speech was not published by him beyond the walls of Parliament, proved his honesty in the matter; and his popularity was undiminished.

In Parliament, at this time, he was, as usual, watchful and active, but not taking a conspicuous part in the proceedings.

Outside the Assembly, he gave most of his attention to his private business. Unfortunately, this business did not answer expectation, and financial troubles again began to wind their toils around him. In the month of October, it became known that he had been obliged to place his affairs in the Insolvency Court. He was trading at the time as Parkes & Co., and doing what appeared to be an extensive business as a general merchant. Friends had assisted him, and he had collected together a large stock of goods; but assured success did not follow; and, after vainly endeavouring to cope with the difficulties which gathered about him through loss of trade and other attendant evils, he was obliged to succumb. He was declared insolvent, his estimated liabilities being £32,000, and his assets £13,300.

Insolvency then, as now, meant to a member of the Legislature that he must resign his seat in Parliament, and, if he wished to return, submit himself to his constituents for re-election. Mr. Parkes resigned his seat for Kiama. Only a short time before Mr. Robertson had, from a similar cause, resigned his seat for West Sydney, and had been re-elected. Mr. Parkes was re elected for Kiama. His seat in the Assembly was declared vacant on October 19th, and he was returned on November 3rd. So far matters were satisfactory.

But his position in Parliament was very considerably affected for the time by the proceedings in relation to his affairs in the Insolvency Court. The details of his indebtedness, which disclosed the names of his creditors, provoked much comment among those who were never backward in seizing upon anything that could be used to injure him. Dislike, on the part of some people, towards him was so intense, that any opportunity affording the means by which he might be placed in unfavourable circumstances, was eagerly seized.

It seemed quite possible to use this second insolvency in his career greatly to his detriment. If his political progress could not be finally stopped it might, at least, be very materially checked. It was nothing to persons who thought in this way that misfortune, rather than any other cause, was the prime reason of his difficulties. Of no concern to them was it that some of those who regretted his position, and were still his firm friends, were among his largest creditors. The chance to do him some harm was apparent, and it must be used. It was used, and, it seemed at the time, with thorough success.

In December the Robertson Government, in which Mr. Charles Cowper was Colonial Secretary, retired from office; and, just before their resignation, Ministers appointed Mr. Cowper to the position of Agent-General of the colony in London.

The appointment raised a loud outcry. Mr. Cowper's fitness for the position was not questioned; but the manner of the appointment was unsparingly condemned as a gross breach of constitutional practice. It was the first instance in New South Wales of a retiring Government appointing one of its number to a permanent office under the Crown; and the danger of Mr. Cowper's case establishing itself as a precedent was urged on all sides.

Mr. Parkes, with the fine sense of constitutional procedure which he always showed, saw the danger as clearly as anybody, and determined to do what he could to remove it. He gave notice in the Assembly of his intention to move—

"(1) That the practice introduced by the Ministry holding office, 1869-70, of appointing its own members to permanent places of profit in the public service, is contrary to the spirit of the Constitution, detrimental to the character and efficiency of government, and ought not to be followed by succeeding Ministries.

"(2) That the foregoing resolution be presented by address to the Governor, praying that His Excellency will cause it to be entered on the minutes of the Executive Council."

No sooner was the notice of this motion given than it was laid hold of, and, in conjunction with the proceedings in the Insolvency Court, used against Mr. Parkes with telling effect.

The editor of the leading journal of the colony was, at this period, as he had been for some years, very hostile to Mr. Parkes. Early, in the latter's public career, the two were mutual admirers, and, to a certain extent, friends. Brought together in the days when the agitation for the cessation of transportation to the colonies was at its height, there was much in the public movements of the time attractive to both. But while the mutual admiration in some degree remained,—for in the character and acts of each, there were points that compelled admiration—the friendship ended, and was never renewed. The editor was remarkable for the bitterness of his pen. His leading articles, while unpolished, and not always meritorious in a literary sense, were invariably able and effective. Disjointed, rough, sometimes even coarse, they nevertheless went straight for the object in view, hurling sneer or epithet, plainly stated charge or innuendo, with such force and continuity, that the unhappy subject of the writer's wrath emerged, at the bottom of the column, as a battered and defeated man might come out from the mauling he has received in the prize ring.

The *Herald* made Mr. Parkes' notice of motion the subject of one of its articles, and tacked to it his position as an insolvent. Already the paper had expressed disapproval of the manner in which

Mr. Cowper had been appointed to the Agent-
Generalship, and to that extent was in agreement
respecting it with Mr. Parkes. But it denied his
right, under the circumstances of his position, to
take such action in the matter as his notice of
motion indicated.

What justification could he have, it asked, for
" taking a position so prominent in the censure of
political immorality " ?   With what title did he
appear in the House as an accuser ?   He had done
distinguished services in the Legislature ; and it
must be admitted that his re-election to the position
of a member gave him all the rights and suggested
the duties of the position. But the public conscience revolted at the anomaly. It could only be
in consequence of an inadvertence on the part of
those who framed the Constitution, that a constituency was given the power to place in the
Legislature an uncertificated insolvent, who might
become the arbiter of the fate of a Ministry and
even its head.

Thus the paper argued.   It referred to the
schedule of his liabilities, to the *personnel* of his
creditors, to the amount of his debts compared with
his assets, and to the manner in which the debts
had been incurred.   It drew attention to the power
associated with a seat in Parliament held by a man
of conspicuous ability and courage ; and, pointing out
how formidable this might be to anyone provoking
his hostility, it hinted at the danger of its even
affecting the administration of Justice. Rumour was

abroad, it stated, that office was to be reserved for Mr. Parkes in the incoming Government, so that he might take his seat in the Cabinet immediately he obtained his certificate from the Insolvency Court ; and it declared that the Governor would be forgetful of all that was honourable in administration, if he were to allow any man to come into the Cabinet under the circumstances.

"It is a misfortune," the article observed in conclusion, "that those who are candidates for office in Government are almost uniformly poor, but, at least, let us take some security that we may have a reasonable presumption that if they are poor they are upright."

Mr. Parkes, in response to the article, promptly resigned his seat in the Assembly. The insinuation that his presence there, while before the Insolvency Court, might influence the officials and the Judge of that Court to the detriment of Justice, seemed to him capable of being answered in no other effective way. Writing to the Speaker of the Legislative Assembly on the day the article appeared, he said :

"The *Sydney Morning Herald* of this morning publishes an article, on a notice standing in my name on the Votes and Proceedings of the Legislative Assembly. In this article, it is affirmed that my holding a seat in Parliament, and exercising the privileges which inseparably belong to such seat, must in various ways prejudicially affect the administration of the law. It is not possible for me to meet the statements, thus made to the world with all the influence of the most widely circulated journal

U

in the colony, except by depriving myself of the power which, in my case, is represented as dangerous to the community. I therefore resign the seat to which I have been elected as member for the electoral district of Kiama."

The resignation, of course, excited remark, and met with approval and disapproval. Those who could not see in it the high sense of political recti- tude which prompted it, sneered at, and ridiculed it. Among them, were some members of the Assembly, notably Mr. Samuel, Mr. Garrett, and Mr. Forster ; and a strong effort was made by these to prevent the letter to the Speaker from appearing upon the Assembly records.

A day or two afterwards, Mr. Parkes wrote a letter to the *Herald*, with the heading "Parting Words,"—an eloquent, manly, forcible explanation and defence of his position, much more in the style of the old-world statesman, than in that of the colonial politician, and brimful of his great ability from beginning to end.

"It is obvious I could not meet the case which had been conjured up against me," he wrote, "by any other course than the one I adopted, and I wished this to be known. It was a thing incapable of being refuted or explained. I do not fear, but that all persons whose opinion is of value, will understand both my motive and my object, and I should not have expected to be understood by the gentlemen who indulged their spitefulness in the Assembly on Friday evening.

"To confound a position so distinct as this with that of weakly giving way before the ordinary animadversions of a public journal," the letter went on to say, "is not more disingenuous than it is absurd. For many years past I have been the subject of your adverse criticisms; so much so indeed that it has appeared to me that any favourable notice of parts of my public conduct of which you could not but approve has been grudgingly bestowed, while my faults have been dealt with in terms of severity not often measured out to the faults of other men.

"My letter to the Assembly," it proceeded, "was the last available peg, it seems, on which my enemies could exhibit the rags of their malice;" and then it referred to Mr. Samuel, and to Mr. Forster, "who, of course had a fling at the fallen object of his long cherished hatred."

"Mr. Forster," the letter declared, "strained his ingenious malignity to the utmost, and dared to suggest to the public mind the suspicion that I have enriched myself at the expense of others. It is bad enough," it continued, "to be in the position I am in, but, whatever may be my misfortunes or my faults, I and those belonging to me are left penniless in the world, and dependent on others for a home. In my extremity, however, I have health; I have such ability as God has bestowed upon me; and I have some friends. And, fortunately for me, there is sufficient evidence, in the possession of a sufficient number of persons, to clear my character from the cruel aspersions flung out so wantonly by Mr. Forster."

"As to my absence from Parliament," it said in conclusion, "I am well aware that my place will be easily supplied. I entered it young, and full of hope ; I leave it no longer young, but not in despair. At least I take nothing away with me. I have neither decoration nor empty title—no honorary post, nor compliment of power. No son of mine is eating the bread of the people he cannot earn. I leave something behind me which cannot be undone or taken from me, and which men will hold in remembrance and honour. For the rest I seek no sympathy, and am prepared to bear the burden alone. No man can control the future, and to resolve against events which cannot be foreseen would be folly; but, for any personal interest that I can possibly have to serve, it would not cause me a single pang of regret if my political existence now terminates."

The *Herald* replied to the letter by publishing another article. Compelled to take some notice of the forcible protest which Mr. Parkes had made against the unsparing censure of some of his enemies, the newspaper sought to explain its course on the ground simply of the inconsistency between Mr. Parkes' position as a member of Parliament and as an insolvent.

The complaint, it said, was not that he had done anything which could not be justified or explained, but that he was " passing to and fro from a high place in the Legislative Chamber to the tribunal of the Insolvent judge." It was again bitterly personal, and closed with the following remarks, the last seven words printed in italics : " We hope we shall not have occasion to return to Mr. Parkes' letter; and we can only express unfeigned regret that a man of abilities so undoubted, of public services so distinguished, and who has obtained such marks of friendly consideration from many, should be able to say that he is ' left penniless in the world and dependent upon others for a home ; ' and we may add that this cannot long be the case with such a man if, with all his other qualities, he could command some share of that worldly wisdom *which often is another word for virtue.*"

Mr. Forster then took up the subject, dealing with it more particularly in respect of the reference which the letter " Parting Words " had made to him and his enmity. His defence of himself was not lost sight of; but it was made the means for a long and scathing attack on Mr. Parkes, which was evidently the principal object of the writer.

Some statements of business relations between the two men in the days of the *Empire*, and an unfortunate pecuniary difficulty which arose in connection with them, drew from Mr. Parkes a rejoinder, with the consequence that the correspondence, comprising several letters of considerable length, was continued almost to the end of the year, with much recrimination, and with no other definite result than the regret of the friends of either writer and the amusement of those who find entertainment in the quarrels of prominent public men.

One feature of the correspondence, from its commencement to its close, was the moderation and dignity in the matter and style of Mr. Parkes' letters as compared with those of Mr. Forster. Through the whole of the latter it was apparent that the chief object in view was to sting ; and the more venom with which the sting could be administered, the more the writer seemed to chuckle and be satisfied. With Mr. Parkes, while he did not fail to reply to Mr. Forster's attacks with what effectiveness he could bring to play, there was an evident desire to leave to the judgment of the public the charges made against him, rather than put himself to the unnecessary task of explaining that respecting which they were well acquainted. And from the first of his letters to the last, there was apparent in them a keen sense of the misfortune of his position, which had deprived him, at least for the time, of political influence, of business, of means of livelihood for those near and dear to him, and of a home.

"I hope," he pathetically said, in the letter which, as far as he was concerned, closed the correspondence,—" I hope I feel the weakness of the position which I occupy, but, if I am not spotless like Mr. Forster, the world, after all, may think that my life has not been without its better purposes and its better actions."

This melancholy close of an eventful year—it was in the Christmas season that this correspondence took place—marked an important period in Mr. Parkes' life. Before twelve more months had

passed he had risen phœnix-like from the difficulties
that had borne him down; he was again in Parliament, his position in politics stronger than ever;
and a few weeks later on, as head of a Government,
he had commenced a long career as Prime Minister
which, while it was of singular benefit to the colony,
placed him in popularity and political reputation
above the most prominent and able of his enemies.

CHAPTER XXII.

DEFEATING THE MARTIN-ROBERTSON COALITION.

THE opportunity to re-enter Parliament came in December, 1871, with a bye-election at Mudgee. The vacancy in the representation of the electorate was caused by the resignation of Mr. Matthew Henry Stephen, now His Honor Mr. Justice Stephen ; and Mr. Parkes, being pressed to allow himself to be· nominated as a candidate, consented, and was elected.

He had been repeatedly urged by his friends to return to public life. By many his absence was regarded as a public loss. Politics were not in a satisfactory state, and the rival parties in the Assembly were so curiously situated that the prospect of useful legislation was very meagre. The want of a man of ability, independence, and courage, such as Mr. Parkes had always shown himself to be, to raise his voice and take his stand in the interest of the people, was very apparent.

The financial policy of the Government was open to grave question ; and indiscreet proceedings on their part towards Victoria, on the subject of border duties, had threatened a serious unfriendliness between the two colonies.   In this respect the condition of affairs gave rise to much condemnatory criticism.

.Worse, however, in the view of a large proportion of the members of the Legislative Assembly, and of the general public, was the circumstance that Sir James Martin and Mr. Robertson had entered into what was regarded as a wholly unjustifiable coalition, and were together in the Government, the former as Attorney-General and Premier, and the latter as Colonial Secretary.

The outcry which this extraordinary alliance caused exceeded the adverse comment which, on any previous occasion, had followed an unusual event in political life.   During the whole of their public careers the two Ministers had been so opposed to each other, so invariably hostile, that their taking office in the same Government, or even sitting on the same side of the House, was never dreamed of. Each had been the leader of a party which had not moderated its opposition, nor lessened its hostility, at any time or under any circumstances ; and, when the coalition of the two leaders was announced, it came as a thunderclap to the two parties as it did to the public.

In common with most persons, Mr. Parkes strongly disapproved of the coalition ; and the condition into which affairs in Parliament had drifted made him, at last, anxious for the opportunity to return there.   Mr. Robertson, he regarded as a deserter from his party ; Sir James Martin was, in his opinion, a traitor.

The nomination for Mudgee was received with general approval. The *Herald*, mentioning the matter as an item of news, said the ranks of the Opposition in Parliament would be greatly strengthened by Mr. Parkes' return. At Mudgee, he was alluded to as the gentleman " upon whose coming the colony waited." Before the electors he spoke vigorously, showing unmistakeably the unabated strength of his position in the public life of the country, and indicating his assured political progress in the future. Nominated for Mudgee on 28th December, 1871, in less than six months from that time he was at the head of a strong and, as it proved, useful Government.

" I know," he declared on the Mudgee hustings, " that I speak to-day with a voice that will be potential in the country. I know that that voice will reach every district, and that it will be listened to in other Australian colonies, with as much interest as if it belonged to those colonies." Notwithstanding his reverses of fortune—his debts and his forced retirements from Parliament—he was still the most popular man in the colony, the man to whom the masses looked for the needful reform of the abuses which were interfering with the proper operations of government.

The Martin-Robertson combination, and the proceedings of the Ministry since they had taken office, he denounced unsparingly.

As it had happened, he was the first person with whom Sir James Martin had any communication after being entrusted by the Governor with the

formation of what afterwards proved to be the
coalition Government; and, during the course of a
conversation upon the difficulties surrounding
the situation, Sir James Martin mentioned Mr.
Robertson and Mr. Forster in such a way as to
lead Mr. Parkes to conclude that the coalition, which
subsequently took place, must have been contemplated by Sir James Martin while sitting in
Opposition and receiving the support of Mr.
Robertson's opponents. Mr. Parkes told Sir James
Martin that the bare mention of such a proceeding
as Mr. Robertson and he coming together in the
same Government, would create a storm amongst
his friends. For two gentlemen who had been
opposing each other " in office, out of office, on the
hustings, in the Assembly,—in fact everywhere, for
a period of twelve years," and had denounced each
other as the worst man in the country, to combine
in this manner, was, to Mr. Parkes, perfectly
startling.

But the coalition taking place, the storm it was
expected to cause immediately raged around the
Government. Mr. Robertson, reluctant to face his
constituents, endeavoured to avoid submitting himself
for re-election by contending that his acceptance in
the new Ministry of the office of Colonial Secretary
was a mere exchange from the office of Secretary
for Lands, which he had held in the preceding
Administration up to the time of its giving place
to its successor. In this contention he was upheld
by the Speaker; but the Assembly, in which he
made his appearance and attempted to proceed with

some business, passed a motion declaring his seat vacant, and thus compelled him to go before the electors. Then he published an address, a paragraph of which brought Mr. Parkes and Sir James Martin into a curious correspondence which was read to the Mudgee electors.

"I have never hidden from the public," the address represented Mr. Robertson as saying, "the hope I entertained that the course of the last Government would have the effect of greatly allaying the unfortunate feeling that had been engendered, and had produced so much acrimony, between class and class, country and country, creed and creed, of the people of our community; and I trust and believe that the determination of the present Government, to deal equally with all classes of the people, will tend to still further cultivate the improved popular feeling in that regard already so gratifyingly apparent."

To Mr. Parkes this appeared to be nothing less than a reproduction of the charge made against the Martin-Parkes Government of 1866, and particularly against himself, in connection with the crime and execution of O'Farrell; and he drew Sir James Martin's attention to it.

"It is impossible," he wrote, "not to recognise in these words the charge which has been persistently made by this gentleman against both you and me, for the worst of party purposes, for the last three years. Under the new circumstances in which he is placed, Mr. Robertson must intend to direct his charge against me alone; but I will not suffer myself to believe that you can have concurred in this artful attempt, in the name of your Government, to exasperate sectarian feeling against one who was long your colleague, and whose support and fidelity in that relation you have frequently acknowledged. Nor can I suppose that you would desire to separate yourself from your former colleagues, in the responsibility that may justly attach to the conduct of your Government. This cannot be considered by me as a light matter, and I am sure it will not be so regarded by you."

Sir James Martin did not put upon the paragraph in the address the interpretation set forth in Mr. Parkes' letter. He did not see in it any attack upon the conduct of the Government of which Mr. Parkes and he had been members; and, "for that conduct," he wrote, "I, as the head of that Government, was of course responsible, and that responsibility I never at any time had the slightest intention of withdrawing from. I think," his letter said, in conclusion, "that the manner in which I have acted on all occasions ought to have rendered your inquiry unnecessary."

This was not satisfactory to Mr. Parkes; and he again wrote to Sir James Martin on the subject, pointing out that the paragraph was distinctly the charge which had been made a hundred times, generally against the former Government of Sir James Martin, and, on other occasions, more specifically against himself. What was the meaning of the words? he asked. To whom did they refer? "If you do not see in these words any attack upon the

Government of which you and I were members, do you see in them any attack upon me as a member of that Government ? "

Sir James Martin responded with emphasis.

" For all official acts of yourself as a member of the Government of which I was the head," he wrote, " I, and all our then colleagues, are just as responsible as you are. All those acts had our fullest concurrence. If Mr. Robertson's address implies—and I am sure it does not—a censure on any of those acts, the present Government has nothing to do with that censure, is no party to it, and repudiates it altogether. If that address implies, as I do not believe it does, a censure on you individually, for some act of your own, not official, and in which your colleagues took no part, then I have nothing to say to it. It is a matter between you and Mr. Robertson ; and does not, and cannot, concern us. I say now, as I have always said, that our Government never did anything to set class against class, or stir up religious animosity in any way. If those things were done, they were not done by our Government, or by you as a member of it, but by persons opposed to us. We did our utmost to preserve the public peace, and act impartially to all parties." And the letter went on : " I would, in conclusion, suggest that if you want to ascertain Mr. Robertson's exact meaning, you should apply to that gentleman himself."

To some extent this second letter from Sir James Martin satisfied Mr. Parkes ; but further correspondence appeared to him to be necessary. Though Sir James Martin clearly exonerated him from any charge such as the paragraph in Mr. Robertson's address seemed to imply, he did not deal with the paragraph itself in the manner Mr. Parkes considered requisite.

"When you take the liberty," Mr. Parkes observed in another letter, " of suggesting to me that I should apply to Mr. Robertson for his exact meaning, I must remind you that for five years you have constantly impressed upon me that his word was not to be depended upon in anything, and that there was nothing in the world which he was not capable of doing." And, thinking he was quite justified in demanding from Sir James Martin an explicit interpretation of the objectionable paragraph, the letter proceeded : " As you say that *you are sure* that the passage in Mr. Robertson's address does not imply a censure on any of the acts of your former Administration, and that you do not believe it applies to me personally, perhaps you will tell me what is its new meaning, so that I may not be } misled by confounding it with the calumny of old times, which was embodied in the same mind, in the same language.

"I think some excuse may be made for the perplexed light in which I am compelled to view the strange things that are passing before me. For more than two years I, and many others, were led by you, and induced to sacrifice our time and convenience, to incur enmities, and often to act against our own discretion and sense of propriety,

for the purpose of ejecting Mr. Robertson from
the place for which, you were never tired of assur-
ing us, he was utterly unfit, and which he could not
hold without danger to the country. During all
that time we were never told—I do not think
any of us suspected—that the real object for
which we were contending was to enable you and
Mr. Robertson to make terms in dividing between
yourselves the offices of State. If Mr. Robertson
was the proper person to be Colonial Secretary, we
might have thought, not unreasonably, that it would
be best to keep him in that office when he had all
the prestige and influence of being also the head of
the Administration to enable him to be useful in it.
But I venture to say that it would have been indignantly resented as an aspersion on your character,
if anyone of your followers had been told that you
were leading him into the arms of Mr. Robertson,
Mr. Garrett, and Mr. Eckford."

The relentlessness of the logic of this statement
of the position was equalled only by the severity of
the castigation which the letter administered. The
whip was one of scorpions.

"You must not think," the letter continued,
"that I am exceeding the limits of propriety in
writing to you in these plain words. You invited
my co-operation, and received my support, on terms
of hostility to Mr. Robertson, in gaining the
position which enabled you to do what you have
done. I therefore am entitled to speak. You may
think that you have formed a strong Government.
If a 'strong Government' can arise from severing

political attachments, from bringing political enemies into combination in the place of friends, from destroying the faith of the people in our public men, and from creating in the popular mind the idea that political life is a juggle, your Government has the prospect of being strong.

"I have written this," he said in conclusion, "without any abatement of my personal regard for yourself, if you will continue to accept it, and without any change in my wishes for your honour and usefulness. Depend upon it, he is the best friend who speaks unreservedly when there is need for it, and you are not likely to hear much plain speaking from others."

When this correspondence was made public at Mudgee, it was twelve months old. The proceedings of the Government during the twelve months had increased Mr. Parkes' disapproval of their position ; and, as he appeared at Mudgee as a candidate who if elected would seek to eject the Ministry from power, he considered the publication of the correspondence to be justifiable and useful.

Mudgee sent him back to Parliament, and the Assembly very quickly became sensible of his presence there again. He had told the Mudgee electors that he had no wish for office for its own sake, but that any man standing in the relations he did, who went into Parliament, must be prepared for office if it legitimately came in his way. It was then, he considered, not only permissible for him to take it, but his duty to do so. Office was not far off.

v

The burning question of the time was that of the border duties. Not only was it setting the two largest and most important colonies of the Australian group by the ears; it was stirring up feeling of such discontent among the people of the southern border districts, as to threaten the dismemberment from New South Wales of a large and valuable section of its territory.

The Martin-Robertson Government had conceived the idea that the amount of money then being paid by Victoria to New South Wales, in lieu of the collection of duties on goods passing into New South Wales over the River Murray, was considerably less than it ought to be. It was £60,000, and the New South Wales Government declared it ought to be at least £100,000. Victoria, though contending that £60,000 fully represented the duties on the goods passing across the border, offered to pay whatever sum a careful investigation of the matter showed to be justifiable, provided New South Wales agreed to receive that sum whether it should prove to be more or less than £60,000. To this Sir James Martin refused to accede; and, at a dinner given him at Albury when on his way to a conference in Melbourne, he declared his determination to have the £100,000.

Nothing would induce him to give way. Victoria, he had got it into his head, was profiting to the extent of at least £40,000 a year at the expense of New South Wales, and this £40,000 he would have, or custom-offices should be established along the border and the duties collected. Intercolonial unfriendliness, or even hostility, he regarded as insignificant compared with the obligation of getting hold of this money. Discontent in the border districts troubled him no more than the time it caused him to expend in taking measures to meet any possible violation of the law. A threat to forcibly evade the payment of duties, if border custom-houses should be established, he replied to by swearing-in special constables and providing other police precautions. Feeling in the country, criticism in the press, or opposition in Parliament, had no effect upon his decision. Having the courage of his convictions he was resolved to carry out his purpose, if it were possible to do so, though in the face of general disapproval and the probability of defeat.

Mr. Parkes caused great amusement at the time by an imaginary description of the ludicrous appearance of Mr. Robertson, dressed in cocked hat and sword, drilling himself at night on the rocks at Watson's Bay, preparatory to marching to Albury at the head of a small military force not long before established in Sydney by the Government. Ridicule, however, was only one of the weapons he employed to defeat the intentions of the Ministry. It did good service, as in such situations it always does. But his trenchant criticism of the Ministerial policy, and his defence of the public interest, did more.

Immediately on the assembling of Parliament after the Christmas holidays of 1871, the Government were met by a hostile motion on the subject of the border duties. Mr. William Forster moved that the terms offered by the Government of

Victoria were reasonable and ought to have been
accepted, that the collection of the duties was
highly inexpedient, and that immediate steps should
be taken to obviate any necessity for collecting
them.   The resolution was carried by twenty-seven
votes to twenty-three, and the Assembly adjourned
in order that the Ministry might consider their
position.   It was expected they would resign ; but,
to the surprise of everybody, it was announced to
the House next day that the Governor, on the
advice of his Ministers, had decided to dissolve
the Parliament.   Supply was to be asked for to
cover the period of the elections, but, whether
granted or not, the dissolution would take place.

The course taken by the Governor aroused great
indignation ; and the Assembly refused supply.

To most members of the House, as to the
majority of the public, a dissolution of Parliament
seemed both unnecessary and unjustifiable.   It did
not appear to be difficult to .form a new and stable
Government from the Opposition in the Assembly,
who could deal with the border duties question in
the way the majority of the House desired.   There
were several measures of importance before Parliament requiring immediate attention.   To close the
Assembly, and plunge the country into the turmoil
of a general election, would aggravate the border
difficulty, and generally injure the public welfare.

.   "Deeply influenced by these various considerations, and anxious in particular to secure
peace and the good-will of our fellow colonists
upon the Border," the Legislative Assembly, by

resolution, respectfully requested His Excellency not to dissolve Parliament at such a critical period.

The reply of the Governor was a proclamation in a *Government Gazette Extraordinary*, the next morning, proroguing Parliament preparatory to sending it to the country. In the afternoon of the day on which the House declined to grant supply, and passed their resolution protesting against dissolution, Lord Belmore left Sydney for his country residence at Sutton Forest; but, very early the next morning, an hour or two after the division, Sir James Martin was speeding by special train to Moss Vale, for the purpose of obtaining the authority of the Governor to the issue of the proclamation necessary to prevent another meeting of the Assembly. Ignorant of the course Ministers were taking, and not doubting that His Excellency would receive, with due deference, the respectful address of the House, and give it fair consideration, hon. members knew nothing of the prorogation until, going to the Assembly Chamber at the usual hour in the afternoon, they found the doors closed, and the *Gazette Extraordinary* informing them that their presence there was no longer required.

The general election which followed ended disastrously for the Government. It was marked with much party zeal and acrimony. In Sydney, the excitement was very great. The question of the border duties was that upon which Parliament had been dissolved; but, for electioneering purposes, the objectionable union upon which the Martin-Robertson Government had been based, and its results generally, were made the principal indictment against the Ministry in the speeches of Opposition candidates at their meetings and on the hustings.

The lead in the attack, and the strength of it, lay with Mr. Parkes. Though, but a few months previously, he was struggling under a burden of debt which had compelled his retirement from Parliament and public life, and had raised about him a hornet's nest of vindictive critics and calumniators, he was now far-and-away the most popular man in the country. His presence before an assemblage of electors was everywhere greeted with enthusiasm. Where other men could not obtain a hearing, he was listened to with admiration, and cheered to the echo.

Much that he said was eloquent, forcible, and such as to safeguard and promote the public good. Some passages in his speeches might, with advantage, have been left unsaid. But electioneering speeches are never without the spice of extravagance. Serious disorders are believed to sometimes require remedies of an extreme nature, and votes, in an election, are frequently won in a good cause by means which those who have employed them are not, after the struggle is over, always disposed to defend.

The electors recognised and supported the efforts of Mr. Parkes to defeat the Ministry. Purity of political life and good government were his watchwords, and they rang through the country from one end to the other. His mission was " to break up the factions existing in the colony, to punish traitors, to vindicate our institutions, and to roll back the tide of corruption which had set in."

To him one of the worse features in the coalition of Sir James Martin and Mr. Robertson, was that it had been brought about with the object of rendering opposition in the Legislative Assembly impossible. For sixteen years—from the time of the introduction of responsible government—he had constantly urged the electors to keep in view, above all other considerations, the necessity for preserving the independence of Parliament. " Bad men may rise to power," he had said ; " bad laws may be enacted ; but you can sooner or later eject the bad men from power, and erase the bad laws from the statute book. Once, however, degrade your Parliamentary institutions, and a wrong is done to the country which will not be remedied during your lifetime."

Occupying a foremost place in the front rank of the opponents of the Government, it was imperative that, in this general election, he should appear as a candidate for East Sydney, where Sir James Martin, with three of his colleagues, expected to be returned. Mr. Parkes announced that he stood for East Sydney to oppose Sir James Martin ; and the electors responded most cordially. When the contest was over he was at the top of the poll, with 3270 votes, while Sir James Martin and his friends were hopelessly defeated. Some days subsequently, Sir James Martin found a seat at East Macquarie ; but three of the Ministers failed to secure election anywhere, and were, therefore, not in Parliament when the elections terminated.

The defeat of the Martin-Robertson Ministry was satisfactory as an emphatic expression of popular disapproval of both the formation of the Government and their proceedings; but it was gratifying in another respect.

At this time there were in existence in the colony, with their headquarters in Sydney, two very active and powerful politico-religious organizations. They still exist, but are not so powerful to-day as they were twenty-five years ago. Now, as then, they seek to rule the political life of the country; but their influence upon Parliamentary elections and the formation of Governments is, at the present time, very much weaker than it was. Their origin can be found in the disturbed state of public feeling which arose from the circumstances surrounding O'Farrell's attempted assassination of the Duke of Edinburgh.

Many of the Protestants of the community, conceiving the idea that the well-being of the country was threatened by all who were of the same religious faith as that professed by the assassin, banded themselves together, with the determination to resist all attempts on the part of Roman Catholics to obtain positions of prominence. In defence of their right to all advantages open to the people in common, the Roman Catholics entered upon an organized procedure which became as aggressive as the association to which they were opposed. Thus the colony came virtually to be divided into two hostile camps, the operations of which were the more objectionable because they were conducted, as far as possible, with secrecy.

The Protestants, being more numerous than the Roman Catholics, were, generally, more powerful. Their leaders were men of considerable influence. Whether this influence was justified, to the extent of the power which they were able to wield over their followers, is doubtful. But the idea prevailed that every man who was a member of the organization was at the bidding of its leaders. The consequence was that Governments were in a large degree subject to them, and elections were special objects of their attention. It was boasted by them that they were able to defeat any candidate, and upset any Government. Whom they would they set up, and whom they would they pulled down. Nothing associated with the Government of the country escaped them. Even the public offices knew them and felt their power, every vacancy being to them a source of concern, and a means for serving their adherents and assisting their cause.

The leaders of the Protestant organization gave their support to the Martin-Robertson Administration, and denounced Mr. Parkes for the severity of his opposition to it. Mr. Parkes, in return, denounced them; and condemned their undue interference with politics and public men. He did so in the Assembly, during the proceedings which led to the defeat of Sir James Martin and his colleagues, and he repeated it on the hustings.

The outcome of the polling at East Sydney, while it was an unmistakeable condemnation of the

Government, was regarded as in a large measure an emphatic declaration, on the part of a majority of the electors, that the time had come when the operations of the two religious organizations should be checked.

Previous to the election Mr. Parkes was warned that he would have to meet their opposition to his return; and, during the election, the strongest efforts they were capable of putting forth were used to bring about his defeat. It was announced that his rejection was certain. But, as was pointed out afterwards, a greater party in the State than either of the two organizations, profoundly influenced by the conviction that there should be in politics no coercion of the kind that had been put in force, and irresistible in their power when once thoroughly aroused, appeared on the scene. Free citizens, they declared, should not be defrauded of their rights by anyone. The cry spread through the electorate, and right-minded Catholics, as well as Protestants, recorded their votes in unison with this assertion of their independence.

The triumphant success of Mr. Parkes, said a writer, commenting on the result of the election and the antagonism of the two organised bodies against him, was, in no small degree, due to "his defiance of pretensions which the city had come to feel were both disgraceful and unfounded."

CHAPTER XXIII.

THE new Parliament met on the last day of April, 1872, and on the day following was officially opened. Mr. Parkes was elected leader of the Opposition.

A few days previously the Martin-Robertson Ministry had tendered the resignation of their offices, but had been requested to remain in their positions until after there had been transacted the business necessary to the opening of the session, and to the passing of a supply bill to cover certain expenditure incurred during the period of the elections. Three of the Ministers having been rejected by the electors, were not present in the House.

Lord Belmore, who had dissolved the previous Parliament, had left the colony for England; and, pending the arrival of his successor, Sir Alfred Stephen, in his capacity of Chief Justice, was acting as Governor. Sir Alfred Stephen, with a view to the formation of a new Government, sent for Mr. Forster.

This he did before Parliament met. Why he should send for Mr. Forster was not quite clear. Mr. Forster was the member of the Opposition who moved the motion which brought about the defeat of Sir James Martin and his colleagues, but the weight of the defeat had proceeded from Mr. Parkes. There was, however, on the part of some influential members of the Legislature an intense feeling against Mr. Parkes, and their dearest wish was to exclude him from any chance of further power.

" I will not," said a member of the Assembly on one occasion, "go the length .of saying that His Excellency will not make the honourable member a Minister, but I will say that I should deeply regret to see him belong to any Administration in this country. Whatever his views may be of the lofty position he thinks he occupies, I, for one, am no believer either in his exalted position or in his capability to benefit the country in or out of office." It would not be right to say that this feeling influenced the Acting Governor, but he must have been aware of its existence.

Mr. Forster accepted the task of forming a new Administration, and failed. His only chance of success was the co-operation of Mr. Parkes, and this he refused to have. Leading members of the Opposition whom he asked to accept office in his Government, and who were ready to do so provided he sought the assistance of Mr. Parkes, urged him to take that course. But, though it was plain to everyone that his success depended upon it, he went his way alone. For several days he tried to get a Ministry together, the Assembly adjourning twice or three times to accommodate him, and, ultimately, was obliged to inform the Acting Governor that his efforts had been futile. Sir Alfred Stephen then sent for Mr. Parkes.

The announcement of this step was received with mixed feelings both inside and outside Parliament. While a majority of the members of the Opposition supported Mr. Parkes, and recognised his claims to office there were as already mentioned, others in the House who would have preferred almost anybody else in the position he now occupied. His great ability was admitted by all; of his powerful influence in politics everyone was aware; but, so bitter was the enmity which many entertained towards him, that his exclusion for the remainder of his life from all chance of place and power would have been to them a matter of the greatest satisfaction.

Dr. Lang, speaking at a meeting of the electors of East Sydney, and alluding to this feeling, referred to Mr. Parkes as "that great grievance, but the friend of the community." The phrase very well describes the subject of the reference. Mr. Parkes was, in truth, a great grievance to those who disliked him; but, by the general public, he was regarded as a friend, ever watchful of their interests, and full of courage and strength to protect them.

Among the great bulk of the community his popularity was unabated,—in consequence of the border duties difficulty it had extended; and the opportunity afforded him to form a Government, of which he would be the head, was greeted with many manifestations of approval.

The leading journal was disappointed and annoyed. It would have preferred to have seen Mr. Forster succeed, or even Sir James Martin and his colleagues remain in office,—in fact almost any Administration rather than a Government under Mr. Parkes. But it was obliged to admit that, in the circumstances, there was nothing for the Acting-Governor to do but send for Mr. Parkes. A new Ministry, it was clear, could not be formed without him, and those who were not satisfied were obliged to accept the inevitable. " It was a matter of opening your mouth and shutting your eyes," it was said. "Such are the turns in the wheel of fortune that the course of a few months has placed in the Premiership the man who seemed least likely to attain that distinction." But there was no alternative, so the leading newspaper of the colony wrote.

To Mr. Parkes himself, the moment was a proud one. In spite of all that had been done openly and covertly to bring about his political destruction, he was now in the situation to be more prominent and powerful than ever. All he had wanted was the opportunity, and it had come constitutionally, honourably, and with public approval.

Immediately he was entrusted with the duty, Mr. Parkes set about forming his Ministry. He met with two rebuffs. Desiring to have Mr. (afterwards Sir) John Hay with him, he offered that gentleman the position of Vice-President of the Executive Council and Representative of the Government in the Upper House. Mr. Hay did not see his

SIR HENRY PARKES.

IN 1839, THE YEAR OF HIS ARRIVAL IN NEW
SOUTH WALES.

SIR HENRY PARKES.

IN 1856, THE YEAR IN WHICH HE ENTERED
THE LEGISLATIVE ASSEMBLY.

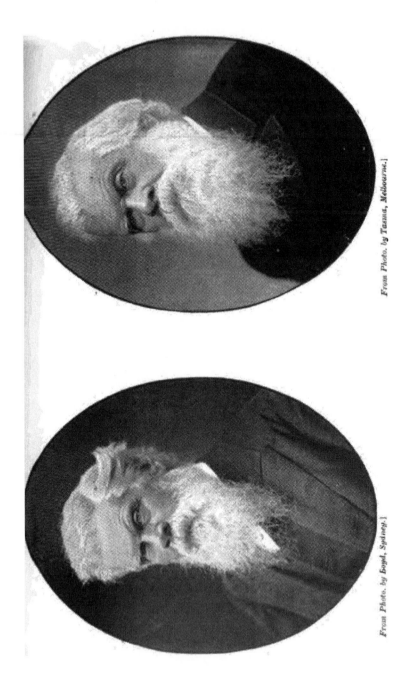

From Photo. by Tesma, Melbourne.]

From Photo. by Boyd, Sydney.]

way to accept the offer. Mr. Parkes then wrote to Mr.
Forster, offering him the office of Colonial Treasurer,
or any other but that of Colonial Secretary. Admitting the personal differences between them, he
pointed out that, in the main, their political opinions
were the same, and urged that personal differences
should not be permitted to stand in the way of
assistance in the formation of a Government. Mr.
Forster met this apparently well-meant communication with a curt refusal.

The following day the new Ministry was
complete.

It consisted of—

MR. PARKES ... Colonial Secretary and
Premier.

MR. S. SAMUEL ... Vice-President of the
Executive Council.

MR. W. R. PIDDINGTON Colonial Treasurer.

MR. J. S. FARNELL ... Secretary for Public
Lands.

MR. J. SUTHERLAND... Secretary for Public
Works.

Mr. G. A. LLOYD ... Postmaster General.

MR. E. BUTLER ... Attorney General.

MR. J. G. L. INNES... Solicitor General.

Formed entirely from the Opposition side of the
House, the new Government consisted almost
wholly of men who had worked together in the
Legislature as members of the same party for the
same objects. Mr. Samuel was the only one of the
Administration who had not always been on

friendly terms with Mr. Parkes ; and nothing had
occurred between them to prevent them from coming
together in the same Government. On the whole,
the Ministry was very favourably received.

There were, of course, those who cavilled at it.
The association, in the same Government, of Mr.
Parkes and Mr. Butler, was complained of, and
denounced, by some, as worse than , the coalition
between Sir James Martin and Mr. Robertson.

Mr. Butler was a native of Ireland and a prominent Roman Catholic. He was a well-known man
by reason of the high position he occupied at the
New South Wales Bar, where he was one of its
leaders ; and also through his having been for some
years in Parliament, where he had shown ability
which had won respectful attention to his speeches
and, on one or two occasions, had led to his being
offered office. But though a gentleman of education,
and generally of liberal tendencies, he was a thorough
Irishman, even to his brogue. Being an Irishman,
and a Roman Catholic, it was not extraordinary
that he should be on the side opposite to Mr. Parkes
in the matter of the alleged conspiracy in connection with the crime of O'Farrell. On all other
questions the two were understood to be in perfect
agreement.

They had known each other intimately for most
of the time from the date of the arrival of Mr.
Butler in the colony. The *Empire* had not been
long started when Mr. Butler landed in Sydney, and
it happened that Mr. Parkes was one of the first
persons with whom he had any communication.

One of the earliest things he did, after his arrival, was to write for the *Empire* ; and, notwithstanding the O'Farrell incident, the acquaintanceship—the friendship it really was—between the two did not cease. This friendship was a sufficient justification for their coming together in the same Government ; and, on this ground, Mr. Butler defended the course he had taken.

It was somewhat remarkable that his inclusion in the Ministry was condemned alike by extreme Roman Catholics and extreme Protestants. But the bulk of those of his own religion saw in his position, as a prominent member of the Ministry, the safeguard of the interests of all of their faith, and were satisfied. Archbishop Polding, who has often been alluded to as the most fair-minded of the prelates who have been at the head of the Roman Catholic Church in New South Wales, was of the same opinion. Mr. Butler's presence in the Ministry, as he himself put it to his constituents, was a guarantee that, while the interests of the people of the colony generally would be attended to, those of his own religion would not be overlooked.

Probably this was not absent from the mind of Mr. Parkes when he offered Mr. Butler the position of Attorney-General. The Ministry was the first formed under Mr. Parkes. He was not, and had not been for some years, in the favour of the Roman Catholic portion of the community. The intro-duction, into the Government, of a gentleman promi-nent among them would placate them and strengthen it. Friendship would justify the offer of office to

w

Mr. Butler, possibly prompt it also; and the advantage to the Government of his acceptance of the offer was undeniable.

So far as was known, there was no good reason for condemning the association of Mr. Parkes and Mr. Butler in the same Ministry. Later on, circumstances occurred which, to some extent, indicated that in accepting office, there might have been in the mind of Mr. Butler, a consideration superior to all others, and one of which the public was not, at the time, aware; but the relations which had existed between him and Mr. Parkes, were alone sufficient to justify the course taken in forming the Government.

The career of the new Ministry commenced under good auspices. The country was in a highly prosperous condition, and the revenue was flourishing. The only cloud upon the general brightness was the difficulty that existed in relation to the border duties. Everything else was satisfactory.

The first act of the Government was to re-open the question of the border duties, and deal with it in the light of the offer which the Victorian Government had made to Sir. James Martin. This was consistent with the wish of the constituencies, as expressed at the general election, and with the attitude Mr. Parkes had assumed in regard to the matter from the first.

Some time elapsed before the necessary arrangement between the two colonies could be made; but, eventually, an agreement was entered into, by which Victoria was to pay New South Wales £60,000 a

year, as compensation for the loss of the duties
which would have to be paid to New South Wales
if the goods sent by Victoria across the river
Murray were not admitted into the colony free.
The tariff of New South Wales at the time was a
protective one, and had been so for some years.
Though not of an extreme kind, for the duties had
been imposed for revenue purposes only, it was
sufficient to class New South Wales as a protectionist colony.   The agreement with Victoria,
therefore, while it had for its chief object the
removal of irritating customs measures from the
population of the southern border was, to a certain
extent, necessary to the New South Wales fiscal
system.

But Mr. Parkes looked beyond the existing
condition of affairs.   Imbued with strong free trade
views, he saw the possibility of liberating the sea-
ports and the inland borders of the colony from the
shackles of a restricted commerce ; and, as head of
the Government, he set himself to the work.   In
his eyes, it was possible to tell Victoria that she
might keep the £60,000 payable under the agreement, and send her goods, in any quantity she
pleased, across the Murray free of charge or any
other hindrance.   It was possible also, with advantage, he was convinced, to throw New South Wales
open to most of the products of the whole world.
The idea was a great one, marked with the courage
and boldness of a far-seeing statesman.   Financial
embarrassment of a serious kind might, for a time,
follow such a course.   Timid men declared it would.

But, on the other hand, there was the prospect of enormously increased trading operations throughout the colony, and the consequent improved general prosperity.

On taking office, it was announced by the new Ministry that they were determined to carry out a policy of free trade; and, consistently with this announcement, Mr. Parkes steadily kept his object in view. One of the results was the termination of the agreement with Victoria, a few months after it was signed, and the free passage of goods across the southern border.

The declaration, by the Ministry, of a free trade policy was followed by the introduction of a budget greatly reducing the customs tariff and virtually making it one of free trade. Victoria, ever alive to her interests, at once saw in the new policy the danger to herself. Unrestricted admission of goods into the port of Sydney might mean the supply of the population along the Murray much more cheaply than they could be supplied from Melbourne, after the goods sent from there had paid the heavy Victorian protective duties. The Victorian Government promptly gave the requisite notice to terminate the agreement respecting the Border duties; and, in thirty days, it was cancelled, having been in force only six months. Very shortly afterwards, in the operation of the new fiscal policy in New South Wales, the compensation which Victoria had paid, in lieu of duties on her trade across the Murray, became unnecessary as it was not required.

This incident, and the spirited policy of the Parkes Government, attracted much notice in the colonies and in England.

The Melbourne *Argus*, writing upon the subject, referred to Mr. Parkes as "animated by a sincere desire to wrest from Victoria the primacy of the Australian group, and to reinstate New South Wales in her former pride of place." "It is a legitimate object of ambition," it said, "and a noble aim; and he could adopt no wiser or safer method of accomplishing it than that of freeing the commerce of the country from all artificial trammels."

The London *Times*, in a long article, was ver eulogistic upon "Mr. Parkes' spirited measures of fiscal reform." "It cannot be said," it observed, "that Mr. Parkes' policy is wanting in boldness; but he has counted the cost, and carries the colony with him with unexpected unanimity. We do not doubt, and we certainly hope, that his courage will be rewarded by a large measure of commercial success."

The *Scotsman* referred to him as "a man with a wonderful history, of great energy, and who was well imbued with sound principles before he left England."

But the most important feature of the articles in the press, was the conviction, in the minds of the writers, of the remarkable advance which New South Wales had made by adopting the new fiscal policy. Not only did they see great advantage to herself, but they saw an improved prospect thoughout the Australian colonies. While New South Wales, by adopting and adhering to a policy of free trade, had everything to gain and nothing to lose, the other colonies witnessing her success would probably be educated into the same policy.

Victoria was the head-centre of protection in Australia; and, on that colony, it was hoped the action of New South Wales would have the good effect of convincing her of the error of her ways. But the *Argus* was doubtful of Victorians taking the matter seriously to heart. It earnestly wished they might, but saw serious obstacles in the pertinacious adherence of the colony to a restrictive tariff.

" Our chief hope of a return to right principles, and to reason, in our fiscal policy," it said, " lies in the lesson which New South Wales appears likely to read us, and in the emulation which her example will provoke ; for the practical benefits which are accruing to her, from the wise and prudent reformation of her tariff in the direction of free trade, are obvious and indisputable. The *Times*, on the same subject, remarked that " even if Victoria, finally stirred to emulation by the prosperity of her rival, should forswear her economical heresies, the latter will still have made solid gains. She will have developed the system of internal communications, and so strengthened all her interests and consolidated all her resources. She will have laid the foundations of a thriving commerce, which Victoria, under a liberal guidance, may share with her, but cannot pretend ever again to monopolise."

In recognition of his service to the cause of free trade, at this period of his life, the Cobden Club tendered to Mr. Parkes its congratulations, elected him an honorary member, and presented him with its gold medal.

Through much of its career success seemed inseparable from the operations of the Government. The term of office of this Ministry was remarkable for a substantial and fast-increasing prosperity throughout the colony, this flourishing state of affairs appearing with the advent of Mr. Parkes to the position of Premier. Money became plentiful; trade and commerce increased and extended their operations; industrial activity, compared with what it had been, assumed a condition which made it necessary to seriously consider the advisableness of introducing a vigorous immigration policy to bring into the country the labour requisite to meet requirements. Through some wonderfully rich finds, gold mining developed to an extent almost incredible, the output of gold being enormous. The seasons were propitious; and the pastoral and agricultural industries were proving sources of wealth to those engaged in them, and of material benefit to the colony.

Of course, so far as the Ministry was concerned, these circumstances were merely fortuitous. But they "boomed" the Government greatly. At the opening of each session of Parliament the Governor's speech announced, in most satisfactory terms, the continued well-being and progress of the colony. "The industrial activity consequent on the continued prosperity of the colony," said His Excellency on one occasion, "has caused a large increase in the public revenue, which is sufficient not only to meet the ordinary objects of government, but to justify the undertaking of important works for the improvement of the country." And each vice-regal utterance contained a similar announcement, the wonderful prosperity of the colony forming the most prominent feature in the speeches to the newly-assembled legislators.

Not only was the Government able to meet ordinary expenditure and to provide for works and services of general advantage; it found opportunity, and the means, for materially reducing taxation, and for making some arrangements for a sinking-fund to lessen the public debt. A vigorous railway policy, consistent with the interests of the colony at this period of its existence, was introduced and set in motion. Ocean mail services, and a perfect system of electric telegraphic cable communication with the mother country, and with New Zealand, received attention. The abolition of the *ad valorem* duties, and of many of the duties of a specific character, which had placed New South Wales in the position, and given it the name, of a protectionist colony, and the simplification of the tariff as much as possible, encouraged outside commerce, and laid the foundations for the large shipping trade, and the extended commercial operations, which are carried on in connection with the colony at the present day.

CHAPTER XXIV.

In November, 1873, there occurred an event which brought about the resignation of Mr. Butler from the Ministry, and for a time threatened its downfall.

Sir Alfred Stephen, who for a number of years had sat upon the Bench of the Supreme Court as Chief Justice, relinquished that position, and it became necessary for the Government to appoint his successor. For some months previous to his actual resignation, it was known that he intended to retire. He had been a Judge of the Supreme Court of New South Wales for thirty-four years, during twenty-nine of which he was Chief Justice. Half of his life had been spent in the service of the country, in one of the most arduous and responsible positions it is possible for a man to occupy; and now, having arrived at the age of seventy-one, he was desirous of spending the remainder of his days in leisure and ease. Full of years, he was also covered with honours. No colonist had done more; few had laboured so faithfully and well. As Chief Justice he had adorned his position; had been held in the highest respect ; and had contributed greatly to the well-being and progress of the colony. The vacancy his retirement caused it was not easy to fill. There were other able Judges on the Bench, and there were men of ability at the Bar ; but, in any community, the characteristics which distinguished Sir Alfred Stephen's judicial career are rare.

Only one man in New South Wales, a leader at the Bar as well as a prominent politician—Sir James Martin—appeared to be really suitable for the office ; and the position being offered to him, it was accepted. The appointment was received with public approval, and it was justified by results. But it was accompanied by a regrettable quarrel between Mr. Parkes and Mr. Butler, and by the latter's resignation from the office of Attorney-General.

Mr. Butler wanted the position of Chief Justice. According to the custom in England he was, he considered, as Attorney-General, entitled to it ; and his right under this practice was strengthened, as he made it known, by what he declared was a direct and repeated promise on the part of Mr. Parkes that he should have it.

The appointment of Sir James Martin was made on the 10th November, and announced on the following day. The Legislative Assembly was informed of the circumstance by the Speaker reading a letter from Sir James Martin resigning his seat in the House, and bidding honorable members farewell. At that time it was not very

generally known that Mr. Butler had been desirous
of the position, or that there was any difficulty
between him and Mr. Parkes respecting it. Members
of the Assembly were aware that he had been
mentioned as the successor to Sir Alfred Stephen;
and the possibility of his appointment had not only
been received with dissatisfaction, but opposition
had been raised to it. The public, however, knew
little. Yet five days before, in consequence of a
letter from Mr. Parkes to him on the subject of the
Chief Justiceship, he had resigned the office of
Attorney-General, and was now merely performing
certain of the duties of the position until the
Government could make arrangements for some one
to succeed him.

The reading of Sir James Martin's letter in the
Assembly gave Mr. Butler an opportunity for
making a statement; and, moving the adjournment
of the House, he explained his position, and placed
the public in possession of a long correspondence
between himself and Mr. Parkes, in which he
declared that, until a few days previous to Sir
James Martin being appointed, he had been led to
believe that he would be the new Chief Justice, and
that the position had been withheld from him for
reasons that were neither sufficient nor honourable.

According to Mr. Butler, he had been called
upon at his chambers by Mr. Parkes, on the day Sir
Alfred Stephen had informed the Government of
his intention to resign, and, without any application
on his part for the position, promised the succession
to the office. On a subsequent occasion, Mr. Parkes,

meeting him in the street, had shaken him by the hand, and congratulated him upon his appointment as a thing in effect accomplished.   Later still, when discussing in Mr. Butler's presence, with one of their colleagues, the possible consequences of his appointment, to which the colleague raised objections, Mr. Parkes, so Mr. Butler asserted, had repelled the apprehensions of the colleague with flattering remarks upon Mr. Butler's qualifications for the office.   His fitness for the office being in this manner admitted, he then, as Attorney-General, had, he contended, according to established usage under responsible government, the first claim to it.

Mr. Parkes, on the other hand, though admitting that he had been, at first, favourable to Mr. Butler's appointment, denied that the position had been promised him; and explained how, on several occasions, he had urged upon Mr. Butler's attention weighty reasons why he should give up all idea of being the Chief Justice, and remain with the Government as Attorney-General.

The correspondence, which was read to the House, told its tale fully.   No one reading it would be disposed to deny that, to a certain extent, Mr. Parkes had been favourable to Mr. Butler succeeding to the Chief Justiceship, and had so expressed himself.   But it does not appear that beyond having been, through his friendly feelings towards Mr. Butler, somewhat impulsive and indiscreet in stating his own view of Mr. Butler's qualifications and claim, he did anything that could justify Mr.

Butler in concluding that an absolute promise of the appointment had been made to him.

Though, as the head of the Government, Mr. Parkes had the appointment in his gift, it was impossible, without risking the destruction of the Government, for him to avoid consulting his colleagues in the matter, and most of the Ministers were opposed to Mr. Butler receiving the position. Opposition to it appeared also both inside and outside Parliament; and, though Mr. Butler's desire for the office was not, at that time, sufficiently known to elicit any strong expression of public opinion on the subject, it was easy to see that his appointment would not give that satisfaction which was desirable. Reflection convinced Mr. Parkes that the requirements of the office would be met, and the public interest best served, by the appointment of Sir James Martin; and, notwithstanding that the difficulty with Mr. Butler afforded an unusual opportunity to the enemies of Mr. Parkes, of which they were not slow to avail themselves, the new Chief Justice was hailed with satisfaction in every part of the colony.

The correspondence commenced with a letter dated 5th November, 1873, to Mr. Butler from Mr. Parkes, in which he said that serious doubts had been awakened in his mind, in a further consideration of the very grave duty devolving upon the Government in filling the vacancy at the head of the Judicial Bench.

" In my first deliberate conversation with you," the letter proceeded, " I expressed my solicitude

that you should remain with your colleagues, and I
represented to you that, in my judgment, you would
be consulting your interest as a public man by
remaining ; but, after listening to your strongly
expressed desire to change your position, I told you,
in conclusion, that I would not stand in your way if
you considered it your duty to accept this high
office, and that I would be no party to the objection
raised against you on the ground of your religious
faith."

Mr. Parkes foresaw that a strong feeling would
manifest itself, in certain quarters, against the
elevation of Mr. Butler to the position of Chief
Justice, and thought it rather inconsiderate on
his part that he should so little regard the disturbing consequences to the Ministry which were
likely to follow his appointment ; but he determined
to resist all sectarian pressure.   Day by day, however, as the appointment to the office came nearer,
and was made more the subject of public discussion,
he became aware, he told Mr. Butler in this
letter, that the objections to him were not by any
means confined to religious grounds, but were
entertained by intelligent persons of his own faith.
These objections were based on the comparative
fitness between him and other members of the
Bar for the position, and were raised and argued
in the interest of the administration of justice and
the public welfare.   One and all, Mr. Parkes said,
who had communicated with him on the subject,
and very many had done so, regarded the possible

appointment of Mr. Butler with disfavour, and not
a single opinion had reached him in approval of it.

"They say, very justly," the letter explained,
"that the office of Chief Justice is the highest in
the community, not only in its judicial functions but
in its relations to the dearest and tenderest interests
of society, and that it ought to be filled by the
member of the Bar possessing, in the highest degree,
the qualifications of learning, professional character,
liberal education, personal standing, and social
recognition; and that neither the Bar nor Society
will admit that you are pointed out by these
considerations."

The phrase "social recognition" was unfortunate, and led to much criticism, and condemnation
of Mr. Parkes for his having used it.   But when
the opportunity came it was shown that he had not
intended it should convey its generally accepted
narrow meaning; his intention was that it should
be taken in the broad sense of recognition by the
general public.   As far as he could form an opinion,
Mr. Butler's brethren at the Bar were opposed to
his elevation to the vacant office, their opposition
arising not from any narrow prejudice, but from a
fair and honourable jealousy of distinctions being
conferred when the requirements of the position
were not met in the person so honoured; and he
did not entertain the faintest doubt that the public
generally objected to the appointment.

"The estimation in which I hold your personal
character, and your great natural abilities," the
letter concluded, "is in no sense altered, and I treat

with scorn the objections urged against you on religious grounds. But I think I am justified in asking you to reconsider the whole matter, when I find that, in the judgment of men of all classes and of all shades of opinion, your appointment would not be the best that could be made for the country, and when, as you are aware, all our colleagues are unfavourable to it."

This letter, evidently, was not expected by Mr Butler, and he replied to it with emphasis.

Stating the circumstances, as they were in his mind, of the interviews with Mr. Parkes, in which, he asserted, the offer of the Chief Justiceship had been made without any previous request for it, he said: "I may then be pardoned for some surprise at your letter of the 5th instant, written, as it seems to me, as an elaborate vindication of a foregone conclusion on your part not to confer the appointment upon me." He excused himself for not answering the objections urged against him. "I have no desire," he wrote, "to be my own advocate. I am quite satisfied to be judged in my social and professional character by those who have no motive to judge me unfairly. When you made me the offer, you had known me longer and better than any of those objectors, after a period of twenty years' intimate acquaintance. The influence which, within a few days, has counteracted your knowledge for that long period, is best known to yourself." He had not been aware, he said, that his colleagues, with perhaps one exception, were opposed to his appointment; he had, in fact, been left under a contrary impression. "As to your request to me to reconsider the whole matter, it is no longer with me one of merely personal consideration. I am convinced, notwithstanding the many disqualifications alleged in your letter, that the 'strong feeling' to which you refer is the real ground of disqualification. Entertaining this opinion, it only remains for me to relieve the Government of all embarrassment by resigning, as I now do, the office of Attorney-General."

Mr. Parkes did not wish Mr. Butler to resign; and, desiring that he should take time for reflection, wrote that he would, for the present, consider the resignation as not received. "I do not ask you to take this longer time for your decision," he pointed out, "in deference to me or my colleagues, but in justice to yourself in a matter to be viewed entirely in the light of the public interest."

Mr. Butler replied that he had no wish to put the Government to any inconvenience, and, if the public service required him to hold office for a few days longer, he was willing to do so.

Writing again, Mr. Parkes addressed Mr. Butler from one of those high constitutional standpoints for which he was always remarkable. "I intended to invite you to consider," he said, "in justice to your own public character, whether in a case where a number of men had, in political agreement, accepted the office of Government, and were still agreed upon questions of principle and policy, it was a wise course for one of them to retire, because objections were conscientiously and re-

x

luctantly raised to his receiving a high judicial
appointment.   I thought I had used language
sufficiently suggestive of the course of reflection to
which I desired to invite you.   I sincerely hope you
will not persist in your resignation.   Nothing has
occurred, so far as I am aware, to lead to disagreement between your colleagues and yourself, on public
questions, and, if our political views remain in unbroken accord, have you really satisfied yourself
that it is your duty to leave the Administration for
reasons almost wholly personal in their nature ? "

He admitted he was to blame in having taken a
course, however sincerely, which naturally led Mr.
Butler to believe that his appointment would not
be objected to by him ; but the interview at Mr.
Butler's chambers, he contended, " did not bear the
same positive and vivid form," in his recollection,
which it did in that of Mr. Butler, and he could not
admit that he had said anything on that occasion
which could be interpretated into " a promise of the
succession to the office of Chief Justice."   As Mr.
Butler knew, he explained, he had argued that
gentleman's case with his colleagues, as long as he
felt he could do so without violating his sense of
public duty.   The obstacle had arisen in " the
public sense of the propriety of the appointment,
and in the more careful examination of the whole
case, and the fuller and clearer knowledge which
have revealed themselves to the Government."

They had not taken office together, he was
careful to point out, to enable one of them to
receive a high permanent appointment ; and, while

he admitted that on hearing Mr. Butler's expressed desire to receive the appointment, he had assured him that he personally would not stand in his way, he had held the opinion that Mr. Butler's elevation to the Bench would lead to serious embarrassment. He admitted also having, on one occasion, shaken Mr. Butler by the hand and congratulated him; "but," he wrote, in explanation of this circumstance, "you ought to have remembered that this was done in a moment of impulse, when you were labouring under strong feelings of excitement at the sectarian prejudices which had been raised against you by others; and I think it is hardly generous to allude to an incident which was so entirely an ebullition of sympathy and friendship."

His feelings with regard to Mr. Butler were, he asserted, unchanged; but the question was "whether in the judgment of the community at large, and in truth," his qualifications for the office of Chief Justice were the highest. He resented the accusation that he had acted on a foregone conclusion, but acknowledged that he ought to have arrived at his doubts earlier. "I am anxious," he declared, "to secure one object as the result of much thought and consideration, and that is the appointment, to the office of Chief Justice, of the person best qualified for that high station, and most acceptable to the colony; and I have no other object."

There was some further correspondence, in which Mr. Butler charged Mr. Parkes with breaking faith in the matter of the appointment, owing to pressure brought to bear on the Government, and otherwise wrote on the subject with considerable bitterness.

" There is only one ground of really personal feeling in what has occurred between us in this business," his letter said. " It is that you did not scruple deliberately and elaborately, and in a letter intended for public use, to disparage my personal and social standing and professional character, when the hostile pressure brought to bear upon the Government made it desirable to find an excuse for breaking faith with me. It was surely open to you to appoint the gentleman you thought most competent, without having recourse to such an elaborately unfriendly proceeding towards one whom you always professed to esteem as your friend."

In the House there was a good deal of party condemnation of Mr. Parkes, and to some extent, it made its appearance outside; but the opinion was almost universal that the right appointment had been made. Virtually everybody admitted that Sir James Martin was the man, above all others in the country, fitted for the position.

The question that arises in the matter is whether after Mr. Parkes had gone so far with regard to Mr. Butler, as he himself admitted he had, he should have held to that gentleman all through, or, in the light of more mature consideration and further information, taken the course he did in giving the position to Sir James Martin. Some persons thought, or, at least said, that he was bound in honour to give the position to Mr. Butler; that, having once led him to understand he was favourable to his succeeding to the office, Mr. Butler should have been appointed. But those who said this were well aware that, had it been done, there would have been a much more severe condemnation of Mr. Parkes for taking a course which only a small section of the people would have considered the right one, and probably no one would have thought the best in the public interest. Then it was said that, in offering the position to Sir James Martin, the chief object of Mr. Parkes had been to get rid of a formidable political opponent. Yet, though not at the time together in the Government, the two statesmen had been friends for many years; and there was no very important advantage to be gained by Mr. Parkes in effecting the removal of Sir James Martin from political life.

If Mr. Parkes had resigned, and left the appointment of the new Chief Justice to another Government, probably it would not have assisted Mr. Butler to the office; and it is quite possible the appointment made would not have been the one that was made. The singular and convincing feature of the whole affair was that, while certain persons thought proper to condemn Mr. Parkes, they admitted he had made the appointment which not only was best in itself but met with public approval. Even Mr. Butler considered the appointment an excellent one.

Mr. David Buchanan brought the subject before the Assembly, in a motion affirming that the conduct of the Colonial Secretary, towards his colleague the Attorney-General, was unworthy, discreditable, and deserving of the censure of the House; but the motion was set aside by the previous question, moved by Mr. Robertson, who was leading the Opposition.

This result to a motion of censure was sufficient to indicate the general feeling. The party politically opposed to Mr. Parkes did not dare go to a vote on the question of condemning him for the course he had taken. Like most other persons, they were obliged to admit that Sir James Martin was the right man. But the debate was useful in one respect. It served to bring to light information which put a clearer complexion upon the correspondence that had taken place between Mr. Parkes and Mr. Butler.

It transpired, that, as far back as the 13th October, Mr. Butler was aware of the strong feeling in Parliament against his appointment. The knowledge came to him during a debate on an amendment to a motion for going into committee of ways and means; and he went away from the House that night, as he said, " a sadder and a wiser man." He at once saw that it was his duty to consider his position, and he did so; with the result that he "made up his mind that come what would he would never yield to such influences." Finding that this feeling against Mr. Butler existed not only inside, but outside, Parliament—that his appointment would not give satisfaction—Mr. Parkes first invited Mr. Butler to reconsider and withdraw the claim he had put forward; and then, seeing that he would not do so, took the decisive step of appointing the man

at the Bar best qualified for the office, and most
likely to meet with public approval. It is difficult
to see what other course, in the public interest, Mr.
Parkes could have taken under the circumstances.

CHAPTER XXV.

CONTRARY to the expectation of many, the Butler incident, though for a time wearing a threatening aspect, did not develop into anything serious. Mr. Butler was not the man to revenge himself by endeavouring to bring about the downfall of the Ministry; and his disposition to let the matter rest at the point it had reached when the correspondence between him and Mr. Parkes was read to the House, disarmed those who would have used it as a weapon of party warfare.

The Government went on with a good working majority, and with fair success, for the average term which, in New South Wales, represents the life of a Ministry. Some difficulty was experienced by the Legislative Council standing in the way of two great measures it was thought by the Government and by the Assembly desirable to pass. One of these was a bill to make the Upper House elective, and the other a bill to amend the electoral law. The latter Mr. Parkes was able to carry through both Houses, and make law, some years afterwards. and, by means of it, to effect some important improve-

ments in the electoral system ; the former, though
not lost sight of in subsequent years, did not, at any
time, make material headway beyond the point it
reached in 1873.

The alterations in the status of the Council,
sought at that time, were very much the same as
those aimed at since.   Existing members were to
continue to hold their seats ; and provision was made
for electing a certain number of others, and for
filling vacancies by the elective process.

The moving spirit in the Council was Mr. Joseph
Docker.   Appointed to that Chamber in 1856, and,
during most of his career there, acting in a ministerial capacity as Representative of the Government,
he was well versed in all the forms and practice of
the House, and ever ready in bringing his knowledge
and experience to bear on the matter before
it.   Adding to these qualifications a keen and
forcible method of debate, and a gentlemanly
bearing, he was a formidable opponent whose
defence of the House he safeguarded it was
exceedingly difficult to overcome.   As Postmaster General in the Martin Ministry of 1866, and
representative of that Government in the Legislative Council, he conducted through the Upper
House the Public Schools Bill of that year ; but his
association in that great work with Mr. Parkes in
1866 did not prevent him from opposing strongly
the attempt of the Government to reform the
Council seven years later.

Military reform was another work to which, at
this period, Mr. Parkes set himself.   A force of

permanent infantry had been established in Sydney, and, so far as drill and discipline could make them, they were an exceptionally fine body of men ; but there were indications about them of an expensiveness which many persons considered was not justifiable, and, in the opinion of others, they were altogether unnecessary.   Permanent artillery might be required for the efficient working of the harbour batteries, and for the proper defence of some vulnerable parts of the coast ; but the duties of infantry could be well and inexpensively performed by volunteer corps.   This opinion was entertained by Mr. Parkes ; and, immediately the opportunity came, he drew the attention of Parliament to the subject.

Permanent military service in a country like Australia, he considered, was in itself an evil, as it tended to withdraw many of the best of the population from occupations, which, rightly carried on, brought about national prosperity and progress. Industry and enterprise, not indolence and mere display, were wanted in New South Wales.   The glamour of war was contemptible, compared with the arts of peace.   The country needed a defence force, but that, with the exception of a small body of men constantly employed taking care of the guns in the batteries, should be composed of the general body of the people trained to arms in the intervals of leisure afforded by their daily work.

Some persons advocated the policy of a small standing army, and defended the existence of a permanent infantry.   Sir James Martin was at the head of these.   To him, indeed, in the main, the country owed both the permanent infantry, and most of the military expenditure of that day. But, with the eloquence of strong conviction, the weight of his popularity, and the confidence he inspired in the community, Mr. Parkes overthrew all obstacles; and the infantry had to go. The officers and men were paid a money compensation, and the force was disbanded.

Perhaps the most telling of all the weapons, which Mr. Parkes used in bringing about this result, was ridicule. A phrase he used in describing the men instantly attached itself to them, and did as much as anything to effect their destruction. He called them "painted soldiers;" and, though the words were used impulsively, in the heat of debate, and were certainly not justified by the capacity, conduct, or appearance of the force, they stood out before the public eye, ever afterwards, in bold letters, as ineffaceable as if stamped upon the uniforms of officers and privates.

A glance at the manner in which the military expenditure of the colony has, of late years, increased will suggest the conclusion that had the infantry of 1873 not been disbanded, the expenses of its establishment during the twenty-three years that have since passed would probably have been something formidable.

Now and then attempts were made by the Opposition, led by Mr. Robertson, to oust the Government from office; but, until the Ministry were actually defeated, these met with little support. At the opening of the session of Parliament, on 9th

September 1873, the leader of the Opposition moved
an amendment on the Address-in-Reply, and was
defeated by a vote of thirty to twelve.   On 3rd
November, 1874, the opening day of another session,
Mr. Robertson again moved an amendment on the
Address-in-Reply, expressing, on several grounds,
dissatisfaction with the administration of affairs ; but
the result was the same as before, the amendment
being negatived by twenty-seven votes to thirteen.

On 27th January, 1875, at the opening of a new
Parliament, the first under the Triennial Parliaments Act, the Opposition leader was more
successful, and the Government found themselves in
a minority of four, in a division in which sixty-two
members voted.

The question upon which they fell was a peculiar
one.   About the middle of 1874 it became generally
known, through a paragraph in an evening newspaper, that the notorious bushranger Frank Gardiner,
then incarcerated in Darlinghurst Gaol, where he
was undergoing a sentence of thirty-two years imprisonment, was about to be released; and immediately
a hubbub arose in protest and condemnation of what,
it was said, the Government intended to do.   It was
of no avail that explanations were made to the effect
that Gardiner was considered to have been
sufficiently punished ; that his liberation had been
recommended by some of the foremost men in the
country, including members of the party in
opposition to the Government ; that his freedom,
after the serving of a certain proportion of his
sentence, had been promised by the Governor ; and

that such precautions would be taken as to prevent the possibility of the prisoner doing any further harm to society.   In certain quarters no effort that could be put forth to inflame the public mind on the subject was neglected ; and, though the Parkes Ministry were simply carrying out what virtually had been determined before they took office, they were made, by their enemies, and opponents, to bear the brunt of the public condemnation.

On the 10th June, 1874, Mr. Edward Combes moved an amendment, on a motion for the House to go into committee of supply, which, by expressing disapproval of the proposed release of the prisoner Gardiner and some other long-sentenced prisoners, was, in reality, a motion of censure.   Mr. Combes was neither an old nor a prominent member of the House ; but this did not prevent his amendment from getting considerable support.   The Opposition threw their whole strength in its favor ; and, when the division was taken, the voting was found to be equal,—twenty-six to twenty-six.   Virtually this was a defeat of the Government ; but the Speaker gave his casting vote with those who voted to go into committee of supply, and for a time no further difficulty arose.   Ministers did not attach much importance to either the division or the amendment, for the reason that as the prerogative of pardon rested, at the time, wholly with the Governor, the Government could not be regarded as responsible for the course which, in Gardiner's case, it had been decided to take.

Trouble more serious was to come next session.
A few days after the division on Mr. Combes'
amendment, Parliament was prorogued; and, on the
day of prorogation, a minute explaining his reasons
for the course he had taken in respect to the prisoner
Gardiner, was sent to the Legislative Assembly, by
the Governor, Sir Hercules Robinson. This minute,
which referred to the protests against the release of
Gardiner as clamour unreasonable and unjust, attracted considerable notice, but did not immediately
affect the Government. Parliament met again on the
3rd November; and, though a hostile amendment
was moved on the Address-in-Reply, nothing was
said in it of the Governor's minute.

Three weeks afterwards, however, Mr. Combes
took the minute in hand, and moved that it should
be taken into consideration by the House in committee of the whole.   The motion was carried by
twenty-eight votes to twenty-six; and, in committee,
resolutions were passed expressing regret that the
Governor should have been advised to communicate
his minute to the Assembly, because it was "in
defensible in certain of its allegations"; because, if
it was "considered to be an answer to the respectful
and earnest petitions of the people," it was "highly
undesirable to convert the records of this House
into a means of conveying censure or reproof to
our constituents;" and because, if it referred to
discussions in the Chamber, then it was "in spirit
and effect a breach of the constitutional privileges
of Parliament."

The division upon these resolutions was twenty-eight votes to twenty-eight ; and, though the Speaker gave his casting vote with the noes, the House, on the motion of Mr. Parkes, at once adjourned, and, a day or two afterwards, Parliament was dissolved.

It is instructive, at the present day, to recall the excitement which was aroused over what has since proved to be a very harmless affair. That the Governor had no intention to wound the feelings of honourable members, insult the dignity of the Legislative Assembly, or question the undoubted rights of the public, is now generally admitted. That the release of Gardiner has had no unfavourable consequence is well-known. To every individual of the population, with the exception of the immediate relatives of the bushranger and the police, the *liberé* has been as dead to the world as the confinee. The public were not made aware of the day when the release from gaol took place; and, beyond a rumour that the released man was shipped to America, nothing has ever been divulged of the convict's movements. Society has been none the worse; and, probably, few among those who joined in the outcry of 1874 really believed it would be the worse. But the opportunity was a favourable one for the opponents of the Government, and the most was made of it. There was nothing to be gained in trying to punish the Governor, but there was a good deal of satisfaction in administering the rod to his advisers.

Ministers did not appear to lose ground in the elections. There was a good deal said in disapproval of the Gardiner proceedings, and some indications were apparent that the attacks upon the Government would be renewed when the new Parliament assembled ; but their general policy seemed to meet with approval.

To the Ministers themselves, it appeared, that on their general policy, a large majority of members were elected in their favour. But at the meeting of the Parliament on 27th January, 1875, the Gardiner question, brought forward again, this time by Mr. Robertson as leader of the Opposition, put the general policy of the Government in the background; and the newly elected of the constituencies were called upon to express their opinions, by their votes, upon the Governor's minute. Mr. Robertson, adopting the words of Mr. Combes' motion which had brought about the dissolution of the previous Parliament, moved them as an amendment on the Address-in-Reply, and the amendment was passed by thirty-three votes to twenty-nine. The Government, of course, then resigned ; and the first Parkes Ministry came to an end.

A notable result of the trouble over the Gardiner question, in addition to the defeat of the Government, was a change in relation to the prerogative of pardon. As Sir Henry Parkes afterwards explained the matter, the Ministers of the day had forced upon them, by a party movement, "the choice between responsibility without authority and the authority of an active judgment coupled with a

just responsibility." Previously the practice had
been for the prerogative to be exercised by the
Governor, irrespective of his constitutional advisers ;
now Mr. Parkes recommended, and the Governor
approved, that it should be employed on the advice
of Ministers. The change was made with some
misgivings as to the wisdom of the proceeding, but
it remains to this day, and operates beneficially.

At this period, Mr. Parkes' speeches displayed
a powerfulness, combined with a wide range of
political knowledge clearly understood and well
applied, which equalled anything in his utterances
of later years, when a more matured experience
raised him nearer what may be regarded as the
zenith of his career. Always eloquent, his speeches
on whatever subject or in whatever circumstances
he spoke, at any period of his life, seldom showed
any sign of weakness ; but those who remember the
Gardiner debates, do not forget the unusual force with
which the attacks upon the Government were repelled, the strength with which their position was defended, or the effect which the scathing denunciation
of the tactics of the Opposition had upon the
House. Ever leonine in his appearance, by reason
of a peculiar cast of countenance, the shape of his
head, and the thick growth and manner of wearing
his hair, it was not at all uncommon for him, in the
indignation of the moment, when he would roam
from one end of the table to the other, his scornful
eloquence thundering from his lips, to suggest in
the minds of those observing him the similarity of
his manner, his voice, and his might, to the

Y

characteristics which mark the strength and superiority of the monarch of the forest. Frequently since then he was referred to as "the old lion," but at no period was he more like his prototype, than when, during the last few days of his first Ministry, he may be said to have been caged but not subdued.

CHAPTER XXVI.

THE defeat of the Government was followed by the
return to power of Mr. Robertson, who formed a
Ministry which held office from February, 1875, to
March, 1877.

The new Government had a politically wild
time, principally in consequence of proceedings on
the part of their Minister for Lands, which gave
rise to much comment outside, as well as inside,
Parliament.

Mr. Parkes was not slow to take his part in this
criticism, and, when necessary, to condemn what he
considered deserved condemnation. The manner in
which his Ministry had been ejected from office, was not
such as to lead him to be very friendly to those who
took its place ; but no active hostility was shown by
him, as leader of the Opposition, for the first few
months, nor until the circumstances of the time
appeared to warrant it.

He gave some attention to the public school
question. The movement to further popularise the
educational system of the colony, which afterwards
developed into the League whose watchwords were

" secular, compulsory, and free," was beginning to show some signs of progress; and Mr. Parkes, opposed to any radical changes in the existing system, appeared to think that the zeal of the reformers might be neutralised, if he could bring about some modifications, which, while not interfering with the great principles underlying the system, would largely increase the number of schools at much less cost, than hitherto had been the case, to the people requiring them. One direction in which this might be done was the repeal of the regulation, then in force, requiring one-third of the cost of the public schools to be raised by the residents of the localities where schools were wanted. Mr. Parkes proposed that this repeal should be effected, and the Assembly agreeing, it was done.

In July, of 1875, rumour was abroad respecting the Minister for Lands, and an appointment said to have been made or procured in the interests of an acquaintance or friend. Eventually it came under the notice of the Assembly, and the Minister was obliged to defend himself. It is right to say that no direct charge was made against him, that little more definite than rumour was connected with the matter, and that he made an explanation, that was not disproved, of the circumstances which appeared to have led to the rumour. The incident is of interest here only so far as it associated itself with Mr. Parkes.

He, as the head of the Opposition, could not fail to take some notice of what was talked of concerning the Minister; and, as was natural, information on the subject was brought to him by some of those acting politically with him.

The Minister for Lands declared that a conspiracy existed to blacken his character, and eject him from office ; and he charged Mr. Parkes with being one of the conspirators. Though quite unfounded, the charge served its purpose. The Minister was a master of parliamentary tactics and political fence ; and a favourite method of his in defending himself from attack was to adroitly hide the allegations against himself behind counter-charges against his accusers. On this occasion, not only did he charge Mr. Parkes with conspiracy, but by means of a rule of Parliament, and the aid of some of his friends, he was able to make the charge without Mr. Parkes being afforded a fair opportunity to reply to it. To Mr. Parkes this mattered little, for the groundlessness of the charge was palpable ; but it was an indication, among others, of a state of feeling in the House not to be commended.

The charge of conspiracy, it scarcely need be said, was not carried beyond the statement of the Minister for Lands and the speeches that followed it. Except for the express purpose for which it was made, it was worthless. It did its work when the Minister succeeded in inducing the House to believe that instead of being in the position of the accused, he was the accuser; and it was then dropped. The allegations against the Minister also resulted in nothing definite ; but it was the destiny of the Ministry to bear him, for much of its existence, like a millstone around its neck, and ultimately to be

ATTACKING THE GOVERNMENT.

ejected from office largely through his proceedings.

Before the year was out, Mr. Parkes made an effort to bring about the defeat of the Government on their policy with regard to immigration and railway construction. The provision made for the former did not appear to him to be desirable, and he objected to a proposed expenditure of £1,100,000 for railways from Sydney to Wollongong, and Junee to Narrandera. Judging from results, the proposal to construct the south coast railway was a wise one; that to construct a line from Junee to Narrandera unwise. Mr. Parkes dealt with these matters by moving an amendment on the motion to go into committee of ways and means, and the amendment was negatived by thirty-four votes to twenty-two.

Just twelve months afterwards, at the opening of a session, he moved an amendment on the Address-in-Reply, expressing dissatisfaction with the manner in which the government of the colony was being administered; and he found himself with a slightly increased following, the voting for the amendment being twenty-five, and against it thirty-two. The Opposition were gaining strength, and there were indications that the Government would not much longer have a majority. They were losing support principally through their Minister for Lands. Several times they suffered defeat on important matters; but, determined to retain their positions, if possible, they remained in office for some months longer.

Becoming weary of this, Mr. Parkes began to think of retiring from the leadership of the Opposition. Some of the party sitting on that side of the House were not as loyal to him as they might have been, and that added to the unsatisfactoriness of the position. In August, 1876, while addressing the people of West Maitland, and at the close of a scathing criticism of the Robertson Government, he said of himself :—

"My tastes, my personal desires, my associations in life would never lead me to the Legislative Assembly. I much prefer my home. I prefer spending my time—what remains of life to me—in a very different way ; and I only attend in my place in Parliament, because I am honoured with the confidence of that portion of the country which, time after time, has sent me there with triumphant majorities. I have long learned the lesson which was taught to a young member of Parliament by Sydney Smith, years ago, when he said : ' Be loyal to your party as far as you can without being untrue to yourself. Do what you conceive to be your duty. Put out whatever abilities you possess in performing it. Think nothing of office. If it comes honourably, take it. If it does not come honourably, do not feel a twinge of regret in refusing it.' "

The Christmas recess of 1876-7 had scarcely commenced when he addressed a circular to members of the Opposition, informing them of his intention to relinquish the position of their leader. He was living at Ashfield ; and, dating the circular from there, he pointed out that, soon after his retirement from office in the beginning of 1875, he intimated to several members of the party his unwillingness to

assume any office in the Assembly which would
entail upon him special labours and responsibilities.
Since that time, however, he had been led to take a
part which had insensibly merged into that of
nominal leadership.　With this position he had
never felt satisfied ; and several circumstances which
had occurred, and to which he did not wish to make
further allusion, combined with personal considerations of which every man must be his own judge,
had induced him to inquire whether, in justice to his
political friends and himself, it was his duty to
continue to occupy it.

A very little examination of the case convinced
him that the duties of leadership, at that time,
required, for their satisfactory performance, abilities
and qualifications which he did not consider he possessed, and must necessarily impose personal sacrifices, and an amount of continuous labour, for which
he was not prepared.　He had, therefore, decided to
limit his political obligations, after the reassembling
of Parliament, to the discharge of his duties as an
individual member.

The circular concluded with the statement that
he had addressed it to all members opposed to the
existing Administration, in order that steps might
be taken, during the Christmas adjournment, to
make such arrangements as might be satisfactory to
the Opposition generally, for the conduct of their
proceedings in the House.

This announcement of his intention to retire
was variously received.　Some persons experienced
a feeling of satisfaction, under the impression that

it would clear the way for new men to come forward. Others professed to doubt the permanency of the retirement, and to express the opinion that, when the right opportunity presented itself, Mr. Parkes would step to the front again and lead as vigorously as ever. Friends or foes, however, could not but feel some regret at the disappearance, even temporarily, of a striking personality, from the fighting rank of his party; and most persons, recognising the great value of his services in Parliament, hoped that he would soon see his way to re-occupy the leading position, for which no one else had shown himself to be so well fitted.

Several meetings were held to elect a new leader; but there was no immediate result, and, for some time, the Opposition was in a state of disorganization. Eventually a ballot was taken, and the choice fell upon Mr. W. R. Piddington. It was, perhaps, the best selection that could be made; but it was of little usefulness.

Mr. Piddington was one of the oldest members of the House; he could boast some experience in the administration of government; and he was well acquainted with Parliamentary rule and practice. But he had none of the more special attributes which are necessary to success as a leader. He never impressed the House, or the public, with a sense of strength or tactical skill. Though earnest and conscientious in the discharge of his duties, he was in no way conspicuous for political ability. Mr. David Buchanan, for many years a member of the Legislative Assembly, and one who possessed much natural talent which found an outlet through a caustic pen, and a tongue that, at times, was a master of invective, once described him as looking like a pilot in his Sunday clothes, with the pretence of being a financier, but, beyond a fluency of utterance, pointless and ineffective in all he did.   There was a never-varying sameness in his style that wearied and annoyed those who listened to him.   Sir John Robertson aptly likened him to an organ-grinder, and his speeches to the tiresome tunes of a hurdy-gurdy ground out in endless repetition.   His favourite subject was finance.   On that he could speak by the hour ; and, so interminable was his criticism, that its value was lost in its length and dreariness.

It was not to be wondered at that the leadership of Mr. Piddington was a failure.   Those who sat on the same side of the House with him, though they elected him to the position of leader, did not show much disposition to follow him; and, while he voted on one side, the majority of them voted on the other.   In February of 1877, he tried the effect of a motion of censure against the Government, for the manner in which they were administering the affairs of the country ; and, on that occasion, his party went with him, the Government escaping by a majority of three in a division of twenty-six to twenty-nine; but it was all along evident, that if the Government were to be overthrown, it would have to be done by some abler hand than his.

The following month, the Opposition met to consider the position of affairs, and it was decided that another motion of censure should be moved.   But the question arose of who was to move it.   Mr.

Piddington had failed a week or two previously, and it did not seem likely that, if he took this second motion in hand, he would be more successful. He himself solved the difficulty by proposing that the motion should be made by Mr. Parkes. There appeared to be no one else with the shadow of a chance of success. The party agreed that Mr. Parkes should be asked to lead the attack; and he consented. It was an early reappearance from the retirement into which his resignation, scarcely three months before, had sent him; but, as the Opposition seemed unable to do without him, he considered it to be his duty, at their request, to resume his former functions.

The House was informed of the circumstances, and notice was given that Mr. Parkes would move—"That the retention of office by Ministers, after having suffered within nine sitting days four several defeats on motions expressive of condemnation and want of confidence, is subversive of the principles of the Constitution." Very little time was occupied by the motion. Moved early in the afternoon of the 6th March, it was taken to a division the same night, and the Government were defeated by thirty-one votes to twenty-eight.

They advised the Governor to dissolve Parliament; and time would have been saved, and the political situation greatly improved, if the advice had been followed.

The Assembly had drifted into a very unsatisfactory state; it had become almost demoralized; and a general election was the only remedy that seemed likely to do any good. But the Governor, though willing to grant a dissolution, attached to his acceptance of the advice of his Ministers to take this course, the condition that they must first obtain supply to cover the period of the elections; and this the Assembly refused. No one with a clear sense of the state of affairs could have expected anything different. Aware that their being sent to the country depended upon the granting of supply, it was not at all probable that members would take a course which would deprive them of their seats. The House declined "to grant supplies to a defeated Government under circumstances which would, in all probability, result in two general elections within a short period of time"; and the Robertson Government were obliged to resign.

This brought Mr. Parkes into power again at the head of his second Ministry. Sent for by the Governor, on the resignation of Mr. Robertson and his colleagues, he formed an Administration in which the offices were allotted as follows :—

HENRY PARKES ... ... Colonial Secretary & Premier.

WILLIAM RICHMAN PIDDINGTON Colonial Treasurer.

FRANCIS BATHURST SUTTOR ... Minister of Justice & Public Instruction.

RICHARD DRIVER ... ... Secretary for Lands.

JAMES HOSKINS ... ... Secretary for Public Works.

WILLIAM CHARLES WINDEYER Attorney-General.

GEORGE ALFRED LLOYD ... Secretary for Mines.

SAUL SAMUEL, C.M.G. ... Postmaster General.

The Ministry was a good one collectively and individually. Three of them were new to office— Mr. Suttor, Mr. Driver, and Mr. Hoskins; but they were men of education and experience, and did not, in any way, weaken the Government as a whole. Had the condition of the Assembly been satisfactory, the new Administration would probably have done good service. As it was, they were able to do but very little; and, in less than five months, were obliged to resign, on a division which took the business of the House out of their hands. This was a motion for adjournment moved by Mr. Robertson. A few days previously they had been defeated on a motion, moved by Mr. Garrett, relative to the interpretation of a section of the Lands Act.

Even had they escaped these difficulties, they could not have made much headway in the existing Assembly. So disorganized had the House, by this time, become, that its business was virtually at a standstill. Obstruction and disorder were frequent, and it was with difficulty that the proceedings were kept under anything like control. Added to this, there was a feeling manifesting itself that the chiefs of the two sides in the House should retire from active leadership, and so make way for others. People began to talk of the see-saw change of office between Mr. Parkes and Mr. Robertson. This had an injurious effect upon politics; and, assisted as it was by the demoralized condition of the Assembly, it added to the difficulties of the Government. It was destined to make itself felt, a few months later, in an unwise, and even cruel, manner at the polls.

At present it was but assisting to hamper the operations of the Ministry.

Mr. Parkes, on being defeated in the Assembly, counselled the Governor, as Mr. Robertson had done, to dissolve Parliament; but, finding that His Excellency would only do this on the same condition as in the case of the Robertson Government, he declined to become a party to a qualified acceptance of the advice of Ministers, and, with his colleagues, resigned. The resignation was followed by another Robertson Ministry, and, in two months, by a general election.

CHAPTER XXVII.

THE two leaders of the Assembly went before the electors knighted. The title of K.C.M.G. had just been conferred upon them. Mr. Parkes had previously been offered the companionship of the order—C.M.G.—and had declined it; not, as he said, because he underrated its value, but because of his disinclination to accept any title.

The knighthood was regarded as a just recognition of the performance of great services in the public interest, but it was not popular. Distinctions of this kind never have been popular in New South Wales, or in any of the Australasian colonies. They do not fit in with the democratic sentiment, or suitably accommodate themselves to the style of address usual, among a people where, it may be said, every man is supposed to be in social rank the equal of his fellow. Certainly the knighthood did not make matters smoother in the Assembly. Business did not show satisfactory signs of progress. The two principal parties were so evenly balanced, and there was such a constant struggle of the one to overthrow the other, that satisfactory work was out of the question.

One great evil was that the balance of power rested with two or three members. These formed a kind of independent or cross-bench party whose intentions, at any time of crisis, were absolutely secret until disclosed by their votes. Virtually they ruled the House. They were not of the stamp of men who could be approached, sounded, and made subservient to influence. When their vote was vital to the result, in any division about to be taken, no method existed of ascertaining how the vote would be given before it was recorded.

They, like others, seemed to think that the frequent change of Government from that of Sir Henry Parkes to that of Sir John Robertson, and from that of Sir John Robertson to that of Sir Henry Parkes, had gone on long enough, and that some new men should be brought forward. It did not appear to occur to those who desired the two veterans to stand aside for others, that it was possible for the two, if they could be brought together in the same Government, to do more towards the stability of an Administration, and the progress of its work, than had been done for many years before. The one idea in their minds was "new blood."

The cry of "new blood" was raised in the elections; and, with the unthinking portion of the public, it had its effect.

Sir Henry Parkes went into the contest with reluctance. At his meetings in East Sydney, for which electorate he was a candidate, he told the electors that his inclination was not to offer himself for election. For some time previously the proceedings in the Assembly had wearied him of his seat there, and led him to feel that it was utterly impossible for any set of men to do in Parliament that work which the electors had a right to see done. For the previous five or six years, he pointed out, no Government had been sufficiently strong to follow their own convictions. They had been obliged to give way on every side, in order to secure a majority and to retain their power. He did not underestimate the honour of being returned for the constituency, but he showed no anxiety for it. At the same time he was confident of succeeding in the contest, for, at one of his meetings, he declared that there would be such a sprinkling of support from every street and alley, from every palace, every workshop, and every poor man's home, that he would be at the head of the poll by 500 votes.

The nomination proceedings took place on 22nd October, and twelve candidates were proposed. Among them were Mr. John Macintosh, Mr. (afterwards Sir) Alexander Stuart, Mr. John Davies, and Mr. James Greenwood.

The last mentioned was making his first appearance as an aspirant for Parliamentary honours. The cause of the Education League, of which he was the founder and the head, had led him to relinquish everything for politics; and his candidature was pushed by his friends to the utmost. His advocacy of educational reform had brought him under the notice of the public generally, and shown him to be possessed of qualities likely to be of

z

great use in Parliament. A graduate of the
University of London, with intellectual qualifications of a high order, and great facility of utterance,
he had arrived in the colony, from England, in the
capacity of a trained Minister of the Gospel, to fill
the pulpit of the leading Baptist Church of
Sydney; and, in that position and as a public
lecturer, had acquired a reputation for scholarship,
a wide range of information, keenness of observation, deep insight into questions of cause and
effect, and unusual power of expression. The large
assemblage which invariably gathered to hear him
was, at no time, the limit of the number of those
who gave heed to his sermons and his platform
addresses; and, for years previous to the formation
of the Public Schools League, he was regarded as
a man of prominence.

He had unbounded confidence in his political
prospects, and his supporters had implicit confidence
in him. No one could hear him speak, or read his
speeches, without being impressed by the wide extent of his knowledge and his deep insight into, and
clear exposition of, great principles. But there ran
through many of his public addresses, particularly
those delivered during this general election, an
indication that he was attempting too much, that
he was over-estimating his powers, and that in the
endeavour to accomplish everything he would in
the end have accomplished nothing. He was,
however, a formidable opponent in the contest at
East Sydney.

Mr. Macintosh, Mr. Stuart, and Mr. Davies were also in the position of being well supported, each for special reasons. Mr. Macintosh, a very worthy colonist, had many friends on the grounds of his being, as he was described in his advertisements, "a hard-working man, an upright man, a good neighbour, a good citizen, a good alderman." Mr. Stuart was a champion of the educational policy favoured by the two great religious bodies in the colony, and a man of some Parliamentary experience and statesmanlike ability. Mr. Davies enjoyed the confidence of important organizations whose influence in colonial politics had always been considerable.

At the nomination proceedings Sir Henry Parkes was not well received. It was with difficulty that he obtained a hearing. But the show of hands was in his favour, and the interruption during his speech from the hustings was attributed, by his friends, to the enmity of certain sections only of the assembled crowd. Three days afterwards the polling took place, and the city and the colony were startled by the announcement that he had been rejected. Four of the candidates were elected, and he was fifth on the poll. Mr. Macintosh headed the list; Mr. Davies came second; Mr, Greenwood was third; and Mr. Stuart fourth. Sir Henry Parkes was eighty-seven votes below the number polled by Mr. Stuart.

It was a bitter moment for him. "I come here," he had told the East Sydney electors at one of his meetings, "after a political connection, which, although severed for short periods, was first riveted by your votes nearly a quarter of a century ago." For more than twenty-four years he had been fighting the battles of the people, devoting the prime of his life to the public interest, and now he was rudely cast aside as one who was no longer wanted. Can it be wondered at that, in the bitterness of his feelings, the sense of the injustice done him, he told the electors they had closed the door of his political life for ever?

Fortunately his political career had not ended, for it was determined by his friends that it should not end in such a manner.

Offers of seats were telegraphed from all parts of the country, and it was not doubted that he would be returned by some constituency and sit in the new Parliament. But, personally, he would take no step to secure his election. He declined all offers. In one day he despatched to the country no fewer than twenty-five refusals.

His friends decided to bring him out for Canterbury, and advertised his candidature for that constituency. Seeing the advertisements, he wrote declaring he was not a candidate, and that he would not consent to be nominated. But his friends persisted. They held meetings in his favour; they proposed him to the Canterbury electors on nomination day; and finally they had him elected. He was returned at the top of the poll, nearly 200 votes ahead of the other candidates.

A wave of regret at the action of the electors of East Sydney had passed over the colony, and everyone now seemed anxious to do what he could to undo the defeat. The people of Canterbury seized with avidity the opportunity to bring him back to Parliamentary life. He, recognizing their public spirit and appreciating their sympathy, appeared before them at the declaration of the poll, and consented to sit for the electorate. "The man must be made of sorry stuff," he said, "who would not be stirred to the depths of his inmost nature by their generous conduct and the triumph accorded him. They had nobly responded to the appeal of his friends, and, by honourably placing him above all others on the poll, had acted in accordance with the desire of the great body of the people throughout the country."

Meantime an examination of the voting at East Sydney revealed the fact that, but for the over-zeal of the supporters of two of the successful candidates, which led them to plump for their favourites, Sir Henry Parkes would not have been rejected. Had his friends known he was exposed to danger in this direction it could have been met by their plumping for him. But, not suspecting anything of the kind, they distributed their votes, and he lost his chance of being returned.

A careful scrutiny of the returns of the voting led to this conclusion. It was estimated that about three-sevenths of those who recorded their votes had voted for Sir Henry Parkes; but the plumping for favourite candidates, the splitting of votes, and other cross purposes in the election, had made it inevitable that he should be beaten. The working man's vote, it was thought had been withheld from him, because of the outspokenness of his views on free trade and immigration; but this he denied. He was, however, of the same opinion as those who attributed his defeat to the plumping resorted to in the interests of his opponents. " Had the election to take place again tomorrow," the *Herald* wrote, it is probable that Sir Henry Parkes would be among the four successful candidates, and, practically, therefore, he owes his defeat less to the separation between him and the working men than to the peculiar tactics of our defective electioneering system."

Before the Canterbury election had taken place, West Sydney, apparently following the example set it by East Sydney, rejected Sir John Robertson. This increased the sensation which the city elections caused, but did not exclude Sir John from the new Parliament. Very quickly he found a seat at both East Macquarie and Mudgee, and, with his colleagues, met the Assembly when the new Parliament opened.

But the general election did not result in giving either Government or Opposition that strength necessary to satisfactorily carry on the affairs of the country. The evenness of the members on each side, which had made the progress of business in the previous Parliament difficult, had, to a certain extent, disappeared; but not sufficiently to enable either the party in office, or that in opposition, to rule.

Parliament assembled on the 27th November, and the Government were immediately met by an amendment on the Address-in-Reply to the Governor's opening speech, expressing want of confidence in them. It was moved by Mr. James S. Farnell.

Just before the session opened, the Opposition met to consider the political position, and, at the meeting, Mr. Farnell submitted the amendment as one he intended to propose. Sir Henry Parkes was present; but the fact that Mr. Farnell's intention to move the amendment was approved by general consent was an indication that Sir Henry was not, at the time, regarded as the chosen leader of the party. They had, in fact, no leader. Sir Henry Parkes was nominally at their head by force of experience and political standing, but they were not in that organised state which makes it necessary to have a duly elected and recognised chief, to whom shall be left the business of leading an attack upon the Government. They were little more than a number of members in general agreement, to any-one of whom it was open to take what hostile action he pleased against the party in power.

Notwithstanding this, however, Sir Henry Parkes interested himself in Mr. Farnell's amendment, so far as to give him some advice as to its composition, and to induce him to alter it in a manner likely to make it more effective. The result was that it proved successful, for it was carried by thirty-three votes to thirty-two. Such a small majority did not indicate a quiet life for the new

Ministry, whoever might compose it ; but, as another dissolution was out of the question, a new Ministry had to be formed.

Sir Henry Parkes was sent for by the Governor, and he accepted the duty of endeavouring to form a new Administration. The choice of His Excellency excited some comment, for, in addition to the feeling that it would be well to see if a stable Government could be formed apart from either Sir Henry Parkes or Sir John Robertson, it was considered by many that, as Mr. Farnell had brought about the defeat of the Robertson party, the formation of the new Government should have been entrusted to him.

His friends determined that he should have the opportunity. Though aware of the fact that the carrying of a vital motion or amendment against a Government, does not entail upon the Crown the necessity to entrust to the mover of the motion the duty of forming a new Administration, they set themselves to prevent Sir Henry Parkes from being successful. No member of the party, of the prominence desirable, would join him. He first endeavoured to secure the co-operation of Mr. Farnell, and did not succeed. Then he sought the assistance of other members of experience and reputation in the House, and again failed. More than ordinary difficulty met him in every direction.

Unwilling to abandon his undertaking, he tried day after day—longer, perhaps, than he ought to have done—and then was obliged to return his commission to the Governor. He could have formed an Administration, he wrote, when informing

His Excellency of his want of success,—one which, so far as he could see, would have the confidence of Parliament in a sufficient degree to proceed with public business; but, owing to circumstances unprecedented in the political annals of the colony, he had failed in bringing together members of the Assembly who, collectively, would have sufficient strength to conduct the affairs of the country for any length of time in an efficient and satisfactory manner.   He therefore was obliged to relinquish his task, and make way for some one else.

That some one else was Mr. Farnell; and the Farnell-Fitzpatrick Ministry came into office, where it was to remain for just twelve months, and then give place to another Government under Sir Henry Parkes.

CHAPTER XXVIII.

A trenchant and very successful method in the hands of Sir Henry Parkes for damaging the prospects of a Ministry, and one frequently employed, was to make a tour through some of the country districts, and delivered a series of political speeches to the people.

Though ostensibly addressing himself to the comparatively small gathering of townsfolk or farmers of some country township or village, his voice reached the ears of the population throughout the colony, and seldom was ineffective. In the country districts he was always popular, and his speeches, backed by his strong personality, damaged many Ministries and carried many elections.

Wherever people existed, and he made his appearance in their neighbourhood, they flocked to hear him; sometimes in crowds, and, at other times, in smaller numbers, just as the population of the place permitted, but always to listen with eagerness and pleasure to what he had to say. Mostly his audiences were large; but he would make before a gathering of less than twenty persons, where he had to wait until a box was found as a rest for the reporter's note-book, a speech, which, for the time, was the best reading matter in the newspapers and a thing of interest throughout the land.

No one in the public life of New South Wales stood so high in the estimation of the people generally; and, though in Sydney there were times when his popularity seemed to have lessened, if only temporarily, in the country districts it never waned. Not being concerned with the strife which occasionally divided the Sydney constituencies, the people of the country looked only at the services he had rendered in the public interest, at the weight of his political experience and judgment, and at the instructive nature of his speeches. They listened, and learned, and profited, and they always held him in admiration.

In many respects these country tours of Sir Henry Parkes resembled those of the great Liberal leader—Mr. Gladstone—in England. Allowing for the difference in the number of the population, there was the same enthusiasm, the same admiration, the same respect. The questions with which the speeches dealt were, in most instances, smaller, by reason of the difference in the political life of the two countries; but the thoughtful exposition of great principles, the earnest advocacy of good government, and the high estimate of the duties of a citizen in a country of free institutions, were identical.

About six months after the Farnell Ministry entered upon the duties of office, Sir Henry Parkes determined upon a tour through some of the

Western Districts of New South Wales; and he visited Orange, Molong, Wellington, Dubbo, Gulgong, and Mudgee. The reverse which he had suffered at the hands of the electors of East Sydney during the general election, and the obstacles that had stood in his way in the Assembly for the previous year or so, found no approval among the people with whom he now placed himself in contact. Receiving him with open arms they met him in procession, presented him with laudatory addresses, entertained him at public banquets, and assembled almost to a man to hear him speak.

It was his first active crusade, in this form, against what he considered to be misgovernment, and in advocacy of the duties of citizenship in the exercise of the franchise. It was also conspicuous for affording examples of other work he engaged in during his political life. This included his speeches on books and reading.

A great reader and lover of books himself, some of the best of his addresses were delivered at the opening of mechanics' institutes and schools of art. His advice with respect to the choice of books, the study of the authors most qualified to teach and improve, and the value of the information acquired by properly directed and systematic reading, was attractive and useful not only to those immediately interested, but to the public generally, who acquainted themselves with his speeches upon these subjects from the reports of them published in the newspapers.

He was equally successful in addressing himself to children. No one was more capable than he of speaking to an assemblage of young people, especially if they were attending one of the public schools. In such a case, he was able not only to interest the children by addressing them in an entertaining manner, but to impart to them, in simple language which they could well understand and appreciate, the great possibilities within their reach from the privileges they enjoyed, if their opportunities for making the most of those privileges were properly recognised and used.

These three classes of oratory marked this western tour; and, for fully a fortnight, the press was engaged chronicling his utterances and his progress from one town or district to another.

Speaking upon the welfare of the colony as a whole, compared with advantages to a single district only, of the importance of Australia as compared with New South Wales, and of the principles which should prevail in legislation and in government, he said—

" Let us cultivate the feeling and conviction that every district in the country will progress best, in the degree in which it is bound up with the prosperity of all the districts in the country. Your great desire should be for the general prosperity; and, if the country is in a state of general prosperity, this district, as all others, must share in that prosperity. I for one go much further than this, and I am not desirous for the prosperity and progress of New South Wales at the expense of the

other colonies. I look to the time when Australian
interests will be identical throughout this land, from
sea to sea, and when those jealousies which have
grown up, to bitter form in some instances, will
have passed away, and each colony will believe that
its prosperity will be best promoted by the prosperity of the free communities around it.

"Just in the same way I am anxious that we
should, more and more, cultivate a feeling of free citizenship, a feeling of nationality, and have more
of New South Wales and less of any particular district in which we live. . . . I believe the true
philosophy of our political system is to elect members for particular districts in order that, in the col-
lective body of the Legislature, we should gather up
a variety of forms of intelligence, a variety in the
knowledge of the condition of the country's resources; but, while that is the case, that the members should legislate for the whole country and not
for any particular district. . . . No interest of
any district ought to be considered beyond its
legitimate claim to consideration.

"The principles which ought to prevail in legislation and in government are as eternal, and as clear,
as the very heavens bending above us. They are
equality of treatment, justice to all, definiteness in
dealing with mankind; and, beyond these great
broad principles of treating all alike, dealing out
even-handed justice to all alike, telling all men in
definite terms what rights they are entitled to,
and giving in definite terms just claims to those
rights, anything in the shape of favouritism—

favouring special interests at the expense of others
—will, in the end, recoil with bitter misfortune on
the whole country."

And, proceeding more closely to the question of
government, he went on ;—

"Free government, under our political system,.
means that the affairs of the country should be
managed by men who, by their services, by their
intelligence, by the proofs that they have given of
integrity, command the confidence of the people.
It does not mean that the affairs of the country
should be in the hands of persons who by promises,
by an improper dispensation of patronage, or by
what there is no other word for than 'jobbing,' can
for the moment get a majority of votes. Government by parliamentary majority, fairly won—won
in the open daylight, by the merits of the persons
who win it, is one of the best forms of government
in the world. Government under our form of
constitution, by men who receive the support of a
majority got together by unseen processes, by back-
door influence, by means which the public know
nothing about, is the worst, or, if not the worst,
nearly the worst form of government."

The great difficulty in a country like this, he
pointed out, was the want of an educated leisured
class properly instructed in politics and the science
of government.

"There is one great drawback to the working
out of our institutions to which older and more
compact countries are not subject. In older and
more compact countries, such for example as

England, there is always a leisured class which is trained to the study of political questions. There is always a class which, from the cradle to the grave, mingles with persons who have made government their chief study : and this class is composed of men who have had every advantage of the highest forms of education. They are, as a rule, men of the most sensitive honour, quick to obey the obligations of public life, thinking more of their public reputation than of any other end ; and hence the government is conducted upon principles of strict purity ; hence it is conducted with a broad and comprehensive attention to the clear ends of government.

"But in a colony like ours, every man has to struggle for existence. Even the men who hold broad acres amongst us, the men in possession of large estates, have lived a more laborious life than men of corresponding wealth in older countries, and have little time to attend to any subject, except those they attend to in prosecuting their own interests. When they get into Parliament, as they occasionally do, they have to turn their attention to political questions for the first time. They turn their attention to these questions under circum-stances and modes of life quite new to them, and frequently are entirely deceived during the first years of their Parliamentary existence,—until, in fact, they probably lose their seats and never appear in Parliament again. Thus our Parliamentary life is made up of novices,—of the actions, purposes, and thoughts of novices,—who are not sufficiently long engaged in it to mature their views, or make themselves thoroughly acquainted with the state of things with which they have to deal; and many of the crudities and mistakes which arise may be traced by thinking persons to these causes." How necessary, under such circumstances, it is for both the people and those they elect to Parliament, to have their respective duties clearly set before them, he fully recognised.

"The duty of every true member of Parliament," he explained on this occasion, "is to support the popular rule, to keep a sharp eye on the growth of abuses, to keep a tight hand upon the public purse; to see that the liberties of the people are in no point affected, that the public money is in no profligate manner expended; and to stand right across the path of any Minister who would indulge in abuses in order to preserve himself in power. It is certainly not the duty of any member of Parliament to be for ever trotting at the heels of a Minister, for ever introducing deputations and asking little favours."

"If the time should ever come," he further said on this subject,—"and I trust it will come as education spreads, and young men of the country grow up with other feelings and other objects of ambition—when we shall have gentlemen forming the Legislature, who consider that government itself can confer no honour upon them, that being freely returned by a body of free electors they have attained the highest position which they can have in a country like this, where they value their independence above all else, you will have a Legislature

AA

more robust, more manly, more deserving, and more patriotic than any you have yet seen. I for one," he went on to say, " do not despair for the successful working of our free institutions; but I look more to the diffusion of knowledge among the people, to a cultivation of the perception of the duties of a citizen, to the greater value attached to an elector's vote, than to any members entering Parliament. Whenever the electors of this country shall form a high idea of their advantages, and cherish in themselves a resolute and manly spirit to perform their duty above all considerations, the result will be a high and independent and proud Parliament."

These words may be read with benefit by everybody; for, though taken from a speech delivered over twenty years ago, they are as applicable to the political life of the colony to-day as they were to that of the time when they were spoken.

The addresses of Sir Henry Parkes upon books and reading frequently contained references to other methods for brightening life, especially life in the more scattered districts of the country. A favourite topic in this direction was cottage-gardening and the beautifying of homes with flowers.

" In a land like ours," he said at the opening of the School of Arts at Molong, " men and women must of necessity, in the remote towns and in other country places, live under circumstances of every-day life which are more rough than elegant, more calculated to imbrute than refine, more calculated to inculcate a taste for the mere physical enjoyments of life than for the higher and finer moral enjoyments. For this reason it is, in the highest sense, desirable that we, all of us, do what we can to bring about our homes those associations of everyday life which have a more refining and more elevating tendency. Hence the man does not perform a light service who by example, by encouragement, endeavours to induce other men and women to some extent to beautify their homes. . . . There is no home in all this land, be it built of slabs or even sheets of bark, that might not be rendered more beautiful, more attractive, or more endearing by the simple act of planting a few flowers around it ; and there is no person so poor, or destitute of resources, that he cannot brighten and enliven his dwelling in this way. . . . I am very sorry to say that this mode of enriching life is too much neglected amidst the rough and hard cares to which men are subject. But neglected as it is, it is really a comforting consideration to think that, in every town of any importance, there are men found who, by their united efforts, create institutions for the eleva- tion of the mind, in the absence of much that might be done, and is not done, for strewing the common path of our life with flowers."

It was not out of place that, in addresses of this kind, to audiences largely composed of working men, he should sometimes allude to the humble circum- stances of his early life, and to his persevering efforts to advance himself.

"There is no passage of my life," he said on this occasion, "of which I am prouder, than that, when I had to undertake a day's manual toil, I always tried

to fulfil my task manfully and well. I was a tradesman, and came to this colony as such; and, if I had
continued so, probably my life would have been spent
more happily. But there is nothing of what I have
accomplished, of which I am prouder, than that I
understood my trade, and could work beside any
of my fellow-labourers. If I no longer occupy a
position of that kind, if I have had to associate with
different persons and perform very different kinds of
duties, I have not the less been a very hard labourer
up to the present hour; and I question whether
there is any man, within the wide limits of society
here, who has toiled harder all his life than the
person addressing these words to you."

The criticisms in the speeches during this tour,
of the Government in office, had considerable effect
in attracting attention to what others, besides Sir
Henry Parkes, regarded as evidence why the
Ministers should be removed from their positions,
and contributed materially to their downfall, which
occurred a few months afterwards.

But unsatisfactory as the Administration in power
seemed to be, the condition of parties in the House
was not such as to indicate that an advantageous
change could be made. Apart from Sir Henry
Parkes and Sir John Robertson, no suitable leader
was apparent; and the followers of the two knights
were so evenly balanced in numbers, that it did not
appear possible for either to return to office with any
chance of remaining there. Unless the Farnell
Ministry were kept where they were, the old oscil-
lation of the ministerial pendulum from Sir Henry

Parkes to Sir John Robertson, and from Sir John Robertson to Sir Henry Parkes, seemed inevitable. And yet the Assembly was not long in deciding that, come what would, Mr. Farnell and his colleagues must go. They did go after, as already mentioned, an existence of just twelve months, when they were defeated by a nearly two-to-one vote upon their Land Bill; and, certain unexpected events taking place, they made way for a Ministry under Sir Henry Parkes, which proved to be the strongest, the longest-lived, and one of the most useful in the parliamentary history of the colony.

CHAPTER XXIX.

GREATER surprises than two experienced in the month of December, 1878, never fell upon the people of New South Wales. Bemoaning the want of a strong and stable Government, and anticipating, with the defeat of the Farnell Ministry, a sustained struggle for office between Sir Henry Parkes and Sir John Robertson, they were suddenly startled by the announcement that Sir John Robertson, determining to retire from public life, had resigned his seat in the Assembly. The sensation was great, for Sir John Robertson was always popular ; and, notwithstanding the inconvenience which arose from his constant efforts for office, his public services were recognised and highly appreciated. His retirement from Parliamentary life, in which he had been one of the most conspicuous figures for nearly a quarter of a century, was the last thing expected ; and, after astonishment, the prominent feeling was regret.

Scarcely, however, had the people begun to recover from this extraordinary incident, than it was made known that Sir John Robertson had consented to join the new Administration, under Sir Henry Parkes, as Vice-President of the Executive Council

and Representative of the Government in the Upper
House. To say that the surprise increased is but
mildly descriptive of the feeling this additional announcement aroused. The public were amazed, but,
with their amazement, came a sense of relief and
satisfaction. A strong Government was assured, for
the union of the two Opposition chiefs promised an
end to disorganization in Parliament, and, consequently, a satisfactory rate of progress with public
business.

What had led to the new position was very simple.
On the defeat of the Farnell Ministry Sir John
Robertson had been commissioned by the Governor
to form a new Government, and had failed. He
succeeded so far as to submit the names of an Administration to His Excellency, but, the House refusing
supply in the form he desired it, he relinquished the
duty placed upon him by the Governor, before he
and those who were to have been his colleagues
were sworn in. At the same time, he determined to
resign from the Assembly. Weary of the disordered
condition of the House, and convinced that the
existence of three parties there was fatal to the possibility of good government, he felt it would be
wise for him to retire. He did so ; and the way was
made clear for Sir Henry Parkes as against Mr.
Farnell. It was cleared also sufficiently for the two
parties forming the Opposition to come together.
The patriotic abnegation of self, which Sir John
Robertson had shown by his resignation, and the
statement of his reasons for the step he had taken,
led his followers and those of Sir Henry Parkes to

consider whether they might not sink their differences, and, for the purposes of good government, join their forces and act in concert. Once the idea was mooted, and began to be considered, it was seen how easily it might be carried into effect. It was agreed that the parties should join on the basis of being equally represented in the Administration, and steps were immediately taken to bring this about.

Sir Henry Parkes was taken by surprise at Sir John Robertson's resignation from the Assembly, and he lost no time in stating this. Apparently, it was done without any intimation of the proceeding being previously made to him ; and he could not see sufficient cause for such an extreme step in the explanation given.

In very generous words, he bore his testimony to the high position Sir John Robertson had filled in public life, and expressed his regret that Sir John's great services should so suddenly, and, at a period when he was still in the full vigour of his faculties, come to an end. Then, alluding to the relations which, in the course of their careers in Parliament, had existed between them, he unconsciously showed how easily the two might have joined in the same Government, and, perhaps, paved the way for what took place afterwards. They had sat for many years in the Assembly, he said, from one cause and another on seats opposite each other, and, whatever those causes were, it would be difficult to trace them to their true source. It had not been in a conspicuous sense from political disagreements, for, on broad grounds, they had been in accord with each other.

Nothing more in fact than a fair rivalry for the position of leader had divided them. Otherwise they were one.

Whether Sir John Robertson entertained any thought of joining Sir Henry Parkes, as he very quickly did, or of any similar arrangement, when resigning his seat in the Assembly, has never been fully explained. Possibly he did not. The reference to the matter in "Fifty Years of Australian History" represents the offer of a place in the Administration to have been made to him by Sir Henry Parkes at Sir Henry's own instance, "without consultation with anyone." In his address to his constituents at Canterbury, Sir Henry Parkes said much the same thing, though with an elaboration which might suggest, to some minds, that the step was not the result of a sudden idea.

"In accepting His Excellency's commission," he stated, "it was impossible for me to close my eyes to the manifest evidences that, both in Parliament and in the country, a strong feeling prevailed in favour of collecting the available elements for the formation of a strong government on the basis of an honourable coalition of parties ; and my first step, therefore, was to place myself in communication with the gentleman who had recently retired from the leadership of the Opposition, and to urge upon him the duty of reconsidering his determination, so far as to assist me by accepting a seat in the Legislative Council as the representative of the new Ministry in that House. Sir John Robertson, at once, and in the most cordial terms, expressed the purpose he had already formed to aid me by using his great influence in promoting the success of my efforts ; and, eventually, he consented to take the position I proposed to him.

The disagreement which had existed between the two having been more personal than political, and the two sections of the Opposition having joined in nominating Sir Henry Parkes leader of the consolidated party, there was really no strong reason why Sir John Robertson should refuse to join the Government. As he was out of the Assembly it was naturally proposed that he should be appointed to the Council ; and the place in the Government submitted for his acceptance, while not conferring full ministerial office, was, next to that of the head of the Ministry, the position of honour. The Government, as a whole, was constructed avowedly on the basis of a fair representation of the two recognised sections of the Opposition; and, to quote Sir Henry Parkes' words, the coalition had been effected " without any violation of principles or any marked differences of opinion on leading political questions among its members."

In connection with the office offered to Sir John Robertson, there was the difficulty that it did not carry with it any salary ; but this was got over by an arrangement among the other members of the Government, by which they contributed a portion of their salaries for the purpose of providing one for Sir John Robertson. In other words, the salaries of the Ministry were combined and shared ; and this arrangement continued for sixteen months, when the passing of the "Public Instruction Act of 1880" caused the office of Minister of Justice and Public Instruction to be divided, and brought about the appointment of Sir John Robertson as Minister of Public Instruction, with the usual ministerial salary.

The Government on its formation, was announced as follows :—

SIR HENRY PARKES... ... Colonial Secretary.

SIR JOHN ROBERTSON ... Vice-President of the Executive Council, & Representative of the Government in the Legislative Council.

JAMES WATSON ... ... Colonial Treasurer.

FRANCIS BATHURST SUTTOR Minister of Justice and Public Instruction.

WILLIAM CHARLES WINDEYER Attorney General.

JAMES HOSKINS ... ... Secretary for Lands

JOHN LACKEY ... ... Secretary for Public Works.

SAUL SAMUEL ... ... Postmaster General.

EZEKIEL ALEXANDER BAKER Secretary for Mines.

All but Mr. Watson had previously been in office, and he, though new to official life, soon showed a special aptitude for the position to which he had been appointed. Most of the Ministers were able men. At first sight, they seemed to be a combination, which, from old personal antagonisms, would find it difficult to work in harmony, but it was wonderful how well they acted together through the long period which comprised their existence.

Many persons, though rejoiced to see the two parliamentary chiefs in the same Government, felt somewhat puzzled at their being together. Some remembered that, in a speech, delivered only ten years before, Sir Henry had emphatically declared that, if he lived fifty years, he could not politically associate himself with Sir John Robertson in any way. Others could not forget that Sir John Robertson had never wearied of denouncing Sir Henry Parkes, and, on one well-known occasion, had gone so far as to threaten him with a criminal prosecution for certain alleged proceedings with papers connected with the Colonial Secretary's Office. Incongruities appeared also in the memories of many concerning the relations between other members of the Ministry.

But these recollections, and the comments they suggested, soon disappeared in the satisfaction created by the useful and important measures which the Government were able to pass. The association of the two chiefs had, in fact, been expected, by some persons who had narrowly watched the Assembly, some twelve months earlier than it took place; but matters were not then quite ripe for it. When Mr. Farnell formed what was known as the Third Party, which subsequently helped him into power, it was thought that Sir Henry Parkes and Sir John Robertson would unite; but the Third Party and the Farnell Government, as events happened, were allowed to run their course, and to drop into the background from sheer inability to retain the position they had assumed.

The new Ministry, though not free from mistakes, produced an exceedingly creditable record of legislative and executive work. They amended the electoral law, passed the Public Instruction Act, under which the present system of state education is administered, materially altered the liquor licensing law, restricted the immigration of Chinese, brought into existence the procedure by which children are boarded out by the state, established the existing systems of water supply and sewerage for the metropolis and the country, introduced the practice under which land for public purposes is acquired by the Government, substituted for the old and inefficient system of honorary police court magistrates the appointment of stipendiary magistrates, extended and regulated the liability of employers in relation to injuries to workmen, regulated the fisheries of the colony, made provision for schools of anatomy, and greatly improved the practice of dealing with the insane. In addition to all this, they were able to leave, when retiring from office, a surplus at the Treasury of nearly £2,000,000.

The change in the public school system was not brought about with the unqualified approval of Sir Henry Parkes. He was satisfied with the law of 1866, which, by the natural development and operation of its principles, was, in his opinion, amply fulfilling all that had been expected of it. Instead of radically altering or "tinkering with" the machinery of what was doing so much good, it was a wiser policy, he had always held, to let the Act continue in the satisfactory way it was working, assisting its

beneficial effects by efforts to improve its administration wherever improvement was possible.   Liberty
of conscience and differences of opinion had been
respected by it, while it had imparted instruction
" to all classes, in all conditions, and under all circumstances," throughout the colony.

He did not sympathize with the maintenance of
purely denominational schools, but he had contended
that, so long as the revenues of the country were
appropriated for the purposes of education, no right
existed to apply them in a way that would exclude
a large proportion of the population from the benefits obtained from that expenditure.

He had not been backward in expressing the
belief that, on this question, the Legislature ought,
as far as it could, to respect the convictions and
associations, and even the prejudices, or what
might be regarded as the unsound opinions, of all
persons.   For the sake of a thin unsustainable
theory, for the sake of carrying out impracticable
whims, were we, he had asked, going to
shut up such magnificent schools as St. Philip's,
St. Mary's, and St. James', and put the country to
the expense of building other school-houses which
could supply no better kind of education?   No advantage could be gained by such a course; the only
result would be to gratify the whim of bigoted
religionists or equally bigoted secularists.

Considering the circumstances of the population,
the differences of opinion, and even the prejudices
which prevailed in the country, we had, he had
argued, a law sufficiently elastic to accomodate

itself to all conditions of our Australian life, sufficiently comprehensive to reach all its proper objects, and economical enough to avoid all extravagant expenditure.

As late as the middle of the year 1875, he had spoken warmly and eloquently in this manner, during a debate in the Legislative Assembly, upon a motion moved by Mr. (now Sir) George Dibbs, for the amendment of the Public Schools Act, in the direction of discontinuing the assistance given from the public funds to denominational schools.

But it came about that the system was made the subject of virulent attack by two powerful, and, curiously enough, directly opposite parties : one the secularists who, while desiring to secularise the system, wanted to make state primary education compulsory and free, and the other the leaders of the Roman Catholic Church in the colony, headed by the late Archbishop Vaughan, whose efforts were untiringly put forth in denouncing the secularism of the public schools, and in endeavouring to secure, for their own schools, a full share of the public expenditure devoted to state education.

Archbishop Vaughan, a man of high education, and one of the most eloquent speakers ever heard in Australia, had denounced the state schools as seed-plots of immorality and crime. He had aroused an interest and activity among the adherents of his Church, and among members of the Church of England, which irritated and alarmed those disposed to stand by the educational system as it existed. So persistent were his attacks, that the indignation of the friends and supporters of the public schools began to give way, in some quarters, and among these that in which Sir Henry Parkes moved, to a determination to increase the safeguards which were intended to preserve the educational system from denominational control or influence. If the large privileges, which the system offered to denominationalists, were to be spurned, with a view to undermining and destroying the system itself, then it was but natural that those, who had given these privileges, should seek to retaliate by abolishing them. But while some persons were influenced by a feeling of retaliation, others saw that, by removing the remnant of denominationalism entirely from the state-supported schools, the system would be both purified and strengthened. While the enemy had a footing in the camp, be it ever so slight, the position was endangered. Exclude him, and it was safe.

It was surprising that Dr. Vaughan did not see, or seem to see, the probable result of the attitude he assumed. From the time of the passing of the Public Schools Act until this period, and from then till now, the vast majority of the population of New South Wales have been warm supporters of the public schools. At no time could the Roman Catholic portion of the people upset the system. Not even when supported in their action by a proportion of the adherents of the Church of England, have they been able to effect any serious harm. But their attacks have been a source of irritation and disquiet; and the very circumstance that the concessions to them, under the law, at this time, gave them a certain right to advance their own interests, though it might be by destroying the interests of others, was regarded as a strong reason why the special privileges afforded them under the Act should be withdrawn.

Archbishop Vaughan, himself, was a splendid type of the fighting Englishman, and the education question afforded him ample opportunity for a display of his fighting qualities.   Expert with his pen, as with his voice, he could attack with judgment, neatness, and effect ; and he could receive, with equanimity and good humour, the chastisement that his opponents were able to give him in return. From his residence at St. John's College, letters to the press, and pamphlets and speeches to his co-religionists, came with a frequency unknown previously in connection with his church in Australia. All were brilliant and forceful, though sectarian from beginning to end, and not always free from features more objectionable ; but their very brilliancy and forcefulness, by stirring the fighting opponents of the Archbishop, and, at their back, the general public, to greater activity, assisted largely to defeat the objects of their author.

The Public Schools League had grown large and strong.   Probably, if Sir Henry Parkes had not included the amendment of the system of state education in the programme of his Government, the matter would have been taken out of his hands, and the work done by someone else.   Inside and outside Parliament, the feeling that the system should be entirely secular, and both compulsory and free,

influenced apparently the majority.   Secularization
would remove the disturbing element of denominationalism; compulsion would extend the benefits of
the instruction given in the schools to every child in
the land; freedom from expense to all but the state
would justify compulsion.

As already mentioned, Mr. James Greenwood
had entered the Legislative Assembly as the
champion of the new doctrine only a year before the
Parkes-Robertson Government assumed office. The
question of state education was a subject of intense
interest to him. He had, in respect of it, all the
earnestness and enthusiasm of the reformer, and the
breadth and strength of view of the statesman.
Extensive reading had made him acquainted with the
fullest information regarding the various educational
systems of the world, and a remarkable capacity for
understanding and dissecting statistics enabled him
to arrive at definite conclusions as to their relative
or individual value.

He could not see why the education provided
and paid for by the state, should not be wholly
national,—by which he meant that it should be
within reach of everybody on the most economical
and equitable terms, without distinction of class or
creed. To associate it in any way with the beliefs
or opinions of any sect was, in his opinion, to do
that with which the state had properly no concern.
The expenditure of public money obtained from the
people by taxation should be, he argued, for the
general and equal benefit of all. No class of the
people could have a just claim to the expenditure of

public funds on denominational or other sectional ground.   Yet under the existing system, as he pointed out, the denominational schools were costing the state far more than the public schools, with much inferior results.

It was equally clear, to his mind, that state education should be compulsory; the necessity for it being apparent in the large number of children of school age in the colony, who were proved by statistics to be growing up in almost total ignorance. National, secular, compulsory, and free were the cardinal principles of his convictions on the subject of public instruction; and having, with the assistance of some friends, formed the League, he carried its banner through the country, and, finally, into Parliament.   James Greenwood, and his followers throughout the land, had, in their way, as much to do with the passing of the Public Instruction Act as Archbishop Vaughan.

Several changes in the composition of the Ministry took place during its long existence.   Some of these were consequent upon the passing of the Public Instruction Act, which led to a division of the offices of Minister of Justice and Public Instruction and the appointment of an additonal Minister.   But others, and these the chief, were owing to trouble which came upon the Administration in 1881 in connection with what was known as the Milburn Creek Copper Mining Company Inquiry.   The member of the Ministry who, when the Government was formed, was appointed Secretary for Mines, became involved in a transaction associated with this

mining company which, eventually, led to his
temporary expulsion from Parliament; but, before
this took place, it brought about the resignation
of Sir John Robertson from the Government,
and the admission into the Ministry, in
consequence, of the present Chief Justice, Sir
Frederick (then Mr.) Darley, and Mr. S. C. Brown.
A rearrangement of portfolios, after the passing of
the Public Instruction Act, brought to the office of
Minister for Justice, Sir J. G. L. Innes, who, less
than twelve months afterwards, was appointed a Judge
of the Supreme Court, and was succeeded in the
Ministry by Mr. (afterwards Mr. Justice) Foster.
Mr. (now Sir) W. C. Windeyer retired in 1879
from the position of Attorney-General, to take
that of Acting Judge of the Supreme Court,
and was appointed to a permanent judgeship two
months before Sir George Innes was elevated to
the Bench. Mr. Windeyer was succeeded in the
Attorney-Generalship by the late Sir (then Mr.)
Robert Wisdom. Mr. (now Sir) Saul Samuel left
the Post Office in August, 1880, to take up the
position of Agent-General of the colony in London;
and his place in the Ministry was filled, first by Mr.
F. B. Suttor, temporarily, and, afterwards, successively
by Mr. S. C. Brown and Mr. Alexander Campbell.
One other member of the Cabinet in its later life,
not in it when the Government was first formed,
was Dr. (now Sir) Arthur Renwick, who became
Secretary for Mines in October, 1881.

So many changes in the composition of a
Ministry, would, in ordinary cases, indicate

weakness in the Administration; but, until Sir John Robertson's resignation, there was no evidence that the strength of the Government had in any degree lessened. Even when Sir John Robertson's retirement seemed, for a time, to threaten the downfall of the Administration, the readiness of Sir Frederick Darley and Mr. S. C. Brown to come forward and assist the Government out of its difficulty removed all fear of disaster. The Government went on very much as before. When, with the termination of the proceedings in Parliament relating to the Milburn Creek inquiry, Sir John Robertson was able to re-enter the Ministry, as he did, its original strength appeared to return; and from that time, until difficulties which arose on the land question began to affect the stability of the Ministry, the union between the two chiefs and their respective parties was not affected by anything likely to shake or destroy it.

The Milburn Creek episode forms a very unpleasant incident in the Parliamentary history of New South Wales. Left as a legacy by the preceding Government, it became the duty of the Government of Sir Henry Parkes and Sir John Robertson, to submit to arbitration a claim of the Milburn Creek Copper Mining Company to compensation for loss of land obtained by them as a mineral lease, and afterwards taken from them by a decision of the Supreme Court in favour of a party who had selected the land as a conditional purchase before the Milburn Creek Company's lease was ratified.

The claim of the company to compensation was regarded by most persons as just and indisputable. It had been inquired into by a select committee of the Assembly, and the committee had decided that the claim merited recognition by the Government. The only question that then required to be determined was the amount of compensation that should be paid. The mine had been carefully examined by Government experts, and the claim investigated in its various bearings; and the arbitrators were empowered, under instructions from the Government, to award any sum not exceeding £26,000. They awarded between £16,000 and £17,000.

An undesirable feature in the matter was the circumstance that the Minister for Mines was one of the principal members of the company. Up to the time the compensation was voted by Parliament, he appeared to act with tact and delicacy of feeling, taking no part whatever in assisting the claim; and afterwards, according to his explanation, he acted simply in justification of the position he held in the company. But no sooner was compensation voted, and the apportionment of the money by the trustees or directors made, than complications arose, strong disapproval being expressed by some of the shareholders.

This might not have been of much effect if it had not found its way into the newspapers. Publicity brought it under the attention of the Legislative Assembly, where from the first some members had regarded the whole matter with suspicion; and it then became necessary, that the published state-

ment of the manner in which the money voted by
Parliament had been divided by the trustees, should
be searchingly investigated.

Anxious to probe the matter to the bottom, if
only to give all concerned in the company an opportunity for speaking out fully and clearly, the
Government issued a Royal Commission to Mr.
(now Sir) Julian E. Salomons; and that gentleman,
after careful inquiry, forwarded to the Government
a report, so sensational in some respects that it
awakened widespread interest. The Minister for
Mines, who had shortly before resigned his ministerial office, was charged with improperly receiving
a share of the money awarded; and a charge of
endeavouring to benefit from the compensation, in a
corrupt manner, was made against another prominent member of the Assembly, the late Mr.
Thomas Garrett.

Sir Henry Parkes took immediate action. He
had entertained no suspicion of anything discreditable in connection with the claim of the company
or the apportionment of the compensation voted.
He had regarded his Minister for Mines as occupying a strictly honourable and proper position in the
matter. He had taken no active part at any stage
of the proceedings but that when the vote of money
was actually before the House for decision; neither
the adoption by the House of the select committee's
report, the appointment of the arbitrators, nor the
issue of the Royal Commission, was his work; but
he had never doubted the propriety of the whole
course of procedure, and it had received his ap-

proval. Now, when the Royal Commissioner charged two members of the House with conduct unworthy of a member, and such as to reflect upon the honour and dignity of Parliament, and when the evidence, as Sir Henry Parkes considered, bore out those charges, he determined upon giving the Legislative Assembly an opportunity for expressing its opinion upon this conduct.

The subject was discussed by the Cabinet, and a certain course decided upon. The attention of the House was to be drawn to the report of the Commissioner, and the House was to be invited to pass resolutions, first expressing the opinion that the conduct of the two members charged had been unworthy, and inconsistent with the honour and dignity of Parliament, and then expelling them.

Sir John Robertson, who could look back upon many years of friendship and association, in and out of office, with the two members, could not permit himself to be in the position of their accuser. The tone of his correspondence at the time indicated his conviction that the case of each looked very unsatisfactory, and he could only hope that they would be able to clear themselves of the imputations against them; but he would not, as a member of the Government, take the action the Goverment proposed to take against them, and he resigned.

" I find myself," he wrote to Sir Henry Parkes, " compelled to make choice between becoming one of the accusers of two gentlemen with whom I have been, for nearly a quarter of a century, connected in public life, and to resign my office, and I have determined on taking the latter course." A chivalrous-minded gentleman throughout his life, generous to a fault whenever friendship was concerned, he separated himself from the Government because he would not, at any risk, take part in what might bring about the ignominious downfall of two who had worked with him hand-in-hand through many, if not most, of the ups and downs of his long political career. He thought the matter ought to be dealt with in the law courts of the country, rather than that the Government should assume in Parliament the position of accuser; but Sir Henry Parkes held that the vindication of the honour and character of Parliament was not a subject for the courts of law, and he could not see that dealing with members criminally in the law courts " would place them in a more honourable or better position than being dealt with by their peers in Parliament."

The resignation of Sir John Robertson embarrassed the Government for a time, and it saved Mr. Garrett; for, becoming known in the House during the course of the proceedings relating to him, and being used with advantage by both Mr. Garrett and his friends, it had the effect of influencing the voting.

In the case of the Minister for Mines, it was of no avail. When that was before the House, members were neither aware of the resignation nor of any want of agreement in the Cabinet. But, if they had known of what had taken place, it is doubtful whether it would have done the Minister any good. The charge against him was different from that against Mr. Garrett, and he was far less popular. Notwithstanding, an explanation which, to his friends, appeared amply satisfactory, he was expelled; and, not until the following Parliament, could he do anything effectual to remove the injury which this proceeding on the part of the Assembly did his reputation. Then the motion which had brought about his expulsion was rescinded, and, subsequently, he was again returned to the House by the constituency he had previously represented.

Mr. Garrett was saved by a majority of two votes in a division of forty to thirty-eight. He owed his escape to Sir John Robertson's resignation, and to the style of speech he adopted in defending himself—an adroit and masterful appeal to the feelings rather than an explanation of his conduct. Throughout his parliamentary career, Mr. Garrett was, in many respects, the ablest member in the House. On this occasion, he surpassed himself; and his speech stands in the records of the proceedings, as one of the cleverest ever delivered within the walls of the Assembly.

CHAPTER XXX.

THE close of the year 1881 found Sir Henry Parkes, still the head of the Government, on a visit to England.

For some time previously he had been in indifferent health, and, his indisposition increasing, he had been warned by his medical advisers that, if he desired any lengthened term of life, it was absolutely necessary for him to seek change of scene and relaxation. To a busy man, such as he had always been, relaxation in any form would be but another kind of work ; but a sea voyage, and the pleasant experiences to which a short stay in the old country would give rise, were certain to be beneficial. His labours in the Colonial Secretary's office, and in Parliament, had overtaxed his strength, and he was suffering from some of the worst effects of overwork.

Away from the Legislative Assembly he lived almost wholly in his office. An anteroom, furnished plainly as a bedroom, gave him sleeping accommodation, and his meals, plain as his sleeping apartment, were provided by his messenger. Though midnight, or any hour of the early morning, might see him in the Assembly, he was invariably in his chair at his office-table long before breakfast-time; and there he sat attending to official papers, receiving callers, or meeting deputations, throughout the day. If the House adjourned early, he was back in his office again, resuming his work until midnight. He frequented no club. He was not of the disposition to fraternise with companions, and stroll away from the Assembly to spend the evening in idle amusement. His life was in his work, and his work was his life. No one enjoyed the satisfaction from labour more than he.

In the gloomy quietness of night, with the flickering gas-light from the street-lamp just making the sombreness of the heavy door perceptible, and the grim-looking policeman, on duty there, measuredly walking to-and-fro, the Colonial Secretary's Office presents anything but an inviting aspect outside; and inside, in the darkness and solitariness of the corridors, it is still more depressing. But any night, or early morning, as the hour of the Assembly's adjourning allowed, the tall well-proportioned figure of the Premier, his head bent as with weariness, and his white hair amply showing from under his capacious silk hat, could be seen approaching the Macquarie Street steps of the building, preceded by the policeman, with latch key in hand, to open the door.

People used to say it was not surprising his health broke down, for how could a man spending most of his time in such a place—night as well as day—expect to keep well. Yet to him the time he spent there did not appear to be distasteful. Some of the pleasantest half-hours or hours were passed with him in his office late at night, by those on such terms of friendship as justified their calling at such a time. He was always glad of a visitor whom he knew, at night, if his work permitted of a chat and an exchange of views. His loneliness may have had something to do with this; but it was accounted for also by the fact that on such occasions, freed from the incessant worry of the office-duties of the day, he was companionable to a degree which not only put the visitor at his ease, but made his visit an unalloyed delight. At such times he was brimful of wise talk on politics and other topics of the day, and of interesting anecdote. The newest of his books, collections of which were constantly being brought to his room, were produced, and the latest of his letters from English celebrities shown. Minutes flew like seconds; the hours, sometimes, like minutes.

His only change from the monotony of his life in Parliament, and in the Colonial Secretary's Office, was a weekly visit to the Blue Mountains. There, at Faulconbridge, not far from the railway, he had taken up a free selection, and built a mountain residence. Constructed of weatherboards, in the bungalow style, inexpensive, and simple, it stood on a commanding eminence, looking abroad upon an attractive prospect of rugged mountain-tops and rocky valleys and glens, and, beyond these, upon a far-off view, which extended to Sydney. The mountain-side he had terraced, and planted with flowers and ornamental trees. The rough rocks he had covered with clinging vines ; and the rocky recesses he had made homes of the fern and the lily. Native trees or flowering shrubs and plants, attractive in any respect, had been preserved with as much care as those obtained from city nurseries were cultivated ; and a blossom-laden Christmas bush, or blushing waratah, was as charming a picture, amidst its forest surroundings, as any of its rivals of the garden. In the same way the native five-corner and the geebung vied with the English currant and the gooseberry. At points of vantage along the winding paths, statuary in bronze and marble had been placed ; and, wherever the trickling of a mountain rill had gathered about it a nest of moss or broidery of ferns, the diamonds and emeralds of the little nook or crook were regarded as precious jewels. So also with the treasures of the larger waterfalls. They, with their fairy-like surroundings, were not absent from the estate ; and one, some distance from the house, approached by a descending pathway, was full of interest to all who appreciated the delicious coolness of the air, the loveliness and variety of the plant life, and the sweetness of the blending sounds of falling water, rustling leaves, and singing birds.

One of Sir Henry Parkes' poems describes with pretty effect some of the natural beauties of the place, and his experiences of them :

> " And have we no visions pleasant
> Of the playful lyre-tailed pheasant,

As some neighbour bird he mocks
Down among the gully rocks,
In the evenings cool and grateful,
When the storm and all its hateful
Gusts of fury are forgotten ?
And of rambles where the rotten
Trees of ancient giant mould,
Felled by ruthless storms of old,
In their robes of golden moss,
Stretch their shattered limbs across
Runlets of sweet water purling
Through the ferns in beauty curling,
Down four hundred feet or more
From our mountain cottage door ?
And of rambles on the ranges,
Where wild Nature's aspect changes,
Every step we onward take
Through the tangled flowery brake,
Every step we press the sweet
Woof of flowers beneath our feet :
Shapes dissolve and colours mingle—
Wooded slope to rocky dingle ;
Trees by tempests toss'd and torn,
Long ere living man was born,
Standing still on steadfast root ;
Currant bushes gemmed with fruit ;
Soft clematis, forming bowers,
With its wreaths of pearly flowers ;
And the waratahs in state,
With their queenly heads elate,
And their flamy blood-red crowns ;
And their stiff-frilled emerald gowns ;
And Australia's Christmas trees,
Budding to the wooing breeze ;
And the robins and the thrushes,
Flitting through the fragrant bushes."

Clad in easily-fitting long coat, and wideawake felt hat, with stick like an alpenstock in hand, Sir Henry Parkes, when at his mountain home, could wander about for hours invigorated in body and mind. Inside the house there were many things to attract and please—rarities in artistic furniture, pictures, marble statuary, bronzes, autograph letters, and choice books. The library teemed with volumes old and new; and adjoining the main residence was a long roomy structure formed into a veritable gallery of art, where oil-paintings, water-colours, and statuary had been collected, and were displayed with both tastefulness and effect. Nothing was more pleasing to Sir Henry than the change from the worry and oppressiveness of Sydney to the quietude, the bracing atmosphere, the beautiful surroundings, and the home comforts of this attractive spot. But it was not often he could get there. Now and then some invited friends would enjoy his company; occasionally he entertained there a large party of political and other personages, and distinguished visitors to the colony; but, as a rule, he was not absent from Sydney on any day but Saturday or Sunday.

It is not therefore difficult to understand that his close attention to parliamentary and office duties ultimately began to affect his health ; and, when ill-health, as it did, prostrated him, the bed in the ante-room of the Colonial Secretary's Office was, for many days, occupied much more than the office-chair. Sympathy with him, it need hardly be said, was universal ; and, when it was made known that, to secure a complete recovery, a trip to England was contemplated, everybody approved.. Mr. David Buchanan, who, on different occasions, had denounced Sir Henry Parkes with considerable bitterness, endeavoured to get, by resolution, the cordial approval of Parliament to a proposal authorising him, while away, to treat with the Government of any country he might visit, if, in so doing, he advanced the interests of New South Wales ; and another ardent member of the House moved a resolution, proposing a grant of £3,000, to defray the expenses of the trip, and enable Sir Henry Parkes to make it with befitting comfort and dignity.

This money was not voted, for Sir Henry Parkes refused to accept it or any sum, and induced the mover to withdraw the resolution ; but there is little doubt that, if the proposal had been pressed, the House would not have hesitated to grant the money, or even a much larger sum, and very few persons inside or outside Parliament would have complained. High in the estimation of all but a small minority of opponents, Parliament was disposed to sanction anything in his honour, so long as it could be done in order ; but he desired to be independent of any grant of public money, as he did of any private donation ; and his determination in this respect enhanced his reputation.

Outside Parliament his friends and admirers started a movement for presenting him with a substantial testimonial from the public. But, as he had met the movement with a similar object in Parliament, so he met this. He declined to accept

cc

anything.   As he had done throughout his career,
he took a dignified view of his position; and
refused his assent to anything which tended to
affect the purity and influence of the important office
he held.

In a letter, addressed to the secretaries and
committee arranging for the testimonial, he wrote
respectfully declining to accept the intended honour.

"Occupying the high place of first Minister of
the Government of the country," his letter stated,
"it is clearly my duty, so far as lies in my power, to
preserve my public position from personal entangle-
ment which, at the present or some future time,
might be made the groundwork of reproach or
suspicion."

"Calumny," the letter proceeded, "is on all occasions sufficiently busy in misrepresenting the actions
of men entrusted with power; and, where the choice
is within my own hands, I must choose to hold myself
entirely free to act, if necessary, against the interests
of individuals who may be my political friends.   As
a matter of principle, which appears the plainer the
more it is examined, I could nòt reconcile the acceptance of a gift of money from the public, with my
sense of propriety and obligations as the occupant of
a high political office."

All he desired was to be permitted to leave the
colony for a short time, without any recommendation to strangers, except such as might be fairly
drawn from his services to his adopted country. He
left the colony for England at his own expense,
taking his daughter with him; the only contribution

in money, from any portion of the public, being a christmas-box of one hundred and fifty sovereigns, presented to his daughter, from some of her friends, at the moment of departure.

In the evening before he embarked on board the steamer, he was entertained at a public banquet, given in his honour, and largely and influentially attended, by the citizens of Sydney. A few nights previous both Houses of Parliament, acting together in the matter, had fêted him in a similar manner in the parliamentary refreshment-room. On each occasion the feeling towards him was remarkably cordial. Nothing was wanting to show the appreciation in which his services to the country were held, or the strength of the position he occupied in public regard.

The parliamentary banquet was presided over by Sir John Hay, a man not given to fulsome adulation, nor even to expressing the merest compliment undeserved; a man of education, of experience, of discernment, and of caution. He drew a portrait of Sir Henry Parkes which, while it does not show all the lines that some might think ought to be indicated, can be easily recognised and approved as one of truth and vigour. He had known Sir Henry Parkes in the early days, and had often been opposed to him. Frequently in the political camps of that period—the Liberal Party as well as the old Conservatives—he had heard him denounced as a dangerous man. But he had never considered him so. He had carefully observed him, and had seen that he had studied politics—that "he had not fallen into politics;" that he had formed political opinions; that he had embraced principles; and was thoroughly imbued with the constitutional principles of English freedom and English Government. Though never known to anyone as a wealthy man, at no time had anyone been able to connect his name with anything that showed a tendency to make a market of politics, to benefit his private interests by the political power he had obtained. He had also, in Sir John Hay's opinion, developed a considerable character for what would be recognised, in all quarters, as statesmanship. Though he might, at times, be mistaken in his views they were taken from a high platform. He looked a considerable distance ahead. He was not confused in his views by paltry details which were being transacted around him. He had looked forward to the future of Australia, with the earnest desire to found therein a new nation which should emulate the character of the people from which he had sprung, which should be distinguished by the sterling qualities of the British race, which should be self-reliant, and which should carry out, as its inheritance, the tempered freedom which our ancestors had enjoyed for so many hundreds of years.

It will not be difficult for most people to see, in this language of Sir John Hay, the strong points of Sir Henry Parkes' character,—points which led the London *Times* to speak of him as the " most commanding figure in Australian politics," and a keen observer of men, and prominent writer on subjects of national concern, to rank him with Mr. Gladstone, and the late Sir John Macdonald, of Canada, as one of the three greatest men in the Empire.

The occasion of the parliamentary banquet brought many recollections to the memory of Sir Henry Parkes. Twenty-seven years had passed since he first entered the Legislature; and of all the men who were then associated with him, only one was at the table that night, only four were in the Legislature, and he alone of this remnant of the band of former days was now in the Legislative Assembly. In the friendless circumstances of his arrival in the colony, and his difficulties in obtaining employment, he had found a sixpence, picked up by him in the street, necessary to prevent him from going without food for the day. Since then he had sat in every Parliament of the country, and had taken an active part in every important measure which Parliament had passed ; and now he was leaving the colony in the position of Prime Minister, with the confidence of both Houses of Parliament and of the people.

One thing he prided himself upon was his faithfulness to the opinions of his early political career. Taking into consideration the arbitrary conditions of ministerial life, which made it necessary for each man in a Ministry to give way to another, there being in every Administration the necessity for compromise, for the purposes of government, he thought he might fairly claim to have been consistent. From the first he had expressed opinions, which anyone curious enough to examine them would find very much in accord with the opinions he now acted upon. But life, he pointed out, was of small value to any man if it were not used to the correction of error, to maturing the judgment, to enlarging the understanding, by all accessible knowledge. For himself, he had been, from year to year, seeking to educate and mature his faculties, so as to best adapt them to the service of his fellow-men and of the world.

To some persons there may seem in this a taint of the egotism with which he was often charged ; but there is in it none the less truth, and it was the truth of the statement which people recognised at the time.

The speech delivered at the banquet given by the citizens was, like that at the parliamentary dinner, to some extent autobiographical, but chiefly remarkable for an announcement of the public improvements which, if he should remain in office, Sir Henry Parkes intended to see carried out in Sydney during the succeeding ten years. This has frequently been sneered at as the outpourings of vanity and boastfulness ; but an examination of it will show that though the opportunity for carrying out the work, essential for the fulfilment of the intention, did not occur, much was ultimately done as at the banquet was indicated.

He would establish for himself, he told his hearers, a stronger hold upon the affection of Australians, during the next ten years, than the proudest warrior in the old world ever attained in the affections of the people with whom he was connected.

With, of course, the assistance of others, he intended to so alter the city of Sydney, in its conditions of life, that the people in the next ten years would not know it as the city of to-day. In all that contributed to the fostering of a taste for the beautiful, its parks and gardens would be made equal with parks and gardens in other parts of the world. The lowest parts of Sydney, which were hotbeds of fever and pestilence, would be wiped out as with a sponge, and their sites used for new structures, that would tend to permanently beautify the city and promote its health, and this without any cost to the public exchequer. The south of the city was to be married to the north by a bridge across the harbour, which would make Sydney and North Shore one. The metropolis would be supplied with an abundance of water and with efficient drainage. Measures were to be introduced to effectively preserve the timber forests of the country, and, in places where it was necessary, forests would be planted for future supply. In addition to all this the Government, he said, were alive to the necessity for a system of irrigation which would convert the arid plains of the interior into fruitful districts capable of sustaining a numerous population.

He was not able to do all this. The ten years have passed away, and the North Shore bridge and the streams for watering the thirsty plains of the interior are still matters for the future. But the other improvements he forecasted have been carried out to some extent, and he had a not inconsiderable share in the work. As a city Sydney is undeniably much in advance of what it was in 1881, and the country generally has advanced with the metropolis.

It has been said that Sir Henry Parkes should not have left the colony in the capacity of Premier, that he should have resigned his Ministerial office before going away; and after his example in this respect was followed by Sir George Dibbs in 1892, he admitted that he was wrong in the course he took.

But, at the time, the wisest plan seemed, to him and to everybody, to keep the Government intact. It had done admirable work ; there was nothing to indicate an inability on its part to do more ; the general desire was that it should retain office. Speaking on the subject, Sir Henry Parkes said it would have been injurious, instead of beneficial, to the public interest, had he taken a step that would have unnecessarily broken up a strong Ministry from which good work was yet to be expected ; and this was the general opinion. Not even his enemies raised the cry that he ought to resign.

Since then, however, he saw reason to change his view of the subject, and to declare that in leaving for England in the position of head of the Ministry, he committed an error, and that as a constitutional principle, the Prime Minister should not leave the seat of Government for any place or period, which precludes him from performing the duties of his office with the closeness of attention, and the responsibility required of him.

The journey to England was made by way of
America; and, while seeking a restoration to health,
Sir Henry Parkes thought he might be of some
public service by endeavouring to influence the
American Government in favour of revising the
protective duties on Australian wool. It did not
seem likely that he would be successful in effecting
this revision, and some persons in Sydney, in their
criticism of the proposal, made his chances of
success more uncertain ; but proper representations
on the subject to the American Government, and
conference with the principal chambers of commerce in the United States, it was thought, might
make the matter better understood, and pave the
way for concessions in the future. In this, he
could see a path of usefulness. The Governments
of South Australia, Queensland, Tasmania, and
New Zealand saw some advantage in what he proposed to do, and, by commission under the great
seal, accredited him their representative. Victoria
held aloof, for she being a strictly protectionist
country, could not, with propriety, ask America to
give to her what she denied to others. But armed
with commissions from five of the Colonial Governments, he was able to adequately fulfil his purpose,
so far as to make full and forcible representation to
the American Cabinet and people. The wool duties
were not removed nor altered; but, in the reports
of Sir Henry Parkes' movements and speeches, more
was made known to Americans, through their
newspapers, of the resources of Australia, and the
opportunities they offered for profitable trade, than

they had previously been aware of, and this must have been beneficial.

The stay of Sir Henry Parkes in America was marked by many pleasant experiences and much honour. He met many of the foremost men of the country, received lavish hospitality, and was paid to the full the attention accorded those of high position and reputation. Though well-known in England, by reason of his public services in New South Wales, he could hardly have expected any special welcome in the United States, where he had never before been, and where comparatively few persons could be acquainted with Australian politics and progress; but members of the Government, governors of states, politicians, merchants, and literary men rivalled each other in making his visit agreeable to him from his landing at San Francisco to his departure from New York.

All that was worth seeing of America's wonderful natural scenery, he saw. The industrial progress of the country revealed itself to him, in visits he made to the various centres, where invention and skill produce and develop countless mechanical marvels. The far-reaching settlement of the population over the land, their active life and general prosperity, the growth and importance of the cities and the vast strength of the whole community as a nation, were apparent to him at every stage of his journey across the continent. And with all the evident greatness of the nation, he witnessed, with not less admiration than surprise, the simplicity and unassertiveness which seemed to characterise everything connected with the highest office of state. The plainest dress and the quietest manner that came under his notice were those of the President.

The stay in America lasted for about six weeks; and during that time, whenever the opportunity presented itself, Sir Henry Parkes did his best to make Australia known to Americans. He spoke of Australia as a whole. Though doing justice to New South Wales, he was careful, in his intercourse with the people of the United States, not to single out his own colony as superior to its neighbours. For the time he represented the group of colonies, overlooking all geographical divisions, and saying nothing of the claims to greater importance of one as compared with another.

In England he followed the same course. It was not so necessary there to say all that was in his knowledge of the resources and progress of the Australians. Though, in some quarters of the mother country, what is known of Australia is often found to be indefinite and distorted, the relationship between the two countries is too close, the intercourse, commercial and social, too extensive, for ignorance of the importance of the colonies to exist amongst those classes of the English people who are important to Australian development. But on various occasions, and in many ways, Sir Henry Parkes was able to do good service in speaking of the resources of his country, of its advancement, and of its probable great future. For doing this his opportunities were unusually good. Houses were opened to

him, and attentions bestowed upon him, in a
manner that brought him into association with
many of the first men of the Empire ; and speeches
which he made in public were published widely in
the newspapers.

One thing in connection with Australia he was
very careful in impressing upon the people of
England, and especially upon men of position and
influence. While ardently desirous of preserving
the ties existing between the Australian colonies
and England, he was emphatic in pointing out that
the more the colonies were left alone the more
closely they were likely to cling to the old land.
" The softer the cords," as he aptly phrased it,
" the stronger will be the union between us and the
parent country." This has not always been the
policy of the Imperial Government ; but the bonds
have been gradually loosened, and now, happily for
both countries, they are but a "silken thread" easy to
bear and yet unseverable.

During the whole of the period of his stay in
England Sir Henry Parkes was one of the lions of
the season. Town houses and country houses
invited and received him as an honoured guest.
Ancient companies and guilds fêted him. From no
important public function was he absent. Royalty,
through the Prince of Wales, the Duke of Edinburgh, and other members of the reigning family,
paid him attention.

But among the pleasures of the time spent in
the mother-land none compared with a few days
stay with the late Poet Laureate at his residence

on the Isle of Wight, and a visit to Stoneleigh, Warwickshire, Sir Henry Parkes' birthplace.

The visit to Farringford, was at the special invitation of the poet. Previously, Sir Henry Parkes had not been acquainted with Tennyson; but there was a friendship between him and the late Thomas Woolner, the sculptor, and Woolner was Tennyson's friend. An introduction through Mr. Woolner led to a pleasant interview in London, and then to the invitation to the poet's residence in the Isle of Wight. The acquaintanceship thus formed, blossomed into friendship, and from that time, until Lord Tennyson's death, this friendship never lessened. The natures of the two men, widely different as the men themselves were in many respects, must, to some extent, have been alike, or at least mutually sympathetic and admiring. Sir Henry Parkes entertained a deep reverence for Tennyson, and the poet undoubtedly saw in Sir Henry Parkes that which called for thoughtful attention and respect. Though going through life by different ways, the two were seeking the same end. Each, in his manner, was devoting his powers to the world's improvement, the work of making things better than they are. One might do it in poetry, the other in politics; the object to be gained was the same. Alfred Tennyson in England, and Henry Parkes in Australia, were each endeavouring to educate and improve. In this, the poet and the statesman were identical, and Tennyson and Parkes became and remained friends, corresponding with each other up to the time of Lord Tennyson's last illness.

Stoneleigh was visited not only because of Sir Henry Parkes' desire to see, in late life, the place of his birth, but in response to an invitation from Lord Leigh to make a short stay at Stoneleigh Abbey. Noticing the arrival of the Australian statesman in England, and being aware of the fact that Stoneleigh was his birth-place, Lord Leigh thought it would be agreeable to Sir Henry to spend a few days at the Abbey, and accordingly sent to him a kindly-worded invitation, which was accepted. At that time there was no idea in the mind of anyone that the daughter of Lord Leigh (the Countess of Jersey) would, within ten years, be assisting her husband in the performance of vice-regal functions at Government House, Sydney; but the stay of Sir Henry Parkes at the Abbey, and the information which, in conversation, no doubt he imparted respecting New South Wales, may reasonably be supposed to have influenced Lord and Lady Jersey, when the expiration of Lord Carrington's term made the appointment of another Governor of the colony necessary. Rambles about the locality disclosed the fact that the farm-house, in which Sir Henry Parkes first saw the light, and the old church in which he was christened, were still as they were in his infancy, and Lady Leigh, greatly interested in the matter, promised to sketch both structures and send the sketches to Sir Henry after his return to Sydney. She did so, and ever afterwards the two drawings were among his treasures.

CHAPTER XXXI.

SIR HENRY PARKES returned to Sydney, from his
visit to America and England, on 17th August,
1882, travelling from Melbourne by rail.

In Melbourne, immediately after his landing
there from the mail steamer, he was waited upon by
a deputation headed by the mayor of the city and
including the President of the Chamber of Commerce.
They, on behalf of the citizens of Melbourne, congratulated him upon his safe arrival, and tendered him a
banquet at the Town Hall. The feeling in the
southern capital being that in what he had done,
while away, he had acted in the interests of all
Australia, the people did not like the idea of his
passing through their city without some expression
of satisfaction on their part and some form of
welcome. So the banquet was given in the evening of the 15th August; and the gathering was
both representative and appreciatory. Throughout
his career, whenever he cared to visit Melbourne,
Sir Henry Parkes was well received; and
frequently he looked to that city for a clearer
and, in his opinion, juster view of some question

or course of procedure in which, at the time, he was concerned, than he observed in Sydney. The welcome on this occasion was very cordial, and was regarded by him, not only as a high personal compliment, but as an expression of generous feeling from one colony to another.

In Sydney, great preparations had been made by his friends and admirers to accord him a fitting reception. The railway station was decorated, the platform crowded with those anxious to give him an early and hearty greeting, and a large assemblage of the public gathered about the station approaches. In the evening he was entertained at a public dinner in the Exhibition Building, Prince Alfred Park.

This hearty welcome-home-again seemed to bode well for the continued stability of the Government. Sir Henry Parkes had been away from the colony for seven months and a half, a longer period than was announced before the trip was taken, or than was expected; but, apparently, the public interest had not suffered. The machinery of government had not ceased its ordinary operations, and the various members of the Ministry had been equal to their respective duties. With Sir John Robertson as Acting Colonial Secretary, the general policy of the Administration had been maintained; and, so far as the public were aware, everything appeared satisfactory.

But appearances are proverbially unreliable. Behind the apparently clear political atmosphere were gathering clouds which rapidly assumed a threatening aspect. Some persons did not approve of the length of the recess; others condemned Sir Henry Parkes for re-admitting Sir John Robertson to the Cabinet after his retirement in connection with the Milburn Creek affair; others again complained of certain acts of administration in some of the Government departments.

More serious than these matters, however, was a feeling of disquietude which had been growing for some time in relation to the land laws.

Money was plentiful, land was cheap, and squatters and others were doing their best to acquire large freehold estates. Lawfully done, this could not fairly be complained of. The condition of the laws, might be condemned, but those acquiring the land would be acting within their rights. In many instances, however, there was reason to believe it was not done lawfully. What was known as " dummyism " was practised to such an extent that it became notorious. In its inception, this plan of acquiring land was the outcome of defects in the laws, which made it imperative on the part of squatters to do something to protect their runs, from undue encroachments by free selectors. When its possible advantages were recognised more fully, its operation was extended as far as could be done with any prospect of safety.

The public had long been aware that much of the freehold land, on some squatting runs, had been secured by a system of mock selection, carried out in the interests of the run holders by their servants; but, for a time, they knew nothing of the extreme lengths to which persons, in their determination to acquire the land, sometimes went.

DD

Someone suddenly discovered that inmates of one or two of the Government asylums were unaccountably leaving the institutions, and going by train, steamer, or coach, into the country. They were old, infirm, and, in some instances, suffering from disease, and, while in the asylums, were known to be without pecuniary means. Yet they left with alacrity, and, apparently, with every provision for their comfort. Their singular departure was a matter for surprise, but, for a time, did not arouse suspicion. They were free to leave the institution, if they so wished, and they were allowed to go without question. It was only when telegrams appeared in the newspapers, announcing the arrival of old and infirm men on some of the stations in the far interior, and selections began to be taken up under very extraordinary names and in a very unusual manner, that the real state of affairs was understood. Putting one thing with another, it was not difficult to connect the selections with the old men, to identify the old men as those who had left the asylums, or to detect in the whole proceeding daring attempts at extensive dummying. The men, it was understood, had been paid a certain sum for their services, and were to be maintained for the remainder of their lives by the persons employing them; they, in return, entering into arrangements by which the land selected by them should fall into the hands of their employers. A loud outcry was made in the press, and, subsequently, in Parliament; and the Lands Minister, Sir John Robertson, indignantly cancelled the selections, where cancellation could be done, and took measures to prevent any recurrence of the evil.

But this did not remove the feeling of unrest in regard to the land laws generally; and dissatisfaction on the subject began to be expressed, from one end of the colony to the other. An amendment of the existing Acts, in the way necessary to put an end to dummyism, and, by providing proper security of tenure for the squatters, remove from them any inducement to dummy, was demanded on all sides.

Unfortunately for the Government, Sir John Robertson would not take the view which almost everyone else adopted. Dummyism was regarded as a direct result of the insecurity in which pastoralists were compelled to carry on their operations; and this insecurity was the outcome of free selection before survey. Public opinion condemned the principle of free selection before survey, as the chief cause of the evils associated with the land system; but Sir John Robertson, as was perhaps natural, refused to disturb this principle, and he was too strong in the Government to be coerced into doing that of which he did not approve. He admitted that the laws might be improved, but denied that it was necessary to alter them to the extent generally stated. He proposed to amend them in some comparatively unimportant particulars, and to consolidate them. Further, he would not go.

In 1872, Sir Henry Parkes told the electors of East Sydney, that the work of alienating the land was " a work of more sacred and tremendous consequence than anything that could fall to the lot of the statesmen of old countries like England and France. As we perform this work," he said, " so

will rise the structure of society, when we are dead;
so will our descendants be free, independent, and
prosperous men, or the reverse; so this colony
will rise to the dignity of a great free country, or
become despised and enslaved, and descend among
the least powerful nations of the earth." In 1877,
he had admitted that the land laws were evidently
bad in their results, in some respects; that, while
the lands were passing away, there was very little
increase in the use to which they were put. "By
the bad operation of the land laws," he declared
"persons of capital have, in reality, been driven to
buy large tracts of land simply to protect themselves against the cultivators of the soil."

This serious evil, apparent to everybody, public
opinion looked to the Government to remove. The
Government met the general demand by the introduction of a bill, good enough in itself, but quite
inadequate to satisfy the popular cry. As a consequence defeat came quickly.

The session opened immediately after Sir Henry
Parkes' return to the colony; and the Governor's
speech announced a list of measures, including a
bill to consolidate and amend the land laws. The
Opposition, disorganised and weak in the previous
session, now assumed both form and strength. Mr.
Alexander Stuart was elected leader, and the
Government found themselves confronted by a body
of opponents compact and determined. An effort
was made to bring about a crisis, by the moving of
an amendment on the Address-in-Reply to the

From Photo. by Rüsfeldt, Sydney.[1]

SIR JOHN ROBERTSON AND SIR HENRY PARKES, IN 1881.

Governor's speech; but that was not successful. A
majority of the House preferred waiting, to see
what the Government measures should prove to be
when introduced ; and for nearly three months, the
business of the House went on with fair progress.

At the end of this time Sir John Robertson
moved the second reading of his land bill. He
spoke vigorously and well, and his figure, on the
floor of the Assembly Chamber, always handsome
and striking, never appeared to greater advantage.
He was a very attractive man. Possessing virtues
which so overshadowed his faults as to render
them almost unnoticeable, it is questionable if he
ever had an enemy in the sense of one who could
see nothing to admire or like in him. No one could
fight harder or more persistently than he ; none
could be more genial and kindly. As the father of
the system under which the lands of the colony
were administered, he naturally defended the good
that system had brought about, and resisted to the
utmost all attempts to unduly expose its defects.
He had many friends in the Assembly, and the
whole House applauded his efforts to pass his bill ;
but neither friendship nor admiration was sufficient
to prevent a majority from declaring, by their votes,
that the measure was altogether insufficient to meet
requirements. On the third night of the debate,
after but few speeches had been delivered, the
House went to a division ; and the bill was rejected
by forty-three votes to thirty-three.

Sir Henry Parkes advised, and obtained, a dissolution. He believed that an appeal to the country

would show that the Government were still popular,
that their programme was not viewed by the constituencies in the same light as it had been by the
Legislative Assembly, and that there was no general
desire to see the Ministry retire from office.

But he was greatly mistaken. Making full
allowance for the party excesses of opponents, who
did not refrain from heaping all the odium possible
upon the heads of Ministers, charging them with
many and serious misdemeanours, still the country
was dead against the Government on the land question. This question it was determined should be
settled in a manner very different from that which
the Government bill proposed ; and, despite strong
efforts made to prevent the elections turning upon
this one subject, the land laws and their radical
amendment were kept to the forefront in every
electorate and influenced every contest.

Sir Henry Parkes sought to obtain the verdict
of the electors on the general work and policy of
the Ministry, rather than upon the Land Bill
alone. He knew that this bill did not go as far
as his opponents considered it should go, perhaps
not as far as he himself thought it might go ; but
he regarded it as a beneficial advance in land
legislation, and was content to let the matter rest
at that point in the hands of the author of the
system. To his mind, there were other matters
equal to the Land Bill in their importance to the
country. The Government had passed into law
several great measures which were promoting the
general good ; and they were prepared, and able, if
opportunity were afforded them, to pass others.

The Opposition, however kept the attention of the public to the subject of the land; and only noticed the general work of the Government to the extent of using it in any way possible to their disadvantage. The very measures which Sir Henry Parkes prided himself upon as having been passed by the Ministry, had raised a crop of enemies around him bent upon his destruction.

"In the part I have taken, as your representative, in the arduous labours," he said, in his address to the electors of East Sydney, and in allusion to the work which the Government had done since their assumption of office, "I have made many implacable opponents." Those who wanted to obtain a giant's hold of the public lands for their own aggrandisement, and those who desired to thrust a giant's hand into the public Treasury for their denominational teaching, he declared were against him, as were those who loved popular ignorance and disliked the sight of orderliness and sobriety.

The friends of denominational teaching in the schools were wroth with the Government for the passing of the Public Instruction Act, which deprived their system of all state aid. The working of the new Licensing Act had incensed the publicans and their adherents. An undercurrent of feeling, among these sections of the community, materially assisted the advocates of land reform at the polling booths.

But what told most against the Government, apart from the weakness of their position on the question of the land, were some singular charges in

relation to a suggested bridge from Sydney to North
Shore, and to an unauthorised purchase of a country
residence for the Governor. They were denounced
also for alleged quarantine mismanagement, for the
destruction, by fire, of the Garden Palace, and with
it many public documents stored therein, and for
proposals to build an Art Gallery on the site of the
Garden Palace, and a Public Library on that of the
Benevolent Asylum. But the North Shore bridge
and the Governor's country residence, were the
subjects of the principal allegations against them.

We hear nothing of these matters now. The
Governor lives at his country seat during the hot
season of the year, and no one thinks of complaining
of it. The North Shore bridge is not yet built;
but he, who, at the present time, should speak of
the sensational announcements respecting this
structure of the future, made during these election
proceedings, as anything more than a party device
and an electioneering squib, would not be credited
with much knowledge of political manœuvre. Yet
the charges against the Government in respect of
these two matters, and especially the bridge, had a
most damaging effect upon the prospects of Ministers
in the constituencies, and particularly upon those of
Sir Henry Parkes. They placed him at the bottom
of the poll.

Before that took place, however, the struggle
was very severe. Probably, never in the parliamentary history of New South Wales has there been a
hotter contest.

With almost the entire press at their back, and a definite pronouncement in their favour from many sections of the people, the success of the Opposition seemed, from the first, to be assured; but this did not lessen their activity, nor cool their zeal. Not a man of their fighting ranks refrained from coming forward; not a particle of material, capable of being used with effect, was overlooked.

Mr. Stuart had a most effective supporter in Mr. G. H. Reid. In his genial, racy, incisive style of oratory, Mr. Reid's speeches had as much to do with the victories of the Opposition as anything else. Mr. Dalley, too, came out; and spoke and wrote as only he could speak and write, and added to the Opposition successes. His brilliant speeches charmed, as well as influenced, both those who listened to them and those who read them in the newspapers. His pen, busy throughout the time, assisted his speeches. He even wrote speeches or addresses to the electors for others. A laughable disclosure of this fact was made on the East Sydney hustings. Carried away by his return as one of the members for that electorate, and referring to the admiration with which his address to the electors of another constituency, for which also he was afterwards elected, had been received, a candidate declared that the much-lauded address had not been written by him, but was the work of Mr. Dalley.

Only one familiar opponent of the Government was absent from the fight—Mr. William Forster. Death had suddenly removed that well-known

figure from the turmoil of politics, a month previously ; and he had been laid to rest, in the
churchyard at Ryde, "Until the daybreak." Those
who remembered him in Parliament, could imagine
how heartily he would have assisted to bring about
the defeat of Sir Henry Parkes. As it was, he had
gone from the scene of party strife for ever ; and it
had fallen to the lot of his old opponent, in announcing to the Assembly his untimely decease, to
speak of him in the kindest words,—of the services
he had rendered to the public, the good qualities
which distinguished him, in many respects, above all
others in the House, and of how ill Parliament
could afford "to lose a member so distinguished by
education, by practical knowledge of the country,
and by ability to give effect to what he believed."

Amid the buzz of the political hornet's nest, in
which he found himself, Sir Henry Parkes could
scarcely get a hearing. His meetings were noisy,
and, to a large extent, antagonistic. Those of other
Ministers, and of ministerial supporters, were very
similar. The friendly cheers of a few weeks
previously, had given place to strong marks of
disapproval, in the face of which the Government
party found it difficult to make headway. Still,
they stood to their programme, and yielded nothing.

At the nomination proceedings at East Sydney
the Premier found the crowd more hostile than at
his meetings. A second Minister, and another
candidate, the two with Sir Henry Parkes forming
the Ministerial bunch, were treated with the same
disfavour. Yet Sir Henry Parkes did not lose

heart. Appearances were decidedly against him ; but he could not believe they were sufficient to justify the idea that he, and those running with him, would be defeated. To the electors he expressed his conviction, that the voting would show a state of things much different from that which the nomination proceedings indicated. Confident of this, he was content to await the verdict of the poll.

His friends were not so sanguine. They saw the danger, and knew that defeat was much more probable than success. In their judgment, it was certain that he would not head the poll ; and it was not unlikely that he would be found among the rejected. To prevent utter defeat, it was necessary to resort to extreme measures ; and, in the voting, many electors, to save him, plumped for him. But all efforts proved futile. Sir Henry, and his companions in the bunch, were badly beaten ; the Opposition candidates, headed by Mr. Reid, being returned in triumph. "The popular breeze of to-day," said Sir Henry Parkes, quoting the words as those of Mr. Wentworth, "may be the adverse wind of to-morrow ;" and one more instance of the fickleness of the political barometer had now to be recorded.

Offers from other electorates came to Sir Henry Parkes, immediately the result of the election at East Sydney was known. There was no desire, in any quarter, to see him out of Parliament ; and a large proportion of the general public were anxious that no time or opportunity should be lost, now that he had failed at East Sydney, in getting him elected.

He himself was in no hurry. Firm in his impression of the good work which the Government had done during their long term of office, and in his belief that their popularity had not lessened as their opponents had endeavoured to show, he did not see in the East Sydney defeat, the beginning of what was to be a complete overthrow; but regarded it as a proceeding, on the part of the electors of that constituency, under the guidance of his enemies, which the electors of other constituencies would condemn and seek to nullify. There would be a reaction, he declared, from one end of the country to the other, and the Government would yet be successful.

From the electorates proffering him assistance he chose St. Leonards. There were others suitable, but he was averse to being nominated for a constituency, where his nomination would interfere with a Government supporter already in the field. At St. Leonards there was not this objection; and, moreover, he was an elector of St. Leonards, and that in itself was a justification of his appearance there as a candidate. He was not free from inclination to retire for a time from public life; but this feeling was overborne by a conviction that he could not take that course, consistently with his duty to the country. It was necessary that, as the head of the Government, he should continue in his position until his services, in this respect, were constitutionally dispensed with; and it was, therefore, incumbent upon him to continue the contest.

About the same time as he appeared as a candidate for St. Leonards, he was spoken of for the electorate of Tenterfield. Representatives of that constituency had, in fact, been in communication with him before he was approached by the people of St. Leonards; and, to a certain extent, he was committed to the electorate of Tenterfield. He told the electors of St. Leonards so; and, in consenting to become a candidate there, he intimated, without reserve, that, if he were elected, he could not promise to sit in Parliament for that constituency. They would have to trust to his public spirit, he said, and to his judgment, as to which of the two constituencies he would represent, supposing he were elected for both. They must ask him no questions on that point. They must either elect him on this understanding, or reject him.

They were content. His candidature for St. Leonards went on; but, before the day of nomination, he was returned unopposed for Tenterfield, the only candidate out for that constitnency, the Mayor of the town, retiring in his favour, and nominating him. Then he withdrew from St. Leonards; but, so earnest were some of his friends there, that, notwithstanding his withdrawal, publicly announced, they persisted in recording their votes for him, and, as a consequence, put him to the expense of £40, which, under the Electoral Act, a candidate receiving a certain proportion of votes below the others was bound to pay.

In one respect it was, perhaps, a fortunate circumstance that he did withdraw from St. Leonards;

for the withdrawal brought back to political life one
who, after a short preliminary term in the Legislative Assembly, had for several years been absent
from Parliament, and who, by Sir Henry Parkes'
election for Tenterfield, had opened to him a career
which was destined to bring him at once into high
ministerial office, and to distinguish him as one of
the foremost of the public men of New South
Wales.

There were four candidates for St. Leonards.
One was Sir Henry Parkes, and another Sir (then
Mr.) George R. Dibbs. Mr. Dibbs, when in the
Assembly, had represented West Sydney, for which
constituency he was elected in 1874. Before the
next general election in 1877, he had made himself,
by his attitude on some questions relating to labour,
so unpopular that he found it impossible to secure
re-election; and he retired into private life. In 1882
he came forward again, for St. Leonards; and, until
Sir Henry Parkes' appearance as a candidate for
that electorate, had a fair chance of being returned.
The candidature of Sir Henry Parkes, however,
threatened to upset everything. If he went to the
poll there was no doubt that he would be elected ;
and it seemed equally certain that the second
member would be a local resident, who, by his
residence and the circumstance of his having spent
money in the district, had a hold on the people
which would find him the requisite number of votes
to ensure his return. Sir Henry Parkes retired,
and Mr. Dibbs, bunching with the local candidate,
was elected. A few days afterwards he was Colonial

Treasurer in the Stuart Ministry, which succeeded that of Sir Henry Parkes; and subsequently, in rapid succession, was Colonial Secretary and Colonial Treasurer in one Government, Colonial Secretary in another, and Colonial Secretary and Premier in two others.

By his election for Tenterfield, Sir Henry Parkes' presence in the new Parliament was assured; but similar success did not come to all the other members of the Ministry. Sir John Robertson was returned for Mudgee, more on personal grounds than anything else—certainly not because the electors were favourable to his land policy; but others, in their appeal to the constituencies, failed irretrievably. When the elections were over, it was found that four of the Ministers had been defeated, and were out of Parliament; and those who had been bold enough to declare adherence to the Government policy, had been rejected in all directions.

The new Parliament had been returned to radically reform the land laws. The Government were hopelessly defeated. Sir John Robertson's return to the ministerial ranks, after the Milburn Creek affair, instead of restoring the old strength of the Ministry, had weakened them to destruction; and the Coalition Government, by his Land Bill, had been carried, as Sir Henry Parkes some time afterwards phrased it, over the " Falls of Niagara," and shattered. There was nothing for it but resignation; and the Government withdrew from office immediately after Parliament met.

CHAPTER XXXII.

POLITICS AND POETRY.

THE new Government proceeded to deal with the
land question; and while they did so, Sir Henry
Parkes, to a large extent, held aloof from active
politics. He felt deeply some of the tactics resorted
to during the elections, to secure his defeat—tactics
which he denounced as discreditable and unjust.
He visited Tenterfield, and thanked the people
there for their public spirit in electing him to
Parliament, without any effort on his part to win
their confidence; and, after a few months, went for
the second time, to England. On that occasion, he
visited the mother country as the representative of
a financial company in Sydney, and was away until
the Land Bill of the Stuart Government was
almost passed.

It was in August, 1884, that he returned; and
the parliamentary session was then rapidly approaching its termination. In the business remaining at that late period to be done, he took some
part; but he did not assume a position of prominence in connection with the Opposition as a party.
Sir John Robertson was the Opposition leader.

Sir Henry Parkes, for the time, had, fallen back from recognised active leadership. 'His absence from his parliamentary duties, caused by his second visit to England, had something to do with this, but the personal influence which Sir John Robertson exercised, over members comprising the Opposition, had more. Sir John Robertson was desirous of Sir Henry Parkes returning to his old place at the head of the party, but Sir Henry declined.

This change of position in the House did not prevent him from adequately criticising the proceedings of the Government, when criticism was necessary, or from voting on those occasions when he considered it right that his vote should be recorded; but it made his presence there less felt.

To a man of his ability and temperament, this could not be agreeable; and, as with a consciousness of a want of due recognition, there was in his mind an impression that the Government were supported by a too-pliant majority, who, in their turn, were accommodated by a too-extravagant Government, he began to manifest a feeling of disgust at the state of affairs in Parliament, and to be again influenced by a strong desire to retire from politics altogether.

His second visit to England occupied fourteen months; and, on his return to Sydney, he was heartily welcomed by his friends, and banqueted in the Town Hall. Fifteen hundred Orangemen received him in the new Masonic Hall, and the members of the New South Wales Local Option League gave him a public breakfast.

But he was not disposed to re-enter the political arena, with the purpose of pushing himself to the front again, or even to actively engage in the business of Parliament in any way. He had not lost the sense of soreness he had experienced from the manner in which he had been defeated in the country on the land question. "The country has had enough of me," he told the company at the Town Hall banquet. "I feel that in my last Administration I received a most unjust reward of bitterness, and I am not disposed to forget it." Of defeat he made no complaint, but no language was too forcible for him to denounce some of the methods by which his defeat had been brought about. At the Orange gathering he declared that he wanted rest and quiet; he was weary of political turmoil. Yet, he said, his energy had not lessened, his courage was still strong; and, if at any time, in the course of the public procedure, something should occur in which someone were wanted to fill the breach, if breach there should be, he would not be backward in filling it.

Very quickly his announced desire for rest was followed by his retirement once more from the Legislature.

The session in progress at the date of his return from England closed in about two months after his reappearance in the Assembly; and, three days subsequently, he published an address to the electors of Tenterfield, declaring his disapproval of the condition of things in Parliament to be so strong, that he not only resigned his seat for Tenterfield, but was determined to neither seek nor accept a seat in any future Parliament. In the present Parliament, he said, political character had almost entirely disappeared from the proceedings of the Legislative Assembly, and personal objects had, to a large extent, absorbed that kind of consideration which had taken the place of deliberation and legitimate debate. " I have," he went on to say, " lately seen immense sums of public money voted away by private pressure and bargaining, in the face of the openly avowed convictions of members so pliantly yielding up their consciences." This was in connection with proposed new railways.

Even if he had strength and disposition for the kind of political warfare he had witnessed, he was not, he informed the electors, prepared to waste the remnant of life which remained to him in contending against such forces. He could not continue to bear the sacrifices of time, and of the capabilities of life itself, which a seat in the Assembly now imposed.

The new Lands Act, he declared, would prove to be more fruitful of abuse, and destructive of revenue, as well as of settlement, than the old law with all its admitted defects; and, while this would be found so, Parliament had with a free and reckless hand increased the salaries of the public servants, created a host of new pensioners, and largely added to the permanent indebtedness of the country. Railways had been sanctioned, which, if carried out, could not for a generation to come pay working expenses, and could only be worked by draining away the earnings from the trunk lines. The safeguards of sound parliamentary government had been blindly and wantonly broken down ; and necessity, with an iron hand, would soon fasten new burdens of taxation around the necks of the people, as the only possible means of escaping from a financial crisis.

He admitted that it might be asked of him, why, if things were as bad as he declared them to be, he did not remain at his post, to assist in bringing about an improvement. But his answer was that he had remained at his post for a generation, much to his personal injury, and until he no longer had strength to confront "the gigantic difficulties which must soon come upon us."

There was a feeling of regret at the step the veteran statesman had thought fit to take, and at the pessimistic tone of his public farewell to his constituents ; but, viewed in the light of former proceedings of the kind, the public were not inclined to take the retirement too seriously. Those who were intimately acquainted with Sir Henry Parkes knew that there was no want of sincerity in the course he had adopted. That he conscientiously deplored what he regarded as the demoralization of the Assembly, and, in consequence of the state of politics, as he viewed it, was determined to clear himself of all connection with the political arena, they did not doubt. But the general body of the people, among them the bulk of his [admirers, though not doubting the genuineness of the step he had taken, felt certain that, in the course of a little time, circumstances would arise which would draw him back again to Parliamentary life.

It was pointed out that the retirement could not have been induced by an impossibility of office. The Ministry, the *Herald* remarked, had been in office for two years, quite the average length of Ministries; two of its members had been crippled by ill-health; and there was sure to be a reaction of feeling through the electorates after the excitement over the Land Bill. Sir Henry Parkes' chance of returning to power could not be considered unfavourable. But office at this time he did not covet. He wanted neither office nor seat in Parliament; all he desired was to rid himself of everything associated with politics and politicians, and to get into a line of life which would afford him rest and quiet.

In a couple of rooms, in one of the buildings in Pitt Street, opposite the *Herald* office, Sir Henry Parkes took up his quarters, acting as the official representative of the financial association in whose interests he had visited England the second time; and there he remained until the beginning of 1887.

As was his habit, whenever leisure permitted, he spent a portion of his hours in writing poems; and, at this period of his life, he produced a third little volume of poetry. He called it "The Beauteous Terrorist and other Poems," and inscribed it "By a Wanderer." It was sent to the newspapers, and was favourably criticised. The actual author was not known. If he had been, he once said, the criticisms might not have been so favourable.

The book is not free from defects, but it contains much that is of interest, as well as of merit.

The principal poem—that which gives the name to
the little volume—is one of those tragic stories
with which all, more or less acquainted with the
desperate efforts in Russia for emancipation from
the thraldom of official tyranny, are familiar. While
being painful in its details, it is attractive in its
heroine, and agreeable in its versification ; but it is
not of particular interest to Australian readers.
Most of the other poems claim attention for the
reason that they deal with subjects nearer home.
One rhymes pleasantly about the author's "Silver
Wedding Day," an extract from which is not unworthy of being reproduced. It was written in
1861.

> " How the light of memory gives
>   All thy girlhood's beauty back !
> Ever fresh the rosebud lives—
>   Ever blooming on life's track !
> Time may thin the soft brown hair,
> Touch the cheek so dewy fair,
> Send a dimness to surprise
> Those for-ever-trusting eyes ;
> But thy rosebud heart's as young
> And thy woman's soul's as strong
> As they were in passion's dawn,
> On our quiet bridal morn."

Lady Parkes, to whom these lines refer, died in
1888, after a married life of 52 years. Her nature
was homely, and she never lost her love of home
and domestic seclusion. During her husband's long
parliamentary career, which commenced more than
a generation before her decease, she appeared but
once at the opening or prorogation of Parliament.

Her happiness was found among her children, in her garden, or in the midst of her household occupations. It has been said that she never seemed to fully realise the change her husband's knighthood brought about, in regard to the manner in which she then became entitled to be addressed, and that it may be doubted whether she ever appreciated the most notable triumphs in his public life. She was in fact, as she was described at the time of he death, an unpretending single-minded woman, with no ambition beyond performing her daily duties as wife and mother, and living to the last under the influence of a Christian training received in early life.

Another poem is entitled "Seventy." It is a portrait of Sir Henry Parkes in the year 1885, drawn by himself.

> "Three score and ten,—the weight of years
> Scarce seems to touch the tireless brain ;
> How bright the future still appears,
> How dim the past of toil and pain !
>
> " In that fair time when all was new,
> Who thought of three score years and ten ?
> Of those who shared the race, how few
> Are numbered now with living men !
>
> " Some fell upon the right, and some
> Upon the left, as year by year
> The chain kept lengthening nearer home—
> Yet home ev'n now may not be near.
>
> " But yesterday I chanced to meet
> A man whose years were ninety-three,
> He walked alone the crowded street—
> His eye was bright, his step was free.

" And well I knew a worthy who,
    Dying in harness, as men say,
    Had lived a hundred years and two,
    Not halting on his toilsome way.

" How much of action undesigned
    Will modify to-morrow's plan !
    The gleams of foresight leave us blind
    When we the far-off path would scan.

" What task of glorious toil for good,
    What service, what achievement high,
    May nerve the will, re-fire the blood,
    Who knows, ere strikes the hour to die !

" The next decade of time and fate,
    The mighty changes manifold,
    The grander growth of Rule and State,
    Perchance these eyes may yet behold ;

" But be it late, or be it soon,
    If striving hard we give our best,
    Why need we sigh for other boon—
    Our title will be good for rest."

In several parts of the little book there are glimpses of the personal character of the author. His admiration for the great men of the old world, whose lives have been spent to the public advantage ; his ambition to add to the results of his own public services, never thinking he had done sufficient, but ever desirous of doing something more, always wanting to move onward ; his delight in nature ; his affection for England ; his love for Australia, and particularly for that part of it with which he was closely connected : all these of his characteristics are to be found in one poem or another of this volume.

But the verses which, after those with the title
" Seventy," attract and hold the attention of anyone who can recognise in them to what they refer,
are some called " The Patriot." They present a
vivid picture of the inconstancy of the popular
mind—of its acclaim to-day and its execration
to-morrow—and of the object of its adulation and
its hate standing erect, through all, in pity at the
spectacle, but otherwise unmoved and unchanged.
It needs little reflection to see, in the vigorous lines
of this poem, the triumphs and the failures which
Sir Henry Parkes experienced in 1882; he, in their
midst, a fine figure, upstanding, resolute, and true to
the purposes of his life, whether applauded or
condemned.

" Fair women cast sweet flowers before his feet ;
From all the housetops 'kerchiefs gaily waved ;
Ten thousand voices hailed him in the street ;
In blear-eyed joy the monster Rabble raved.

" The town was mad with triumph where ne passed,
The very flags flew out as wild with glee ;
The few who dared dissent fell back aghast,
Like weeds washed past by a tumultuous sea.

" A year !—and jibe, and jeer, and savage yell
Salute his ears ; and missiles rank and foul
Fall thick about him where the garlands fell ;
No cheer breaks through the monster Rabble's howl.

" And yet it is the same unswerving soul !
He only kept his faith when others changed,
And heeded not in scorn the ominous roll
Of jarring threats, from foes, and friends estranged.

" He only kept his onward path, when they,
Who could not see the grandeur of his aim,
Turned to the new-fledged creatures of the day
And drank their slanders, feeling not the shame.

> " So ever rise the Feeble 'gainst the Fit ;
> So ever first the noblest blood is shed ;
> So surged the angry waters round De Witt :
> So tortured France was robbed of Danton's head."

A little later it fell to his lot, as it fell on several occasions through his eventful life, to make public reference to another patriot, one of the foremost of those conspicuous in the annals of New South Wales—Sir James Martin. The reference was made in verse. He had known Sir James Martin through almost all his life. He had been acquainted with his early aspirations, and his efforts to improve his condition. He had been his associate in many of his public acts and proceedings ; and had assisted him to attain the success which he eventually won. In the first instance, these verses were published in the *Sydney Morning Herald*, without signature or any information as to their authorship. They bring out with distinctness and force, the strong characteristics of Sir James Martin. The struggle of his young life in the immature existence of the colony, when in no respect were things very bright and satisfactory, and his dogged persistency in overcoming the difficulties which then beset him; his indomitable courage when facing the determined efforts that, at an important period of his subsequent career, were made to prevent him from attaining any position of influence ; and his ultimate splendid success, are presented in such a manner as to bring the subject of the poem vividly before the mind, and to impress the reader with the undeniable greatness of the man the verses pourtray. There is also about the lines a literary finish which is very noticeable. They were sent to the *Herald*, written upon a sheet of notepaper, in the curiously rugged and somewhat unreadable handwriting of the author; and, as they are an interesting specimen of this, as well as of his literary style, a *fac-simile* of them is here given.

The buried Chief.

Nov. 6. 1886.

"Speechless lips and solemn tread,
They brought the lawyer-statesman home,
Laid him with the gather'd dead
Where rich and poor like brothers come.

So bravely did the stripling climb
From step to step, the rugged hill,
So gaze thro' that benighted time,
Fix'd on the far-off beacon still.

He faced the storm, that o'er him burst,
    With pride to match the proudest bore,
He bore unblench'd Detraction's worst,—
    Paid blow for blow, and scorn for scorn!

He scaled the summit while the sun
    Yet shone upon his conquer'd track;
Nor falter'd till the goal was won,
    Nor, struggling upward, once look'd back.

But what avails the "pride of place,"
    Or winged chariot rolling past?
He heeds not now who wins the race,
    Alike to him the first or last!

In type, they read as follows :—

THE BURIED CHIEF.

Nov. 6, 1886

With speechless lips and solemn tread,
They brought the lawyer-statesman home ;
They laid him with the gather'd dead
Where rich and poor like brothers come.

How bravely did the stripling climb,
From step to step, the rugged hill,
His gaze, thro' that benighted time,
Fix'd on the far-off beacon still.

He faced the storm that o'er him burst,
With pride to match the proudest born ;
He bore unblench'd Detraction's worst,—
Paid blow for blow, and scorn for scorn !

He scaled the summit while the sun
Yet shone upon his conquer'd track,
Nor falter'd till the goal was won,
Nor, struggling upward, once look'd back.

But what avails the " pride of place,"
Or wingéd chariot rolling past ?
He heeds not now who wins the race,
Alike to him the First or Last.

CHAPTER XXXIII.

TWO NOTABLE ELECTIONS—ARGYLE, AND ST. LEONARDS.

SCARCELY had three months passed after the resignation of the seat for Tenterfield, than there arose circumstances which recalled Sir Henry Parkes to public life. The "breach" to which he alluded when addressing the Orangemen of the metropolis, in the Masonic Hall, on his return from England, had appeared, and he at once stepped forward to occupy it.

The Soudan Contingent movement had commenced. Suddenly, without the publication previously of even a hint of what was going to be done, the country learned that an offer had been made to the Imperial Government, by the Government of New South Wales, of two batteries of artillery and a battalion of infantry, for service in the Soudan. The death of General Gordon had just been announced; and a suggestion, made in a letter to the press, that New South Wales might patriotically offer the assistance of troops to England, had been seized and acted upon by Mr. W. B. Dalley.

The announcement of the offer was received by the public with enthusiasm. The same spirit which manifests itself in England, on an approaching out-break of war, was apparent through New South Wales from one end of the country to the other. There was no question of the wisdom of the pro-ceeding, no counting of the cost. Fired with the desire to assert the power of the nation, the British courage of the people urged them to action. England was not really in need of the proffered assistance, but would, doubtless, be glad of it; and New South Wales, by her offer of troops, would exhibit to the world the wide-reaching strength of the British Empire and the imperishable virtues of the race. Everybody seemed either to want to go to the Soudan as a soldier, or to applaud and to assist those going. Those who could not be ex-pected to bear arms, were disposed to lavish time and money in promoting the success of the move-ment. The colonies adjoining New South Wales, catching the fever of the time, telegraphed to England offers similar to that sent from Sydney. Canada followed in the same direction.

A few persons kept cool during the general excitement; and one or two were venturesome enough, after the first outburst of popular feeling, to utter a word of warning. They saw the seriousness of the proceeding, and, beneath the glamour of it all, the probable ultimate difficulties, debt, and disaster.

But, of those who raised their voices or used their pens in protest, none was so prominent or pronounced as Sir Henry Parkes. Loyal to the backbone to the old country, he yet saw, in the step the Government had taken, a serious inroad upon the constitution, a danger to the well-being of the people, and a very probable legacy of future trouble.

England, he pointed out, was not in want of the troops, and the offer of them was, therefore, unnecessary. Further, without the authority of Parliament, and in the absence of the head of the Government—for Parliament was not in session at the time, and Sir Alexander Stuart, the Premier, was in New Zealand travelling for the benefit of his health— it was unconstitutional for the Government to raise a body of troops, and more reprehensible to send them for service out of the country. It was inconsistent, he also urged, to send men away from the colony when we were, by our system of immigration, anxious to bring people here. The result must, inevitably, be largely increased and unjustifiable taxation, to provide, first for the expenditure on the equipment and maintenance of the troops, and afterwards for the effects of casualties.

He did not want the country, he said on one occasion, to make a reputation on a military basis. He wanted it to establish its reputation " by the splendour of its resources, by the soundness of its commercial policy, by its efforts at planting a free people within the land, and by its sober spirit in avoiding any meretricious military display." He desired it to be known as " a community of solid sensible British people, where the people of the three nations may mix as British Australians, and where their object will be the industrial progress of the country."

The objections put forward to the raising and despatch of the Contingent were undoubtedly forcible; but the martial fever of the time was too high, to allow of them having any great effect in the direction sought. People read them, or listened to them, and, for the most part, pooh-poohed them. If Sir Henry Parkes had only found the opportunity, it was asked, would he not have seized it with more than Mr. Dalley's alacrity? It was envy, not a desire to serve the country, it was said, that had prompted his protests.

Yet there were some, even among the members of the Ministry, who were not wholly in accord with Mr. Dalley in the step he had taken.

Mr. Dalley did not anticipate an acceptance of his offer. It would be a splendid thing for the country to make it, and he had consulted the two officers at the head of the military forces as to the men and material that, if wanted, would be available; but he thought it extremely probable the offer would be declined with thanks. When the telegram from England, announcing the acceptance of the troops, was received in Sydney, Mr. Dalley was at Burrowa, and it was sent on to him there. "I hope," he wired back to the Minister in Sydney, from whom he had received the news—"I hope to God the Contingent will be forthcoming."

It was forthcoming. In a marvellously short period of time, the force was organized, equipped, and sent away in a manner which would have done credit to any Government and any country.

GG

Once the colony was committed to the proceeding, the desire to make it a thorough success
was practically universal. Ministers united in
pushing it forward ; the press heartily gave it
support ; and the people joined almost as one man.
The unconstitutional nature of the proceeding was
condoned by Parliament, in a special session convened
for the purpose. The evils which Sir Henry Parkes
pointed to, as likely to result from casualties in the
force, did not appear, for the reason that, by the time
the Contingent arrived at the seat of war, most of
the fighting was over ; and a patriotic fund, which
had been raised in Sydney, was more than sufficient
to meet all claims for gratuities or pensions.
Furthermore, the *éclat* of the whole movement was
so pronounced, that undoubtedly the general result
to New South Wales was very beneficial.

But this did not alter Sir Henry Parkes' opinion
of what the Government had done, nor induce him to
withdraw, in any respect, from his attitude of disapproval. Convinced that the Government had
acted unjustifiably, and deserved censure, he determined to seize the first opportunity for testing the
feelings of the people, upon the subject, at the polling
booths. This, if he succeeded, would bring him
back to Parliament, against his recently-expressed
intentions to remain away ; but it would have the
effect of showing that the public were not altogether
against him, in the course he had taken. That
would be a great satisfaction ; and he felt certain,
that in their calmer moments, when excitement had

given place to sober reflection, the public generally
would be found on his side.

The opportunity to test the feeling of the
electors presented itself at Argyle, in March, 1885;
and thither Sir Henry Parkes went, as an avowed
opponent of the Government in the matter of the
Soudan Contingent.

His chances of success did not appear to be very
bright. The widespread popularity of the step the
Government had taken, seemed much more than
sufficient to overshadow the comparatively few expressions of disapproval, even though they came
from such an important source as Sir Henry Parkes.
He, in fact, by his opposition, had apparently made
himself very unpopular. The press attacked him
very severely. Public opinion, to judge from the
conversation and exchange of views in places where
people meet, unequivocally condemned him. For
a time, he was very much in the position of one
without friends or apologists. Yet, in spite of all,
he vindicated himself. He was returned for Argyle,
though he was strongly opposed; and the principal
question upon which the votes of the electors were
asked, was the despatch of the military force to
Egypt.

The Argyle election took place on 31st March,
1885; and, on 8th September, of the same year, Sir
Henry Parkes took his seat, as Member for Argyle,
in the Legislative Assembly.

No sooner did he do so than he found himself
called upon to answer a charge which, if endorsed
by the House, and carried to a legitimate conclusion,

involved his expulsion from the Parliament to which
he had just been returned. His address to the
electors of Tenterfield was brought under the notice
of the House by the Premier, Sir Alexander
Stuart. The statements in the address, reflecting on
the conduct of members, seemed to Sir Alexander
Stuart to be of a character which compelled him to
draw attention to them, and he did so as a matter
of privilege.

As results showed, the proceeding was not a wise
one. Sir Alexander Stuart was of opinion that Sir
Henry Parkes should be afforded an opportunity,
and should be called upon, to explain, if he chose to
do so, what he had intended to convey by the objectionable statements in his address; and that the
House should then consider whether, and by what
means, it should purge itself of the charges made
against it.

Sir Henry Parkes admitted the questioned statements; contended that he had said no more than had
often been said in English parliamentary circles of
political conduct strongly disapproved; and declared
that he had nothing to retract or to say in qualification of his language. He had not reflected
on the Assembly as a whole; he was very careful in
explaining that. He was as anxious, he said, to
preserve the character and independence of the
Assembly, as any one; but he could not shut his
eyes, or close his mouth, to the proceedings of a
considerable section of the Assembly, if he thought
proper to condemn their conduct either in the
Assembly Chamber or out of doors. As a citizen

of the country, he pointed out, he had, in a matter of this kind, a privilege outside Parliament, equal to the right of criticism and complaint he would possess as a member of Parliament.

It is scarcely necessary to consider whether his view of his rights, in this respect, was correct. If, as a private citizen, he were not able to go so far, in his criticism of parliamentary proceedings, as to say that political character had almost disappeared from them, and that personal objects had to a large extent taken the place of deliberation and legitimate debate, then there can be no justification, on the part of the public, to express disapproval, in any way, of anything associated with politics.

Sir Alexander Stuart, ill-advised, having drawn the attention of the House to the matter, was bound to go on with it. Sir Henry Parkes not only admitted publishing what had appeared in his address, but reiterated it. The words were sufficiently plain, he said; sufficiently clear to convey his meaning. That was his meaning then; it was his meaning now; and he saw no reason to say anything in qualification of it, still less to withdraw the words. Sir Alexander Stuart moved a resolution, affirming that the words were a gross libel on the House; and, after considerable debate, in which the peculiar position of the Government in the course they had taken was forcibly shown, the resolution was passed by a majority of four votes, in a division of thirty-one to twenty-seven.

The natural sequence to this was a motion proposing that Sir Henry Parkes be expelled. He had been adjudged guilty of grossly libelling the House; the step now to take was to expel him from Parliament. Sir Henry Parkes snapped his fingers at the resolution carried by the majority of four, and dared the Government to proceed with his expulsion. The Government proposed to let the matter rest at the point it had reached. They had succeeded in their course so far ; they were doubtful of success if they proceeded further. The House, knowing Sir Henry Parkes' popularity in the country at any time, were not likely to send him back to his constituents only to be returned again, probably in a manner severely condemnatory of themselves. But Sir Henry Parkes urged the Government to do so. If they stopped at the resolution which had been passed, they were making a laughing stock of Parliament. " I snap my fingers at the motion," he declared, "and I appeal from you to your masters, the electors of the country."

Still the Government made no sign of going further. The indignation of Sir Henry Parkes, and the taunts of other members of the Opposition, were alike unavailing. To have secured a vote which declared the veteran ex-Premier to have grossly libelled the Assembly, was satisfaction enough for one sitting. It was something like an adequate return for the denunciations of the Ministry, in which the honourable member had been indulging, not only in the Tenterfield address, but on various occasions between the publication of that address and the Argyle election. To attempt anything beyond this might result in failure, which would destroy the effect of the motion already carried. So the Government could not be induced to stir from the position at which the House had arrived. One of the supporters of the Ministry gave the House the opportunity which Sir Alexander Stuart had declined to give, and moved that Sir Henry Parkes be expelled; but no one voted for the motion except the mover and the seconder. The Government voted against it.

As Member for Argyle, Sir Henry Parkes resumed in the Assembly his old habit of activity, and, though Sir John Robertson was still leader of the Opposition, a position of influence.

This influence, however, was more in relation to the business of the House than upon members personally. His long experience and extensive political knowledge were always of great assistance, and his speeches, more than those of any other member, were instructive and useful; but, with all this, he attracted to himself very few members as close associates. With a man like Sir John Robertson sitting on the same side of the House, in the position of leader of the party, it was not easy for another to make headway.

At the same time there was nothing to indicate that Sir Henry Parkes entertained any desire to displace Sir John Robertson. Being in Parliament again, and having resumed his wonted activity, it was natural to consider that circumstances must arise, sooner or later, under which he would once more be called to the first position in the ranks of his party; but for that he was content to wait. Not much more

than a year was to pass before he was again the acknowledged leader of those with whom he sat, and
but two years before he was at the head of another
Ministry ; but during that short period, as events
transpired, there were three changes of Government,
and the honourable gentleman had some curious experiences both inside and outside the Assembly.

In October, 1885, Parliament was dissolved; and
the Stuart Government coming to an end, through
the illness of Sir Alexander Stuart and of Mr.
Dalley, a reconstruction of the Administration was
carried out by Mr. G. R. Dibbs.   This reconstruction was effected immediately after the prorogation preparatory to Parliament being dissolved.
The   Prime   Minister,   at whose   instance   the
prorogation took place, was not the Prime Minister
who brought about the dissolution.   The first was
known to Parliament ; the second was not.

Sir Henry condemned this proceeding as unprecedented and revolutionary.   No such thing, he
contended, had ever before occurred in either New
South Wales or England ; and in a letter sent by
him to the press, he used words of censure upon the
Governor, Lord Augustus Loftus, for being a party
to it.

The " Ministerial metempsychosis," as he styled
it, determined him to do his best to defeat the new
Government in the elections; and he announced
himself as a candidate for St. Leonards, in opposition
to the Premier, Mr. Dibbs.   Broadly stated, the
issue put by him before the electors was, whether

the free institutions of the country were to be worked out in accordance with constitutional Government, or at the instance and in the interests of a particular set of men.

But he adopted other tactics also. They were condemned in some quarters at the time, and notably by the leading journals, as tainted by inexcusable localism.

An interesting question at St. Leonards in those days, as it is now, though not so prominent now as then, was the connection of the North Shore with Sydney by a bridge. Sir Henry Parkes, of course, knew this. He knew also that the people of the electorate were anxious for a railway to open up the district. They have the railway now, but then it was a matter of talk and promise. Sir Henry Parkes advocated both bridge and railway, particularly the former, in a manner that caught the approval and support of the electors completely. It would not be correct to say that his condemnation of the Government, on constitutional grounds, did not carry with it great weight. Sir Henry Parkes never spoke on constitutional questions or procedure in any part of the country, at any time, without being accepted as an authority entitled to speak, whose views might be regarded as sound. But the North Shore bridge and the railway were matters which appealed to the every day convenience and comfort of the residents, and his attitude in regard to those works had a marked effect in the election. Parodying the well-known lines of Macaulay, he

exclaimed at the nomination proceedings, amidst
the cheers of the populace :—

> " In that straight path a thousand
> May cross as soon as three,
> Now who will stand at my right hand,
> And build the bridge with me !
>
> Out spake the bold electors,
> ' Four thousand strong are we ;
> We'll all abide on every side,
> And build the bridge with thee ! ' "

The appeal was irresistible.   The announcement.
of the result of the polling showed Sir Henry
Parkes to be at the top, 476 votes in excess of the
number recorded for Mr. Dibbs, and that gentleman
defeated.   Mr. Dibbs' defeat was not a matter of
general satisfaction, and it was with pleasure that.
the public soon afterwards learned of his return for
the Murrumbidgee ; but the triumph of Sir Henry
Parkes was unmistakeable.   It constituted him the-
chief figure in the elections.   There appeared to be
a very fair prospect of his becoming again, in a very
short time, the head of a new Government.   To this
he told the electors he did not aspire, though, if the-
position came to him in the natural course of events,
well and good ; but he was ambitious of being the-
leader of the country, in the contests proceeding in
the choice of the new Parliament.

CHAPTER XXXIV.

THE FLAG OF FREE TRADE.

THE new Parliament opened on 17th November, 1885. The Government had suffered severely in the elections, and it was scarcely possible they could remain in office. Many persons had expected their resignation before Parliament assembled; but, notwithstanding the reverses he had experienced, Mr. Dibbs declared his intention of meeting the new House, and definitely testing, there, his position.

Some of the opponents of the Ministry taunted them with a desire to retain their offices long enough to receive Lord Carrington, who was about to arrive in Sydney, as Governor of New South Wales.

If the near arrival of Lord Carrington had any influence in this direction, the circumstance, to a certain extent, was excusable. Never before had an expected Governor been regarded with such widespread and engrossing interest. The appointment, and the landing in Sydney, of Lord Carrington, may be said to have marked an era in the history of the colony.

Lord Carrington was the successor to Lord Augustus Loftus; and his antecedents, and the manner in which his appointment had been heralded, raised the expectations of the colonists to the highest pitch. It was the first time a rich, fashionable nobleman, fond of gaiety, and with a disposition to spend money freely, and live in the best style, and withal strive to make himself popular, had been placed in the vice-regal position. Government House had been occupied previously by noblemen; but they had not been in touch with the people, and their expenditure had been of such a nature that it had created impressions the reverse of complimentary. The most absurd stories had been current of the manner in which some Governors had lived. But, with the appointment of Lord Carrington, an entirely new style of things was anticipated. He was known to be an intimate companion of the Prince of Wales, and a personage at Court; and, therefore, one who moved in the best society in England. He was a thorough sportsman. He liked horseracing. He was fond of driving, and his horses and equipages were of the best description. He had an income of £40,000 a year, it was said; and he was prepared to spend the whole, or most of it, during his stay in the colony. His wife was described, by Lord Rosebery, as an English lily, delicately nurtured, sweet in disposition, everything that an English lady ought to be; and, it may be said at once, she justified every word that had been said in her praise. Previous Governors had been content

with one aide-de-camp. It was announced that
Lord Carrington would have four. So numerous
in fact did they and the household generally of the
new Governor appear, that it became a habit, when
referring to them, to discard the term "staff," and
speak of them as the Governor's *entourage*. Certainly there was some reason why the Ministry
should desire to remain in office, long enough to
receive a Governor of such unusual importance.

A week after Lord Carrington arrived the Dibbs
Ministry resigned.

The determined opposition Sir Henry Parkes
had shown them in the elections he continued in
Parliament; and the strongest speeches against
them were spoken by him. But Sir John Robertson
was regarded as the leader of the Opposition, and
he was commissioned to form the new Government.
His chances of success depended upon Sir Henry
Parkes. Knowing that without Sir Henry's
assistance, he might as well abandon his commission,
he offered him any position in the Government he
cared to choose.

Sir Henry Parkes declined to rejoin Sir John
Robertson. Though willing to support the new
Administration, if its composition and policy should
prove such as to meet with his approval, he was not
prepared to become a member of it. He was not,
at this time, desirous of office; but it was the
general opinion among politicians that he could have
got together a capable and strong Government, if
the task of forming the new Ministry had been
entrusted to him. As it was, his non-acceptance of

a portfolio with Sir John Robertson was fatal to the
new Government. His refusal to join the Administration was a serious stumbling block in its way;
the circumstance, that, on its formation, and the
announcement of its policy, he found that he could
not give it his support, materially assisted in
bringing it to an end. He found it necessary to
vote with those opposed to it; and the Government
was obliged to retire, the course taken by Sir Henry
Parkes giving rise to bitter feelings on the part of
Sir John Robertson.

The retiring Ministry had lasted two months,
and was then succeeded by an Administration at the
head of which was Sir Patrick Jennings. The
division between Sir John Robertson and Sir Henry
Parkes had led the former, on the defeat of his
Ministry, to seek a coalition with Sir Patrick
Jennings; and, for a day or two, it had appeared
probable that the coalition would be effected. If it
had been accomplished, Sir Henry Parkes would
have been left on the Opposition side of the House
for some time, with a very small following. But it
was found to be impracticable. At the last moment,
a dispute arose in regard to the office of Attorney-
General, and this brought the negotiations for a
combination of the two parties to an end.

In these proceedings there was a strong desire,
and a determined effort, to keep Sir Henry Parkes
from power. The Robertson party were incensed
at him, for the attitude he had assumed against
them; the party comprising the main portion of
the Opposition disliked him, for the course he had

taken in the elections. Sir John Robertson had
greatly damaged Sir Henry Parkes' chances of
favourable cónsideration at Government House, by
submitting to the Governor a statement of parties
in the Assembly, in which Sir Henry was
represented as being associated with a section
numbering seven, including himself. Outside
Parliament, there were powerful influences at work
in the same direction. The consequence was that,
when Sir Patrick Jennings had formed his Administration, which he did from the portion of the
Opposition that had been part of, or had supported,
the Dibbs and Stuart Ministries, Sir Henry Parkes
was left on the Opposition side of the Assembly,
little more, for the time, than a unit among those
antagonistic to the new Government.

But a change very quickly took place. Considering what had occurred, it was scarcely possible
for Sir John Robertson and Sir Henry Parkes to
again work together with anything like cordiality;
it was quite impossible that they could ever again
join in the formation of a Government. It was
equally impossible for Sir John Robertson to succeed in the formation, or the carrying on, of a
Government, without the assistance of Sir Henry
Parkes. Apparently recognising this, Sir John
Robertson, a few months after the entry into office
of Sir Patrick Jennings and his colleagues, resigned
his seat in the Assembly, and finally retired from
parliamentary life.

Thus the way was once more cleared for Sir

Henry Parkes. He became leader of the Opposition ; and immediately there opened a period of his career which for vigour, brilliance, and success was unsurpassed in his history. Yet at this time he was 71 years of age.

The Jennings Ministry remained in office for a little less than eleven months. The year was one of financial need, and, for revenue purposes, Sir Patrick Jennings and his colleagues introduced in Parliament, and passed into law, a Customs Duties Bill, under which an *ad valorem* duty of 5 per cent. was imposed, and the tariff altered in relation to certain specific duties.

The appearance of this measure aroused a storm of indignant protest and opposition on the part of Sir Henry Parkes, and of the party of which he was leader. With the exception of about a dozen Members, the whole House professed the principles of free trade ; but, while the Opposition declared the proposals in the bill to be of a protective character, the Government denied that they were, in any sense, associated with protection. They could have no protective effect upon industries, it was argued, and they were not of a nature to cause any disturbance of trade. They were, however, supported by the protectionist Members of the Assembly, and regarded by them as the first instalment of a protective policy. Thus the Government were charged with "sneaking in protection;" and, for the time the bill was before the House, Ministers found the proceedings hampered by every method of resistance which the rules, or the practice, of Parliament, permitted. The sittings became unexampled for length, and notorious for scenes of excitement and disorder. For the first and only time, in the history of the Assembly, a sitting of the House extended to Sunday morning. Determined to destroy the bill, if that were at all possible, the Opposition laid hold of it at every point that offered; and, at every step, intercepted its progress. Quite as firm as their opponents, the Government were resolved to defeat these tactics. So the struggle went on.

Eventually the bill was passed, and the new tariff enforced. It cannot be said that it did any immediate harm. The *ad valorem* duty was not appreciably felt, and protectionists were not, in any material way, benefited. But the duties were not regarded with satisfaction. The press, as well as the Opposition in Parliament, kept the objections that might be fairly raised against them, well before the people. There was a feeling abroad, through the colony, that the tariff under which the country had lived, and, on the whole, prospered, having been one of free trade, there should have been no alteration in a direction in which the general advantage was, at least, very doubtful; and, before long, it became apparent that this feeling would manifest itself unmistakeably at the next elections.

Rather more than three months after the Customs Duties Act had been assented to, the Jennings Ministry retired from office; ostensibly through a disagreement between Sir Patrick Jennings and Mr. Dibbs, but largely owing to

HH

fiscal differences between the head of the Government and some of his colleagues.

Lord Carrington then sent for Sir Henry Parkes, the summons reaching him late on a Saturday afternoon. The Governor's aide-de-camp, Lord Bertie, had been looking for him all day; but, as he was spending the day at the Blue Mountains, did not find him until his return. At this date he was living at Parramatta; and Lord Bertie met him on his way back from the Mountains, in the train, at Blacktown. He saw Lord Carrington at 9 o'clock in the evening of the Saturday, and, by Monday evening, the new Ministry was virtually formed. By Tuesday everything was complete.

The House met on that day, and Sir Henry Parkes, through Sir Patrick Jennings, sought to obtain from the Assembly the supply necessary to cover the period which would be occupied by the re-election of the new Ministers. Sir Patrick Jennings, friendly enough to the incoming Ministry, endeavoured to do as he had been requested; but some members objected. The names of the new Ministers had not been announced to Parliament, and this was used as a reason why the House should refuse the request for supply. It was used also for another purpose. The new Government were in the peculiar position of being, as far as parties in the Assembly existed, in a serious minority. Sir Patrick Jennings had retired from office, while having a large and loyally working majority at his back. Some members professed not to be able to see how, in the existing state of things, Sir Henry Parkes was going to make any headway. In their opinion,

it was but trifling with Parliament for him to
attempt to form a Government. The first test
motion, which they considered was sure to come,
would, they argued, result in sending him back to
the Opposition benches, with the comparatively
small party which, since Sir John Robertson's retirement from public life, he had been leading.

He, and those who could intelligently read the
situation, knew better. That he and his party in
the House were in a minority was undeniable ;
but it was equally plain that he could not have
accepted the Governor's commission, to form a new
Administration, without an understanding with his
Excellency, that, in the event of an adverse vote or
serious obstacle to his proceeding with business, the
House should be sent to the country. He had a
dissolution in his pocket, in fact, from the time of
leaving Government House on the Saturday night.
Some members opposed to him either could not, or
would not, see this. They persisted in objecting to
the supply asked for being granted, and it was
refused.

The following afternoon Sir Henry Parkes appeared in the Assembly. Anticipating some such
course as the House had taken, he had, for the time,
refrained from having himself sworn in as Colonial
Secretary ; and he took his seat, still as Member for
St. Leonards, and as Vice-President of the Executive Council. Naturally there was some outcry,
and his right to appear in the Chamber was
challenged. But it could not be denied. Remaining
there, he demanded the supply he had asked Sir
Patrick Jennings to procure ; he dared the House

to refuse it ; and he told honourable members, that, granted or not, they would be sent before their constituents.

There was in this much that irritated many, and not a little that savoured of dictatorship. But there was some excuse for it, especially as most of those who were the cause of it were in no sense friendly to the change of Ministers. Supply was granted ; Parliament was dissolved ; and the country was immediately stirred by a general election as exciting and significant in its results as any which had preceded it.

It was a long time since the country had been so agitated by political questions. The composition of the Ministry was as follows :—

SIR HENRY PARKES, G.C.M.G.	Colonial Secretary and Premier.
MR. J. F. BURNS ...	... Colonial Treasurer.
MR. W. J. FOSTER ...	... Attorney General.
MR. T. GARRETT ...	... Minister for Lands.
MR. JOHN SUTHERLAND	... Minister for Works.
MR. WILLIAM CLARKE	... Minister of Justice.
MR. JAMES INGLIS ...	... Minister of Public Instruction.
MR. FRANCIS ABIGAIL	... Secretary for Mines.
MR. C. J. ROBERTS, C.M.G.	Postmaster General
MR. J. E. SALAMONS, Q.C. ...	Vice President of the Executive Council, and Representative of the Government in the Legislative Council.

On the publication of the names of the Administration, some doubt was felt as to its free trade principles, for among the Ministers were at least three reputed protectionists. But the doubts quickly disappeared. There could be but one opinion of the Ministerial policy, from the moment it was announced definitely. Two plain general issues, as Sir Henry Parkes decribed them, were submitted to the people: "the restoration of their affairs to an economical, pure, and sound constitutional state of Goverment, and the restoration to the colony of the old policy of free trade." The Free Trade Flag was to be nailed to the mast, and carried to victory. "The Ministry," wrote the leading journal, "is worthy, in our opinion, of the confidence of the country, and the country, if we are not mistaken, will give its confidence."

Sir Henry Parkes' address to his constituents at St. Leonards, and manifesto to the country, was an eloquent and stirring appeal. "I have undertaken the labours of office," he said, "at a time of unexampled difficulty." Four years previously, when retiring from office, his Government had left in the Treasury a surplus of nearly £2,000,000. Now he returned to power to face a deficit, as he stated in his address, of at least £2,500,000, a public expenditure which had increased more than 50 per cent., and a public debt which, under £19,000,000 when he last left the Treasury benches, had become £41,000,000. Of course these sensational increases in the country's liabilities were capable of explanation and defence, but, regarded alone, they constituted a formidable indictment against those mainly responsible for them.

The first duty of the new Government was to be to extricate the country from "its deplorable condition," and to " restore it to a position worthy of its splendid resources and the generous spirit of its people." An amended Land Act, to facilitate permanent agricultural settlement, and to secure, in an improved manner, the rights of the pastoral tenants, while, at the same time, getting adequate revenue, without charging excessive rents or imposing oppressive conditions, was promised. There was also to be introduced a Railway Bill, which would effectually withdraw the railways from political influence. The Civil Service was to be inquired into and reformed ; and the question of the " unemployed" was to be dealt with. " In a land," wrote Sir Henry Parkes, "where, on all sides, nothing is so much needed as human labour, no pair of healthy human hands ought to be seeking employment in vain," and " in dealing with the temporary dearth of employment amongst the working population, the Government will avoid giving any measure of relief the character of pauperism, and will endeavour to absorb this spasmodic labour in some form or other of permanent value."

Town and country flocked to the free trade standard. Protection was more noticeable in some of the constituencies than at any previous election, but with little chance of becoming formidable. The prominence into which the protectionist proclivities of the Jennings Ministry had been brought by the criticism of their opponents, had imparted to protection a stimulus that had lifted it into more notice than had before been given to it ; but no one believed that it had any consider-able hold in the country. Still it was necessary to fight it.

From the sounding of the first note of the bugle of free trade, Sir Henry Parkes was at the front, and in the thick of the conflict. It was wonderful how he managed to find the physical strength neces-sary to the work he accomplished. It was remarkable how the constituencies turned towards him, and hailed him as the statesman and leader that was wanted. They were for free trade and prosperity, with the few and convenient fiscal burdens which are associated with the liberal policy, but they were as strong, or stronger, for Sir Henry Parkes. His personal popularity at this time, was surprising. So pronounced, in fact, was public approval in his favour, that very quickly it was recognised by candi-dates for the new Parliament, that supporting Parkes was the high road to success, and dis-approving of him certain defeat. This had a somewhat demoralizing tendency. There were, of course, men above attempts to gain a seat in the new Assembly by simply attaching themselves to the Premier's coat-tails, but there were many others, whose principles were much weaker than their desire to be elected by whatever means the election could be brought about.

Sir Henry Parkes, himself, flitted from one electorate to another, with extraordinary rapidity. To-night he would speak to the electors of a metropolitan constituency; to-morrow night he would address the people in an electorate hundreds of miles away in the country. In all directions he travelled. No distance was too great; no obstacle too serious. Everything gave way to his desire to assist the Government candidates by defeating their opponents. Most of his speeches were admirable in matter and style. Some were blurred with personal attacks and references which might very well have been omitted. These did not meet with general approval. But as he who delivered the speeches was received enthusiastically, almost everywhere, success to the Government candidate rarely failed to follow as a consequence of his efforts. The failures were chiefly in districts which may be said to have been protective by nature as well as by politics. "The old worn-out empirical doctrine," as he termed protection, had its grasp on some parts of the colony, and the time had not arrived for that grasp to be loosened.

Victory for Sir Henry Parkes and free trade, through the constituencies generally, was assured from the opening of the struggle; the people triumphantly declaring for government by a statesman understood and appreciated, and for unrestricted commerce. As usual, at that period, the elections were carried out in batches; and the first day's polling showed the Ministry to be a long way ahead. Out of twenty-six seats, twenty-four were won by the freetraders, and the other two were lost for reasons not connected with the fiscal question. The majorities gained in the voting were overwhelming ; and the success in the metropolitan constituencies paved the way for successes in the country. When the elections terminated, the free trade party returned to the new Parliament were, compared with the protectionists, as two to one. Of 124 members comprising the Assembly eighty-three were classed as free traders or ministerialists, and forty-one as protectionists. The majority for the Government was consequently very strong.

The protectionists were a much larger body than at any previous general election had been returned to Parliament ; and, for the first time in New South Wales' history, they were likely to act as a united and compact party, carrying with them some weight if not exercising much influence. In this position, while it was improbable they could do any harm, they could not fail to attract attention.

CHAPTER XXXV.

THE Ministry remained in office for two years. They commenced well, and went on well; retiring, eventually, on a very simple matter connected with which their resignation was neither desired nor expected, but was brought about by the punctilious regard Sir Henry Parkes always had for the duty of a Government, when they had been attacked and beaten on a vital question.

The two years constituted one of the most important and interesting periods in the colony's history.

A return to free trade was, of course, the necessary consequence of the Ministry coming into office. The protectionist policy of the Jennings Government was reversed, and once more freedom reigned at the Custom House, as far as, under the circumstances of the time, it could be brought into operation. Contentment and gradual progress became apparent. There was a serious difficulty existing in relation to the unemployed; but no time was lost in dealing with it, and arrangements were made under which employment was found for men

out of work in clearing Crown land, which, afterwards, in its more valuable condition, by reason of
having been cleared, could be sold to public advantage. In some respects the scheme was beneficial;
but the general result was unsatisfactory, and was
the cause of some unpleasantness both inside and
outside Parliament.

The Civil Service was taken in hand by appointing
a Commission, whose duty it was to inquire into the
condition of the various departments, with a view to
the necessary improvement. In this matter also, the
success desired and expected was not achieved. It
was found that while there was no difficulty in learning
the state of the departments, and in making the
necessary recommendations regarding them, it was
not practicable to publish the evidence upon which
the recommendations were based. The only
way, apparently, in which the truth and the
whole truth concerning the service could be
obtained, was by getting each officer to speak freely;
and this freedom of speech depended upon a
guarantee, that what an officer stated to the Commission should go no further. Consequently all the
Commission did was to hear the evidence, have it
recorded for their own information and discussion,
and make their report upon it. The record of the
evidence was destroyed. A state of things was
thus brought about which made the proceedings of
the Commission useless. The reports, as they were
drawn up, were sent to the Government, and remained
with them. Members of the Assembly demanded that
they should be laid before Parliament; but Ministers

declined to produce them without the evidence, and, under the compact of the Commission with the witnesses, the evidence was not available. The reports have, therefore, never been made public. In a few instances, recommendations made by the Commission were acted upon by Ministers, in a re-arrangement of their departments, but the bulk of the recommendations in no way emerged from the paper upon which they were written.

But, though the results of the measures taken to deal with the unemployed and with the Civil Service, were not satisfactory, there was much else in these two years of administration of the affairs of government which met with approval.

One matter was that of effectually regulating the Chinese question. At this time, as throughout his political life, Sir Henry Parkes was opposed to aliens of inferior race coming to New South Wales in exces- sive numbers. Population, to any extent, was welcome from any part of the globe, so long as it was of a kind that could satisfactorily merge itself in the community already in the colony. In his eyes, the Chinese were incapable of mixing with a British population without causing it to deteriorate. They were not, in his opinion, less law-abiding, industrious, or thrifty than British colonists; but he maintained that, in a country like New South Wales, the type of the British nation should be preserved in the people, and, therefore, that, for no consideration whatever, should there be admitted into the country any element that, in an appreciable degree, would lower that type. Further, he held that

there should not be admitted any class of persons to
whom the community were not prepared to give the
full privileges and rights of citizenship ; and he saw
how unfairly, considering their manner of life, the
Chinese competed with the population of the soil in
the labour market. The Chinese, he had made up
his mind, must be kept out of the country. They
were here in large numbers ; if allowed to come unrestricted they would be here in numbers much
greater, and would probably overrun the country.
For some time signs had been apparent, in all the
colonies, of a serious increase in the number of them
coming to Australia. The matter had become one
of urgency. Popular agitations on the subject made
it the more necessary for the different Governments
to take action.

New South Wales, while, to a certain extent,
acting in concert with its neighbours, took an
independent course. Chinese passengers to Melbourne, quarantined there with the object of forcing
them away from Victoria, and afterwards compelled
to leave that colony, were refused a landing when
the steamers, on board of which they were, arrived
at Sydney. The Government were warned that
they were acting illegally, and, that if applied to,
the Supreme Court, under the existing state of the
law, would authorise the landing. Sir Henry Parkes
declared that, until the question was decided by the
Supreme Court, no Chinaman should set his foot on
shore.

He sought the aid of the Imperial Government,
in preventing Chinese from coming to the colony.

The Imperial Government seemed more inclined to listen to the Chinese Ambassador in London, than to the Prime Minister of New South Wales ; and Sir Henry Parkes sent to London, a message declaring that, at all hazards, the Government here would put an end to Chinese immigration. His attitude in this respect was not approved by some persons, and led to notice being given in the Assembly of a motion of censure by a prominent member of his own party ; but he had the public with him, and he carried his determination into effect.

A bill was passed containing stringent provisions against Chinese coming to the colony ; and, from that time to this, it has been the law of the land. China protested a little ; Great Britain viewed the matter dubiously. But the relations between the two nations were not affected by what was done, and, undoubtedly, New South Wales has benefited.

Though earnestly desiring to preserve the integrity of the Empire, Sir Henry Parkes could not see why he should not be faithful to the interests of his colony. "We must be loyal to ourselves," he said, when speaking on the subject in the Assembly; "we must be loyal to the constitution under which we live ; and the only way in which we can be true to ourselves, as Her Majesty's free. subjects, is to show that we have a lively appreciation of the great liberties, of the great privileges, which we possess, and which we will never forfeit, nor suffer to be impaired."

Payment of members became a prominent question during the period in which this Government was in office. Sir Henry Parkes, as he had always been, was opposed to it; but, to a considerable extent, the constituencies were favourable, and there was a strong majority supporting it in the Assembly. In a sense, the Government were forced to bring the question forward, and give Parliament the opportunity to vote upon it. A few days after they were sworn in, a motion in favour of payment of members, introduced by a private member, was passed by a majority of twenty; and the Government were placed in the position of deciding either to bring in the bill, or to resign their offices. In the circumstances, resignation of office would have been highly injurious to the country; and the only other course was to bring in the bill.

Ministers were divided in their attitude towards the measure, the majority being opposed to it. Sir Henry Parkes made it known that, for his part, if it had not been for other considerations, he would much rather have left office than be a party to the introduction of the bill. He could neither see that it was necessary, nor admit that it would lead to an improvement in the representation of the constituencies. In his view, the proposed payment was inadequate as a salary for parliamentary services, and, as a means of introducing men of value to the public life of the country, who otherwise would not make their appearance, would be an entire failure. The character of Parliament would not, by it, be improved one whit.

The argument that, to pay members a salary, would have the effect of raising the tone of Parliament, by bringing into the Legislative Assembly the most capable men obtainable, was the highest ground taken by the friends of the bill. There were several other reasons, which did not reach this standard, for the support given to the measure. A conversation between a member of the Assembly and an acquaintance, during the time the bill was under discussion, imparted to the claim for payment an aspect both significant and amusing.

"We must have payment of members," said the member emphatically; "oh! we must have it. Do you know my correspondence is so great that it takes up every moment of my time."

"I have no doubt of it," it was remarked.

"Oh! every moment of my time."

"But you mean to say," the member was asked, "that you attend to all of it?"

"Attend to it!" he exclaimed; "of course I do. I have to. First you will have a long letter from a fellow who wants a billet; then another from a rascal who has got the sack, perhaps for being drunk —he wants to be reinstated. Then another writes, asking for the cancellation of a lease; and another scoundrel wants his lease extended. So it goes on."

"It really must take up all your time."

"Take up all my time! My feet are actually sore walking about the Government offices."

"They must be if you attend to everything that is asked of you in that way."

"I must attend to it, you know, or I should be simply kicked out at the next election. Oh! there ought to be payment of members, and there must be."

The bill providing for payment ultimately became law. Some obstacles stood in its way in the Legislative Council; but, eventually, it was carried through the necessary stages, the opponents of the measure in the Upper House making an unsuccessful effort to secure the important point of restricting the operation of its provisions to future parliaments.

But the *magnum opus* of this Government was the passing of the Government Railways Act and the Public Works Act, two measures which have done, and promise yet to do, as much for the colony, in the public interest, as any legislation effected in its history. They may even do more. Dependent as the country is upon the successful working of its great railway system, for the maintenance of its chief asset, and upon a judicious carrying out of large public works, these Acts have had the result of removing the railways from the baneful effects of political influence, and placing them under an administration based upon business principles; and of subjecting public works proposals, the expenditure upon which is estimated at or beyond £20,000, to the keen scrutiny of a committee elected by both Houses of Parliament. Had these measures been in existence fifteen or twenty years ago, the results from railway construction and management, and from the prevention of unnecessary expenditure on public works of one kind or another, would be repre-

I I

sented now by a very much smaller debt than that
which confronts the colony, a much easier burden of
taxation than the people at the present time have to
bear, and an absence of some works, constructed under
the old system, which have been little better than
millstones upon the necks of the general community.

The colony of Victoria had placed its railways
under Commissioners, with a view to removing their
administration from political influence, before the
idea assumed definite form in New South Wales ;
and the measure which Sir Henry Parkes introduced, and carried into law, was preceded by one
brought forward by the Minister for Works in the
Government of Sir Patrick Jennings.   That, however, was different in some essential particulars.   It
followed very closely the Victorian Act.   Sir Henry
Parkes adopted some portions of the Act of Victoria,
but added new and effective provisions of his own.
He saw weak spots in the Victorian system, and
avoided them.   Visiting Melbourne, for the purpose
of inquiring respecting the new law and its operation, he conferred with both the Government and
the Railway Commissioners ; and, having learned
all there was to learn, returned to Sydney, and
framed his bill upon the information he had obtained
and his own conception of what the New South
Wales railways needed.

The Public Works Act he claimed wholly as his
own.   Certainly there is no such Act in any other
colony of Australasia, and probably in no country
outside Australasia.   The Standing Committee,

which each parliament has appointed under the provisions of the measure, may be somewhat similar in form to a Grand Committee of the House of Commons, but, in the main, its functions are distinct from those of any committee in any other parliament in the world. Nothing has shown this more clearly, than the applications which have been received from all quarters, for copies of the New South Wales Act, in order to learn its provisions, and of the reports of the Committee, to be informed as to its method of work and the results of its operations.

Under the Railways Act, three railway commissioners were appointed, the Chief Commissioner being obtained from England, the second found in the person of one who had been some years previously in a high position on the railways of Victoria, and the third transferred from one of the principal offices in the New South Wales Civil Service.

The appointment of the second commissioner brought about unexpectedly—it may almost be said accidentally, for this result from it was not desired —the defeat and resignation of the Government. Rumour associated the second railway commissioner with practices, in connection with railway freight on wool, which had led to the prosecution of a well-known commercial firm ; and this rumour was brought under the notice of the Legislative Assembly. Though satisfied of the commissioner's integrity, Sir Henry Parkes promised that inquiry should be made ; and inquiry confirmed him in the belief that the character of the commissioner was above reproach. This, however did not satisfy everybody ; and the matter was again referred to in the House. Sir Henry Parkes was annoyed. Having, after much consideration and trouble,. secured for the position of railway commissioners three gentlemen whom he believed to be admirably suited for it, and then, when the character of one of them had been assailed, proved by careful inquiry the falseness of the allegations made, he resented what seemed to him to be unreasonable persistency in a course unjust to both the commissioner and the Government. The matter was brought before the Assembly on a motion for adjournment; and, indifferent as to what the result might be, Sir Henry Parkes remained silent, and allowed the motion to go to a division, which placed the Government in a minority of fourteen, and induced Sir Henry Parkes to resign.

The Ministry had done good work in the two years of their existence, and they had done their work in the face of many obstacles and trials. Opposition from their opponents on the other side of the House was natural. , But difficulties arose from other sources than the action of the Opposition. They made their appearance among the Ministers themselves. The Attorney-General threw up his portfolio, because he did not receive an appointment to a vacant Judgeship to which he considered himself entitled ; and his successor resigned, after nine months of office, on the ground that the remuneration attached to the position was insufficient. The

Minister for Lands, the ablest parliamentarian in the Legislature, so neglected his duties that he endangered the existence of the Government, and was obliged to retire. In addition to this, allegations of an unpleasant and damaging kind were made in connection with the course taken by the Government in relieving the unemployed, and in relation to some other matters of administration.

No Government in New South Wales is free from charges of this nature. At one period or other of the existence of all Ministries, acts savouring of corruption are alleged against them. The charges are not proved; except, perhaps, by those whose natures prevent them from thinking anything but evil of their fellows, they are not believed; but, nevertheless, they do a certain amount of harm. They give rise to a feeling of dissatisfaction and of unrest, and they assist all movements of a directly hostile character against the Government. They assisted in the division connected with the case of the Railway Commissioner.

But that, which, in these proceedings, struck the public more forcibly than anything else, was the inglorious ending, brought about by the defeat on the motion for adjournment, to the proud career which had marked the life of the Government, from their triumphant return from the elections to the passing of the two great measures which, more than anything else, particularise this period of the colony's political history. The flag of free trade, which had been raised so conspicuously, and around which so many of the constituencies had rallied, seemed to disappear in an atmosphere of indifference. Free-traders complained; and there were those who blamed Sir Henry Parkes for allowing the motion. for adjournment to go to a division. He, himself, charged some of the free trade party—those who had voted for the adjournment, and there were some who took that course—and those who were not in the House to vote against it—with a want of loyalty which justified him in the action he had taken.

From whatever point of view advocates of free trade may regard the situation, it was not satisfactory. The state of parties in the House still showed the free traders to be in a large majority; but, Mr. Dibbs being commissioned to form the new Government, an appeal to the country was inevitable; and, in the peculiar circumstances of the time, there was no saying what the result of that appeal might be. As it happened, Sir Henry Parkes was brought back to office.

CHAPTER XXXVI.

THE month of March, 1889, saw Sir Henry Parkes in the position of Prime Minister of New South Wales, for the fifth time, and the champion of Australian Federation.

The general election, which followed the resignation of the Parkes Government, and the entry into office of a Government under Mr. Dibbs, made the two parties in the Assembly almost even. The freetraders were still in the majority, but it was very small.

Through the elections, there had been apparent a feeling not as friendly to Sir Henry Parkes as formerly; for, rightly or wrongly, he was blamed in many of the constituencies, as he was by many of his immediate friends, for having abandoned the free trade position, and thereby seriously injured its chances of a long and progressive prosperity. It is, of course, easy to condemn, and there is nothing more common than to overlook circumstances which may very well justify the proceedings complained of. Yet he had to listen to many well-grounded expressions of regret at the course he had taken, and to much rebuke.   He was still popular wherever he went, and whenever he spoke; but there was not, at this time, noticeable, the enthusiasm manifested two years before, when he was attacking the protectionist strongholds in all quarters of the country, and leading his party to victory.   Now, as then, he achieved successes; but, in many places, he was weak where before he was strong ; and, when the elections terminated, so much had the protectionist party advanced, that there was but a difference of two or three between them and their opponents, who were in the majority.   This did not prove the existence of a desire on the part of the people of the colony to abandon the policy of free trade, but it indicated an important advance of the advocates of protection, with a material strengthening of their position.

The Dibbs Ministry were defeated in the elections, on the question of protection; but this did not prevent them from making an effort to continue in office.   It seemed possible to proceed with general legislation for the time, and to deal with the fiscal question later on.   At any rate, they thought that course might be fairly taken, and they made the attempt.   They proposed to "sink the fiscal issue," or, in other words, deal with general legislation, and leave the tariff alone.   The attempt failed. Conscious of their majority, as shown by the election returns, the freetraders were sanguine that a test motion would remove the protectionist Ministry from office, and bring about their own return to power ; and they determined to try the strength of the Assembly without delay.

SIR HENRY PARKES AND HIS DOG MAORI.

Sir Henry Parkes was not inclined for another term of office. He was anxious for rest; and he regarded the circumstances that had brought about the defeat of the Government; in the matter relating to one of the Railway Commissioners, such as to justify him in refusing to re-occupy a position in which he might be again subjected to this objectionable treatment. He expressed himself as unwilling to be other than an ordinary member of the free trade party. But the party wished a continuance of his leadership; and, as they unanimously re-elected him leader, he accepted the situation, and, moving by way of an amendment on the Address-in-reply to the Governor's speech at the opening of the new Parliament, a direct want of confidence in the Government, he found himself, within a few days, at the head of his fifth Ministry, one of the ablest that have held office in New South Wales. Members of the free trade party, who previously had no desire for ministerial position, had consented to take a share in the work of government, for the purpose of safeguarding what they deemed to be the policy favoured by the country; and a Ministry was formed individually capable and collectively strong, The list was as follows :—

SIR HENRY PARKES, G.C.M.G. Colonial Secretary.

WILLIAM McMILLAN... ... Colonial Treasurer.

JOSEPH HECTOR CARRUTHERS... Minister of Public Instruction.

ALBERT JOHN GOULD... ... Minister of Justice.

GEORGE BOWEN SIMPSON, Q.C. Attorney-General.

JAMES NIXON BRUNKER ... Secretary for Lands.

BRUCE SMITH...	...	... Secretary for Public Works.
DANIEL O'CONNOR ...		... Postmaster-General.
SYDNEY SMITH	...	... Secretary for Mines.
WILLIAM HENRY SUTTOR		... Vice-President of the Executive Council.

Taking office on 8th March, 1889, the new Ministry remained in power until 22nd October, 1891. Their career was eventful. Commencing under fair auspices, they went on with little difficulty for twelve months; passing, during that time, the Land Bill which established the present Land Appeal Court, and carrying out various other important matters of legislation as well as of administration. Then they received a serious check by Sir Henry Parkes meeting with an accident, which broke his right leg and incapacitated him for many weeks from legislative work of any kind.

The accident happened on the 18th May, 1890; and, for several weeks, Sir Henry was confined to his bed. A fortnight previously he had moved, in the Legislative Assembly, resolutions approving of the proceedings of a Conference on the subject of a federation of the Australasian Colonies, shortly before held in Melbourne, and appointing himself, and three other members of the Assembly, delegates to the Federation Convention which sat in Sydney in 1891; and the House was in the midst of the debate upon the resolutions when he was stricken down.

All his public life he had been an advocate of federation. Recognising to the full, the obstacles

to provincial prosperity, as to national progress,
which the disunion of the colonies promoted, he
had, at various times, pressed the advantages of
federation upon the attention of the public of his
own colony ; and, as far as practicable, upon that of
the Governments and people of the other colonies.
During the editorship of the *Empire*, he had, on
several occasions, raised the question of the ultimate federation of Australia ; and it was he who first
applied to Albury the name of the Federal City.
In 1867, while a member of an Intercolonial.
Conference, held in Melbourne, at which all the
colonies but West Australia were represented, he
urged that the time had arrived when they should
be united by "some federal bond connection."
During the same year, at the instance of the
Government of Sir James Martin, in which he was.
Colonial Secretary, the New South Wales Parliament passed an Act authorising the Government
to appoint one or more of its members to represent
the colony in an Australasian Federal Council,.
whose duty it should be to arrive at an understanding on the subject of mail communication with
Great Britain. In 1881, at an Intercolonial Conference held in Sydney, Sir Henry Parkes framed a
set of resolutions for the creation of a Federal Council ;.
and, the resolutions being adopted, he drafted a
bill to make them law. This bill, after further
consideration of the whole question, he became
convinced would prove a failure, and, so far as he
was concerned, it was abandoned ; but it was taken up
at another Conference, held in Sydney in 1883,.

while he was on a visit to England, and the present Federal Council came into existence, under an Act which, though of wider range than the draft bill of 1881, was, in some important respects, very much its counterpart.

To him, as to most persons in New South Wales, this Federal Council was never attractive ; for, while it possesses certain extended powers of legislation, it can exercise no executive authority to give the legislation due effect. In his view the creation of this body was a false step ; and, at the first opportunity which presented itself, he endeavoured to effect a remedy.

In the early part of 1889, he proposed, to the Premier of Victoria, the creation of a Federal Parliament of two Houses, with an executive Federal Government; and, later in the year, in consequence of a report by Major-General Edwards, C.B., on the military forces of the colonies, and the necessity for legislation to ensure combined action in time of war, he invited the Governments of Victoria, Queensland, South Australia, Tasmania, and New Zealand to send, through the Parliaments of those colonies, representatives to a National Convention empowered to frame and report upon an adequate scheme of Federal Government. This invitation resulted in a conference at Melbourne known as the Federation Conference of 1890, and this conference led to the resolutions moved by him, in the Legislative Assembly of New South Wales, shortly before his accident.

Previous to 1889, it had appeared to him that matters were not ripe for "the construction of a Federal Constitution with a Federal Parliament," but, in that year, he was convinced the time had arrived when this should be done.

Military defence, and such organization as would provide for the effective employment of the troops of all the colonies in any part of Australasia, in periods of necessity, were, in his mind now, the primary reasons for federal action; but he did not fail to recognise that there were other important matters, with which a Federal Executive could deal with advantage to the colonies as a whole. Great benefit, he was aware, might be expected from the control by a Federal Government of the railways, in the direction of a uniformity of rolling stock and permanent way, the classification of goods, and the arrangement of rates. The rich fisheries, in the seas which wash the Australian coasts, required development and protection, and only a Government of all the colonies could do this. Further, there was the necessity for establishing a Federal Court of Appeal, and for combined action on the questions of the influx of foreign criminals and of aliens of inferior races.

One great Commonwealth, under one flag, and one Government, based on the experience gained in Canada and the United States—" a union under the Crown:" this was his proposal. There would be a Governor General, and an Australian Privy Council, a Federal Parliament, consisting of an Upper House or Senate and a Lower House or

House of Commons, and an Australian Judicial Court of Appeal. Such a federal system would provide all that was requisite for the government of Australia, or Australasia, as one great community, and yet in no way limit, or impair, the rights and powers of the several provincial governments and parliaments in relation to matters of purely local concern. They would deal with their own affairs as now ; the Federal Government would " simply rise to a higher level, and do the great things required to be done by Australia as a nation."

And how improved would be the position of Australia with federation ! " We should have a higher stature before the world. We should have a grander name. We should have an outline of empire such as we could never hope for as isolated colonies ; and our place would be admitted in the rank of nations, under the noble and glorious flag of the mother land."

Logical, as eloquent, throughout the earnestness and activity he displayed in bringing this great subject under public attention, he convinced the majority of those who heard or read his speeches, and impressed all. The obstacles in the way he regarded as trifling ; the advantages to be gained immense.

" We know," he told the people of Melbourne at a federation banquet given in the Queen's Hall, Parliament House, " it is a wise dispensation that these large colonies sprang into existence, and we admired them when they were fighting their own battles and working out their own prosperity independently of New South Wales ; but the time has now arrived when we are no longer isolated. The crimson thread of kinship runs through us all."

For his own colony he sought no selfish advantage; he proposed no conditions. Aware of the transcendent importance of bringing the different provinces together, he was content to leave those matters in which New South Wales might be specially interested—such as the tariff or the question of the Federal Capital—to the wisdom and patriotism of the Federal Government and the Federal Parliament. The question of a common tariff of free trade, or of protection, he said on many occasions, was a mere trifle compared with the great overshadowing importance of a living and eternal national existence.

Strong freetrader as he was, he was prepared, as he put it, to go into this national union without making any bargain whatever, without stipulating for any advantage for New South Wales, but trusting to the good faith and justice of a Federal Parliament for a right decision upon all questions with which the mother colony was particularly concerned. Let the colonies federate, and he did not fear that the national fiscal policy would be opposed to that which New South Wales had chiefly favoured. Federalist first and freetrader afterwards, he was anxious that those who joined in the federal campaign should move, untrammelled by anything which could well be laid aside, until the great object in view had been effected ; and, therefore, he saw no reason why freetraders and protectionists should not, in this sustained effort for union, go hand-in-hand

The news of the unfortunate accident of May,
1890, startled the conmunity. The sudden and
serious check, which it indicated, in a long public
career, now more than ever attracting attention,
aroused universal regret. The debate upon
the federation resolutions in the Legislative
Assembly was in its initial stages, and the feeling
of sympathy for Sir Henry Parkes prompted a
suggestion that it should be adjourned until he was
able to return to the House. He, however, was
anxious that it should proceed ; and this course was
adopted.

Meanwhile, he lay enduring the pain and the
tedium of a slow recovery. Messages, and visits of
sympathy and encouragement, were constant. Lord
and Lady Carrington were, in many ways, most
kind. Every morning, an orderly from Government House visited Hampton Villa, the residence of
Sir Henry Parkes at Balmain, with a kind note of
inquiry, and, more frequently than not, some little
present suitable to the sufferer's wants.

Most people regarded the accident as the close
of the aged statesman's career; but those who knew
of his splendid constitution, and his remarkable will
power, were not afraid that he would not resume his
place in Parliament and in public life. Ill, as he
was, he transacted on his sick bed, day by day, the
ordinary business of the Chief Secretary's Office ;
and, from the beginning to the end of a great strike
of seamen that took place in 1890, he controlled
the operations of the police and the military. His
jealous regard for his right to exercise the powers of

his Ministerial office, caused him, in response to an intimation from the Colonial Treasurer to a deputation, which seemed to him to trespass upon his position as head of the Government and Chief Secretary, to administer so sharp a rebuke that the Treasurer tendered his resignation ; and the existence of the Ministry was, for a time, threatened. Happily, mediation and explanation removed this difficulty ; but the determination to personally do the work pertaining to the office he held, was apparent throughout his long illness.

Fourteen weeks after the date of the accident, on August 27th, 1890, Sir Henry Parkes reappeared in the Legislative Assembly, a large House according him on the occasion a great welcome.   He walked with crutches, and had to be assisted to a specially prepared seat by the Sergeant-at-Arms and a private attendant ; but, apart from this, and a paleness of face, the result of his long confinement indoors, he looked well, and, in a few words of acknowledgment of the consideration shown to him by the House, spoke well.

" For more than a hundred days," he said, " I have suffered from an accident which, to me, has been a heavy misfortune, but which placed me in the far more painful position of holding a great public office that I felt I could not resign with honour, and yet the obligations of which I had not the physical strength to perform.   Throughout that time no breath of impatience has been evinced by this great House ; and I have received an amount of consideration which I trust will never fade from

KK

my mind, and which I shall endeavour to so utilise
as to soften, and, I hope, give a high tone to, all my
intercourse with hon. members."

One reason for his return to the Legislative
Assembly, at this time, was his desire to bring the
debate upon the federation resolutions to a close.
The members of the House, with a few exceptions,
concurred in the proposals, so far as they related to
the subject of federation, but there was a strong
feeling, on both sides, against the exclusion from the
delegates who should represent the colony at the
proposed convention, of the leader of the Opposition,
Mr. Dibbs. Sir Henry Parkes had maintained that,
in view of the attitude Mr. Dibbs had assumed on
the federation question, he could not possibly have
nominated him; and he held to this opinion. A
majority of members thought that, friendly or unfriendly to federation, Mr. Dibbs should be
appointed a delegate as the rightful representative
of the Opposition side of the House; and this
difference of opinion, between the Premier and the
friends of Mr. Dibbs, interfered with the otherwise
harmonious course of the debate.

Fortunately, the difficulty was surmounted, by
submitting the choice of delegates to the ballot;
and the way to this was smoothed, by circumstances,
connected with Sir Henry Parkes' illness, preventing
him from attending in the Assembly, to speak in
reply, when the debate upon the resolutions came to
an end. His absence was a great disappointment,
for it was felt, by all, that the opportunity presented
for a great speech was unique, and that he might

never again be able to appear to such advantage ;
but an unfavourable condition of a wound in his heel,
arising from the fracture in the leg, confined him to
his bed, and compelled him to remain away. A
division on the resolutions was taken on the 10th
September, with the result, after deciding to
appoint the delegates by ballot, that they were
passed by ninety-seven votes to eleven. The delegates chosen were Sir Henry Parkes, Mr. McMillan,
Mr. (afterward Sir) J. P. Abbott, and Mr. G. R.
Dibbs ; and they acted in the convention with
three delegates appointed by the Legislative
Council—Mr. Edmund Barton, Sir Patrick Jennings,
and Mr. W. H. Suttor.

Satisfaction at the favourable ending of the
proceedings in the House was expressed on all sides.
Lord Carrington, ever observant of public affairs,
and an ardent supporter of federation, wrote on the
morning after the division—

"My dear Sir Henry,

It is with very great regret, I heard last night, that
you did not feel equal to winding up the Federation
debate in the Assembly. It is indeed hard, and must be
a great disappointment ; but still you now have the satisfaction of seeing your own project passed, and passed
with enthusiasm by all the Australian Parliaments. The
good seed which you have sown, is fast springing up; and
you (and you only) will for ever live in history, as the
originator and creator of the movement which will change
these colonies into a nation.

We have all been thinking of you for the last two
days. Your courage and endurance of pain are a public
example ; but still it must be terrible to bear. Mr.
McMillan writes that Dr. MacLaurin has been called in

to consult by Dr. O'Connor. I am glad of this, as though
the case has been very well treated (as the healing of the
fracture shows), still fresh advice may bring relief.

Lady Carrington and the children send every kind
message, and the inquiries last night, at St. Vincent's
Ball, were incessant. The public sympathy is a direct
evidence of the gratitude which the colony owes to you.

Is there anything that we can do ? I can only trust
you are a little easier to-day, though I fear last night was
a bad one.

Yours most sincerely,

CARRINGTON."

Very complimentary also, were the comments of
the newspapers, on the services which the suffering
Premier had rendered to the great cause. " Even
the hardening influence of political antagonism,"
the *Herald* wrote, " could not render men insensi-
ble to what the cause of Federation owes to the
initiative, the great power, and the influential
personality of Sir Henry Parkes." All would re-
joice, it said, to find him aiding by his great ability,
experience, and force of character, in carrying on to
its end the work he had so successfully begun ; but
with a foresight, remarkable when considered in the
light of subsequent events, it pointed out that all
must be prepared to see the work drawn out into
length, and to move very slowly, and that though
the movement had been commenced, and commenced
well, it would be vain to speculate by whom, or in
what form, it would be ended. " But," the paper
added, " when it is brought to a happy issue, and

the new Australian union starts out on its life as a
great federal dominion, then will be the time to
remember, and to remember with patriotic recognition, what the great work owes to the strong
initiative, and compelling impetus it received from
the hand of Sir Henry Parkes."

CHAPTER XXXVII.

A YEAR had not gone by before, in the light of
events, it was apparent how correctly the newspapers had forecasted the probable progress of the
federation movement. Six months after the
passing of the resolutions in the Legislative
Assembly, the National Australasian Convention,
presided over by Sir Henry Parkes, sat in Sydney,
and adopted, in the form of a draft bill, a constitution for a proposed Commonwealth of Australia,
with the understanding that, as soon as possible,
it should be submitted, for approval, to the
Parliaments of the several colonies favourable to
federation ; and another month saw the great
question relegated to a position of seclusion from
which it has only recently emerged.

The Convention was the most distinguished
gathering, political or otherwise, that had met in
any of the Australasian colonies, at any period of
their history ; and its work attracted attention
throughout the civilised world. In the future it
will rank with those great Assemblies which
brought into existence the United States of

America and the Dominion of Canada. Sir Henry Parkes entered it with the same liberal-mindedness he had previously shown. Though, in no respect indifferent to the interests of New South Wales, he recognised the necessity for com- promise, and materially assisted in bringing about the results which were the outcome of the Con- vention's labours. To him fell the duty of moving resolutions that, with some amendment, formed the basis upon which the draft constitution was after- wards framed ; and, in speaking upon the occasion, he appealed to the representatives of every colony to meet the work, then about to begin, in a broad federal spirit, losing sight of local interests, and keeping in view only the better government of the whole Australian people.

" One People one Destiny," was the toast at a great federation banquet held in the Sydney Town Hall, during the sittings of the Convention, and attended by the Governors, as well as by the principal statesmen, of the different colonies ; and the senti- ment could not have been more cordially received. Sir Henry Parkes, adopting it as the subject of one of his sonnets, asks ;—

> " One People working out one Destiny,—
> Shall we not live within the ample shores
> Of our fair land, with no remembered sores
> Of once-distempered blood ; no enemy,
> Nor speech nor hearts divided ; earth, sea, sky,
> Our own ; the coming Nation's plenteous stores
> Of courage, richer than her golden ores,
> Expanding with her fame and industry ?
> Name of the Future, to inspire and charm

> The teeming emulous people of the West,
> To fill the Orient with her peaceful rays,
> To lead the King-Apostles to disarm,
> To teach the Masses to exalt the Best,
> To herald in the round of happy days."

The work of the Convention was undoubtedly well done, but it did not meet with the approval of everybody. In a matter connected with which there was necessarily considerable conflict of opinion and clashing of claims, compromise was unavoidable. But this compromise was the very thing that raised, in some minds, feelings of alarm. While in Sydney, and through the colony of New South Wales, there were many persons who warmly approved of the efforts in the direction of union, there were others in the position of active opponents, and very many who were indifferent.

One of the strongest of those who opposed the proceedings was Sir John Robertson; and he, at this time, was a political sage, exercising great influence upon the minds of younger men more or less prominent in public life. In his view there was neither desire nor necessity for federation. The people, he was convinced, did not want it, and those trying to force it upon them, would, if successful, permanently and largely injure the colony's interests. No prospect could he see from it of anything but evil. "What does Sir Henry Parkes mean by what he is doing?" he asked, hotly, on one occasion. "What does it all mean? The whole thing comes from England. That old Derby commenced it." And then, waxing hotter as he proceeded :—

" Look at the number of boy-governors they are
sending out here now, everyone of them supporting Parkes' policy. The fools! They think there
will be Imperial federation, and they will find a
United States of Australia and separation. Then
see," he said, as a parting shot at the New South
Wales federalists, " if federation should come about,
what a howl there will be here when the seat of
government is removed to Melbourne, as it certainly
will be."

Two others almost as antagonistic as he to the
federation movement at this period, were Mr. G.
H. Reid and Mr. J. H. Want. The former, while
not opposed to federation if it could be effected
without injustice to New South Wales, objected
strongly to the bill drawn up by the Convention,
and vehemently denounced it ; the latter, believing
that the progress and prosperity of the colony
depended upon its remaining unhampered by the
obligations of union with the sister states, and therefore with no wish to see the colonies federated, disapproved of the whole proceeding. Mr. Reid
opposed the bill in public meeting, and then carried
his opposition into the Legislative Assembly. Parliament met, after the close of the Convention, on
19th May, 1891, and, on the Address-in-Reply to
the Governor's speech, he moved an amendment
hostile to the Commonwealth Bill, and of such a
nature that, if passed, it would have caused the
Government to resign.

This course of action was variously received.
Some applauded it, but more condemned it. Gener-

ally there was a feeling through the community in favour of federation. No enthusiasm was noticeable; but people were beginning to think on the question, and to recognise that, in this direction, the destiny of Australia lay. The amendment was defeated by a large majority, with an expression of opinion from almost all the leading members of the House strongly in favour of union.

At once the way appeared clear for dealing with the draft federal constitution, and, as far as the Parliament of New South Wales was concerned, for determining the basis upon which, with the approval of the public, the colony should join in the proposed scheme. Everything seemed favourable for proceeding to the desired end. Everybody looked for the next step, which should show New South Wales to be undeterred in the resolve to lead the other colonies in the work which, more or less, all had in hand.

Yet scarcely a week had elapsed, before Sir Henry Parkes announced to the House, that, in view of the action of the mover of the amendment on the Address-in-Reply, and the delay thereby caused to public business, the Government had decided to withdraw from their original intention to proceed with the subject of federation as the first business of the session, and to postpone it until a local or district government bill, and an electoral bill, had been dealt with. After the trial of strength upon Mr. Reid's amendment, the Government, he announced, did not consider themselves justified in delaying several measures which the country

urgently wanted, and which Ministers desired to
bring forward and to pass into law without having
in their way the disturbing influence of a second
edition of the feeling displayed in the recent debate.
They proposed to pass a bill to provide for adequate
municipal government, and another to amend the
electoral law so as to establish single constituencies
and bring into operation the principle of one man
one vote. Sir George Grey, who had attended the
Federation Convention, as one of the representatives
of New Zealand, had aroused the populace to enthusiasm on the one man one vote question ; and
legislation in that direction was imperative.

An outburst of anger, inside and outside Parliament, followed this announcement. No good reason
could be seen for delaying what seemed easy of
accomplishment. Put federation off, it was said,
and it might never again be seriously taken in
hand. Push on with it at once, and there was
every prospect of its being carried to the desired
conclusion. Without, perhaps, adequately reflecting upon the causes which led Sir Henry Parkes
to alter the course of procedure laid down in the
Governor's speech, he was denounced as the
betrayer of the cause of which he had been the
champion ; and, seizing the opportunity, the leader
of the Opposition, Mr. Dibbs, moved, in the
Assembly, a motion of want of confidence which,
defeated only by the casting vote of the Speaker,
resulted in a dissolution of Parliament.

When the circumstances of the time come to be
fully examined, there will probably be found sufficient reason for the Government's apparent change

of front. Even from what is known now, it is easy to see how difficult it was for Sir Henry Parkes to adhere to his original programme of proceeding with federation before anything else. His Ministry was a strong one individually. Most members of it were men of opinions, and of backbone. With little experience of office, their strength of character and impetuousness sometimes led them to courses of action which did not promote harmony between them and their chief. Kicking over the traces, was, according to common report, much more frequent than running quietly in harness. The Cabinet, it was said, were not a united body on federation. Some of the more prominent of the Ministry did not approve of federation being pushed on to the delay of other business, and several went so far as to disapprove of federation itself.

The general election ended unfavourably for the Government. After two attempts the Postmaster General failed in obtaining a seat; and, in a comparison of the relative strength of the two principal parties in Parliament, the Ministerialists were in a minority. But a labour party had been returned,—to some extent a result of the great strike which had shortly before raged in Sydney, though more as a consequence of the introduction into parliamentary life of the principal of payment of members; and it was thought, by the Government, quite possible to secure from that quarter sufficient support to enable them to proceed with public business. The policy of the labour members was support for concessions, but this it was considered might be accommodated if not overcome.

Difficulties soon appeared, however. The attitude of the labour section of the House, towards the Government, very quickly had upon Sir Henry Parkes and his colleagues a very irritating effect. Without their support the Ministry were powerless; with it, they were humiliated. For a time the situation was accepted, and the Government strove to make the best of it; but, sooner or later, it was certain to become unbearable, and, in a little more than three months, they cast the yoke from their necks and set themselves free.

A strong effort was made to push on with general legislation. Federation was laid aside, awaiting a more favourable opportunity. No lack of earnestness in the cause existed on the part of Sir Henry Parkes; but the difficulties of the Ministerial position made it impracticable to proceed with federation until other questions had been dealt with. The speech at the opening of Parliament indicated the intention of the Government to pass, among other measures, an Electoral Bill which was to abolish plural voting, a Local Government Bill, a bill to put an end to labour disputes by establishing courts of conciliation, a bill for the regulation of coal mining, and bills to provide for mining on private property and to regulate manufactories and workshops.

Such a programme of legislation, in the interests of the working classes, could not but be acceptable to the Labour Party ; and their approval of it was very soon shown by the support which they gave the Government, in rejecting an amendment, on the Address-in-Reply to the Speech, moved by the leader of the Opposition. Regarding this as an assurance of continued support, general business was pushed forward ; but obstacles appeared, and grew as the work of the House proceeded. No opportunity was lost by the Labour Members to assert their independence, and their determination to give their support only so long as they received for it an adequate return. To the Electoral Bill and the Coal Mines Regulation Bill they gave special attention ; and, in connection with the last-mentioned measure, a clause was carried by them limiting the hours of labour in mines to eight, and making an infringement of that or of any of the other provisions of the bill, penal. This brought about a crisis. Strongly opposed to the compulsory time limit of work, Sir Henry Parkes desired that the bill should be recommitted so that the objectionable clause might be reconsidered, and warned the House that, if an adjournment to enable this to be done were refused, the bill would be abandoned.. The adjournment was refused ; and the Government resigned.

The situation was a serious one. By their demands, the labour members had aroused a feeling of alarm. Many of those who had watched the course of politics feared that existing institutions were about to be undermined. Lord Jersey, who at this date had succeeded Lord Carrington, in the

Governorship of New South Wales, wrote to Sir Henry Parkes, on the morning after the division upon the motion for the adjournment of the debate upon the Coal Mines Bill :—

"Last night's vote was extraordinary, or, at least, seems so to me who have only read the circumstances as reported in the papers. . . . . I shall be here all the morning ; but, unless you specially wish to see me, I think that I had better wait to hear from you the result of the meeting of the Cabinet. The position of affairs seems doubly acute. I need not, I feel sure, express to you my readiness to do anything in my power to lessen the tension, and to assist in preserving the principles of good government. If, therefore, you are of opinion that a conversation now can be of service, I am ready to see you. I admire your speech."

The Government were not long in deciding upon the step they should take. Their position had become intolerable, and resignation was the only means of relief.

To Sir Henry Parkes, the situation had been far more unpleasant than it had been to his colleagues. Outside the Cabinet, he had endured the irritating proceedings of the labour members ; inside, he had been subjected to the annoyance caused by the independent attitude of some of his colleagues towards important portions of the Ministerial programme. For some time he had contemplated resignation, and retirement from political life. In the early part of 1889, he had distinctly refused to

place himself in any position which would entail the
responsibility of leadership upon him ; and, prior to
the elections in 1891, he had asked his colleagues to
consent to his retirement from the Government.
He was getting very tired of it all ; and, on the
occasion of his setting out on an electioneering tour
to some of the southern electorates, said that when
the elections were over, he should give up his
position as Premier, and let some one else take his
place.   His idea was that, should he take this step,
it would be open to the Governor to send for Mr.
McMillan or Mr. Brunker to reconstruct the
Ministry, so that the free trade party in the
House need not suffer by the change.   Both worried
and ill, he longed for rest ; and he had determined that, if he retired, his retirement should
be permanent.

During September, of 1889, he wrote to Mr.
Brunker a letter, which pathetically indicated the
nature of his position, in office, at this period.   He had
not been feeling well—his heart was showing signs
of weakness—and his colleague, an old and valued
friend, had written inquiring after his health.   His
doctor had made a careful examination, and had
found things "not so bad as they might have been."
On previous occasions of a similar character, he
had remarked "it is all right ;" now, the opinion
was "it is not so bad," or "it might be worse."
And the letter went on to say that the writer knew
of no parallel instance, in English public life, of a
person remaining in active work, in office, as Premier,
at his age, except the cases of Lord John Russell

and Lord Palmerston; and they, in their later years, did little, and were pampered and looked after in every way likely to contribute to their comfort. Mr. Gladstone was another instance that might be mentioned, " but he," the letter said, " nurses himself in every way now."

Just at this time Sir Henry Parkes was reading the life of Mr. Gladstone, written by Mr. G. W. Russell; and his perusal of the book had filled his mind with curious reflections.

" I was thinking, when reading it," he said in conversation shortly afterwards, " of a comparison between Mr. Gladstone's life and my own. When he was at Eton, preparing himself for Oxford, enjoying all the advantages of a good education, with plenty of money, and being trained in every way for his future position as a statesman, I was working on a rope-walk at fourpence a day, and suffered such cruel treatment that I was knocked down with a crowbar, and did not recover my senses for half an hour. From the rope-walk I went to labour in a brick-yard, where I was again brutally used ; and, when Mr. Gladstone was at Oxford, I was breaking stones on the Queen's highway, with hardly enough clothing to protect me from the cold."

The relief which the resignation of the Government brought him was very great. A published extract from his private diary shows how keenly he relished his freedom. At the Cabinet meeting, held to consider the position of the Ministry, after the unfavourable vote upon the Coal Mines Bill, and at which their resignation was decided upon, he pointed out,

LL

that though, under the circumstances, their retirement was not necessary, yet it was quite open to them to take that course. They had gone as far as men could go, without losing all sense of honour and self-respect, to meet the demands of the labour party, and he could not see that they were called upon to go further.

"As we had not a majority without their inconsistent votes, coupled with their rapacious demands," his diary record stated, "the course best calculated to maintain our own reputations, and to serve the public interest and the true cause of parliamentary government, was to tender our resignations." His colleagues unanimously concurred in this view; and the Governor, while expressing his deep regret at the step taken, acknowledged it to be one which, under all the circumstances, honourable men were justified in taking. In the Legislative Assemby, Sir Henry Parkes announced the resignation, "and went home happy." Next morning he arose early, "after a long night's refreshing sleep," so different "from the weary waking after a tumultuous night in the Assembly;" and, home again from the House before six in the evening, free from the burden and cares of office, his diary gives vent to his feeling of satisfaction in the exclamation, "What a blessed change!"

CHAPTER XXXVIII.

FROM LEADER TO PRIVATE MEMBER.

WHILE Sir Henry Parkes was struggling against the difficulties which beset him during the later part of the period comprising the existence of his Ministry, it again fell to his lot to see pass away from this life, some of those who had been his contemporaries in the great political contests of the early days. Others had gone before; more soon followed.

Frequently, in the course of his career, it was, for him, a melancholy occupation to reflect upon the number of instances in which old faces and figures, well known to him in his younger as well as in his more matured political life—some of them opponents, some friends—had dropped out of sight, disappearing in the darkness of the tomb. Almost every year someone had gone. In 1888, Mr. W. B. Dalley and Mr. James Squire Farnell passed away; in 1889, Mr. John Sutherland; in 1891, Sir John Robertson and Sir William Macleay. The battles had been fiercely fought; the warriors had fallen on this side and on that; and he, whitehaired and old, was left on the field almost the sole survivor.

Of late years, Mr. Dalley had been more of an opponent than a friend ; but Sir Henry Parkes had always recognised the abilities and services of his fellow commissioner of 1861, and admitted the distinguished position he had attained. The success of the Opposition party in the elections of 1882, which preceded the entry into office of Sir Alexander Stuart, was largely due to Mr. Dalley ; and very hard he worked as Attorney-General of the Stuart Ministry, and, subsequently, as the counsellor and assistant of Sir George Dibbs in the first Dibbs Ministry, and of Sir Patrick Jennings in the Administration which preceded the fourth Ministry under Sir Henry Parkes. Yet his help to the opponents of Sir Henry Parkes did not push him to an attitude of personal enmity. Sir John Robertson was a much closer associate than Mr. Dalley had ever been. Many times he had opposed Sir Henry Parkes, and used unfriendly language towards him ; but their coming together in the same Government, and the four years' association which that brought about, removed the effects of the former want of political agreement ; and, when Sir John Robertson died, Sir Henry Parkes was able to speak of him as a friend of forty years, who, though not without defects of character, had done so well as to entitle him to the veneration of posterity.

Three months after the death of Sir John Robertson, there assembled at the residence of Sir Henry Parkes, by his invitation, a singular luncheon party. Fourteen persons sat round the table, the remnant in the colony of those who, in one way or

other, were prominently associated with the introduction of constitutional government into New
South Wales, or with the progress of the colony
under constitutional government from the time of its
introduction.   United, their ages represented 1100
years; and ten of them have since died.   Sir John
Hay, Sir William Manning, Mr. Richard Jones,
Mr. Geoffrey Eagar, and Mr. Peter Faucett were
among them ; and they have gone.   All these were
in the first Legislative Assembly, some in the
earlier mixed Legislature; and all were Ministers
in the young days of responsible government.
Fond of preserving recollections of the past,
Sir Henry Parkes had brought his guests together;
he, with them, a group of aged men "standing
within the shadows of another world," under
circumstances and surrounded by recollections, it
was remarked at the time, such as could not apply
to any other fourteen men in all the population of
Australia.   They feelingly honoured " the memory
of the early friends of Australian Freedom," and
now most of them also live only in the memory.

The resignation of Sir Henry Parkes from office
in 1891, would have been followed by his retirement
from parliamentary life, but for some obstacles unexpectedly appearing in the way.   One of these was
a strongly expressed desire, on the part of leading
persons among his constituents, that he should
refrain from taking the contemplated step.   Though
extremely anxious to retire, he could not
altogether disregard the wishes of those who had
elected him to the Assembly ; and, in the end, he
gave way to them.

Some of his friends thought that, in contemplating retirement, he must be conscious of some regret. But in reality, it was otherwise. "Why should I?" he asked one day, when the matter was mentioned to him. "Because you have been in Parliament so long; you are so identified with the place; you are so wedded to it." "I am not wedded to it." he replied quickly, and with some severity. "That is a great mistake. I am not wedded to it, and never was. I never really liked it. I never was so tired of anything, and shall be exceedingly glad to get away from it."

The leadership of the Free Trade party was not retained by him. In his desire for rest, he was now averse to occupying any position which would entail the necessity for prolonged parliamentary sittings and extreme physical exertion. If he remained in Parliament, he wished to do so, for the present at least, as a private member, with no responsibility upon him other than that associated with private membership. At the same time he was not pressed by the Free Trade party to remain as their leader.

Latterly, he had shown signs of much physical weakness, the outcome of his accident of the previous year and of his advancing age; and a feeling existed, in the minds of some of those who had supported him, that he should be replaced by a younger and more active man. In the ordinary course, on the the retirement of the Government from office, he would but cross the floor of the House from the head of the Government benches to the head of the benches used by the Opposition, his right to continue his leadership unquestioned. Now, his contemplated early retirement from Parliament, as well as the feeling amongst his party, was regarded as sufficient justification for making a change. Some deference, however, was due to him in view of the position he had filled; and a deputation waited upon him, at his private residence, to obtain from him a definite statement of his intentions respecting his future relations with his party. His reply was by letter; and, in this, he distinctly declined to resume the position of leader. The leader of the Opposition, he explained, should be not only a man of great political capability, but one prepared to remain at his post throughout the sittings; and he feared that one of that kind would not be found in him at his time of life.

But, irrespective of the state of his health, and the inconveniences arising from his accident, there were other and weighty reasons which led him to decline the position under existing circumstances. These other reasons he did not explain; but they were to be found in the annoyance and worry to which he had been subjected, and a repetition of which he feared, from the peculiar condition of the Assembly in consequence of the presence there of a third party.

He did not say that if circumstances of difficulty arose in the future, sufficiently serious as to justify the step, he would not again accept the burden of office; but, he distinctly declared that, as things were at this time, he was anxious to avoid any position of responsibility, other than that of a simple member of Parliament. He afterwards said that one reason for his declining to lead the party at this date, was their determination to immediately attack, with a view to upset, the Government which had come into power under Mr. Dibbs. The coming into office of that Government he regarded as perfectly constitutional, and he refused to do anything to dislodge them. He therefore stood aside, and Mr. G. H. Reid was elected to take his place.

This election of Mr. Reid was not expected, and, to Sir Henry Parkes, was anything but agreeable. Promptly and publicly he intimated that he would not follow the new leader; and some scenes of considerable bitterness between them occurred, in the course of debate, in the Assembly. The leadership of Mr. McMillan, or of Mr. Bruce Smith, would have been much more acceptable.

Regarding Sir Henry Parkes as in very much the same position as Mr. Gladstone when his retirement, through ill health, becoming necessary, the Marquis of Hartington was temporarily elected leader of the English Liberal Party, some persons thought that, as in the English case, when a change of Government came about, the Marquis of Hartington stood aside for his great chief to form the new Administration, so the new leader of the Free Trade Party might very well, when the time came, make way for Sir Henry Parkes. Naturally, it would have been agreeable to Sir Henry Parkes if matters could have been so arranged. But though, in view of his distinguished public services, and long experience at the head of his party, there was much to recommend such an arrangement, circumstances generally were unfavourable for it; and the relations existing between him and Mr. Reid, rendered it practically impossible. So he fell away from the main body of the Free Trade Party, and assumed an attitude of independence.

A striking feature in his career, at this period, as indeed it had been throughout his life, was the unsatisfactory condition in which he stood pecuniarily, and the disregard of this circumstance which was apparent in his public acts. Retirement from the leadership of his party, as resignation from office, meant a state of circumstances in his home and amongst his family, which, at times, bordered upon poverty; but, in his strong adherence to the principles of sound parliamentary procedure, this did not cause him to hesitate in taking what he considered to be the right course. The path of duty was to him ever preferable to that of convenience. Straight ahead he always went, without a thought of the troubles in the way, influenced only by his belief in the soundness of the step he was taking, and its value as something which, in the public interest, might, in similar circumstances, be followed with advantage in the future.

In the desire to so act in public matters that his action should be a safe precedent for the future, no one has stood higher in general estimation. "When I left office lately," he said one day, talking to a friend, "if you will believe me I had scarcely £10 to my credit. I have no money. I am a poor man." During the previous week he had sold some of his

household goods.   He had always been in the habit
of getting together little treasures of one kind and
another, very valuable in themselves to him ; and
he had been obliged to sell some of them "to get
bread," for he had "the butcher and the baker to pay,
and mouths to feed."   Just at this time he had found
a purchaser for a valuable collection of Australian
autograph letters, many of them those of prominent
men of the early days, and for some other interesting
relics that had adorned his home, for which he had
received a hundred guineas,—a fairly large sum ;
but more satisfactory to him than the money, was
the assurance that he had parted with the letters
and the other articles to a gentleman who, he was
confident, would take care of them.

In the situation of a private member of Parliament, attending the sittings of the Assembly, and
taking a fair share in the debates associated with its
business, and, outside the House, interesting himself
in public affairs as they came under notice at public
meetings, Sir Henry Parkes passed the period which
marked the life of the Dibbs' Ministry—a little less
than three years.   In August, 1892, his disapproval
of the visit of Mr. Dibbs to England, and his
view of the principles of parliamentary government, led him to intimate an intention to move a
motion of censure upon the Government; but, learning that a similar proceeding was intended by the
leader of the Opposition, he gave way, and allowed
the other motion to be made, he speaking and voting
in favour of it.   Of the general policy of the Government he did not approve, and he gave it his strong

opposition, moving on one occasion in Committee of Ways and Means a motion which, if carried, would have resulted in their downfall ; and, in the early part of 1893, he joined in a movement of the Free Trade party to bring about a dissolution of Parliament.

His usefulness in the public life of the colony as an authority and critic on constitutional procedure was, at this time, very noticeable ; and, as by his isolated position in the Assembly, he had little or no chance of office, he was secure from the accusation of condemning the Government for personal advantage.

CHAPTER XXXIX.

In 1889, Sir Henry Parkes published a collection of his poems under the title "Fragmentary Thoughts," and in 1895, a small volume of "Sonnets and Other Verse." The former was dedicated to the late Lord Tennyson.

"Permit me," Sir Henry Parkes wrote on the page preceding the preface, "to dedicate this volume to you, in remembrance of golden hours of life spent with you in various ways. Our happy walks together, in the groves and over the downs in the neighbourhood of Farringford, and through the bowery lanes and across the green fields around Aldworth; the hours of rare enjoyment vouchsafed to me when, under your honoured roof, I have listened to your reading of your immortal poems; the delicate kindnesses extended to me by the gracious lady who, for so many years, has made the spiritual sunshine of your illustrious life—all remain to me as memories whose beauty can never die."

Charmed with this gracefully-worded compliment, the Laureate wrote, in reply :—" I send you from over the convex of our little world, which you are

My wife &
the Union thank
kindest sympathy
when it help & to
you the fast presence
of the Australian
Dominion

My dear Sir Henry

I send you from over the convex
of our little world which you fare doing
your best to make better, my choicest thanks
for your volume of Poems & your kind &
affectionate dedication, & moreover congratulate
you that you have, not unsuccessfully,
interwoven the laurel of the Muses with
the civic wreath which you wear as a
Statesman
               Yours always
                    Tennyson

Jan^y — 1890

doing your best to make better, my choicest thanks
for your volume of poems and your kind and affectionate dedication, and, moreover, congratulate you
that you have, not unsuccessfully, interwoven the
laurel of the Muses with the civic wreath which you
wear as a Statesman."

Reproduced as it came to Sir Henry Parkes, the
letter was in the form shown in the illustration.

Thomas Woolner, referring to the dedication, in
a letter acknowledging the receipt of a copy of the
book, wrote:—"Allow me to say that though the dedication to Tennyson is not in the form of verse, it is
so true, genuine, impulsive, and so beautifully expressed, that it seems to me almost like one of the
illustrious poet's immortal poems. I do not wonder
that he was much pleased with it, for such a compliment from any man would naturally be welcome,
but from one who has so many claims upon the
gratitude of mankind, it must be doubly dear."

The book, the author stated in his preface, he
sent into the world like a friendless child, with no
claim to notice and no expectation of favour, but
with all the fond attachment of a hopeless parent.
If the quality of poetry were denied to it no one
would take the trouble to question the verdict, the
object of its publication being something different
from the establishment of a poet's reputation. Care-
less of public praise, no more was desired than that
the verses should go forth as they were in themselves,
with their excellence or their blemishes as the lines
portrayed them, a curious feature in the author's
hard and chequered life, a part of himself.

"They have been written," he informed his readers, "on occasions which have been as breaks in the chain of nearly sixty years of incessant labour, and struggling effort, in fields far removed from literary study. They form, in some measure, the broken record of the inner life of a busy public career, which men, at times, have treated too indulgently, and, at other times, have blindly and perversely misjudged, but which few have critically understood." Imperfect expression had been found in them for "the hidden burning passion, the pulsations of prescient thought, the unsullied yearning for the higher part, the involuntary scorn of worldly-mantled meanness, the better aspirations of the unsatisfied spirit." To those who desired to know the author in his political character, it was explained, they would have an interpretable interest, and in the investigations of the curious, they might serve to throw light on transactions and proposals which are now as little heard of as if they were forgotten.

Most of the poems were culled from the volumes which saw the light from 1842 to 1885. Others were new. One, "To a Beautiful Friendless Child," elicited some criticism from Woolner. The poem was suggested by a visit to Sir Henry Parkes, while Colonial Secretary, in 1888, of a poor man, whose wife had recently died, with an adopted child—a boy—whom, no longer able to support, he wished to hand over to the care of the Government, under the system which operates in New South Wales for the maintenance of destitute children by the State. The boy, a fine looking little fellow of four years, excited the admiration of both Sir Henry Parkes and his colleagues, and the feelings of the former found expression in these verses, one of which reads :—

> "What need of star or coronet,
> Or dross from India's mines?
> On thee, in rosy splendours set,
> God's stainless order shines."

Alluding to this verse, Woolner, in a letter to Sir Henry Parkes, said—"There is one point that struck me in the 'Beautiful Friendless Child,' on page 20, which I thought it worth while bringing under your notice. You say,—

> 'What need of star, or coronet,
> Or dross from India's mines?'

"Meaning that the child lives in such rosy splendours he has no need of such adventitious decoration. But surely no one would expect dross to add to any one's splendour; and why call a lovely gem dross? Doing so weakens your own beautiful idea; whereas if you call the gem by its true name you assist your idea, and the lines would read more musically and with sweeter cadence.

> "What need of star or coronet
> Or gems of Indian mines?
> On thee in rosy splendour see
> Immortal glory shines."

"By thus slightly changing the last line you avoid the sibilant, and remove the notion of 'order' which is unnecessary in the first line, and interferes with the largeness of the conception; moreover, it sounds more poetical because more suggestive, as immortal glory could come only from God. Pray pardon my bold criticism," he continued, "but as an old versemaker I feel jealous and anxious that my friends should polish up theirs to the highest pitch. The poems, as you suggest, give a most interesting glimpse of your inner aspirations, and, above all, the warm and passionate desire you have always felt to improve the hard fate of the poor, and bestow upon them your sympathy, which, in some respects, is by them even more highly valued."

But, perhaps, the most interesting communication Sir Henry Parkes received in relation to "Fragmentary Thoughts," was a letter from Sir Charles Dilke. In his work "Problems of Greater Britain," he had made a somewhat contemptuous reference to Sir Henry Parkes' poetry; and, on the publication of "Fragmentary Thoughts," Sir Henry sent him a copy without letter or comment. Sir Charles Dilke acknowledged the gift by a graceful explanation of the unpleasant passage in "Greater Britain," which changed the objectionable allusion from a sneer to a compliment. "I am touched and charmed," he wrote, by your sending me the volume of poems. I have no doubt that you saw the 'impertinent' adjective I applied to your earlier poems; but you must excuse me, if I repeat, that even pretty poems seem to me 'trashy' if weighed along with your services to what we hope will soon be the Australian State."

At the time of the publication of his "Problems of Greater Britain," Sir Charles Dilke had observed, in a letter to Lord Carrington, in Sydney, accompanying a copy of his book—"I am told that Parkes will not like what I have said of him ; but, in reality, what I have said I meant for high praise, for I consider Parkes and Macdonald the two biggest men in the Empire after Mr. G."

"Sonnets and Other Verse" is the title of a little book, published in London, and representing the poetical compositions of Sir Henry Parkes during the spare hours of the years 1894 and 1895. It appeared about the middle of 1895, and was dedicated to "The Right Honourable Hallam, Lord Tennyson, with kindest regards." The contents are varied, but chiefly of a political character, several of the subjects rather old. One of the strongest of the sonnets is entitled "The Glory of Bonaparte."

> "The twenty years of Bonaparte, O God!
> What matchless meanness, unexampled crime,
> And shameless pomp defamed that fateful time !
> O'er Freedom his devouring armies trod,
> And men and nations trembled at the rod
> Of the destroyer ! Hofer's death sublime
> Attests how bravely heroes, in their prime
> Of courage, fought to free their native sod.
> But Bonaparte ! what his absorbing aim
> In all his blind destruction unwithstood ?—
> To conquer, subjugate for worthless ends,
> Make to himself a world-resounding name,
> And found a Dynasty in tears and blood !
> How swiftly Heaven the dread Avenger sends !"

Some lines entitled "Unfit for Freedom," present a striking picture of human nature as it is in Aus-

M M

tralia, in common with other countries—the ambitious
strivings of the wealthy, the hard lot of many of the
poorer classes, the debasing effects of the struggle
for that which never rises above the level of sel-
fishness.

> "Inscrutable and Omnipresent God !
>   Who dost behold, as Thou sustainest, all ;
>   With Thee it will not weigh, or great or small,
>   Or rich or poor. Thy creatures plan and plod
>   In building temples, while the labourer's hod
>   Hard grinds the shoulder's flesh.   On Thee they call,
>   When terrors in their worldly path appall,
>   But few devoutly kiss Thy chastening rod !
>   A people poor in heart, O God of Truth !
>   Not fashioned like our fathers for great deeds,
>   We know not how nobly to live and die :
>   Of different clay were men in the world's youth ;
>   Too much of knowledge and too many creeds
>   Have we, unawed by Freedom's majesty !"

One of the sonnets was written to mark the
author's eightieth birthday. The lines are not
strong and attractive, as are the verses written ten
years before under the title "Seventy"; but they
are interesting, inasmuch as they indicate that,
even at eighty years of age, Sir Henry Parkes was
unconscious of any noticeable sign of decay in himself, mental or physical.

> "I count the mercifullest part of all
>   God's mercies, in this coil of eighty years,
>   Is that no sense of being disappears
>   Or fails—I see the signal, hear the call,—
>   Can calmly estimate the rise and fall
>   Of moth-like mortals in this 'vale of tears.'"

The volume closes with some verses entitled " Weary," plain enough for anyone to understand to whom they refer.

"Weary of the ceaseless war
   Beating down the baffled soul,—
Thoughts that like a scimitar
   Smite us fainting at the goal.

" Weary of the joys that pain—
   Dead sea fruits whose ashes fall,
Drying up the summer's rain—
   Charnel dust in cups of gall !

" Weary of the hopes that fail,
   Leading from the narrow way,
Tempting strength to actions frail—
   Hand to err, and foot to stray.

" Weary of the battling throng,
   False and true in mingled fight ;
Weary of the wail of wrong,
   And the yearning for the night !

" Weary, weary, weary heart !
   Lacerated, crush'd, and dumb ;
None to know thee as thou art !
   When will rest unbroken come ?"

CHAPTER XL.

FREE from the trammels of office, or the obligations of Opposition leadership, Sir Henry Parkes now determined to devote the remaining years of his life to the cause of Federation.

Before everything else he intended to place the union of the colonies. In his eightieth year there was no time to lose; and less because of the dilatoriness in the national work, apparent in the action of others. Many were now the supporters of union, but few were the active workers; and none saw, as he did, the limited period and opportunity for doing what required to be done, while his life lasted. The safer, the more progressive, the higher existence which federated Australia would enter upon, transcended, in his mind, all else. While still as earnest as ever in promoting the interests of his own colony, he was, without detriment to New South Wales, federalist first and a citizen of the mother colony afterwards. No injury to her from union could he see ; and, freetrader as he was, he was content to leave the question of free trade to the Parliament which would be elected by the federated states, convinced that its action in framing a national fiscal policy would be in the direction of commercial freedom.

Federation he put in the forefront of his address to his constituents at St. Leonards, at the 1894 elections, and federation was his political cry ever afterwards. " We have reached a period in the history of Australian growth and development," he said in that address, "when these colonies present to the world all the proportions of national life, and when their coming together, under a federal form of government, is a question pressing for settlement in the realm of practical politics." So most men believed ; but party considerations often thrust conviction aside, and aim. at nothing but party interest.

" The formative stages of federal opinion are passed," he wrote, " and the national sentiment is alive and strong in the hearts of all thinking men."

He himself was convinced the country was in accord with his views; that the best, and the majority, of the people were ready, and anxious, to support him, in his efforts to bring the colonies into union ; and from what was indicated by the attitude of the press, the tone of public meetings, and the expression of individual opinion, there was much to justify his conviction. Yet under a system of parliamentary government, such as operates in the Australian colonies, the opinion of the thinking portion of the community, or, it may be, of the majority, is not always the strongest factor in politics. Of this he was well aware ; but, believing that the country as a whole was in favour of federation, he resolved to push on.

Nothing could drive from his mind the incalculable advantages of bringing the colonies together. Other measures for their advancement were necessary, but none so essential as the first great step which would make them one.

"The inviolability of the soil as the home of one Australian people," he said in his address to the electors of St. Leonards, "the restriction of inferior races, the opening of new fields for the employment of the people and for the investment of capital, the lighting of our coasts, the improvement of our harbours, the avenues of enterprise in connection with the commerce of the South Seas and of neighbouring markets, the name and influence of Australia among the nations of the earth : these, and a crowd of federal questions, are waiting for the consummation of union."

Much, during the period occupied by the 1894 elections, he did to bring this great question before the attention of the people ; and, everywhere he went, his utterances met with approval. The elections resulted in favour of the Free Trade party, and, as he and many others believed, in support of federation first and free trade subsequently.

But the after-circumstances were disappointing. Mr. Reid was still the recognised leader of the free traders ; and, having been in the front of the party in the elections, he had a claim to prominence in the victory, which it was difficult to overlook. Sir Henry Parkes was the more conspicuous figure in the contest and its result ; Mr. Reid, the one who really held the position when victory was assured.

Sir Henry Parkes, driving through the streets of Sydney on the night of the declaration of the poll, was overwhelmed with popular applause ; Mr. Reid, when the beaten Protectionist Government retired from office, was sent for by the Governor and formed a new Administration.

This, in Sir Henry Parkes' view, indicated another check to federation, though it was not necessarily more than one of a temporary character.

Federation was included in the programme which the new Government put before Parliament, but it was not accorded the place desired by Sir Henry Parkes and those who thought with him ; and he was not satisfied. To him it was also unpleasant to find that several of his old colleagues and friends had joined Mr. Reid in his Government, and there-fore, to that extent, severed their connection with him. This naturally tended to further alienate him from the Ministry. Regarding them with strong disfavour, he refrained from occupying the position of a supporter of them ; and their efforts, in due course, to alter the existing protectionist tariff to one of almost absolute free trade, led him, in the interests of federation, to make a determined attempt to drive them from office.

Justifiable though this was, in the light of his long professed intention to press forward federation before free trade or anything else, it brought upon him much obloquy. Yet he went on. A champion of union, such as he had long been, he could, in his position, be no partisan. Federation not being a party question, it did not seem wrong to look for its

supporters among the protectionist members of the
Legislature, any more than to find them among the
free traders.   All he wanted was earnest men in the
cause, from whatever quarter they might come.

A suggestion was made that, if a policy of
federation were put before the House, the protectionist party, as well as many free traders, would
vote for it.   The chief members of the protectionist
party were ardent federalists ; and it was known
that some of the party supporting the Government
were not pleased with the proceedings of the
Ministry in relation to this question, and were disposed, if the opportunity offered, to transfer their
allegiance to Sir Henry Parkes.

Mr. Reid had brought about, and attended, a
meeting of the Premiers of the different colonies,
at Hobart, to consider the question of union ; and
a plan had been agreed upon, by which the whole
question was to be considered by the several Parliaments *de novo*.   An influential portion of the Press
described this as breaking wholly with the past, and
making inadequate preparation for the future ; and
Sir Henry Parkes, comparing the Hobart conference with the convention which sat in Sydney
in 1891, likened it to a *coterie* of mice claiming for
itself the mastery over a gathering of lions.

Strongly in favour of the basis for federation
set forth in the draft bill of the convention of 1891,
he resented any attempt to set the labours of the
past aside ; and he listened to the overtures, which
came to him, of support, to overthrow those whom
he regarded as enemies of the cause to which he
had devoted the remainder of his days.

The protectionist party, it need scarcely be said, though ready enough to vote for federation, had in view interests of their own. The continuance in power of the Free Trade Government meant the abolition of the tariff which the Dibbs Ministry had introduced, and which helped to keep certain industries alive; a policy of federation would leave things as they were, until a Federal Parliament should be in a position to deal with the tariff question as it affected outside trade.

To Sir Henry Parkes the intended alteration of the New South Wales tariff, to one of free trade, appeared a serious blow to the prospects of federation. New South Wales, Mr. Reid had declared, was going to sail into the port of federation with the flag of free trade flying. Suppose, asked Sir Henry Parkes, the colony of Victoria should declare she intended to sail into the same port with the flag of protection flying :—what chance would remain for federation, on any terms? Instead of union it must be perpetual disunion ; and, recognising this, he saw the wisdom of letting the tariff, though it was that of a Protectionist Ministry, alone, until the colonies could be brought together, and the matter dealt with in the interests of them all, as one nation.

"The question of a fitting Government for an intelligent, rapidly-growing, aspiring people," he wrote, "is far above any fiscal considerations, or the adjustment, in a code of policy, of any economic principles." The young states, if they meant to achieve success, must "meet in the spirit of brotherhood ; each respecting the other, and all admitting

the ground of equality." And, where all met as
equals, there could be no attempt to stipulate for
special advantage, or to lay down conditions of
favour to one or more.

As he had told his constituents at the election of
1894, the time had passed for an "unwholesome
conflict between free trade and protection;" and,
free trader himself, he called upon all free traders to
reserve their strength, for the advocacy of their
cause, in the election of the Federal Parliament.
On that battlefield, he said, he should use all his
faculties of mind and body, all his energies and all
his courage, "to fight the good fight of free trade,
and to crown the struggle with victory in the House
of Representatives." That the protectionists would
do their utmost, on the same field, to ensure the
adoption of their policy, he of course expected; but
he did not, on that account, despise their assistance
in the work of establishing the union.

In this spirit, and under these circumstances, he
fell in with the movement which arose among the
federalists of the Legislative Assembly, in February,
1895.

Soon after the assembling of Parliament in 1894,
he was urged to confer with Sir George Dibbs on
the situation, in order that a basis of action against
the Reid Government might be discussed and
agreed upon; but he declined, neither of them, at
this time, being disposed to act with the other. For
years previously they had not spoken to each other,
some circumstances in their political strivings, not
clearly known to either them or their friends, having

led to the suspension between them of the ordinary courtesies of life. So they remained aloof. But, in the meantime, friends of both kept alive the idea of bringing them together ; and several attempts were made, to induce them to sink their differences and join their forces. In the early part of 1895, the prospects of their coming together seemed more favourable ; but subsequent events showed that it was yet too soon for anything of the kind. In a position in which, if the hostile movement against the Government should be successful, one must give up the leadership of the new Administration to the other, and both desired it, united action was exceedingly difficult.

Sir Henry Parkes was conscious of the necessity for some definite action against the Government, but showed considerable reluctance to enter upon the struggle. Writing about this time, he said : " Although, to my mind, the confusion of government business is the deeper the more it is examined, still the question comes out of the very examination, am I the man called upon to kill the rattlesnake? Is it that I who was betrayed, deserted, and thrust aside, a few months ago, by those who owed me allegiance, should leap into the gulf now?"

But the year was still young, when, appealed to by a number of members of the Assembly, to submit a motion of want of confidence in the Ministry, and, believing from the representations made to him, that a majority of the Assembly were favourable to such a proceeding, he drafted a resolution expressing dissatisfaction at the state of public business and distrust of the future.

Those who heard of the contemplated step, were of opinion that there were reasonable grounds for thinking the Government to be in danger. From one cause and another, public business had not proceeded with the expedition that had been expected; and doubt existed in the minds of people, outside the House as well as inside, as to the chances of the Ministry doing much in the future.

The draft resolution met with the approval of Sir Henry Parkes' friends, and might have been moved; but, before any definite action could be taken upon it in the Assembly, notice of a motion of censure, against the Government, was given by Sir George Dibbs. This, necessarily, prevented any similar proceeding on the part of Sir Henry Parkes, as, without the approval and support of the leader of the Opposition, any motion of the kind would be regarded by the Government as that of a private member, and treated accordingly.

It was in the month of May before the opportunity for action, on the part of Sir Henry Parkes, came.

The motion made by Sir George Dibbs received but scant support; and, on its failure, the attention of the opponents of the Ministry was once more directed to the only man considered likely to be successful. Again it was urged upon the recognised leader of the Opposition, that if anything effective was to be done against the Government, and its policy, Sir Henry Parkes was the only man to do it. The matter had become one of urgency. So earnest were some members of the Opposition in regard to it, that they talked of leaving the protectionist party as it existed, and going over in a body to Sir Henry Parkes. But this was not necessary. Having himself failed, Sir George Dibbs was now ready to give his support to anyone likely to succeed. The success of a hostile motion against the Government would be as beneficial to the protectionists, in the maintenance of their tariff, for a time at least, as it would be gratifying to the advocates of federation, who saw, in the wished-for victory, only the interests of the great cause they had at heart; and the Opposition leader no longer held back. A meeting of the Opposition was held ; support to Sir Henry Parkes was agreed upon ; and he was informed of the turn things had taken.

Two months before, in a letter to the public press, he had made no secret of his intention "in the lasting interest of good government" to get rid of the Ministry, and he had invited men from all sides, who believed in the objects associated with federation, to join him " in rendering this service to New South Wales and Australia." He, therefore, showed no reluctance to accept the proffered support of the protectionist party, as a response to his invitation; and, with the aid he expected from a number of free traders, he determined to challenge the Government.

On 16th May, 1895, he made a motion of censure, to the effect that the continuance in office of the Government would retard the progress of much needed legislation, and seriously prejudice the cause of Australian Federation.

The occasion was a great one, and the proceedings aroused wide-spread interest. In ordinary circumstances, coming from the source it did, the motion might have succeeded ; at least it would have fared better than was actually the case. But, from physical weakness, Sir Henry Parkes was not effective in his speech; and, the announced intention of the Opposition to support the motion, raised loud and bitter cries of disapproval at what was termed an unholy coalition. That, in face of his life-long advocacy of free trade, Sir Henry Parkes could join the leader of the protectionists, in an attempt to overthrow a free trade Ministry, was what the newspapers, with one or two exceptions, from one end of the country to the other, professed their inability to understand, except on the ground that Sir Henry was a deserter from the ranks of free trade, and now a protectionist.

Though, in reality, he was but acting consistently with the course of action he had, for three years past, laid down for himself, and many times had explained publicly, he was denounced in the strongest terms. Federation, and a cessation of fiscal strife until the tariff could be dealt with by the Federal Parliament, instead of altering the tariff now, and, by that alteration, raising a formidable barrier to union : that was his aim. But his opponents in the press, concerned only for the existence of the Ministry, shut their eyes to his consistency, and refused to see, in the course he had taken, anything but perfidy. And, while he was bitterly assailed, those free traders who were likely to give him their support were warned of the dire consequences likely to fall upon them at the next elections. Naturally this had its effect. Only two members of the free trade party voted for the motion, and they, with the protectionists, were so insufficient to effect the object sought, that the motion was defeated by a majority of nearly two to one.

The result was more disappointing than was apparent merely from the numbers in the division ; for the position of the federal party was now worse than before. The Ministry were strengthened most materially. From the representations made to Sir Henry Parkes he had counted upon defeating the Government easily. Instead of that his motion had shown what before was not evident—that they had behind them a large and solid majority, determined to assist them in carrying out their policy ; and that policy they immediately began to press forward, with increased energy and confidence.

CHAPTER XLI.

" THERE are times," wrote Sir Henry Parkes to a political acquaintance, in the course of his efforts to place Federation in advance of all other questions in the public policy of New South Wales, "when men are called upon to sacrifice everything—life itself—for their country;" and, though defeated upon the motion he had made in the Assembly, he was not turned from his purpose. The one remaining object of his life, it was at the same time the greatest, and, in any circumstances, it was worth fighting for.

In the light of a conviction, which nothing could drive from his mind, that the country was with him in the matter, that the decision of the Assembly upon his motion was contrary to the wish of the people, it would have been traitorous for him to abandon his work. It was inevitable that he should go on. Like the famous American President, when he only was not disheartened at failure after failure of the measures taken to preserve the Union—an example often quoted by Sir Henry Parkes—he must "keep pegging away."

For some little time an organization, known as the Federal League of Australasia, had been in existence. It had been formed by Sir Henry Parkes, and consisted of some of the more ardent supporters of federation, in the Assembly, and advocates of the cause outside Parliament. In numbers it was not large ; but it was regarded as the nucleus of something more extensive in the immediate future, and, for the present, it was expected to assist in carrying the federation movement forward. The members of it were known as Progressive Federalists. By means of this organization, Sir Henry Parkes determined to keep the work of union before the people, and to continue to advance its interests. The leading provisions in the programme of the League, shortly stated were :—

1. The Federation of Australia to be held first, above and before all other questions.

2. The trade between the Australian Colonies to be absolutely free.

3. The customs tariff of Australia to be left unconditionally to the Federal Parliament, without reference to or in any way fettering the opinion of individuals.

4. Their territorial rights and possessions to be secured by the Federal Constitution to the respective Colonies.

5. The Colonies separately to have the rights of taxation over land, personal income, negotiable instruments, and individual property of all kinds.

6. The main trunk lines of railway to be at the service of the Federal Government for Federal purposes.

NN

And in respect of New South Wales as one of the Union States :—

(a) Compulsory local government embracing the whole territory under Divisional Councils.

(b) Labour Colonies to be founded and governed on the principle of remunerative improvement, where all persons in want of employment may earn, by regular labour at equitable rates of wages, the necessary means to support themselves and families, while establishing, in the interest of the State, industrial communities.

(c) The gradual cessation of public borrowing outside the Colony.

(d) In the Civil Service, the inhabitants of the Colony to have the preference, all other things being equal, in all appointments and promotions.

(e) The Defence Forces—under whatever designation—to be formed from the young men of the Colony.

The members of the League met frequently, and arrangements were made for giving life to the movement throughout New South Wales.

Meantime, political matters were approaching a crisis. The Legislative Council had shown signs of an indisposition to sanction the direct taxation policy of the Government, and it was soon evident that, when the opportunity should arrive for decisive action on the part of that House, the financial measures, which the Government desired to pass into law, would be rejected. An opening for the advance of the federalists here seemed probable.

Quite consistently with his repeatedly announced opinion that the time was inopportune for making tariff alterations, and, by so acting, raising additional

barriers against the union of the colonies, Sir Henry
Parkes did not view with disapproval the course the
Upper House appeared disposed to take; and
when, by its rejection of a bill providing for the
machinery necessary for the collection of land and
income taxes, a crisis arrived, he closed up the ranks
of his party, and prepared for the general election
that was unavoidable.

Parliament was dissolved on the 5th July, and
the arrangements for the elections quickly followed.

For some days Sir Henry Parkes quietly watched
the form the elections were taking. Arrived at
a time of life when extreme physical exertion must,
as much as possible, be avoided, it was not to be expected that he should plunge into the contest with
the promptness and vigour of the earlier years; and
there were other reasons which discouraged activity.
But everybody anticipated action of some kind, and
waited for it with impatience. Though not regarded
as a probable source of much injury or inconvenience
to the Government, whatever course he should take
his position was certain to impart to the struggle an
interest which only he could give it.

His chance of being re-elected for St. Leonards
was viewed by many as doubtful. Some of the
more prominent of the electors, who had previously
supported him, disapproving of the attempt, with
the aid of the protectionists, to upset the Government, had announced their intention to oppose him;
and, though he might not be defeated, it was evident
he would, at least, have to fight very hard for the
seat. This was not likely to trouble him, for there

were several electorates that would be glad of the
opportunity to return him; and anticipations
were abroad that, in any case, he would, in this
election, abandon St. Leonards, and come out for the
constituency in which he could appear as the leader
of the side opposed to the Ministry.

Writing to one of the nembers of his St.
Leonards Committee, he said that, for many reasons, he could wish to be relieved from parliamentary
obligations altogether; but then he knew that there
were duties which must be undertaken, and public
work which must be done, and naturally men who,
like himself, had steadily endeavoured to enforce the
true principles of free government in the work of
legislation, hesitated to abandon the direction of
political affairs to hands that might be incompetent
or untrustworthy. He could not say he might not
be influenced to seek a seat in the new Parliament,
if it should appear to him that his services could be
of special value to the cause of good government, but
he had decided not to be a candidate for St.
Leonards. No doubt was in his mind that, if he
presented himself for re-election, he would be returned; but, as he was then situated, he was not
prepared to go through an unpleasant contest that
could have no wider result than his personal success.

He was not indisposed to engage in the elections
as duty might call him, but he was not likely to do
it with anything approaching the old enthusiasm.

Domestic affliction was, at this time, so affecting
him, as to make politics far more of a burden than a
source of pleasure. For some months previously,

there had been signs about his home of the approach of the dreaded last messenger to one who was very dear to him ; and now the shadow was deepening, and the end very near. His wife was dying.

They had married late in his life, and she had been his devoted companion for six years. She had brought him both happiness and trouble. His home was very bright with her presence and her tasteful ways. Throughout his long confinement from his broken leg, she had nursed him with all tenderness. She had been a sympathiser and a helpmate in his work, inside and outside Parliament. A natural cleverness and cheerful manner, made her, to all, a pleasant acquaintance ; a kind heart and a generous disposition proved her a good friend. Her husband's books and pictures contained many tributes to her worth. Yet, though he was happy in her presence and affection, and though all who knew her intimately were drawn towards her by her good qualities, she did not secure the goodwill of Society. Where, before their marriage, her husband was the principal figure, he was not now seen. She was not invited, and he remained away. In May, 1889, replying to an invitation from Government House, he wrote to the Governor, Lord Carrington :—

"Sir Henry Parkes regrets that he cannot accept the invitation of his Excellency the Governor to dinner on the 24th May. He owes it to his wife, whatever may be the occasion, not to enter the door which is closed against her ; but he desires at the same time to be understood as not seeking a reversal of her exclusion, while he insists upon sharing any indignity to which she is subjected."

From that time until after the death of Lady
Parkes, except on one occasion, in the period of the
Earl of Jersey's stay in Sydney, when the Governor
having been present during the day on the grounds
of Sir Henry Parkes' residence, at a fête given to
the boys of the training school ship Vernon, he
returned the courtesy by attending the Queen's
Birthday dinner in the evening, Government House,
during any of its entertainments, was not visited
by Sir Henry Parkes.

This denial of the social recognition due to him,
as much as to his wife, was as annoying as, in some
respects, it was unjust ; but, in his published collection of sonnets, it finds fitting answer in indignant
and touching lines.

"TO ELEANOR.

"And thou hast suffer'd bravely, tender Heart !
But well thou know'st the world is not for them— -
The social nonconformists who contemn
Or disobey the whitened laws, that part
The saints from sinners, in its painted mart.
Be thou content with Jesus' apothegm ;
And whoso comes from out Jerusalem
To stone thee, stand the woman that thou art.
Thou, who would'st give thy last sore-needed crust
To feed the hungry in thy woman's pity,
Stand with thy noble boys at Jesus' feet !
Pray they may join the army of the just,
To serve this land, this sorrow-laden city,
And that beyond the grave we all may meet !"

In the midst of the trouble caused by the
rapidly approaching death of his wife, it was urged
upon him that he should allow himself to be

nominated as a candidate for the King Division of
the city of Sydney, in opposition to the head of the
Government, Mr. Reid.

Popular as the policy of the Government was,
the opponents of it, inside and outside Parliament,
were very anxious to find a strong man to put forward against the Premier. Several persons were
approached, and among them Sir Henry Parkes.
He hesitated; advanced objections to such a course;
promised to think over it; and, finally, mentioned
the matter to his wife. She counselled him to do
as he was urged.. There was no possibility of her
sharing the satisfaction of victory, if the election
should be won, or of being there to condole with
him in defeat. But, while she lived, she could, as
she had always done, advise him; and, with all the
strength she could bring to bear, her advice was
that he should enter the contest as proposed, and,
unmindful of her condition, fight with the earnestness and vigour necessary to ensure success.

Next morning his candidature was definitely
announced; and, at once, the King Division became the centre to which public attention was
directed. The contests in other electorates faded
from notice. All eyes were fixed on the fight
which, by the defeat of the Premier, must inflict
a fatal hurt upon the Government, or, by his
victory, exclude Sir Henry Parkes from the new
Parliament, and, perhaps, close his parliamentary
career. However the election might end, the
issues must be momentous; the struggle, therefore,
was certain to be severe.

Both candidates buckled for the fray. Putting before the electors a federalist manifesto, in which he declared that, in view of the early federation of the colonies, nothing whatever ought to be done which would create obstacles to union, Sir Henry Parkes entered upon the contest—the thirty-sixth in which he had engaged—with confidence and energy. So energetic in fact was he, that, at the first meeting of his committee, he announced his desire to direct the plan of operations himself, and direct it he did until the election was over.

His attitude presented a unique spectacle of courage and pathos. Vigorous, eloquent, and vituperative at his meetings, his language in denunciation of Mr. Reid equalling in bitterness anything he had said at any time during his public career,—in his home he was never free from the harrowing sense of the rapid approach of death to his suffering wife. Alarming phases in her illness interrupted the work of his committee by preventing his attendance; and, in the midst of their preparations, she died. Yet, though stricken by this calamity, he was not disposed to withdraw from the struggle he had entered upon. Let him bury his "dear dead," he wrote to his committee, and he was ready to return to his election labours at once. He was prepared to resume the fight immediately after the funeral. Up to the last moment of consciousness, the counsel of his wife had been—no surrender; and, apart from his grief at her death, there was no reason why he should not continue to be as active as the necessities of the case demanded. Few things in political history, it was remarked at the time, are more pathetic than the advice and encouragement of the dying wife to her husband in this election.

He followed the advice to the letter. The day after the funeral he was again at work, almost as active as ever, the excitement of the contest proving to some extent an antidote to his trouble. Ably supported by some of the foremost men in the public life of New South Wales, he now addressed meeting after meeting, amidst popular excitement, uproar, and enthusiasm. To rally round the cause of a United Australia and of New South Wales as one of the sister states, was what he urged upon the electors;—federation, instead of trifling over a provincial fiscal battle which could have no result when union should take place. It was the same high topic upon which he had often spoken, and he pressed it upon public attention now with the same sincerity.

But though many listened and applauded, few were influenced. The policy of the Government, supported as it was by a majority of the newspapers, including the most influential, was too attractive among the masses to be easily set aside, and the popularity of the Premier, Mr. Reid, too great for anyone to make much headway against him.

The friends of Sir Henry Parkes were sanguine of success, but their hopefulness was based upon information which, ultimately, was found to be unreliable. The reports of the canvassers promised not only victory; it was to be victory by a considerable majority. But, in a parliamentary election, there is no certainty of success until the votes have been polled, and the numbers are known ; and, once more in political experience, promises proved very different from performances. On the eve of the polling, so favourable did the prospects of the contest appear to them, the committee of Sir Henry Parkes were unanimous in believing he would be elected on the morrow,—that he could not fail ; and, when the morrow came, and the poll was declared, he had been defeated by 140 votes.

With the recollection of the hot fight, and the indications all through it of probable success, this was hard to bear. Sir Henry Parkes bore it best. At once he imparted to the situation a tone fully in keeping with the great cause which, as a candidate in the election, he had advocated. Compared with the importance of that question, the result of the election was to him nothing. "Think no more of the result," he urged upon his committee ; "think of the cause we have in hand." There was no need, he said, to concern themselves about him. He was nobody in the matter. He would pass away. But they would remain, and, taking up the question where he had tried to place it, must carry it on.

As one of the public journals observed, his defeat contributed to the election an element of tragic pathos, for his domestic affliction had enlisted public sympathy, and his absence from the new Parliament, at his great age, was indicative of the close of his active public life.

CHAPTER XLII.

ILLNESS AND DEATH.

THE lost election and the death of his wife were borne by Sir Henry Parkes with fortitude; but, together, they, for a time, had a very depressing effect. A return to the Legislative Assembly, flushed with the achievement of having defeated the Prime Minister, would have kept his mind from dwelling too much upon his domestic trouble, and would have rekindled in him some of the old fire which, in the parliamentary battles of earlier days, had made him the chief figure in the country's political life. But defeat, and of so decided a character, looked like a peremptory dismissal from politics, and the end of his career.

Most persons were of opinion that he would not again be seen in Parliament. He, himself, though, at times, despondent over the change in his political fortunes, never thought his popularity had lessened, nor doubted that, before long, he would be at the head of his sixth Ministry. "If I live and my health does not fail," he said to a friend one day, "you will see me in power again within two years." Sanguine always as to his political future, it never occurred to him that in his way were obstacles insurmountable.

His defeat in the election for the King Division took place in September. In a little more than six months afterwards, his future was decided by the end coming, not only to all hope of further service in Parliament, but to his life. And what an eventful six months these were! In the short period of time which they represent, he appeared as a candidate at two more elections, from one of which he retired, and in the other was again badly defeated; he contracted a third marriage; he returned to Government House and to Society; he became so destitute of the means of living as to be obliged to sell most of his books and furniture, and to seek a grant of money from Parliament; and, finally, he died in absolute poverty, lamented by everybody, and reconciled to his great political opponent, Mr. Reid.

His poverty was the saddest feature of the last few weeks of his life. More or less, he had always been in want of money, but, in one way or another, had managed to get along. "How strange it is," he once wrote in reply to a letter sent him with a present of wine on his birthday, "that I should occupy the high position I do, and be so poor as to be compelled to receive presents from my friends!" A serious decrease in the amount of income which he derived from money collected for him by public subscription in 1887, and invested by trustees in bank shares, was the principal trouble. From £540, it had dwindled to £212, and this was all he had to provide for his household, afford some assistance to relations outside his immediate family circle, and pay some of his debts. "The diminution of my income, which I foolishly calculated upon, and of my strength to earn money," he said in a conversation last December, "is making things harder with me than they ever were in my life." Only by selling the valuable little articles he had collected in past years, and by borrowing sums of money at different times from friends, had he been able to live.

It was in December, of 1895, that the movement arose to procure for him a grant of money from Parliament, and it was this conversation, during which he explicitly stated his position, and his willingness to accept a grant, that led to the steps which were taken to obtain it.

"If such a thing as a grant of money had been hinted to me a few years ago, I should have rejected it with something like utter disapproval," he said on this occasion. "It has been several times, in an indirect way, suggested to me, and once on behalf of the Dibbs Ministry; but I did not entertain it. Now I am compelled to look for something of the kind. I cannot throw myself into new employment—I am too old. If I cared to do so, I have no doubt I could rally the country now, and form a good party; but as all my old friends are dead, I am reluctant to do this. I am willing to leave it to the people on the stage to fight it out as best they can. If this grant were offered to me now, in consequence of my necessities, I should accept it, and I should consider that it severed my connection with party strife."

Great indeed were his necessities. He had no money at his command; the tradesmen who supplied the household were threatening to stop supplies; and a pressing creditor had taken action which was expected to result in a bailiff entering the house and seizing the furniture. It was a question, as Sir Henry Parkes, himself, put it, of his having to go to the workhouse or accepting the grant of money.

But the grant of money was not made. The Government were willing to propose it, but the parliamentary session was within two or three days of its close, and, on members of the Assembly being sounded as to the prospects of the money being voted, it was ascertained that the motion would meet with opposition which must keep the House sitting beyond the time appointed for the prorogation. In view of this, it was thought advisable to await a more favourable opportunity.

Had the money been voted he might not have died so soon, and his long and useful life might have closed peacefully and happily, after a few years well-deserved rest, free from the troubles that attend pecuniary embarrassment. For, in anticipation of the grant, he had talked of again visiting England; and his mind was full of literary projects of one kind and another. As it was, however, he died in circumstances which made it necessary for the Government to step forward and provide him with the ordinary comforts of a sick room, and his family with daily food.

It was in the month of April, 1896, that he fell
ill ; and though, at no time, before the end came,
was his condition alarming, his great age, and weak
heart, made the case a serious one from the first.

One of the earliest of the callers at "Kenilworth,"
where Sir Henry Parkes was lying, was Mr. G. H.
Reid.   " I have come," he said to Lady Parkes,
" to inquire concerning the announcement of Sir
Henry's illness, in this morning's papers.   I was
indeed sorry to see it.   How is he ?   I scarcely
like to ask him to see me, if he is very ill."

They did, however, see each other, though it took
some minutes to persuade Sir Henry Parkes to
receive his visitor, the bitterness of the political
relations between them not having yet been forgiven or forgotten.   The two statesmen met, and
the meeting was of a nature worthy to be recorded
by the brush of the painter as much as by the pen
of the historian.

Entering the chamber, where the great man
lay attended by his wife and his physician, not more
than a day or two from death, Mr. Reid made his
way to the bed ; and, grasping the hand extended
to him, bent over it, and touched it with his lips.

This kindly act, which seemed to speak of deep
respect, of regret for the harsh things of the past,
and of sorrow for the present illness, touched the
heart of the dying veteran.   The feeling which had
made him reluctant to see his visitor melted away ;
the hand-grasp tightened ; and tears came from
the eyes of both.   For some seconds,—it seemed
like minutes—no word was spoken ; but the heart

of each went out to the other, and, when the visit had ended, and Mr. Reid had taken his leave, with an expressed desire to call again, Sir Henry Parkes was able to say, "I am glad he called; I am glad I saw him; I have misunderstood him."

Each day all eyes were directed to the latest bulletins from the sick room; all hearts beat in sympathy; and when, on Monday, April 27th, it was announced that death had come at 4 o'clock that morning, there was sorrow universal; for the end of this great life was the close of an epoch of Australian history, and, by it, the people seemed to feel that they had lost their stoutest champion and truest friend.

"A good soft pillow for that good white head!" The errors which, here and there, had shaded the deceased statesman's career, were forgotten, and only his virtues remembered—his public services, the unselfishness of his career, his sterling worth. Messages of sympathy came from all the Australasian colonies and from England. The Government offered a public funeral.

But Sir Henry Parkes had been opposed to public funerals. In 1893, he made a will; and, so particular was he with regard to the proceedings which should follow his decease, that, in this document, he enjoined his trustees that, when death took place, not even the newspapers should be informed, but that his body should be enclosed in an inexpensive coffin, and buried in any consecrated ground the trustees should decide upon, the funeral to be carried out as privately and simply as possible. A further-

"KENILWORTH," ANNANDALE, SYDNEY.
THE HOUSE IN WHICH SIR HENRY PARKES DIED.

direction was that, on no account, should the trustees consent to any monument or other public honour being conferred upon him by the Government or Parliament of New South Wales. This will lapsed with the death of Sir Henry Parkes' second wife ; but his known opinions with regard to public funerals led to the offer of the Government being declined, and to the funeral being of a private nature, though necessarily attended by a very large number of mourners representing all classes of the community.

In this form, the last ceremony in relation to the deceased statesman was carried out ; the interment taking place at Faulconbridge, where the remains were laid by the side of those of the first Lady Parkes, in ground which, from the time of her burial, was regarded as her husband's final resting-place.

CHAPTER XLIII.

Nearly half a century has passed since Sir Henry Parkes first appeared before the public of New South Wales, and, during that long period, no one in the political history of the colony has presented such a forceful personality. Had the circumstances of his early life been such as to have sent him into the House of Commons, he would have excelled there. But he was better fitted for a House of Legislature in Australia. The new land offered all the requisite opportunities for the employment of his faculties. Work of a special nature required to be done, and there were few capable of doing it. In the public life of England, he never could have risen to the height he did in New South Wales, where, for so many years, he was engaged shaping the destinies of one of the most important portions of what, eventually, will be a great nation.

The work he did has been widely recognised; but, at no time, was he free from detractors. All do not now praise him. Notwithstanding his great services, there are some who question their merit.

Often, in the course of his career, he was denied
the credit of originating the most important of the
measures he was instrumental in having passed.
Appropriating other men's ideas, it was said, he
merely gave them vital form.   To say that he
did so, in the spirit in which the charge has been
made, is not correct; but, if the assertion were true,
it could be answered by pointing to the fact that
most of the work of the world has been done in a
similar way.   If he should have done nothing
more than put into active shape what others
had suggested, he did but follow the path trod-
den by a long line of statesmen.   But that is not
the sum and substance of his work.   He himself
conceived, and carried his conceptions into effect to
the lasting benefit of his fellow-men.

Had he been born and brought up under circumstances which would have provided him with a good
education and training for the career which, eventually, he followed, many of his friends are of opinion
he might have been a much more prominent man
than he was.   Possibly so.   But easy circumstances
and scholastic advantages are not, to some natures,
the levers which poverty and the necessity to push
one's way have shown themselves to be.   Wealth
and education would not have caused the young
emigrant to leave his native land for the little
known Australia in 1839.   The *Empire* newspaper
would never have entered upon its useful mission.
The Public Schools Act, or something like it, might
have been passed, but probably not quite in the
same form nor at the same time.   The Railways

Act, the Public Works Act, and a number of other Acts of the first magnitude which owe their existence to him, might have come, in the course of years, from other men; but he it was who was instrumental in making them law years ago, and he it is who is entitled to the credit arising from their beneficial operation.

It has been said that he might have done more. So it may be said of all men. Frequently he was charged with promising, year after year, important legislation which is now as far off as ever it was. Those who know anything of the difficulties of government, must be aware of the manner in which the best intentions are upset by unexpected circumstances. He did what he could—far more than has been accomplished by any other man, now, or heretofore, in the public life of New South Wales; and, it has been remarked (with little exaggeration) that if the measures for which he is responsible were removed from the statute book of the colony, the pages of the book would be left almost a blank.

Next to his services, a great fact in his career was his pecuniary condition—his poverty. Though he entered Parliament in 1854, and six times occupied the position of a Minister of the Crown—five times as Prime Minister—he was as poor, when he died, as he was the first day he entered the old Legislative Council. With unlimited opportunities for acquiring wealth, he availed himself of none. Had he held office in England, he could, on retiring, have obtained a pension of several thousands a year. In the colony to which he gave his energies,

for the whole of his life, retirement from office was
the cessation of his means of existence. Yet many
as were the charges made against him, no one ever
accused him of clinging to office. On two occasions
public subscriptions provided him with a fairly
large sum of money; but, in the first instance, this
was only of temporary benefit, and, in the second,
through the investment of the money proving less
fortunate than was expected, little was obtained
from it.

This want of adequate means was a cause of
much trouble, and, at times, exposed him to the
charge of seeking office for the sake of its emolu-
ments.

He was not a man of expensive habits. In
only one direction can his expenditure be said to
have been in any degree excessive, and that was in
the purchase of books and works of art. His desire
for new books that are worth having, in the type and
binding of their first editions, filled his library with
a very valuable collection of the best literature, to
which additions were constantly being made, and
his taste for artistic work beautified his home with
pictures, busts, and other articles of *vertu.*

His books were the source of his extensive
knowledge. Few men were better read, especially
on subjects of a political nature; and his habit of
thinking was apparent, not only in his speeches, but
in his conversation. When speaking to a friend or
acquaintance, his utterance was so deliberate as to at
once suggest the idea that he had carefully thought
out the subject before he said a word respecting it;

and, with this thoughtful expression, there went a continuity of ideas which, however it might be interrupted by an interjected observation from someone else, proceeded connectedly from beginning to conclusion.

Except when he was called upon by the excitement of the moment to speak, his speeches were carefully considered. So closely was this practice followed, that it was even his custom, on special occasions, to prepare for use certain phrases which, with unerring skill, he employed at the very moment and in the very parts of his speech where they proved most effective. This careful preparation was almost necessarily accompanied by a desire to be reported accurately and fully. So well arranged was the matter of his speeches, and so well expressed all he said, that he was one of those very few public speakers, either in New South Wales or elsewhere, who will bear being reported *verbatim*. As a rule, he spoke with the assistance of a few notes which suggested the main topics of his speech, and might contain a prepared phrase or two, and one or more quotations.

His speeches have been said to be of that kind described as unadorned eloquence, but they are more than that. Though, as in the public utterances of most men, they are not free from disfigurements, especially attacks upon political opponents, many of them contain passages that, for oratorical gracefulness and force, arouse the admiration of the reader almost to the extent to which they must have moved those who heard them spoken. Up to

recent years—say to 1890, the year of the accident
which had so serious an effect upon his physical
activity and strength that, at no time afterwards, was
he the same man—no one who sat in the Legislative
Assembly of New South Wales was more able to
hold the attention of a crowded House, to bring it
back from disorder to a sense of its responsibilities,
to rouse it to enthusiasm, or to sway it in the
direction he desired.   The merit in the speeches
that, in most instances, they can be read in cold
type with admiration, and, in all, with the advantage
that they are instructive—that while they can be
admired, much can be learned from them that is
useful and important—is a high test of their
excellence, for it places them far above the level of
ordinary public speaking, and gives them a lasting
value. Many of them are text-books upon parliamentary government, the principles of constitutional rule,
and the duties of citizenship.   In this respect they
have had, and will yet have, a great educative effect
inside and outside the Legislature.

During the last few years of his life, in order to
meet the demands of the up-to-date journalism in
Australia, Sir Henry Parkes, in common with other
public men, sometimes found it necessary to
anticipate a speech in public, by putting forward his
views upon certain events or proceedings through
an interviewer ; but even these interviews, as they
appeared in print, were not destitute of the signs of
the impassioned utterance and the effectiveness
which strikingly characterised what he said upon
the floor of Parliament or on the public platform.

His strong literary tastes not only drew him to
his books, but impelled him to do what was in his
power to encourage colonial literature. His admiration for some of the earlier poets of New South
Wales may be found expressed in some of his poems;
and, when Henry Kendall was drifting down the
stream of poverty and neglect, fast bringing to a
close a self-blighted life, a hand was stretched out to
him from the Colonial Secretary's Office, and he
was placed for the remainder of his days in a
Government position which not only gave him the
means of subsistence but provided him with an
occupation among the woods and streams, the flowers
and the birds, which have enriched his verses with
the beauties of nature as it is in Australia.

Sir Henry Parkes' own contributions to literature
include, besides his poems, many magazine articles, a
volume of speeches covering a period of twenty-five
years of his political life, published in 1876, and his
" Fifty Years in the making of Australian History,"
which appeared in 1892. The speeches met with a
favourable   reception,   but   the   " Fifty   Years,"
although well received by the great English
journals, raised, in the colonies, much hostile criticism which the book did not deserve.

As he did that which was in his power for the
encouragement of literature, so he gave a helping
hand to art. Through his appreciation of the educative and refining influences of artistic work, and
especially of its value in a community where time
and effort are devoted chiefly to the pursuit of
material wealth, the National Art Gallery received

much assistance from him when in power, and the public offices and the parks and gardens owe to the same source many of those features which adorn them and form their principal attractions. The national gratitude for public services, which finds expression in the erection of commemorative statues to public men, had a sympathiser in him; and, had his Government of 1891 remained a little longer in office, he would have had erected, in the splendid avenue on the north side of the Sydney General Post Office, statues of three of the most prominent men who have appeared in the public life of New South Wales—Mr. W. C. Wentworth, Sir Charles Cowper, and Sir James Martin. It is a defect in the beautiful city of Sydney, that there is little in the form of statues to commemorate the services of its public men, beyond some sandstone figures filling niches in the walls of one or two of the public buildings; and this defect Sir Henry Parkes showed a desire to remove, believing that, in doing so, he would but give effect to the wishes of an appreciative and public-spirited people.

In all things associated with the public life of Sir Henry Parkes there is much to admire. That his career was not free from circumstances which may fairly meet with disapproval, or even condemnation, goes without saying. What man who has engaged in the turmoil of political strife for nearly half a century has so acted that none of his proceedings are open to question? Such monsters as perfect characters or perfect statesmen, it has been well said, do not exist. He made mistakes—many of them. He

himself frequently freely admitted his errors. On one
of these occasions, when acknowledging the approval
with which his services had been received by the
people, he remarked that though, at times, he had
been censured when he did not deserve it, upon the
whole the judgment spontaneously and cordially
passed upon him was such as a far worthier man
might accept with unbounded gratitude. He never
was slow to confess his faults; but, whatever those
faults were, they pale into insignificance when compared with the good he did.

His presence in Parliament was ever an assurance
of unbroken watchfulness for the prevention of any
departure from recognised procedure, and his entrance
into office a guarantee that nothing of a violent
nature need be feared in either legislation or administration. At no time was this more noticeable than
during the progress of labour strikes and distur-
bances, when, as head of the military and the police,
he showed, in combination with a due regard for the
interests of each side in the disputes, a moderation
that did not interfere with the preservation of law
and order, and yet prevented any resort to extreme
measures which would have resulted in excesses to
be never afterwards forgotten. Able to calmly view
the strife, he always understood how best to bring it
to an end, with the least injury to anyone engaged
in it. It was ever recognised by him that, among
those taking part in a great labour uprising, are
many of the best of the working population, and
that it is only a question of a little time when their
excitement will pass off, and they will resume the

duties of peaceful and industrious citizenship. While, therefore, he saw that effective measures were taken by the police, or by the police and the military, no policeman or soldier ever fired a shot into a riotous crowd, and the trouble ended without the use of anything more formidable than police-men's batons.

So long was Sir Henry Parkes identified with the public life of New South Wales, that it is difficult to realise that he will never again be in the Government, and still more so the existence of Parliaments . from which his venerable and commanding figure will be absent. Yet though the walls which have re-sounded to his eloquence shall listen to him no more, the echoes of his voice remain to teach all who come after him, adherence to principle, consistency of conduct, patriotism, faithfulness to the responsibilities of public service.

The story of his life is one from which many useful lessons may be learned, of importance to all interested in the well-being and progress of young communities.

BEATTY, RICHARDSON AND CO.,

PRINTERS,

PALING'S BUILDINGS, SYDNEY.